The CAREERS DIRECTORY 2009/10
- the one-stop guide to professional careers

edited by
Ken Reynolds
and John Mainstone

opening doors of opportunity

The CAREERS DIRECTORY 2009/10

This edition published in 2009 by Cambridge Occupational Analysts Ltd
Sparham, Norwich, NR9 5PR

Editorial and Publishing Team

Editors Ken Reynolds and John Mainstone
Design and typesetting Simon Foster and Paul Rankin

British Library Cataloguing in Publication Data
A catalogue record for this book is available from the British Library.

ISBN 978-1-906711-00-9

Typeset by Cambridge Occupational Analysts Ltd, Sparham, Norwich, NR9 5PR
Printed and bound in Great Britain by Clays Ltd, Bungay, Suffolk, NR35 1ED

Contents

Most people, when they look back on their lives, agree that there is a gap between what they once aspired to and what they eventually settled for. The bigger the gap, the more likely they are to feel dissatisfied.

Career planning, while not claiming to guarantee a lifetime of success and fulfilment, can help you to clarify your aspirations and can identify relevant routes for you to achieve your goals. We are convinced that The Careers Directory can make a major contribution to setting out the options available to you and can suggest suitable directions for the road ahead.

Making career decisions is never easy. Apart from reading this book, you will find that it helps to talk things through with friends, family, teachers, lecturers, training providers, employers and - last but certainly not least - a professional careers or personal adviser.

Conscious that careers information is constantly changing, we are committed to keeping The Careers Directory as up to date as possible. For this edition, completed in early May 2009, we have checked every entry, with a particular emphasis on assessing the impact on future prospects of the economic downturn of 2009, updating salary information and making sure that every web address is current.

We have made every effort, in keeping with established practice in professional career guidance, to ensure that the information in The Careers Directory is accurate, up to date, objective and impartial.

Ken Reynolds and John Mainstone, Editors

Introduction

Welcome to *The Careers Directory 2009/2010*.

The world of work has changed dramatically since we prepared the previous edition of this book only 12 months ago. While the global economy had been expected to show some slow down, no-one anticipated the level of exposure that the financial markets had to the bad debt created by the collapse of the sub-prime mortgage market in the United States. Not only have industrialised economies seen turmoil in their financial markets in recent months, but those economies previously considered 'decoupled' from the West, such as China and India, have proved just as vulnerable to the spreading contagion, with falling share prices on their stock exchanges and shrinking export markets. The UK economy has proved one of the most exposed to the debt crisis and, according to the Organisation for Economic Cooperation and Development (OECD), is likely to suffer one of the worst contractions among the major European economies. By the end of 2009, it is likely that the UK economy will have experienced a contraction that will affect the immediate career prospects of many young people seeking to enter the labour market for the first time.

For example, the number of graduate vacancies in the UK will drop this year for the first time since 2003, according to data published by the Association of Graduate Recruiters. Vacancies overall are expected to decrease by over 5%, with most employers blaming the economic downturn for the cuts. At the same time, graduate starting salaries are likely to remain frozen. This year's median starting salary is stuck at the 2008 figure of £25,000, while some employers, notably in banking and financial services, will be cutting graduate salaries - by up to 8% in some cases. The salary freeze will be a particular blow to 2009 graduates, who are the first to have contributed tuition fees for the full three years of their degree courses.

Unsurprisingly, vacancies have been badly hit in the financial sector, with a 28% cut in vacancies in investment banking and a 10.7% decrease in financial services. Construction has also been hard hit, with 16.6% fewer vacancies predicted this year. There are also gloomy reports from sectors as varied as law, manufacturing, tourism and property services.

It would be a mistake, however, to believe that activity will decline across all areas of employment. We are heartened to hear skills in Information and Communications Technology described as 'credit crunch resistant' and we know that recruiters to certain shortage subjects in teaching will be delighted by the upsurge in interest from graduates who might otherwise have sought lucrative careers in the City.

We must also acknowledge the fact that most readers of this book will not be entering the labour market before 2011. If you are about to undertake a period of sixth-form or further education study, followed by three or four years in higher education, you won't be looking for a job until around 2015. We certainly hope that the current forecasts prove correct and that the recession of 2009 will by then be nothing more than a statistic for the history books.

The expectation is that the worst will be over by the second half of 2010, credit conditions will have eased and the economy will start expanding again. Demand will start to return and projects mothballed during the recession will be reactivated fairly quickly. In other words, recovery should be well established by the time you leave full-time education and there is every reason to make confident plans for your future career.

The Workbrief Analysis

In this publication, we cover some 300 career ideas in 173 carefully chosen chapters, each analysed under our unique WORKBRIEF headings. We cover a further 167 careers in the Additional Career Outlines section.

What is Involved?

What sort of work would I be doing? What kind of responsibilities would I have to deal with in a typical day or week?

Opportunities for Training

What sort of courses and qualifications are available? Do I need qualifications before I start? Can I work towards these on a part-time basis? Is there a choice of qualifications and/or routes?

Requirements for Entry

What exams would I have to pass in order to be considered for entry to this kind of course or work? Are there any other specific requirements?

Kind of Person

What personal qualities would help me succeed in this type of work? What skills are particularly important?

Broad Outlook

Is there likely to be a demand for this type of work in the future? What are the promotion prospects? Is there a chance of self-employment?

Related Occupations

Are there any similar careers for me to consider at this stage?

Impact on Lifestyle

How would this type of work affect my overall lifestyle? Would my work limit my free time, especially in the evening or at weekends? Is it likely to be hot/cold, dirty/clean, noisy, active, dangerous or whatever? What levels of stress would be involved?

Earnings Potential

How much would I be paid? Am I likely to be on salary/commission/bonus or whatever? Could this type of career give me an adequate or very good lifestyle? Are there any benefits apart from the salary?

Further Information

Where can I obtain more detailed information about this type of work? (Especially in terms of website addresses)

Why Workbrief?

Well, the chapters are *brief* and they're about *work*! Much more than that, Workbrief allows us to *brief* you about a type of work by answering questions about both the 'hard' facts (What will I be doing? What entry qualifications do I need?) and the equally important 'soft' aspects (Will doing this job affect my family or social life? What personal qualities might be important?). With each title analysed under identical headings in a double-page format, you get a clear briefing about a specific occupational area and you should find it easy and beneficial to compare and contrast a number of different career options.

The Workbrief Focus

The Careers Directory is aimed at young people who anticipate achieving or already have a range of GCSEs/S grades or equivalent at A-C/1-3, who hope to achieve AS/A level/Higher/Advanced Higher or equivalent qualifications and who are likely to progress to higher education. (See our comments below regarding equivalent qualifications). Much of the information is also relevant to undergraduate and postgraduate students.

University isn't for everyone and, if you feel this way, you might try exploring NotGoingToUni.co.uk. The award-winning jobs portal provides advice on alternatives to the traditional university route. The site is split into two sections: advice and jobs. The advice pages offer guidance on the opportunities available, while the job site brings together apprenticeships, school leaver jobs, training schemes, employer-funded degrees and more.

For full details, visit the website at: www.notgoingtouni.co.uk

Preparing for university

Given that many of the careers covered in this book require a degree as a starting point, we are concerned that universities report finding increasing numbers of candidates taking less than ideal combinations of A level subjects or equivalent.

The so-called 'Russell Group' of prestigious universities are consequently posting entry profiles on the UCAS website, giving detailed guidance on how you might best tailor your post-16 study to meet their admissions requirements.

No Russell Group institution bars any particular A level subject, although *General Studies* and *Critical Thinking* are not normally accepted as approved subjects for entry purposes.

With fierce competition for places at Russell Group universities - particularly for subjects such as Medicine, English and Law - it is difficult for admissions tutors to choose between uniformly excellent candidates. It is therefore worth taking care, if you are likely to be applying to these institutions, to ensure that you do not put yourself at a potential disadvantage by choosing a combination of subjects at A level that will not best equip you to excel on your chosen course.

Cambridge University and the London School of Economics, in particular, publish lists of less-preferred subjects. Cambridge's list has 20 A levels which could be considered 'less effective' in applications, including accounting, business, dance, ICT, media studies, sports studies and travel and tourism.

Equivalent Qualifications

While we are aware that the majority of our readers will progress from GCSEs/S grades to AS/A level/Higher/Advanced Higher examinations, we acknowledge that there are many equivalent qualifications - notably the International Baccalaureate (IB), European Baccalaureate (EB), Irish Leaving Certificate (ILC), National Vocational Qualifications (NVQ) and Scottish Vocational Qualifications (SVQ). For certain types of work, moreover, the Apprenticeship route might be more appropriate than traditional full-time study. You might also find that an Access course could help you return to higher education opportunities after taking a break from your studies.

The 2008/9 academic year has seen the introduction in England of the first five Diplomas - in engineering, construction, information technology, creative and media studies, and society, health and development. There will be 17 in place by 2011.

These new qualifications are intended to be an alternative to GCSEs and A levels for 14 to 19 year-olds, blending hands-on learning and theory. There are four different levels of diploma: foundation (level 1), higher (level 2) and progression/advanced (both level 3).

A Foundation Diploma is regarded as the equivalent of five GCSEs at grades D-G, a Higher Diploma is worth seven GCSEs at A*-C, a Progression Diploma equals 2.5 A levels, and an Advanced Diploma counts as 3.5 A levels. From 2011, an Extended Advanced Diploma will be worth 4.5 A levels. Diplomas will also involve 10 days' work experience, ideally in a field related to the diploma subject.

To find out more about Diplomas, visit the website at: http://yp.direct.gov.uk/diplomas

At the same time, A levels designed to stretch and challenge the most able students feature a greater variety of questions, including open-ended essays and case studies, asking you to analyse, evaluate or discuss topics. It is hoped that the new A* grade will be widely accepted by universities.

Some schools and colleges have abandoned A levels in favour of the Cambridge Pre-U, a new qualification devised by Cambridge University and seen as a return to traditional A level standards. Pre-U is currently being taught at 50 schools, 15 from the state sector and 35 independent, with another 100 schools preparing to offer Cambridge Pre-U within the next two to three years.

To be eligible for the two-year Diploma, students complete three Principal Subjects and a Global Perspectives and Research (GPR) component, a course focusing on global issues, which leads to an independent research report on a topic chosen by the student. The Diploma is flexible enough to accommodate students who wish to import existing A levels.

To find out more about Cambridge Pre-U, visit the website at: www.cie.org.uk

Unlike other baccalaureate qualifications, such as the IB or Welsh Bac, AQA Bacc retains A levels at its heart. The successful completion of three A levels, in any combination, is key to success in the Baccalaureate, with three additional elements required:

• An Enrichment Programme, recognising students' accomplishments away from the classroom, perhaps through the Duke of Edinburgh Award, work-related activities, community involvement or sporting achievement. The Bacc encourages students to go out into the world, to develop people skills in a non-academic context and to broaden the scope of their interests

• An Extended Project, developing students' abilities to manage tasks using their own initiative and resources

• Broader Study, designed to develop critical thinking/citizenship skills through an AS level examination in General Studies, Critical Thinking or Citizenship.

For full details, visit the website at: www.aqa.org.uk/qual/bacc.php

Rather than fill each page of this book with lengthy and repetitive listings of every possible alternative qualification, we mention the most commonly cited entrance requirements and add 'or equivalent'. Professional bodies and higher education institutions are fair and flexible when considering entry qualifications, so it is always worth making specific enquiries if you feel uncertain about matching the requirements for entry to a course or career.

In the requirements sections of each Workbrief chapter we refer to A levels. We do not normally mention Advanced Subsidiary (AS) level qualifications because these usually provide the first half of the eventual A levels awarded. AS subjects which are not converted to A levels can of course be counted for UCAS tariff points purposes, as explained later in this chapter.

You should be aware that the entry levels shown do not guarantee automatic acceptance by professional bodies or higher education institutions.

You can find out more about these qualifications and the most recent changes from:

Department for Children, Schools and Families
Website: www.dcsf.gov.uk

Qualifications and Curriculum Authority
Website: www.qca.org.uk

Learning and Skills Council
Website: www.lsc.gov.uk

Apprenticeships
Website: www.apprenticeships.org.uk

Welsh Assembly Government
Website: http://new.wales.gov.uk/topics/educationandskills

Northern Ireland Council for the Curriculum, Examinations and Assessment
Website: www.ccea.org.uk

Scottish Qualifications Authority
Website: www.sqa.org.uk

UCAS and Higher Education

Many of the articles in this book highlight the need for a higher education qualification. You can access a complete database of UK higher education provision and full details of how to apply at the Universities and Colleges Admissions Service (UCAS) website at: www.ucas.com

The Open University is not part of UCAS but you can explore the courses it offers at: www.open.ac.uk

The UCAS Tariff

UCAS operates a points system known as the UCAS Tariff for entry to higher education. This allows you to use a range of different qualifications to help secure a place on an undergraduate course.

Universities and colleges use the UCAS Tariff to make comparisons between applicants with different qualifications. Tariff points are often used in entry requirements, although other factors are often taken into account. You will find that Entry Profiles on the UCAS database provide a fuller picture of what admissions tutors are seeking.

The Tariff helps universities and colleges when deciding on course entry requirements and making conditional offers, although conditional offers that use Tariff points will often require a minimum level of achievement in a specified subject (for example '300 points to include grade A at A level chemistry', or '260 points including SQA Higher grade B in mathematics).

Use of the Tariff may also vary from department to department within any one university or college, and may in some cases be dependent on the programme being offered.

Key features of the UCAS Tariff:

- You can collect Tariff points from a range of different qualifications

- There is no ceiling to the number of points that can be accumulated

- Double counting is not allowed. Where you have different qualifications in the same subject, only the qualification with the higher Tariff score will be counted. This principle applies to: AS and A level, Scottish Highers and Advanced Highers, Key Skills at level 2, 3 and 4, speech, drama and music awards at grades 6, 7 and 8

- Tariff points for the Advanced Diploma come from the Progression Diploma score plus the relevant Additional and Specialist Learning (ASL) Tariff points

- Where the Tariff tables refer to specific awarding bodies, only qualifications from these awarding bodies attract Tariff points. Qualifications with a similar title, but from a different qualification awarding body do not attract Tariff points

To find out more about the Tariff and how it relates to your qualifications, visit the website at: www.ucas.com/students/ucas_tariff/tarifftables

To give you some idea of how the system works, here are some examples of Tariff points:

Advanced Extension Awards*

Grade	Tariff points
Distinction	40
Merit	20

*Points for Advanced Extension Awards are over and above those gained from the A level grade

Cambridge Pre-U Diploma*

Grade	Principal Subject	Global Perspectives and Research	Short Course
D1	To be confirmed	To be confirmed	To be confirmed
D2	145	140	To be confirmed
D3	130	126	60
M1	115	112	53
M2	101	98	46
M3	87	84	39
P1	73	70	32
P2	59	56	26
P3	46	42	20

*Points for Cambridge Pre-U Diploma come into effect for entry into higher education from 2010 onwards

Diploma in Foundation Studies (Art & Design, and Art, Design & Media)*

Grade	Tariff points
Distinction	285
Merit	225
Pass	165

*Points are awarded for Edexcel Level 3 BTEC Diploma in Foundation Studies (Art & Design) and Level 3 Diploma in Foundation Studies (Art, Design & Media) awarded by ABC Awards and WJEC

GCE AS, A level and VCE

Grade					Tariff points
GCE & AVCE Double Award	A level with additional AS (9 units)	GCE A level and AVCE	GCE AS Double Award	GCE AS & AS VCE	
A*A*					280
A*A					260
AA					240
AB					220
BB	A*A				200
BC	AA				180
	AB				170
CC					160
	BB				150
CD	BC	A*			140
DD	CC	A	AA		120
	CD		AB		110
DE		B	BB		100
	DD		BC		90
EE	DE	C	CC		80
			CD		70
	EE	D	DD	A	60
			DE	B	50
		E	EE	C	40
				D	30
				E	20

International Baccalaureate (IB) Diploma*

Grade	Tariff points
45	768
44	744
43	722
42	698
41	675
40	652
39	628
38	605
37	582
36	559
35	535
34	512
33	489
32	466
31	442
30	419
29	396
28	373
27	350
26	326
25	303
24	280

*The points for the International Baccalaureate (IB) are awarded to candidates who achieve the IB Diploma

Irish Leaving Certificate

Grade		Tariff points
Higher	Ordinary	
A1		90
A2		77
B1		71
B2		64
B3		58
C1		52
C2		45
C3	A1	39
D1		33
D2	A2	26
D3	B1	20
	B2	14
	B3	7

Scottish Higher and Advanced Higher (2010 onwards)

Grade	Higher	Advanced Higher
A	80	130
B	65	110
C	50	90
D	36	72

Welsh Baccalaureate Core*

Grade	Tariff points
Pass	120

*Points for the Core are awarded only when a candidate achieves the Welsh Baccalaureate Advanced Diploma

Engineering Qualifications

When covering engineering careers in this publication, we are concerned particularly with training and working as a professional engineer. There are many other valuable roles in engineering - at operative, craft and technician levels - but they are outside the immediate scope of this book. The professional level can be divided into two groups: chartered and incorporated.

As a *chartered engineer*, you would be involved with the processes of innovation, creativity and change that drive technological progress. You would develop and apply new technologies, promote advanced designs, improve production efficiency and pioneer new management methods. You could lead projects and work towards a senior management role in your organisation.

As an *incorporated engineer*, you would be more concerned with maintaining and managing applications of current technology, seeking to extract maximum efficiency from existing systems and processes. As with a chartered engineer, you could work towards a leading management role.

Aspects of the roles often overlap in practice and there is a corresponding closeness in the training routes available. The quickest route to either qualification is to obtain a degree accredited to Engineering Council standards by one of the professional engineering institutions. If you want to be a chartered engineer, you should select a four-year MEng course, for which you would need high grades at A level/Advanced Higher/Higher or equivalent. Maths is generally an essential requirement.

If you want to be an incorporated engineer, you should select a three-year BEng (or BSc or BTech) course. This would be more involved with practical applications than the more mathematical and theoretical syllabus of the MEng. Entry requirements for BEng courses are usually lower and more flexible.

You can convert your incorporated engineer qualification to chartered status by following an extra period of learning, known as a *matching section*, to bridge the gap between the BEng and MEng standard. You can do this over several years, while you are working, if you wish.

Whichever route you take, you could seek sponsorship for all or part of your course. You would gain industrial experience by working for your sponsor during the summer vacation and you would receive a salary to offset your student loan. You could also extend your course by a year in order to incorporate longer periods of industrial experience in a sandwich course.

When you have finished your degree, you would enter a period of *initial professional development* with an employer, during which you would apply your knowledge to solve real problems in a working environment. The final stage of this process is a professional review, in which you would have to show that you have the necessary competence and commitment. When this is successfully completed, you can call yourself a *chartered* or *incorporated* engineer and add the letters CEng or IEng after your name. Chartered status would also entitle you to register with the Fédération Européene d'Associations Nationales d'Ingénieurs and claim the title European Engineer (EurIng).

Further Information

Royal Academy of Engineering
Website: www.raengbest.org.uk

Year in Industry
Website: www.yini.org.uk

Engineering and Technology Board
Website: www.etechb.co.uk

Engineering Council UK, London WC2R 3ER
Website: www.engc.org.uk

Institution of Engineering and Technology, London WC2R 0BL
Website: www.theiet.org

About the Editors

Ken Reynolds is an experienced careers adviser, writer and consultant. He was Assistant Principal Careers Officer in Cornwall before moving on to edit *Careers Adviser*, *School Leaver* and *Which Course* magazines for Independent Educational Publishing. He has served as a member of the Institute of Career Guidance Editorial Board and as one of the judges for the annual National Career Awards.

John Mainstone is Chairman and a founder member of Cambridge Occupational Analysts Ltd (COA), formed in 1986. He has considerable experience in advising students in both careers and higher education matters - the fields in which COA specialises. His background includes industrial management, fine art publishing, teaching and career advisory work.

Contributors

The entries in the Careers Directory are based on original articles supplied by:

Jennie Barnes
Annie Edgar
Sue Eynon
Graham Garrett
Jill Garrett
Bob Jackson
Joyce Lane
John Mainstone
Ken Reynolds
Joanna Roberts
Godfrey Thomas

Acknowledgements

We acknowledge the considerable help given by the following organisations:

Armed Services Careers Office, Norwich
Association of Accounting Technicians
Association of Clinical Biochemists
Bar Council
British Dental Association
British Medical Association
British Pharmacological Society
British Psychological Society
Chartered Institute of Architectural Technologists
Chartered Institute of Building
Chartered Institute of Environmental Health
Chartered Institute of Librarians and Information Professionals
Chartered Institute of Personnel and Development
Chartered Society of Physiotherapy
College of Dispensing Opticians
College of Occupational Therapists
College of Optometrists
Council for British Archaeology
Dental Technician Training and Advisory Board
E Skills
Faculty of Advocates
Forensic Science Service
General Osteopathic Council
Hotel and Catering International Management Association
Institute of Actuaries
Institute of Barristers' Clerks
Institute of Biology
Institute of Chartered Secretaries and Administrators
Institute of Legal Executives
Institute of Management Consultants
Institute of Physics
Institute of Practitioners in Advertising
Institute of Public Relations
Institution of Agricultural Engineers
Institution of Engineering and Technology
Institution of Mechanical Engineers
Institution of Mining and Metallurgy
Market Research Society
Meteorological Office
National Council for the Training of Journalists
Qualifications and Curriculum Authority (QCA)
Royal Aeronautical Society
Royal College of Speech and Language Therapists
Royal Institute of British Architects
Royal Institute of Naval Architects
Royal Institution of Chartered Surveyors
Royal Pharmaceutical Society
Royal Town Planning Institute
Scottish Qualifications Authority (SQA)
Society of Chiropodists and Podiatrists
Society of General Microbiology
Society of Radiographers
UCAS

The WORKBRIEF Career Descriptions

What is Involved?

What sort of work would I be doing? What kind of responsibilities would I have to deal with in a typical day or week?

Opportunities for Training

What sort of courses and qualifications are available? Do I need qualifications before I start? Can I work towards these on a part-time basis? Is there a choice of qualifications and/or routes?

Requirements for Entry

What exams would I have to pass in order to be considered for entry to this kind of course or work? Are there any other specific requirements?

Kind of Person

What personal qualities would help me succeed in this type of work? What skills are particularly important?

Broad Outlook

Is there likely to be a demand for this type of work in the future? What are the promotion prospects? Is there a chance of self-employment?

Related Occupations

Are there any similar careers for me to consider at this stage?

Impact on Lifestyle

How would this type of work affect my overall lifestyle? Would my work limit my free time, especially in the evening or at weekends? Is it likely to be hot/cold, dirty/clean, noisy, active, dangerous or whatever? What levels of stress would be involved?

Earnings Potential

How much would I be paid? Am I likely to be on salary/commission/bonus or whatever? Could this type of career give me an adequate or very good lifestyle? Are there any benefits apart from the salary?

Further Information

Where can I obtain more detailed information about this type of work? (Especially in terms of website addresses)

Accountant (Professional)

What is Involved?

As a professionally qualified accountant, you would be working with financial and management information, using your specialist knowledge to advise a range of clients, from individuals to large organisations. There are several different professional bodies in accountancy and your initial employment could be linked to the specialist activities of the body you choose. You would find, however, that there is considerable overlap between the various professional qualifications and you could move between sectors later in your career.

Major areas of work include private practice (also known as public practice, which is not terribly helpful), the public sector and industry/commerce. In the first of these, you would work in a specialist firm of accountants offering services ranging from basic bookkeeping to audit (independent assessment of your client's current financial position), taxation advice, management consultancy and corporate financial planning. Working in the public sector could see you handling very large budgets in local or central government, the National Health Service, colleges or universities. As an accountant in industry/commerce, you could be involved in keeping financial records for a company, overseeing credit control systems and possibly participating in strategic planning for the organisation's future development.

Opportunities for Training

To gain recognition as a qualified accountant, you would need to spend several years pursuing the professional training route of one of the six main bodies, all listed in the Further Information section.

With so many different bodies, there are many routes to professional qualification. Most take three to five years and usually involve work experience in an approved organisation, part-time study and lots of exams. You may also opt to start as an accounting technician and then work your way towards professional status.

Requirements for Entry

As with training routes, entry requirements vary from one body to another. You would need at least two A level/Advanced Higher, three Higher or equivalent qualifications, together with three GCSE/S Grade passes A-C/1-3, including English and maths, to enter a training contract with ICAEW, ACCA, CIMA or CIPFA.

ICAS, on the other hand, would require a degree, unless you come through the accounting technician route. In practice, the most common entry route to professional accountancy training is with a degree in any academic subject. If you choose an accountancy-related degree subject, you should gain exemption from some of the exams set by the professional bodies.

Kind of Person

You need to be very computer, figure and systems literate. You do not have to be brilliant at maths but you should enjoy working with figures and problem solving, as well as being diligent and accurate. Employers have indicated that they are looking for good academic results together with other skills such as leadership, communication, numeracy, interest in finance and business, self-motivation and commitment.

Broad Outlook

An accountancy qualification is a very useful tool and demand for accountants is currently growing in all sectors. As your career develops, you could choose to work for a very large organisation, you could become self-employed and work as a freelance consultant or you could take advantage of the worldwide recognition of UK accountancy qualifications and travel extensively.

Related Occupations

You might also wish to consider: accounting technician, investment analyst, banking executive, chartered secretary, economist, stockbroker, tax inspector, insurance underwriter, actuary, management consultant or financial adviser.

Impact on Lifestyle

Normal working hours are Monday to Friday, nine to five, but your lifestyle as an accountant would depend very much on the sort of organisation you join and the area of specialisation you choose. Audits can take you all over the country and a large international partnership would expect you to travel. High salaries are possible but are usually associated with increased stress and longer working hours. You may have to move a few times to develop your career. One of the main lifestyle challenges for trainees is balancing part-time professional study commitments with the pressures of the day-to-day job.

Earnings Potential

Accountancy positions tend to pay well, which can mean anything from a reasonable to a considerable salary. Starting salaries for graduate trainees vary from around £19,000 to £25,000; salaries for school leaver trainees are rather lower. On achieving full qualification, you could expect to earn between £30,000 and £45,000 and, if you rise to become a partner in private practice or a senior manager in industry or the public sector, you could command a salary ranging from £60,000 to £100,000 plus.

Further Information

Institute of Chartered Accountants in England and Wales, Milton Keynes MK9 2FZ
Website: www.icaew.com

Institute of Chartered Accountants in Scotland, Edinburgh EH12 5BH
Website: www.icas.org.uk

Institute of Chartered Accountants in Ireland, Dublin 4
Website: www.icai.ie

Association of Chartered Certified Accountants, London WC2A 3EE
Website: www.accaglobal.com

Chartered Institute of Management Accountants, London SW1P 4NP
Website: www.cimaglobal.com

Chartered Institute of Public Finance & Accountancy, London WC2N 6RL
Website: www.cipfa.org.uk

Alternative/equivalent entrance requirements can include: ILC, IB, EB, NC/ND and many other similar international systems. For further details see the Equivalent Qualifications section in the Introduction.

Accounting Technician

What is Involved?

As an accounting technician, you could be working alongside professionally qualified accountants in activities such as keeping financial records, auditing accounts, preparing tax returns or providing information for management reports. You could be running a payroll or credit control system. There are opportunities in virtually every sector of the labour market: you might be based in a specialist accountancy practice, in industry or commerce, in the public or voluntary sectors or you could work from your own home for a variety of clients. Unlike a professional accountant, you would not be legally qualified to conduct a full-scale audit but you could be responsible for much of the groundwork. As a broad rule, you would be more likely to be involved with the detailed, practical applications of day-to-day accounting issues than with the wider areas of financial management dealt with by professionally qualified accountants. As your career develops, you may choose to specialise in a particular area of work, such as taxation or insolvency.

Opportunities for Training

The Association of Accounting Technicians (AAT) and the Association of Chartered Certified Accountants (ACCA) both offer training and qualification routes for accounting technicians. Several major chartered accountancy bodies sponsor the AAT and the qualification would make you eligible for entry to their professional examinations. You would work your way through N/SVQ foundation and intermediate levels 2 and 3 to become a technician at level 4. The completion of these levels, together with a year's relevant experience, achieves the qualification. The training scheme is offered at many different centres, including local colleges, the workplace and training providers. There is also a diploma route if you are not currently working in finance. With ACCA, you would work towards their Certified Accounting Technician qualification (CAT). Once you have this, you would be eligible for direct entry to Part 2 of the ACCA professional accountancy examination. Study is flexible and can be full- or part-time at a local college or training provider, by correspondence or online.

Requirements for Entry

There are no formal academic requirements for training with one of the organisations that award qualifications as an accounting technician, although you must be over 16 years old and should be reasonably numerate with a good command of English.

You may be able to gain exemption from part of the AAT qualification if you have relevant work experience or suitable A level/Advanced Higher, Higher or equivalent qualifications.

Kind of Person

As an accounting technician, you would need to feel completely at ease when working with numbers. You would also need to be accurate, with a sharp eye for detail, and you would need good communication skills in order to explain details of accountancy and finance to those less numerate than yourself. You would usually be working as part of a team. Good computer skills are essential. The work would often require you to keep to strict deadlines.

Broad Outlook

Opportunities for accounting technicians have grown in recent years, in line with the trend of shifting financial responsibility and decision making away from large central offices towards local, independent control. Qualifying as an accounting technician can be a step on the career ladder leading to full professional status, although many technicians enjoy their work as it is and do not wish to take further exams. With experience, you could move to a senior management position in a company or you could pursue the option of self-employment.

Related Occupations

You might wish to consider: professional accountant, bookkeeper, insurance clerk, banking executive or financial adviser.

Impact on Lifestyle

Accounting technicians are office based, working traditional office hours five days a week. You may have to move across the private and public sectors - and possibly to different parts of the country - in order to gain experience and develop your career. There may be opportunities for working from home and for part-time work.

The work can often be intense and pressurised with a constant need to meet important deadlines.

Earnings Potential

You may start on £11,000 to £15,000 as a trainee, with your salary rising from around £12,500 to £22,500 at the foundation stage, £13,500 to £25,500 at the intermediate stage and £20,000 to £28,000 or more once fully qualified and experienced. You can earn considerably more in a senior management post or if you are successful in running your own business. AAT and ACCA qualifications are recognised globally, meaning that you could work overseas if you wish.

Further Information

Association of Accounting Technicians, London EC1A 4HY
Website: www.aat.org.uk

Association of Chartered Certified Accountants, London WC2A 3EE
Website: www.accaglobal.com

Accounting Technician Online
Website: www.accountingtechnician.co.uk

Institute of Accounting Technicians in Ireland
Website: www.iati.ie

Alternative/equivalent entrance requirements can include: ILC, IB, EB, NC/ND and many other similar international systems. For further details see the Equivalent Qualifications section in the Introduction.

Actor

What is Involved?

As an actor, you would be a creative interpreter of dramatic works, comedies or musicals, performing in the theatre, in films, on television, video and radio. You should be prepared not merely to act but also to sing, dance and maybe undertake fights and stunt work. Glamour, fame and self-fulfilment might spur you on but can seem far away when you are rehearsing lines or sitting around while scenery and lights are adjusted. The varied working life of an actor might also see you doing voice-overs for advertisements, recording talking books or narrating documentary films.

Opportunities for Training

It is possible to become an actor without any formal training but you would be well advised to consider an accredited training course at a drama school. This would give you a much better chance of gaining employment and acquiring an Equity (the actors' union) Card.

Courses vary a good deal in style, so you should do plenty of research to determine which would be the best for you. Straight from school at the minimum age of 18, you would normally follow a three-year course. There are shorter courses available for graduates and mature candidates. The syllabus should include movement, voice projection, improvisation, singing, dancing, audition techniques, and make-up.

You must be careful not to confuse accredited drama school courses with the many drama or performing arts degrees offered by universities and colleges. These tend to be academic, concentrating on the history of drama and the analysis of texts rather than vocational training.

Requirements for Entry

Entry to accredited courses is fiercely competitive and you may find that you are one of 20 or so applicants competing for a single place. Admission is usually by audition and interview, with experience of performing regularly in amateur productions or youth theatre a great advantage. You may not need any special academic qualifications, although some drama schools ask for five GCSE/S Grade passes A-C/1-3 or equivalent and even two A level/Advanced Higher or three Higher or equivalent qualifications.

Kind of Person

Apart from possessing outstanding acting talent - the intelligence, sensitivity and imagination to understand and interpret various roles and the ability to present them to a theatre full of people or to a camera - you must be dedicated, determined and disciplined.

You would need to be strong enough, both physically and mentally, to withstand the long hours of rehearsal, the emotional demands of public performance, the disappointment of rejection at audition and the pain of negative criticism. A good memory is clearly important, together with a mixture of self-confidence and willingness to work in an ensemble. A feeling for music and movement would also be of great benefit.

Broad Outlook

You can build a name for yourself by working hard and giving good performances. There is often a degree of luck involved in having the right talents and being available at the right time for a particular project. Many actors, it must be said, spend more time looking for work than they do performing. You need to bring yourself to the notice of casting directors and producers whenever possible and you might find it useful to have an agent to help you get work. Networking and personal contacts are also invaluable tools in the hunt for work. Many actors provide themselves with other qualifications as well, so that they can earn some money in other fields when the going gets tough.

Related Occupations

You might also consider: drama teacher, dramatherapist or speech and language therapist. If being in the theatre is your main motivation, you might look at: stage manager, musician, dancer, production assistant or TV/film camera operator.

Impact on Lifestyle

As an actor, you would probably be seen as a member of a glamorous profession. There certainly are great rewards for some in terms of fame and personal fulfilment but you should be aware of the restrictions this could put on your private life. Most performances take place in the evening and at the weekend, and a long run in the theatre could take you out of social circulation for weeks on end. You may find that you would spend a considerable time away from home, staying in a variety of surroundings.

Earnings Potential

Be prepared for the fact that, on average, actors work professionally for only 11.3 weeks per year. When working, you should be entitled to the pay rates negotiated by Equity, with a current minimum wage of, for example, £400 a week in a London West End theatre or £350 in subsidised repertory in the provinces. Lodgings allowances could be available if you are on tour and your agent may be able to negotiate a rate for you above the minimum level. If you are not a member of Equity, you may be expected to work for less than the minimum rate. Stardom would entitle you to demand whatever sum you or your agent can command!

Further Information

National Council for Drama Training, London WC1H 0JJ
Website: www.ncdt.co.uk

British Actors' Equity Association, London WC2H 9EG
Website: www.equity.org.uk

Conference of Drama Schools, London NW5 1XJ
Website: www.drama.ac.uk

Get Into Theatre
Website: www.getintotheatre.org

Gaiety School of Acting, Dublin 2
Website: www.gaietyschool.com

Alternative/equivalent entrance requirements can include: ILC, IB, EB, NC/ND and many other similar international systems. For further details see the Equivalent Qualifications section in the Introduction

Actuary

What is Involved?

As an actuary, you would use your specialist statistical skills to make financial sense of the future. Using a database of previously accumulated information, statistics, probability theory and compound interest, you would design solutions to questions of financial risk, particularly in the fields of insurance, pensions, risk assessment and investment. For example, you might be asked to consider how much money a company would need to invest in order to pay its employees a reasonable pension when they retire.

You could work for the Government Actuary's Department (GAD), reporting to Parliament on such matters as projected population growth or forecasting funding needs for the National Health Service. Alternatively, you might advise an insurance company on the premiums required to make life insurance policies competitive while still offering a reasonable return for customers and shareholders.

Opportunities for Training

There are two professional bodies - the Institute of Actuaries in England and Wales and the Faculty of Actuaries in Scotland - and in order to qualify you would need to become a fellow with one of them. The two bodies are likely to merge in the very near future. Working towards fellowship would mean finding employment with a firm of actuaries and passing a series of professional exams, mainly via correspondence courses and tutorials, taking about 15 to 20 hours a week. The examination system is flexible in that you can take as many exams as you like at one sitting.

In addition to your degree course, it would usually take three to six years to obtain your full professional qualification.

Requirements for Entry

For entry to a degree course, you would need at least two or three A level/Advanced Higher or three or four Higher or equivalent qualifications, including a good pass in maths, together with five GCSE/S Grade passes at A-C/1-3 or equivalent, including maths and English. While any degree subject is acceptable, you would find it advantageous to obtain a good honours degree in maths, actuarial science or a related subject such as economics or statistics. You would be expected to gain relevant work experience during your university holidays.

To help you check whether you meet the rigorous entry requirements, the professional body invites people who have not yet joined the profession to take its Financial Mathematics exam. Full details of how to apply can be found on the Institute/Faculty website.

Kind of Person

You would need to be the sort of person who finds solving difficult numerical problems very satisfying. Employers would expect you to be highly numerate and analytical, with sufficient people and communication skills to explain your work to non-mathematicians, work with other professionals and manage teams of colleagues. Accuracy and attention to detail would be very important, as would excellent time management, prioritising and IT skills. The training is long and difficult and you would need determination to see it through.

Broad Outlook

Employment prospects are excellent. Actuaries can work for the public or private sectors and are involved in all sorts of areas, including corporate finance, asset management, international business and investment. The Financial Services Act and the Pensions Review have both had a big impact and the actuarial market is a growth area.

Very few actuaries are unemployed and hardly anyone feels the need, once qualified, to leave actuarial work. As the UK qualification is highly valued throughout the world, it is possible to spend part or all of your career abroad.

As a Fellow, you would be one of only 9,000 qualified actuaries in the UK. About 60% of your colleagues would be working for insurance companies and 30% in consultancy, where they would advise clients mainly on pension provision or insurance requirements. GAD is a unique organisation, both a government department and an actuarial consulting firm operating on commercial lines.

As part of a campaign to attract more high-flying graduates, the profession now has a Facebook page, providing an opportunity for you to learn about actuarial work and to engage directly with people currently pursuing an actuarial career.

Related Occupations

You may wish to consider: accountant, chartered secretary, insurance underwriter, investment analyst, stockbroker or financial adviser.

Impact on Lifestyle

You could expect your life as an actuarial student to be dominated by long hours and examinations, which could mean temporarily giving up any aspects of your social life that conflict with your professional studies. A good training package from your employer would be very important as you would need their support and study leave for exams. This is very responsible and demanding work, which can be stressful, especially when huge financial risks are involved.

Earnings Potential

The actuarial profession is very well paid. Figures from the latest salary survey show £30,500 to £35,000 for a student actuary, rising to £46,000 to £55,000 on qualification. A senior actuary/junior consultant typically earns around £90,000 a year and a chief actuary/senior partner £160,000 plus.

Further Information

Institute of Actuaries, Oxford OX1 2AW
Website: www.actuaries.org.uk

Faculty of Actuaries in Scotland, Edinburgh EH1 3PP
Website: www.actuaries.org.uk

Government Actuary's Department, London EC4A 1AB
Website: www.gad.gov.uk

Association of Consulting Actuaries
Website: www.aca.org.uk

Alternative/equivalent entrance requirements can include: ILC, IB, EB, NC/ND and many other similar international systems. For further details see the Equivalent Qualifications section in the Introduction

Advertising Executive

What is Involved?

Advertising agencies are employed by their clients to promote almost anything, from products, services and information to health warnings, entitlements to state assistance, job vacancies, sales of houses, flats, holidays, travel and educational opportunities.

- As an *Account Executive*, you would liaise with a client to assess the message the client wishes to promote and then work out and cost, with the help of your colleagues, a suitable campaign. You would report back to your client for final approval. You would then monitor the whole programme and ensure it is completed on time and within budget.

- As an *Advertising Copywriter*, you would write the words for advertisements using suitable slogans, jingles, or scripts for TV commercials - helping to make the advertisements both memorable and persuasive.

- As an *Art Director*, you would plan the visual aspects of a campaign. You would need an artistic training for this career, which could be highly creative, whether in terms of TV commercials, illustration of the script, layout of advertisements, sales literature or the artistic layout of the client's website.

- As a *Media Executive*, you would need knowledge and experience of the media and would know how to place advertisements to influence the maximum number of potential buyers at the most economic cost to your client. You would then buy time on television, cinema or radio, or book space in magazines or newspapers.

- As an *Account Planner* or *Market Researcher*, you would be responsible for ensuring that the advertising campaign is targeted at the right market place or audience. You would carry out market research into the client's field of activity, assess consumer attitudes and look at the techniques used by competitors for similar work.

Opportunities for Training

There are no essential training routes, although most agencies have a defined professional development programme that runs alongside the day-to-day on the job experience. You may be able to work towards the CAM (Communication Advertising and Marketing) Diploma or to access the professional development programme offered by the Institute of Practitioners in Advertising (IPA).

Requirements for Entry

Advertising and media agencies will generally look for people with a degree, yet this can be in almost any area. The industry tends to recruit from a broad base of degree subjects in order to achieve diversity of thinking and ideas. Several universities and colleges offer relevant courses, some with modules focusing on either the creative or the business side of advertising. For art director posts, you would probably start your training with an art and design foundation course followed by a relevant degree.

Kind of Person

In all of these fields, you would need a combination of commercial and creative skills. On the creative side, you must have an original imagination with strong visual or writing powers; on the business side, you would need excellent communication skills and a high level of numeracy. Developing campaigns calls for the imagination to see how others would react to your ideas and being flexible enough to change quickly if you get things wrong.

Broad Outlook

Advertising is an extremely popular career choice, with many applicants competing for every vacancy. Once you are in employment, promotion tends to be based on experience and proven track record. There is a tendency for creative and commercial functions to merge, so you would improve your prospects if you can combine imaginative flair with sound business sense. Agencies differ in size and speciality and executives often seek promotion by moving between agencies. With sufficient experience, you could start your own business.

Related Occupations

In the creative field, you might consider: artist/illustrator, graphic designer, photographer, web designer or journalist.

In the more commercial arena, you might consider: marketing or sales manager, public relations officer or market research executive.

Impact on Lifestyle

This job is mainly office based, although you would have to travel to meet clients. To bring in a campaign on time, you might have to work long, irregular hours. Advertising is a young person's world and the great majority of people employed in this field are under 40. A job in advertising tends to be seen as glamorous, but it is recognised as a demanding and difficult world to enter.

Earnings Potential

Earnings differ greatly from agency to agency. Those based in London tend to pay the most and as a graduate recruit you could expect to earn between £18,000 and £25,000. With experience you could earn about £45,000 to £75,000, while the most senior posts pay £150,000 plus.

Further Information

Institute of Practitioners in Advertising, London SW1X 8QS
Website: www.ipa.co.uk

Communication, Advertising and Marketing Education Foundation (CAM), Maidenhead SL6 9QH
Website: www.camfoundation.com

Advertising Association, London SW1P 1RT
Website: www.adassoc.org.uk

Design and Art Directors Association, London SE11 5EE
Website: www.dandad.org

Young Creative Network, London EC2A 3AY
Website: www.ycnonline.com

Creative Circle, London W1T 4HF
Website: www.creativecircle.co.uk

Creative Choices
Website: www.creative-choices.co.uk

Alternative/equivalent entrance requirements can include: ILC, IB, EB, NC/ND and many other similar international systems. For further details see the Equivalent Qualifications section in the Introduction.

Advocate

See also Barrister for England, Wales, Northern Ireland and Republic of Ireland

What is Involved?

As an advocate, you would work as a member of the Scottish Bar, representing clients in courts of law and giving specialist legal advice. You would work as an expert in a specific area of the law and would be consulted by solicitors or other professionals. You would not work directly for the general public. As well as appearing in court, you might be consulted on a particular point of law or you may appear at a tribunal or enquiry. Advocates can also find employment working for the government or as part of the in-house legal team in a large organisation.

Most advocates work as self-employed independent professionals, based in the Advocates' Library in Edinburgh. A group of advocates who share a clerk are known as a 'stable'. This system offers some support to newly qualified advocates but you would need to build your own reputation in order to get work. It would help to establish a good relationship with the clerk of your stable, who would be, to some extent, responsible for allocating the work that comes in.

Opportunities for Training

The process of becoming an advocate is currently under review. At the moment, after completing a degree of the requisite standard in Scottish law and the one-year, full-time Diploma in Legal Practice at a Scottish university, you must undertake a period of full-time training (usually 21 months) in a solicitor's office approved by the Faculty of Advocates. After you have been formally admitted by the Faculty as an Intrant (trainee advocate) and passed certain examinations there comes a further eight/nine month period of unpaid practical training ('devilling') with an experienced advocate (a devilmaster) and finally a competency assessment, which covers written and oral advocacy skills. Current advice is that you should complete a two-year solicitor's traineeship so that you can qualify and practise for some years as a solicitor before going to the Bar.

Requirements for Entry

Degrees in Scottish law are popular and you would need to get good results in your Higher/Advanced Higher subjects in order to be accepted. It would also be helpful if you could show, through work experience, that you have a genuine interest in the law and its processes.

Kind of Person

You would need complete integrity of character and must be deemed to carry the 'seven lamps' of advocacy: honesty, courage, industry, wit, eloquence, judgment and fellowship. Self-confidence, the intellectual capacity to assimilate large volumes of information in a short time, and the ability to work long hours with tight deadlines and high levels of responsibility are all essential. In addition, you would need the motivation and determination to succeed in what can be a daunting profession, particularly in the early years.

Broad Outlook

In the early days as an advocate, you may have to work for a reduced fee or work in lower courts in order to get yourself known. It can be hard work for little reward for the first few years, after which it is usually clear whether you are going to be successful.

There are no guarantees of employment, meaning that your job security would depend entirely on your own ability and reputation. You would be part of a small profession, with only 460 advocates currently in practice at the Bar. This compares with around 8,000 solicitors in practice in Scotland.

Related Occupations

You might consider solicitor, civil service administrator, barrister or legal executive (England and Wales).

Impact on Lifestyle

The hours of work can be very long, especially when you are starting out, and can be unsocial as you have to prepare late into the evenings and travel to courts. However, you should be able to do quite a lot of work from home and, if you are successful, to be selective in the sort of work you prefer to do. Payment often comes in some time after the work has been done and this can be a particular problem in the early years.

Advocates who are employed would have the security of receiving a regular wage but may not have the potential for the very high earnings that are possible for advocates in legal practice.

Earnings Potential

Whilst you are working as an intrant in a solicitor's office, you would receive a guaranteed minimum salary. This would be around £15,000 at present for the first year, rising to around £18,000 in the second year. You would not receive any money during your nine months of devilling. There are scholarships available but you are more likely to be funding yourself. As a practising advocate, you would be self-employed so your earnings would vary enormously, depending on the nature and extent of the instructions you receive and the reputation you develop.

Further Information

Faculty of Advocates, Edinburgh EH1 1RF
Website: www.advocates.org.uk

Alternative/equivalent entrance requirements can include: ILC, IB, EB, NC/ND and many other similar international systems. For further details see the Equivalent Qualifications section in the Introduction.

Aeronautical Engineer

What is Involved?

As an aeronautical or aerospace engineer, you would be concerned with all aspects of making things fly and keeping them flying. This could range from missiles or one-man microlites right up to the largest passenger planes. You could be involved at all stages of the planning, design and testing of the aircraft. In addition you might be concerned with developing new technology. You would need to consider factors such as aerodynamics, the most appropriate materials to use, electrical systems and the means of propulsion. You could find yourself involved with the design of any aspect of the aircraft, from the wings to the guidance system used. You might choose to become a specialist in one particular field, such as thermodynamics or onboard computer technology. You could find yourself developing ideas for either for civil or military aircraft. This is an industry where you would be likely to be working with new, cutting edge technology.

Opportunities for Training

There are 33 UK universities offering degrees in aeronautical or aerospace engineering. Some focus more on production and some on electronics or research, so you should read the prospectuses carefully; there is also a variation in the degree of specialisation as some courses are designed to show the integrated nature of engineering degrees. You should certainly check that your course is accredited with the Royal Aeronautical Society.

In order to become a chartered engineer (CEng), you would need to complete at least four years of academic study on a course leading to an MEng. There are also three-year courses leading to a BEng degree, which could take you to incorporated engineer (IEng) status.

Requirements for Entry

In order to study for a degree course in aeronautical engineering or one that incorporates aeronautics options, you are likely to need at least five GCSE/S grades A-C/1-3 plus three A level/Advanced Higher, four Higher or equivalent qualifications, to include maths, physics, and/or another science or technology subject.

Kind of Person

You would need a keen interest in aviation, a very logical and practical approach to problem solving and an ability to understand and to keep up to date with modern technology. You would need to be able to check technical specifications accurately and to follow detailed designs. You might be involved with conducting lengthy equipment tests and would need to show attention to detail. You are likely to be involved with analysing data, so would need to be numerate and able to use computer technology in your work. In addition to your scientific and practical engineering skills, you are likely to be working as a member of a team so you would need to be able to get on well with others. You would be expected to communicate both with fellow professionals and with others who do not have your specialised knowledge.

Broad Outlook

This is a relatively small and specialised field but there are good opportunities for well-qualified graduates, particularly if you can demonstrate some work experience. Aeronautical engineers may work for manufacturing companies, airline operators, the armed forces and the Defence Evaluation and Research Agency. There are also opportunities to work abroad. Many employers would be interested in sponsoring you for at least some of your time at university. There has been a low unemployment rate for qualified engineers in recent years but economic factors can cause cutbacks in aircraft production.

Related Occupations

You might wish to consider: RAF officer, airline pilot, mechanical engineer, electrical/electronic engineer engineer, naval architect, materials scientist or metallurgist.

Impact on Lifestyle

Whilst you may have set conditions of work, there are times when you may need to work long hours in order to meet a deadline or to solve a particular problem. You might be based in a laboratory but you could have to work outside or possibly on a wind tunnel project for example. You might be expected to travel to conferences or meetings, which could be in another part of the country or abroad.

Earnings Potential

As a recent graduate you could expect to start on around £22,000 to £30,000, rising after a few years to £35,000 to £55,000. Once you are experienced, your salary is likely to rise to £50,000 to £65,000. Average earnings for incorporated engineers are around £42,000.

Further Information

Royal Aeronautical Society, London W1J 7BQ
Website: www.aerosociety.com

Society of British Aerospace Companies, London SE1 7SP
Website: www.sbac.co.uk

British National Space Centre, London SW1W 9SS
Website: www.bnsc.gov.uk

Alternative/equivalent entrance requirements can include: ILC, IB, EB, NC/ND and many other similar international systems. For further details see the Equivalent Qualifications section in the Introduction.

Agricultural/Land-based Engineer

What is Involved?

As an agricultural engineer (or land-based engineer), you would be working as a specialist in technology related to agriculture or one of the allied land based industries, including forestry, food engineering and technology, renewable energy, horticulture and the environment. These are highly mechanised industries and you would be involved with the design, development and maintenance of the specialised equipment currently in use. You could expect to be involved with: tractors and tillage machines, harvesting equipment, crop processing, animal welfare (handling and transport), irrigation and drainage schemes, earth moving and other construction equipment, pioneer road and bridge construction, forestry machines, horticultural machines and fish farming equipment.

You could also work in areas such as field engineering, land reclamation, drainage and irrigation and the systems used for this or the management of the field-to-table supply chain. You could combine your technical engineering skills with management and economic knowledge and play a valuable role in many aspects of an industry that is undergoing rapid change at the moment.

Opportunities for Training

This is a specialised area and there are few universities or HE colleges that run courses in engineering for the land-based sector. It is possible to take a three-year course that leads to the BEng or a four-year course leading to the MEng degree. There are also sandwich courses available, which allow for time to be spent working in industry as part of the course, and you could combine agricultural engineering with another subject, such as management. In order to become a chartered engineer, you would need to take an accredited course and to complete at least four years of academic study; to become an incorporated engineer, you would need at least a three-year accredited course (see separate article on engineering qualifications).

A new chartered environmentalist (CEnv) award is now available from the Society for the Environment. It is available through a number of professional institutions, and is open to members of the Institution of Agricultural Engineers involved in environmental work.

Requirements for Entry

Some universities would require you to have maths at A level/Advanced Higher, Higher or equivalent qualification, but even those that do not actually insist on maths would prefer you to have it. Most universities would also prefer you to have physics at A level/Advanced Higher, Higher or equivalent as well.

Kind of Person

You would need to have a strong interest in and understanding of agriculture, horticulture or forestry and the ways that these industries work. You should have a very practical and logical approach to problem solving and a strong mechanical interest. You would need to be able to analyse problems clearly and then to produce workable solutions. In addition to your technical and engineering skills, you would need to be able to communicate your ideas to others. You may well find yourself working as part of a small team, in which case you would be required to tell others what you think and to listen to their points of view. You could find yourself explaining your proposals to others who do not have your expert knowledge, or having to 'sell' your ideas in other cases.

Broad Outlook

As with most engineering disciplines, there is a serious shortage of engineering skills in the land-based sector. This is particularly evident in the area of servicing. There are good opportunities for well-qualified and knowledgeable engineers who can help to bring solutions to the range of problems facing agriculture, horticulture and forestry today. The industry needs to change and adapt to different demands and conditions both in the UK and abroad. There is a constant need to find more efficient and sustainable ways of using natural resources and more profitable ways of farming, with implications for recycling and environmental concerns. There are opportunities to work abroad, particularly in developing countries.

We are likely to see in the near future a new profession of biosystems engineers, combining knowledge of biological systems and processes with a strong engineering background. This will allow practitioners to be involved with issues concerning human health and welfare, including biomedical engineering, regenerative medicine, innovative materials and biomaterials, bio-mechatronics, bio-fuels and alternative energy sources.

Related Occupations

You might be interested in working in another branch of engineering as, for example, a mechanical, automotive, manufacturing or mining engineer. Alternatively, you might like to become a farm, commercial horticulture or estate manager.

You might consider becoming an agricultural adviser, an equipment seller or a food researcher.

Impact on Lifestyle

Whilst you might find yourself working normal office hours, you are also likely to be required to travel out to farms or factories, which could involve longer hours. You may need to be outside in all kinds of weather, which may involve you getting wet, cold and dirty, or hot and dusty in developing countries with primitive facilities. You may have to travel to get to your clients or to the areas where they need your advice. At times you might find yourself working with potentially dangerous equipment and be required to take the necessary safety precautions.

Earnings Potential

You are likely to be paid around £22,000 to £24,000 when you first graduate. This can rise as you gain experience to around £50,000 to £55,000 for a chartered engineer and £36,000 to £38,000 for an incorporated engineer.

Further Information

Institution of Agricultural Engineers, Bedford MK45 4FH
Website: www.iagre.org

Agricultural Engineers' Association, Peterborough PE2 5LT
Website: www.aea.uk.com

Society for the Environment, Warwickshire CV9 1AH
Website: www.socenv.org.uk

Alternative/equivalent entrance requirements can include: ILC, IB, EB, NC/ND and many other similar international systems. For further details see the Equivalent Qualifications section in the Introduction.

Air Traffic Controller

What is Involved?

As an air traffic controller (ATCO), you would be part of a team ensuring the safety of all aircraft taking off, landing and overflying the United Kingdom. You could work at the main control centre at Swanwick, near Southampton, in Manchester or at Prestwick, near Glasgow, monitoring flights en route to their destinations; alternatively, you may be based at a specific airport, dealing with arriving and departing flights. In all situations, you would be communicating with pilots by radio, providing them with a radar-based picture of all the air traffic in their vicinity and authorising their movements in relation to the flight plans they submit before take-off.

Most air traffic controllers work for National Air Traffic Services (NATS) and this article is concerned primarily with a typical NATS career structure.

Opportunities for Training

Under the NATS training scheme, you would begin your training with a 6 to 12-month course at the NATS College of Air Traffic Control, next to Bournemouth International Airport. You would develop teamwork skills, undertake practical training in simulators, do some private flying and visit air traffic control units. In the process, you would work towards ratings for the specific type of work you choose to do: aerodrome approach, approach control, approach radar control or area radar control. You can't do everything and your specialist rating would determine whether you work at a control centre or an airport.

On successful completion of the student phase, you would be posted to an operational unit as a trainee controller and would continue to develop your skills as you work towards your Certificate of Competency as an operational controller.

Requirements for Entry

You must be at least 18 and under 36 when you apply, in good overall health, with particular reference to hearing, eyesight and colour vision. Glasses or contact lenses are acceptable within certain limits. You would need at least five GCSE/S Grade passes A-C/1-3, including English and maths and to have studied through to examination two A level/Advanced Higher, three Higher or equivalent qualifications. You must be eligible to work in the UK and you must be security vetted. Following a series of psychometric tests and personality assessments, you would proceed to a second stage of interviews and computer tests.

Kind of Person

Because of the intense nature of the work, much of it sitting at radar screens and computer displays, you would need a high level of concentration and the ability to stay alert for sustained periods. You would need to be able to work both quickly and accurately under pressure and stay calm and focused; to think logically and to react quickly if required. Although the international language of air traffic control is English, you would need to be tolerant when communicating with pilots whose English is not strong, particularly in emergency situations. You must have a clear speaking voice.

You should be a good team player but able to work on your own. You should also have an aptitude to work with complex radar systems and the ability to think in 3D and calculate distances and angles.

Broad Outlook

With the continuous increase in air travel, despite the recent economic downturn, the further development of air traffic control is assured. The new 'state of the art' centre at Swanwick is the largest and most hi-tech in the world. All European air traffic control will be integrated at some stage in the future and NATS will have to compete for contracts against other member states of the European Union.

Once qualified, some 80% of ATCOs remain operational throughout their career. However, opportunities do exist for those who are interested in moving on to other areas. You could, for example, become a watch manager, or even a unit manager. Air traffic controllers can also apply to become trainers of new controllers.

Reducing the impact of air traffic operations on the environment is a top priority for the future and NATS has pledged to reduce the total CO_2 emissions by aircraft it controls by an average of 10% per flight by 2020. NATS is the first company in its sector to create this kind of environmental aim.

Related Occupations

You might wish to consider: air traffic controller in the armed forces, airline pilot, RAF officer or other posts in civil aviation.

Impact on Lifestyle

Although you would work a 40-hour week, you would be expected to complete this in eight-hour shifts, including nights, weekends and public holidays. The work is entirely indoors, mostly wearing headphones and speaking into a microphone. It is extremely tiring and you would normally expect a break of at least 30 minutes after two hours of sitting in front of a radar screen.

You must be prepared to work at any NATS operational unit, depending on vacancies and your specialist qualifications. NATS has over 40 manned sites across the UK, including radar and radio stations, control towers at airports, area control centres, corporate headquarters, and the College of Air Traffic Control.

Earnings Potential

You would start on a basic salary of £10,500 per annum for your initial period at college, rising to £15,000 to £18,000 when you start your unit training. On the third anniversary of your career with NATS, and on appointment as an ATCO, you would be on a salary scale ranging from £39,992 to £44,857 plus £5247 shift pay. At Swanwick and Heathrow, potential earnings including shift pay are over £85,000. Outer London weighting is also payable at Heathrow.

Further Information

National Air Traffic Services Ltd, London WC2B 4AP
Website: www.natscareers.co.uk

Alternative/equivalent entrance requirements can include: ILC, IB, EB, NC/ND and many other similar international systems. For further details see the Equivalent Qualifications section in the Introduction.

Airline Pilot

What is Involved?

As an airline pilot, you would fly aircraft on scheduled and chartered flights, transporting passengers and cargo. You would normally be one of two pilots on the flight deck, starting as first officer or co-pilot and working up to promotion as captain or commander. You would be in overall charge as captain, responsible for the safety of the aircraft and everyone on board. A typical flight would follow a logical sequence of tasks: before take-off, for example, you would decide on a flight plan, taking into account the weather conditions, the number of passengers and amount of cargo. You would supervise loading and fuelling operations, brief the cabin crew and carry out all the necessary pre-flight checks of operating systems. When ready for take-off, you would liaise with air traffic control for permission to proceed to the runway. During the flight, you would maintain a series of checks on the aircraft's position and technical performance, monitor weather conditions and other air traffic, communicate with air traffic controllers and advise passengers of flight details. Finally, you would land under instruction from air traffic control and would write a report on the flight.

Opportunities for Training

You would need to complete a lengthy and expensive training programme in order to obtain your Airline Transport Pilot's Licence (ATPL), which is essential to work as a captain. Among the different routes, you could start with a Private Pilot's Licence (PPL) and 150 hours of flying experience, working up to the ATPL through part-time attendance (totalling about 26 weeks) at an air training school. If you do not already have a PPL, you can take a longer training course of 47 to 60 weeks at an air training school. In either case, you should emerge with a 'frozen' ATPL, which you would convert to the full qualification by accumulating 1500 hours of flying experience, about a third of which would be as a co-pilot. Because of the very high cost of pilot training, you might want to seek full or partial sponsorship by an airline. Schemes vary but you could normally expect to repay up to half of your training costs once you start working. A popular alternative route is to qualify as a pilot in the armed forces and take a conversion course at the end of your military career.

Requirements for Entry

You must hold a medical certificate from the European Aviation Safety Agency, confirming that you are physically fit, with normal colour vision and good hearing and eyesight. Glasses may be allowed and some airlines specify minimum height requirements. Most flying schools look for a minimum of five GCSE/S Grade passes at A-C/1-3, including English, maths and a science. Airlines offering sponsorship usually ask for more than this and would normally expect two A level/Advanced Higher, three Higher or equivalent qualifications, preferably including maths and physics.

Kind of Person

Your spatial aptitude must be very high, including the ability to think clearly in three dimensions and to interpret maps quickly and accurately. You would also need a high level of numeracy for making mathematical calculations. Excellent communication skills would be essential for linking with air traffic control, briefing the cabin crew liaising with passengers and producing written reports. Qualities of leadership, initiative, adaptability and the ability to work well with other people would be required, together with high levels of concentration and attention to detail, the ability to stay calm under pressure and the authority to take charge in an emergency.

Broad Outlook

It would normally take you about seven years to reach the required number of flying hours to progress from first officer to captain. You may have to change employers several times during your career, either for better pay or to make the step up to captain.

The airline industry is undergoing considerable change and has been severely affected by the current economic downturn. (2008 was the first year since 1991 to show a decline in passenger numbers at UK airports) Market conditions at present tend to favour new, low-cost companies rather than the traditional 'flag carriers.' Job prospects should, however, improve as the global economy recovers and more people choose to fly.

Related Occupations

You may consider air traffic controller, pilot in the armed services, or RAF officer.

Impact on Lifestyle

You would be away from home for extended periods of time, especially on long-haul flights. Your social and family life would have to be fitted around your job. Your hours of work would vary enormously but would usually include nights and weekends. While your time in the air would be restricted to 900 flying hours per year, your workload would not necessarily be spread evenly throughout the year; on charter airlines, for example, the summer months tend to be busier than the winter months. As a short- or long-haul pilot, you could expect to have 12 to 15 days off per month, but you would be lucky to have a regular day or night off each week. Long-haul pilots may suffer tiredness, particularly when flying regularly through different time zones.

Earnings Potential

Your salary would vary according to the type of aircraft you are flying, the airline you are working for and your experience. You would be paid more for flying jet aircraft than for flying turboprop planes. As an example, with one popular low-cost airline, the salary of a fully qualified captain is £74,000 and of a first officer with a frozen ATPL £36,500. A rival airline pays experienced captains up to £140,000. Many airlines expect you either to pay for your own 'type training' to qualify you to fly a certain type of aircraft, or to pay the airline a bond of £15,000 to £30,000 to cover part of your training. Your bond would be repaid to you over a period of several years if you continue to fly with that airline.

Further Information

British Air Line Pilots Association, Hayes UB3 5BG
Website: www.balpa.org.uk
Civil Aviation Authority, London WC2B 6TE
Website: www.caa.co.uk
European Aviation Safety Agency
Website: www.easa.eu.int/home/index.html
Guild of Air Pilots and Air Navigators, London WC1R 5DJ
Website: www.gapan.org
Royal Aeronautical Society, London W1J 7BQ
Website: www.raes.org.uk
Pilot Training College of Ireland, Waterford
Website: www.pilottraining.ie

Alternative/equivalent entrance requirements can include: ILC, IB, EB, NC/ND and many other similar international systems. For further details see the Equivalent Qualifications section in the Introduction

Ambulance Paramedic

What is Involved?

As an ambulance technician/paramedic, you would respond to 999 and other urgent calls, travelling by ambulance, helicopter, car or motorbike to be at the scene of an emergency as soon as possible. You would be highly trained in all aspects of pre-hospital emergency care from crush injuries to cardiac arrest. Your aim would be to treat and stabilise patients before movement but not to delay hospital admission unnecessarily in order to achieve this. You would be working primarily in a vehicle designed to provide a clinical workplace with maximum mobility. It would be equipped with a wide range of emergency care equipment, including a heart defibrillator, spinal and traction splints, rescue equipment, intravenous drips, oxygen and a range of drugs for medical and traumatic emergencies. You would carry sophisticated patient monitoring equipment such as a pulse oximeter and cardiac and blood pressure monitors.

Opportunities for Training

Traditionally, staff joining the ambulance service could work their way up with experience and additional training from care assistant, through ambulance technician to paramedic. However, this route is no longer open to new entrants. Anyone wishing to work as a paramedic will now need either to secure a student paramedic position with an ambulance service trust, or to attend an approved full-time course in paramedic science at a university.

Courses tend to be modular, with flexible entry and exit point related to your academic qualifications and any relevant experience. They last from two to five years, depending on whether you study full- or part-time. The training comprises both theory and practical clinical experience, including several weeks in various hospital departments. Much of the training of paramedics is carried out under the supervision of senior doctors.

As a paramedic, you would have to register with the Health Professions Council, sitting a one-day paramedic refresher every year, and a five-day paramedic refresher every three years.

Requirements for Entry

The range of paramedic science courses at university varies in terms of entry requirements and you must contact each university directly for information on their admissions policy.

In order to drive an ambulance, whether emergency or non-emergency, you will need a full, manual driving licence. Ambulance services use vehicles of different gross weights and you must hold a driving licence with the appropriate classifications to enable you to drive ambulances in your chosen service. In some ambulance services, a 'standard' driving licence may be acceptable, but if you passed your test after 1996, you will need an extra driving qualification to drive larger vehicles and carry passengers. Some services may provide support for staff who need to gain further licence classifications but this is not standard across the UK.

Kind of Person

You would have to be highly skilled, quick thinking and decisive, yet able to provide a calm and reassuring environment for the patient and relatives. You would also need to be a good team worker, with excellent communication skills. Physical fitness would be essential to deal with moving and lifting patients and equipment. At the same time, you would need the manual dexterity to carry out treatment in awkward conditions.

Broad Outlook

As the ambulance service is run on a local basis, the demand for staff varies across the country, with more vacancies occurring in London and other urban areas. You should contact your local ambulance service for more details. There are some opportunities with ambulance services run by private hospitals or with large industrial companies who run their own on-site ambulance service. There is also some scope to train and work within the armed forces. Promotion to senior management positions can come after successful experience.

With further experience, you might take on one of the developing roles in the community such as an emergency care practitioner. Here you could be based in one of a number of different settings, such as a GP surgery, minor injuries unit or hospital accident and emergency department. You would usually need extra training and qualifications for this.

Related Occupations

You might also wish to consider: fire officer, health visitor, nurse, or police officer.

Impact on Lifestyle

You would have to work on rotating shifts, going out in all weathers at night, over the weekend and during public holidays. Most of the population respect ambulance personnel for the vital work they do but you should be prepared for the occasional hostile reception, especially when dealing with people under the influence of drink or drugs. As you would be wearing uniform, you would be immediately identifiable. The work can be stressful in that you would rarely know in advance the severity of the emergency to which you were responding; you could be dealing with a train crash or motorway pile-up involving seriously injured casualties.

Earnings Potential

NHS Trusts with vacancies for paramedic posts are likely to advertise these in Band 5, ranging from £20,710 to £26,839. An ambulance service area manager would be in Band 7, earning from £29,789 to £39,273. Additional allowances are paid for appointments in and around London, ranging from 20% of basic salary for Inner London, to 15% for Outer London and 5% for the London Fringe. In addition, up to 25% more can be earned as an unsocial hours allowance if shifts are worked.

Further Information

Ambulance Service Network, London SW1E 5DD
Website: wwww.nhsconfed.org/networks/ambulanceservice
British Paramedic Association, Derbyshire DE23 8GF
Website: www.britishparamedic.org
Scottish Ambulance Service, Edinburgh EH10 5UU
Website: www.scottishambulance.com
Welsh Ambulance Services, Denbighshire LL17 0WA
Website: www.ambulance.wales.nhs.uk
NHS Careers, PO Box 2311, Bristol BS2 2ZX
Website: www.nhscareers.nhs.uk
British Paramedic Resource Centre
Website: www.paramedic-resource-centre.com

Alternative/equivalent entrance requirements can include: ILC, IB, EB, NC/ND and many other similar international systems. For further details see the Equivalent Qualifications section in the Introduction.

Archaeologist

What is Involved?

Archaeology is the study of the past through objects left behind by previous generations. Studying the remains of the past can involve anything from old coins to buried cities. As an archaeologist, you could choose to take up teaching, lecturing, museum work, research or fieldwork. You would need a broad academic understanding of your subject before specialising in an area such as conservation, heritage management, underwater, computing or environmental archaeology; other specialisms include coins, weapons, ancient languages, chemical analysis and dating of specimens, as well as geographical areas (eg Egyptology) or historical periods (eg the Iron Age).

To show evidence of your commitment and enthusiasm, it would be a very good idea to do as much voluntary work as possible during your university holidays. The Council for British Archaeology (CBA) can help you arrange this, providing information about excavations requiring volunteers.

Opportunities for Training

Nearly all archaeologists are graduates and most have a first degree in archaeology. For some areas of archaeology (eg museum work) a postgraduate qualification is normally required.

There is great variation in the course content but most single honours courses include a basic core of archaeological methods, a broad geographical and chronological view of the subject, science, history and the role of archaeology in today's society. There is a trend also towards the more scientific aspects of archaeology, with several institutions offering BSc courses in archaeological science. Most courses offer a varying amount of practical fieldwork experience, often on research projects in Britain and abroad.

The Qualification in Archaeological Practice is a vocational qualification developed by the Archaeology Training Forum. It is awarded by Education Development International, currently the awarding body for cultural heritage NVQs in the museums sector. The qualification is offered at levels 3 (entry level) and 4 (experienced professional) with level 5 (strategic management) in development. Each level consists of core units and a range of options. This new qualification will enable you to demonstrate that you have particular sets of skills, competencies or experience, which will be of benefit when applying for jobs, promotion or membership of the Institute for Archaeologists (IfA).

Requirements for Entry

The minimum requirement for a degree course in archaeology is normally three A level/Advanced Higher or four Higher or equivalent qualifications, together with five GCSE/S Grade passes A-C/1-3, including English and maths. Geography, history and a foreign language are all useful subjects. Some science based degree courses ask for physics and chemistry. Archaeology has become a popular subject and high grades are, therefore, required.

Kind of Person

Archaeologists need a dual approach: digs require physical stamina and teamwork, whereas writing up your finds requires attention to detail and patience. You would need to have an academic interest in the past and it is important to realise that the finds made are not always glamorous. You would examine pieces of pottery, coins, human skeletons and bone fragments, which may reveal DNA evidence, together with organic matter which may need dating by processes such as isotopic analysis.

Broad Outlook

There are many archaeology graduates but fewer than 5,000 professional archaeologists employed in the UK. The main areas of work for archaeologists are in commercial archaeology units, museums, providing planning and development control advice through local authorities or specialist consultants. Many also work for the national heritage agencies (English Heritage, Historic Scotland and Cadw) or conservation charities, of which the National Trust is probably the biggest employer.

A number of archaeologists continue with academic research after graduation and some of these go on to teach in colleges and university departments. Some archaeologists are self-employed and many of these work as specialist consultants in their particular field, such as pottery or bone analysis. Most archaeology graduates enter the general graduate market, taking up commercial, financial, managerial and teaching careers (eg history, ancient history or classical studies).

Related Occupations

You may be interested in other careers in this field, such as historical researcher, museum/art curator or archaeological surveyor.

Impact on Lifestyle

Your hours of work would vary according to the type of archaeological activity being undertaken. Museum work usually involves a 36-hour week and some weekends. If you work for a local authority or national agency, you could also expect to work normal office hours. Work on excavations, however, is likely to involve long and sometimes unsocial hours, not to mention a potentially muddy, wet and windswept or achingly hot and unshaded workplace.

Earnings Potential

This varies depending on who you work for and your level of seniority. Generally, the pay tends to be low and you can expect to earn between £15,000 and £18,000 on graduating, rising to between £20,000 and £30,000. If you were working in education, you would be paid on the normal academic scale. The IfA stipulates minimum recommended starting salaries of £15,054 for a practitioner grade post, £17,534 for an associate member grade and £22,704 for a full member level post. In a recent job evaluation survey, the IfA acknowledges that its minimum rates are up to 53% lower than those for comparable posts in other sectors. British Archaeological Jobs and Resources also publishes recommended salary scales on its website.

Further Information

Council for British Archaeology, York YO30 7BZ
Website: www.britarch.ac.uk
Training Online Resource Centre for Archaeology
Website: www.torc.org.uk
Institute for Archaeologists, University of Reading RG6 6AB
Website: www.archaeologists.net
British Archaeological Jobs Resource
Website: www.bajr.org
Education Development International
Website: www.ediplc.com

Alternative/equivalent entrance requirements can include: ILC, IB, EB, NC/ND and many other similar international systems. For further details see the Equivalent Qualifications section in the Introduction.

Architect

What is Involved?

As an architect, you would be involved with designing and constructing new buildings or restoring old ones. You would have the power and the responsibility to shape the environments in which people spend their daily lives. Your designs must be attractive, practical, soundly conceived and not too expensive to turn into reality. You would need to combine both the creativity of using shape, colour, materials and space to meet your client's design requirements and the practicality of understanding planning and building regulations while meeting the physical demands of the construction process.

Opportunities for Training

In order to practise as an architect you would need to complete a seven-year training programme, which involves three stages:

- Firstly, a five-year degree at a recognised school of architecture; this consists of a three year intermediate degree (Part 1) and a two year further degree (Part 2);

- Secondly, two years in professional practice in an architect's office. The first year usually follows Part 1 and the second year follows Part 2;

- Thirdly, the Professional Practice Examination (Part 3).

The title 'architect' is protected in the UK by law. It is only by following this route - or an equivalent route recognised by the Royal Institute of British Architects (RIBA) and the Architects Registration Board (ARB) - that you could be eligible to call yourself an architect.

Requirements for Entry

To be accepted for a degree course at a school of architecture, you would need a minimum of two A level/Advanced Higher, three Higher or equivalent qualifications, plus five GCSE/S grades A-C/1-3 to include maths, English language, double award science or a single science in either chemistry or physics. Some courses may require maths or physics at A level/Advanced Higher or Higher, or art at A level/Advanced Higher/Higher or equivalent.

You could expect an interview by the schools you have applied to and they may want to see your portfolio. Your portfolio may include a mixture of photos, sketches of buildings, short notes, collages, still life and life drawings. They would be looking for evidence of creative skills together with an awareness of architecture. Work experience in an architect's office would be especially valuable here.

Kind of Person

Three-dimensional awareness is important, together with the ability to explain complex structures in the form of drawings. A balance of creative flair and technical skill is essential and you would almost certainly be using computers quite extensively. You should enjoy problem solving and you must have a keen interest in how people react in different types of built environment. You would also need an awareness of and interest in current trends and fashions.

Architects must be able to work as part of a team. They need to be good communicators both with clients and with construction personnel on site. Good management skills are also important. You would need to be able to work to deadlines.

You would need to be physically fit for the site inspections, which would involve climbing around part-constructed buildings, and the ability to drive would be a considerable asset.

Broad Outlook

Like the construction industry generally, architecture has highs and lows reflecting the state of the national economy. In the recession at the start of 2009, building has slowed down considerably and with it opportunities for architects. When the economy picks up again, there should be more than enough work for everyone. Training is very long with no guarantee of employment at the end. Most architects work in small private practices with usually fewer than ten staff. To start with, you might be on a short-term contract and then progress with experience to junior and then senior partnerships. Alternatively, you could start your own practice. You would be working on a variety of industrial and commercial projects as well as for private individuals. Other architects work in the public sector and are involved with schools, housing, hospitals and so on. Many architects are self-employed.

Related Occupations

You may consider: architectural technologist, civil engineer, interior designer, surveyor and landscape architect.

Impact on Lifestyle

Architecture is regarded in any community as a prestigious and highly regarded profession. Training does, however, take a long time and you can expect to still be a student when your friends are working. Most architects work normal office hours unless there are deadlines to be met. As a self-employed freelance architect, you might experience periods of inactivity and other periods of high workload.

You could expect to work some of the time in a light, bright office and some of the time on a potentially hazardous construction site.

Earnings Potential

As a Part 1, first year out student, you should earn £17,000 to £20,000. This should rise to £23,000 to £27,000 for a Part 2 student and to £30,000 to £34,000 for a Part 3, newly qualified architect, varying according to location and size of your employer. The public sector tends to pay less. With experience you could expect to earn £40,000 to £80,000 and, at the top of the profession, considerably more. RIBA publishes an annual salary survey.

Further Information

Royal Institute of British Architects (RIBA), London, W1B 1AD
Website: www.architecture.com

Architects Registration Board, London W1B 1PP
Website: www.arb.org.uk

Royal Incorporation of Architects in Scotland, Edinburgh, EH1 2BE
Website: www.rias.org.uk

Alternative/equivalent entrance requirements can include: ILC, IB, EB, NC/ND and many other similar international systems. For further details see the Equivalent Qualifications section in the Introduction.

Architectural Technologist

What is Involved?

As an architectural technologist, whether designing new buildings or altering existing ones, you would be a member of the architectural team. You would in fact be trained to complete a project from start to finish, in making sure that the building is properly constructed and works as specified in the original design.

The design process requires many activities to be undertaken by the architectural team: you would start by deciding exactly what is required, establishing with the client such factors as how the building might be used, how much it would cost, how it would be built and what sort of site might be available, before thinking about its outward appearance.

In addition to the design drawings, detailed specifications and documents would have to be prepared in conjunction with other consultants. You would have to negotiate with the planning and building authorities and you would work closely with other professionals such as architects and building surveyors. Finally, a 'package' would be prepared to enable the building project to be carried out, often including a management role for your team in supervising work on site. Much of your office work would be carried out using computer-aided-design technology (CAD).

Opportunities for Training

To graduate as an architectural technologist, you will need to enrol on an honours degree in Architectural Technology. This programme can be studied over a period of three or four years, full- or part-time. The four-year degree will include a sandwich year (excluding Scotland); allowing you to gain industry experience before returning to complete the degree. Studying on an accredited programme is part of the preferred route to becoming a chartered architectural technologist. There are currently 26 accredited degree programmes across the UK and upon graduation from one of these programmes you will have acquired the underpinning knowledge to help your progression to the next stage of your professional assessment.

This next stage of assessment can take up to three years to complete, depending on experience. If you are successful in demonstrating your competence, you will be granted the title chartered architectural technologist and be able to use the designation MCIAT.

Requirements for Entry

While there are no specific minimum qualifications, you would be unlikely to be accepted for any training route with less than four GCSE/S Grade passes A-C/1-3. To be accepted for a degree course, you would need at least two A level/Advanced Higher, three Higher or equivalent qualifications, together with three GCSE/two S Grade passes (A-C/1-3). English and maths are often required and sometimes a science. The HNC/D route usually requires at least one A level/Advanced Higher, two Highers or equivalent qualifications. A driving licence would be useful.

Kind of Person

Entry to an architectural technology programme is subject to individual university requirements but you should have a broad secondary education with particular focus on science and technology subjects. It is recommended that your GCSE/S Grade passes should include art, design and technology, English, information technology, mathematics and science (double or triple). A/AS levels/Highers or equivalent should be in relevant subjects such as science, technology, building services engineering or construction.

Broad Outlook

Prospects in architectural technology are linked to the overall health of the construction industry. The current economic climate is far from encouraging but there will be times when competition for jobs becomes much less intense. Employment can be found in a variety of national and international organisations, from private architectural practices to local authorities and construction companies, and can include new build, conversion, adaptation, restoration or management and maintenance work on many types of commercial, industrial and residential property.

In addition, there are opportunities in teaching, manufacturing and research.

You could eventually set up your own practice or work in partnership or as director with fellow architectural technologists, architects and other professionals within the construction industry.

Related Occupations

You might also consider: architect, landscape architect, civil engineer, chartered surveyor or structural engineer.

Impact on Lifestyle

Your working week might vary from one contract to another but you would be mostly office-based and could expect a fairly typical Monday to Friday, nine to five timetable. Particular schedules might demand unsocial hours from time to time to meet deadlines and you might be required to travel to site meetings.

Working conditions on building sites can be hazardous, wet, muddy and cold. You may have to climb ladders and scaffolding, and would need to comply with all health and safety requirements.

Earnings Potential

There are no set salary scales and how much you earn could depend on your employer and how good you are. As a guide, a junior architectural technologist could expect to earn around £15,000 to £22,000, rising to £24,000 to £28,000 with some three years' experience. In a more senior post, you could expect to earn £35,000 to £42,000. To attract the highest salary, you would need both considerable experience and the ability to run complex contracts.

Further Information

Chartered Institute of Architectural Technologists, London EC1V 1NH
Website: www.biat.org.uk

Alternative/equivalent entrance requirements can include: ILC, IB, EB, NC/ND and many other similar international systems. For further details see the Equivalent Qualifications section in the Introduction.

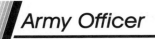
Army Officer

What is Involved?

As an army officer you would be part of the service responsible for the defence of Britain and its allies at home and abroad and playing an increasingly important part in combat, humanitarian and peacekeeping operations around the world.

The army divides its career opportunities into seven areas:

Combat - on the front line as part of a fighting force, keeping the peace in war-torn areas or delivering humanitarian aid

Engineering - providing engineering expertise for the machinery and hardware used by the army

Logistics and support - getting materials and supplies from A to B, and making sure the army has the equipment it needs

Intelligence, IT and communications - ensuring effective communication between allies, the field and those back at base, or listening in on the enemy

Human resources and finance - recruiting and training human resources, administrative, finance and IT specialists

Medical - doctors, nurses, dentists and veterinary surgeons protecting the lives, health and well-being of soldiers, civilians and the animals that serve in the army

Music and ceremonial - taking part in ceremonial occasions and representing the public face of the Army at concerts and military parades

Opportunities for Training

Most officers follow the commissioning course at the Royal Military Academy Sandhurst (RMAS), which consists of three 14-week terms. The course includes training in leadership and management, tactics, weapons and fitness. After leaving RMAS, you would complete an additional course and receive a commission. There are three main types of commission:

- A short service commission (SSC) - the normal first commission, awarded for at least three years (eight in the Army Air Corps) after leaving Sandhurst, with opportunities for extension
- An intermediate regular commission (IRC) - applications can be made after at least two years on an SSC. Officers can serve on an IRC for up to 16 years, and have the opportunity to convert to a regular commission
- A regular commission (Reg C) - offering a full career, potentially up to the age of 60. It is awarded to officers who have had at least two years' IRC service

At the age of 16, you could apply to attend the Defence sixth-form college at Welbeck to study A level sciences. There are also opportunities to take a short gap year commission.

Requirements for Entry

The minimum entry requirements are seven GCSE/S Grade passes A*-C/1-3 and two A level/Advanced Higher, three Higher or equivalent qualifications. Nearly all new entrants are graduates and you must be of degree calibre even if you choose not to go to university. For some specialist sections a degree in a relevant subject, e.g. in engineering, would be necessary, while some jobs require you to be professionally qualified before applying.

You must pass the Army Officer Selection Board, where you would be put through a series of selection tests and interviewed at length about your motivation and interests.

Kind of Person

Above all else, the qualities of leadership are important. A high standard of physical fitness is also vital and the programme at Sandhurst ensures that you would leave not only in top physical condition but also able to supervise the fitness training of the soldiers placed under your command. Expeditions involving climbing, sailing, caving, kayaking, diving, trekking and other activities are all encouraged at Sandhurst, with the success or failure of each expedition depending entirely upon your initiative, resourcefulness and courage.

As an officer you must be able to command the respect of those in your care, through your ability to lead in difficult and potentially dangerous situations. You must be able to exercise responsibility, be fit, prepared to work closely with others in combat and mix easily with all sorts of people in whatever context. You must be a team player but able to work alone if required, able to listen but also to make on-the-spot decisions.

Broad Outlook

After commissioning, you would become a second lieutenant (for up to two years of service), before seeking promotion to lieutenant, captain, major, lieutenant colonel (typically after 16 to 18 years' service) and brigadier. Promotion is achieved primarily by examination, experience, training and merit.

Many opportunities exist for officers upon retirement from the armed forces because of the management and professional training and experience gained during their period of service.

Related Occupations

You might consider RAF officer, Royal Navy officer, police officer.

Impact on Lifestyle

You would be paid to be available 24 hours a day, seven days a week, although when you are not on exercise or operations you are likely to work a fairly normal five-day week.

You could expect to be posted, often at short notice, anywhere around the world, in combat or in humanitarian work like peacekeeping or famine relief. You would need to be highly adaptable and broad-minded for you may not always be welcomed by the local community.

Earnings Potential

How much you get paid as an officer in the Army is determined by your rank and how long you have served. Sixth form sponsorships and undergraduate sponsorship and bursaries are offered to suitable candidates and special rates of pay may be offered to undergraduates whilst studying. An Officer Cadet currently earns £15,268 and a Second Lieutenant/Graduate Officer Cadet £24,133. A newly appointed Lieutenant earns £29,006, rising to £32,062; at the top of the tree, a Brigadier is paid up to £98,984. Many allowances are provided in terms of accommodation and food.

Further Information

Available from school and university careers and liaison services and local Armed Forces Careers Offices
British Army
Website: www.army.mod.uk
Welbeck - the Defence Sixth Form College
Website: www.welbeck.mod.uk
Defence Forces of Ireland
Website: www.military.ie

Alternative/equivalent entrance requirements can include: ILC, IB, EB, NC/ND and many other similar international systems. For further details see the Equivalent Qualifications section in the Introduction.

Artist/Illustrator

What is Involved?

As an artist, you would probably wish to develop your own creative ideas, perhaps in a specialised area such as sculpture or portraiture. You might receive commissions for some of your work from individuals, private companies or public authorities, although it would be more likely that you would have to persuade galleries or art dealers to exhibit your work for sale, or engage an agent to do this for you. In any case, you would probably have to subsidise your earnings by undertaking some other work such as teaching, illustration or theatre set design.

As an illustrator, you would be employed to carry out a brief or project set by a client. This could include work on magazines, books, greetings cards, technical publications and so on. Most illustrators work as freelances, in their own homes or studios. As either an artist or illustrator, you would spend some time travelling or contacting potential clients to show them examples of the work in your portfolio.

Opportunities for Training

Some successful artists/illustrators are entirely self-taught but talent is seldom enough and a good starting point would normally be to take an art foundation course before going on to a further course of training at an art school or university. Most foundation courses allow you to explore several areas of artistic work before you choose a specialised degree or higher national diploma (HND) course.

Requirements for Entry

Entry to foundation courses can be from GCSE/S Grade or A level/Advanced Higher/Higher or equivalent qualifications, with great importance placed on a current portfolio of your own artistic work. The courses last for one or two years full-time, and can be found at sixth form colleges, further and higher education colleges, art colleges and some universities.

Entry to an HND course would normally require a minimum of four GCSE/S Grade passes A-C/1-3 and one or two A level/Advanced Higher or two or three Higher or equivalent qualifications. The course would last for two or three years, with the possibility of conversion to a degree course. Entry to a degree course would normally require a minimum of five GCSE/S Grade and two or three A level/Advanced Higher or three or four Higher or equivalent qualifications. These requirements might be waived if you have foundation course experience and/or an impressive portfolio.

Kind of Person

You would clearly need a high degree of creative artistic talent but there is also a call for other skills. As an illustrator, in particular, you would need to be very well organised, able to stick to deadlines and to interpret the wishes of your clients. IT skills would almost certainly be helpful. As either an artist or an illustrator, you would need to be very determined but able to deal with disappointment if a client or dealer rejected your work. Communication skills, particularly powers of persuasion, would be very important, as you would have to deal with a wide variety of people. Some business sense and an understanding of budgets would also be a great asset.

Broad Outlook

The traditional image of the starving artist in a lonely garret still has some relevance. It is not easy to make a living purely as an artist but that should not stop you trying if you feel that you have necessary talent and determination. The position is somewhat less bleak for illustrators, although permanent contracts are still something of a luxury.

Related Occupations

You might wish to consider: art director, art therapist, cartographer, fashion designer, graphic designer, interior designer, photographer, textile designer, theatre set or costume designer.

Impact on Lifestyle

Working as an artist or illustrator would put you in a very competitive field, with very little security. You would most likely work on a freelance basis, with extremely variable hours, and you might have to work during the evenings or at weekends if you had a deadline to meet. Also, your earnings might be far from regular and you would have to plan your budget and your domestic and social activities accordingly.

Earnings Potential

The price you could ask for your work is governed by many factors and could vary tremendously, possibly requiring you to supplement your income by undertaking some other work. As an illustrator, you would usually receive a fee for each piece of work, the amount being dependent upon the size and scope of the commission. Alternatively, you might charge a daily rate, ranging from, say, £200 upwards. You should also remember that any artists' agent you might employ would charge you a fee. The Association of Illustrators has extensive information about pricing on its website. The Artists Information Company website has an interactive artist's toolkit, designed to help artists calculate how to price their work. It is suggested that artists might reasonably aim at a similar income to teachers.

Further Information

Association of Illustrators, London EC2A 3AR
Website: www.theaoi.com

Your Creative Future
Website: www.yourcreativefuture.org

Creative and Cultural Skills
Website: www.ccskills.org.uk

Scottish Arts Council, Edinburgh EH3 7DD
Website: www.sac.org.uk

Artists Information Company
Website: www.a-n.co.uk/artists

Alternative/equivalent entrance requirements can include: ILC, IB, EB, NC/ND and many other similar international systems. For further details see the Equivalent Qualifications section in the Introduction.

Auctioneer/Valuer

What is Involved?

As an auctioneer, you would be expected to sell at auction such items as bankrupt stock, commodities, collectables, furniture, household goods, property, land, motor cars, farming equipment or whatever else owners wish to sell in this way. You might work for a firm of surveyors or estate agents who undertake general auctioneering, or for a specialist auction house in the worlds of fine art, furniture, sculpture, antiques, literature, philately, postcards, militaria and celebrity memorabilia, where you would need a very high level of expertise.

In addition to conducting the auction itself, you would assess the value of items for sale, advise clients on setting reserve prices, arrange items into lots, organise a catalogue, insure the goods against loss or damage, arrange the transport of sold and unsold lots and ensure adequate pre-sale publicity.

Opportunities for Training

There are many possible routes to a qualification such as the Royal Institution of Chartered Surveyors (RICS) diploma in valuation or fine arts and chattels valuation. You could, for example, complete a degree or diploma course accredited by the RICS or, if your degree is not accredited, a postgraduate conversion course. You would then undertake two years of practical, on-the-job training leading to the RICS Assessment of Professional Competence. Auction houses, like Christie's and Sotheby's, run their own courses in fine art, inviting selected participants to join them as trainees in their London or provincial offices. Opportunities range from unpaid work experience to various kinds of internship. Sotheby's Institute of Art runs six MA degree programmes, while Christie's Education offers a variety of courses, ranging from evening classes to postgraduate qualifications.

Requirements for Entry

Two to three A level/Advanced Higher, three to four Higher or equivalent qualifications, together with supporting GCSE/S Grade A-C/1-3, would normally be required to secure entry to most relevant degree or diploma courses. There are no specific requirements for open learning, although employers may determine their own minimum standards.

Kind of Person

You would need to be capable of inspiring confidence in your clients and of understanding the minds of collectors or purchasers. A sound grasp of the market and its trends and fashions would be essential, as well as a willingness to steep yourself in your specialist field. You would need to have good commercial and business flair. You should be a good public speaker, capable of controlling the auction room and able to explain the special features of items for sale. You should be extremely quick-witted and observant in spotting bids, with excellent hearing and eyesight.

It would be important to know the particular features involved in establishing authenticity, supply and demand, market price and provenance of important or valuable items for sale, especially in the fields of fine art and antique furniture. Writing skills would be needed to produce catalogues, numerical skills to assess bids quickly and IT skills to keep accounts, produce inventories and perhaps maintain a website.

Broad Outlook

There are openings from time to time for those with the necessary drive and enthusiasm in this relatively small field of employment. Late starts are feasible in the smaller undertakings but far less easy in the major international auction houses. In many top auction houses it may take up to five or six years to acquire the necessary expert knowledge in a specialised field, such as in 18th century painting or furniture, and even then becoming an auctioneer would not be automatic.

General auctioneering within an estate agency would usually be less demanding. Securing employment in one of the large international auction houses is extremely competitive and you may have to work in a range of practical activities before being accepted into a specialist department where you could learn about and value artistic objects.

Related Occupations

You might also consider: chartered surveyor, estate agent or museum/art gallery curator.

Impact on Lifestyle

Within a big organisation, travel is likely to be a major consideration. In all auction houses, much pressurised time would be devoted to preparatory activities in itemising and valuing the goods for sale, producing catalogues and displaying and storing the items to avoid awkward delays during sales. Conducting an auction can be very demanding on you mentally and physically.

Earnings Potential

There are huge variations in potential earnings, depending on the location, the level of business and the profit margins involved. As an auctioneer in a big company, you are likely to start on around £20,000, moving on to £30,000 with some experience and £40,000 as a senior manager. Where you are running your own business or are an employed director of a firm of auctioneers, hard work and a successful track record would largely determine your financial rewards. The auctioneer normally takes a percentage of the value of each item sold and your own earnings could be directly related to the sale prices you achieve.

Further Information

Royal Institution of Chartered Surveyors, Coventry CV4 8JE
Website: www.rics.org

College of Estate Management, Reading RG6 2AW
Website: www.cem.ac.uk

National Association of Valuers and Auctioneers
Website: www.nava.org.uk

Sotheby's Institute of Art, London WC1B 3EE
Website: www.sothebysinstitute.com

Christie's Education, London W1W 5BD
Website: www.christies.com/education

Alternative/equivalent entrance requirements can include: ILC, IB, EB, NC/ND and many other similar international systems. For further details see the Equivalent Qualifications section in the Introduction.

Audiologist

What is Involved?

As an audiologist, you would work directly with patients to identify and measure hearing loss, detect balance problems and neurological diseases and work closely with patients to develop rehabilitation programmes. You would be qualified to see people of all ages but most of your work would be with children and older people because hearing problems are most common in these groups. The rehabilitation of hearing-impaired adults would require both the prescription and evaluation of hearing aids, using objective and subjective methods and measures. You would have to be proficient in all procedures for testing hearing and balance, together with interpreting and reporting the results of these tests.

As you progress through the career grades, you would be expected to undertake more complex and non-routine tasks. These may include electrophysiological testing of the auditory pathways and the fitting of more complex hearing aids. Senior grade audiologists are also involved with the training and supervision of junior grades.

You could develop a special interest and expertise in one area of audiology, such as paediatrics, balance disorders or complex procedures like cochlear implants.

Opportunities for Training

You could take a four-year BSc degree in audiology, with the first two years spent at university, learning about the science behind tests and treatments that are used in hospitals and acquiring the knowledge needed to work with patients in a therapeutic relationship. The third year is spent on clinical placement in an audiology setting, learning how to carry out some of the procedures a qualified audiologist performs and learning how audiology services work in the NHS. The final year is spent back at university, learning about more advanced aspects of audiology and completing a dissertation.

It is also possible for graduates with an appropriate first or upper-second class science degree to apply for training through the Clinical Scientist Training Scheme. This initially takes one year, leading to an MSc, followed by 18-24 months supervised in-service clinical placement.

Audiologists who have trained through one of the above routes are eligible to apply for registration with the Registration Council for Clinical Physiologists. Clinical scientists in audiology must register with the Health Professions Council (HPC) in order to practise.

Requirements for Entry

The usual entry requirements for the BSc are three A level/Advanced Higher/five Higher or equivalent qualifications, normally including at least one science-related subject. However, universities consider each application individually and credit can be given for relevant experience and non-traditional qualifications.

Kind of Person

You would need the ability to listen carefully to problems and, when necessary, to break bad news in a caring and sensitive way. You must be deaf aware, comfortable looking directly at your patient and speaking at a normal level but slightly slower. You should be easy to lip-read. In the assessment of children, you would need a wide range of skills and strategies to test babies, toddlers and older infants.

In all types of audiology work, a scientific, evidence-based approach would be essential, together with a keen interest in working with people in a clinical environment. You should have the enthusiasm to keep up with modern trends and technological developments.

Broad Outlook

The profession of audiology is currently undergoing a period of considerable change and this is a good time to join a rapidly expanding speciality. The Government is supporting major changes in Hearing and Balance services, and funding the training of new staff to support these improvements. The recent introduction, for example, of hearing screening for every baby born in England and Wales, alongside the increasing availability of cochlear implants and therapy for balance problems, underline the need for a strong and enthusiastic workforce of well-educated and well-trained audiologists in the UK.

Audiologists can also work outside the NHS, in the private sector or in a university where you could undertake teaching and research.

Related Occupations

You might also consider: speech and language therapist, physiotherapist, teacher of the deaf or ear, nose and throat doctor.

Impact on Lifestyle

Most audiologists work office hours from Monday to Friday in a hospital outpatient department. Some audiology work is also carried out on hospital wards, during surgery or in a community setting. In order to progress to higher grades, you would often be expected to attend courses and meetings at weekends or study outside working hours.

Earnings Potential

As an eligible student on the BSc course, you would have your course fees paid and would receive an NHS means-tested bursary in years 1,2 and 4. You would receive a trainee salary in year 3.

Working as a registered audiologist in the NHS, you would be paid on the Healthcare Scientist scale in Band 5, which runs from £20,710 to £26,839. With further training and experience, you could move up the career structure to Band 7, earning from £29,789 to £39,273. Additional allowances are paid for appointments in and around London, ranging from 20% of basic salary for Inner London, to 15% for Outer London and 5% for the London Fringe.

Further Information

British Academy of Audiology
Website: www.baaudiology.org

NHS Student Bursaries
Website: www.nhspa.gov.uk/sgu

Alternative/equivalent entrance requirements can include: ILC, IB, EB, NC/ND and many other similar international systems. For further details see the Equivalent Qualifications section in the Introduction.

Automotive Engineer

What is Involved?

Working as an automotive engineer, you would be involved in a specialised area of mechanical engineering that deals with all aspects of the production of motor vehicles and their components. Your job would be to apply mechanical principles to issues related to the design, development or maintenance of all aspects of motor vehicles. You could be involved with designing new cars or with developing a specific part of a vehicle, such as the transmission system. You would be likely to be working as part of a small team on a particular project, seeing it through from the beginning to the production phase.

Opportunities for Training

There are a number of universities offering degrees in automotive engineering, sometimes combined with mechanical engineering. In order to become a chartered engineer, primarily concerned with research, design and development, you would need to complete at least four years of academic study and would usually achieve this via an MEng degree. If you want to be more involved with the day-to-day management of production processes as an incorporated engineer, you could take a three-year BEng degree.

You don't always have to choose your specific training route from the start, so you should read prospectuses carefully. See also our separate article on engineering qualifications. There are sandwich courses available for both types of degree; these add an extra year but give the opportunity for a period of work experience, which can be very valuable when you are looking for a job. After graduating, you would need to complete a period of industrial training and responsible work experience before you achieve chartered or incorporated engineer status.

Requirements for Entry

For degree entry, you are likely to need A level/Advanced Higher/Higher or equivalent qualifications, including maths and/or physics plus one or two other subjects. If maths and physics are not required, they are certainly preferred by universities. In addition, you would need at least five GCSE/S Grade passes at A-C/1-3. You would normally need higher grades for MEng than for BEng admission.

Kind of Person

Your job would involve understanding and solving complex engineering problems. For this you would need a practical and logical mind that might need to show creative approaches to problems. You are likely to find yourself using maths and statistics in your work and you would make extensive use of computers, including specialised and sophisticated software packages.

You are likely to find yourself working as part of a multi-disciplinary team, which means that you would need to be able to communicate with a variety of people. These could be fellow engineers, who would share your technical expertise and understanding, or non-technical specialists in other fields, who would expect you to explain your ideas clearly to them. You could also find yourself managing a team of people working on a project. In addition, you may need to take into account the costs and budget of a project, so you would need some business skills.

*B*road Outlook

The UK excels in the design and development of motor vehicles, as evidenced by the number of Formula One racing teams based here. Most global manufacturers carry out research, design and development activities in the UK and there are also specialist consultants, such as Lotus Engineering, who employ around 1,000 engineers. There has in the past been strong demand for qualified automotive and mechanical engineers, although the motor industry has been severely hit by the economic downturn at the start of 2009.

You may choose to develop skills in emerging fields in order to stay ahead of the game or take advantage of skills gaps. Environmentally friendly vehicles, for example, are currently the subject of intense interest within the automotive sector.

*R*elated Occupations

You might also consider: manufacturing, mechanical, aeronautical, electrical or electronic engineer. Alternatively, you might want to consider working as an industrial designer, perhaps specialising in motor vehicle design.

*I*mpact on Lifestyle

Whilst you may have set hours of work, you could expect to be under pressure sometimes to meet commercial deadlines and may have to work overtime. You could be based in an office but you are also likely to be working in a more practical, hands-on environment for a large part of your working week. You may occasionally be expected to wear protective clothing of some sort.

*E*arnings Potential

Average salaries on graduation are currently in the range of £23,000 to £30,000, rising to £35,000 to £40,000 after four or five years. Managerial positions usually offer £50,000 to £60,000. A top engineer in a Formula One racing team, with 10-15 years experience, can earn over £100,000 a year.

*F*urther Information

Institution of Mechanical Engineers, London SW1H 9JJ
Website: www.imeche.org.uk

Engineering Council UK, London WC2R 3ER
Website: www.engc.org.uk

Lotus Engineering
Website: www.grouplotus.com

Institute of the Motor Industry
Website: www.motor.org.uk

Alternative/equivalent entrance requirements can include: ILC, IB, EB, NC/ND and many other similar international systems. For further details see the Equivalent Qualifications section in the Introduction.

Banking Executive

What is Involved?

The banking industry has undergone radical change over the last ten years, with many mergers and acquisitions taking place and increased competition from supermarkets, building societies, insurance companies and large retailers to provide financial services to individuals and organisations.

As a banking executive, you might choose to build your career in an area such as:

- **Clearing, retail and private banking** - involving the transfer, borrowing and lending of money (sterling and foreign currency) to private customers, sole traders and partnerships

- **Corporate and commercial banking** - dealing with business clients ranging from small start-up companies to major international corporations

- **Investment or merchant banking** - involving corporate finance, investment management and dealing in capital markets, usually on a global basis

Opportunities for Training

There is such diversity in the banking sector that there are many possible training routes. All banks/financial institutions recruit school leavers and graduates in varying numbers from year to year. However, each institution has its own specific recruitment and training preferences and you should contact individual banks for current details and an application pack. You can access the websites of all major organisations through the British Bankers Association.

Most management training schemes require a degree as a starting point. The exact subject is not critically important but study in such fields as economics, finance, business or marketing could prove useful. Once in post, you would normally work towards membership of the Chartered Institute of Bankers.

It is sometimes possible to join a management training scheme through internal promotion after gaining experience as a cashier or customer services adviser.

Requirements for Entry

For entry to a degree course you would need two to three A level/Advanced Higher, three to four Higher or equivalent qualifications, together with a minimum of five GCSE/S Grade passes A-C/1-3. The degree would usually last three years, although you might like to consider a sandwich course, which would last four years, including a period of paid work experience.

Kind of Person

Since much of your work would be concerned with dealing with a wide variety of people, both colleagues and customers, you would need excellent communication skills, as well as a good head for figures and an understanding of the economic climate. Accuracy and organisational skills would be very important.

As a manager you should be able to inspire confidence and loyalty in your team, and also be capable of selling the bank's services effectively. A high degree of computer literacy would be of benefit, as would proficiency in a foreign language. You would generally be expected to maintain a neat, formal appearance at all times.

Broad Outlook

Technology has dramatically changed the face of banking over the past few years and has resulted in such initiatives as telephone and e-banking. If you enter the banking industry, you would almost certainly face the prospect of continuing change.

Banking has been at the heart of the financial crisis that has severely affected the world economy in 2009. Consequently, careers in banking have lost a great deal of their allure and may take some years to recover.

Related Occupations

You might also consider: accountant, actuary, economist, financial adviser, insurance broker, insurance underwriter or stockbroker.

Impact on Lifestyle

In retail banking, you might work normal office hours from Monday to Friday, although increasing competition may mean evening and weekend work. Promotion in this sector of the industry often entails moving to another part of the country.

In investment or merchant banking, you would need to be available when colleagues and clients are at work in other parts of the world, which could involve evening and night-time attendance at the office. You may be required to travel extensively.

Earnings Potential

Pay scales would vary widely according to your experience, level of responsibility and the type of banking in which you specialise. Starting salaries for new entrants to graduate management trainee programmes range from £23,000 to £30,000. You may also qualify for a London allowance, funding for study for professional qualifications, and relocation expenses. Typical salaries at senior level range from £50,000 to £100,000, depending on your level of responsibility. Salaries in investment and merchant banking have traditionally been considerably higher, although it remains to be seen whether these will continue in post-recession Britain.

Further Information

British Bankers Association, London EC2N 1EX
Website: www.bba.org.uk

Financial Services Skills Council, London EC2V 7HQ
Website: careers.fssc.org.uk

Bank of England, London EC2R 8AH
Website: www.bankofengland.co.uk

London Investment Banking Association, London EC2R 8BT
Website: www.liba.org.uk

Chartered Institute of Bankers in Scotland, Edinburgh EH3 7SW
Website: www.ciobs.org.uk

Alternative/equivalent entrance requirements can include: ILC, IB, EB, NC/ND and many other similar international systems. For further details see the Equivalent Qualifications section in the Introduction.

Barrister

England, Wales, Northern Ireland and Republic of Ireland. See also Advocate for Scotland.

What is Involved?

As a barrister, you would work as an expert in a specific area of law and would be consulted by solicitors or other professionals. As well as appearing in court, you might be consulted on particular points of law or you may appear at a tribunal or enquiry. Your job as a barrister in a higher court would be to present the facts of the case to the judge and jury, using evidence collected by a solicitor. You would cross-examine witnesses and seek to persuade the court to find in favour of your client.

Opportunities for Training

You must either take an approved first degree in law or a degree in another subject, which you then 'convert' by taking a postgraduate qualification known as the Common Professional Examination (CPE) or the Graduate Diploma in Law (GDL).

You must join one of the four Inns of Court (Gray's Inn, Inner Temple, Lincoln's Inn, Middle Temple) and take the Bar Vocational Course (BVC), a one-year full-time or two-year part-time course of study, which includes practical training in mock trials, drawing up evidence and interviewing clients. It also covers litigation, sentencing and specialist options. Once you have successfully completed the BVC, you will be 'Called to the Bar' by your Inn. During the BVC year and before Call can take place you will also have to undertake 12 qualifying sessions (previously known as 'dining') with your Inn.

Having completed the BVC you must, if you intend to practise, complete two pupillages of six months each, working under supervision while you gain experience in all aspects of the job. After this you must find a tenancy in a set of chambers, from where you must work for at least three years while you follow a compulsory system of professional development. It is not essential to complete a pupillage if you are going to work in commerce or industry but you would not then be able to appear in court. Most chambers select their junior tenants through the process of pupillage.

A similar system applies in the Republic of Ireland. For details, visit the Irish websites listed below.

Requirements for Entry

You would need a minimum of a 2.2 Honours degree but in fact most chambers are looking for at least a 2.1. Competition for places to read Law is exceptionally strong and university admissions tutors expect high grades at A level/Advanced Higher, Higher or equivalent. No particular subjects are specified. You will have to take the National Admissions Test for Law (LNAT) to secure a place on a Law degree at 10 of the most prestigious UK universities.

Kind of Person

Bar Council research shows that the following abilities make an important contribution to success as a barrister: intellectual ability and the ability to cope with large volumes of information to be assimilated in a short time; the ability to withstand the stress of working long hours with tight deadlines and high levels of responsibility; the ability to deal with a wide range of people, to listen to them and then to put across a point of view convincingly. In addition, barristers need the motivation and determination to succeed in what can be a daunting profession, particularly in the early years. You need to be confident both in your work and socially.

Broad Outlook

Most barristers work as self-employed independent professionals, often based in chambers, which means they share the offices and costs of support staff. However, you have to build your own reputation in order to get work. Traditionally, barristers start their working life in London but there are opportunities to work in other cities on the legal circuit. It can be very hard work for little reward in your early days as you build up your practice. You may need to work for a reduced fee or in lower courts to build up your reputation. It is usually clear after a few years whether you will make a successful barrister. For many barristers, the eventual aim is to become a Queen's Counsel (QC), which involves leading in very serious cases, or entering the judiciary as an assistant recorder prior to becoming a judge.

Related Occupations

You might be interested in other legal professions such as solicitor, barristers' clerk or legal executive.

Impact on Lifestyle

The hours of work can be very long, especially when you are starting out, and can be unsocial, as you have to prepare late into the evening and travel to courts. Your life may very well start to revolve around your chambers. However, if you are successful, you can later be selective in the work you choose to do. Payment for work often comes in some time after the work has been completed, which can present problems in the early years.

Earnings Potential

All pupils must be paid no less than £833.33 per month plus reasonable travel expenses. As practising barristers are self-employed, your later earnings can vary enormously. Typical earnings/receipts for self-employed barristers, before deduction of tax and chambers' charges, range from £40,000 to £200,000 gross within five years of call. Typical earnings/receipts at senior levels range from £65,000 to £1,000,000 gross after ten or more years of call. A top QC can earn in excess of £1,000,000 per year. Barristers who are employed have the security of receiving a regular wage but may not have the potential for the very high earnings that are possible for the self-employed.

Further Information

Bar Standards Board, London EC4A 1NE
Website: www.barstandardsboard.org.uk

Pupillage listings
Website: www.pupillages.com

Law Library of Ireland
Website: www.lawlibrary.ie

Honorable Society of King's Inns, Dublin
Website: www.kingsinns.ie

Alternative/equivalent entrance requirements can include: ILC, IB, EB, NC/ND and many other similar international systems. For further details see the Equivalent Qualifications section in the Introduction.

Barristers' Clerk

What is Involved?

As a barristers' clerk (*advocates' clerk in Scotland*) you would work for a set of barristers practising in chambers; *the equivalent in Scotland is to work for a stable of advocates based in the Advocates' Library in Edinburgh.* Your job would be to operate as a member of a small team keeping the chamber or stable running efficiently as a business. Each barrister/advocate is self-employed and the senior clerk acts as an agent for them. As such, you would be expected to make and maintain contacts with solicitors to ensure that briefs come to your set or stable. Negotiation of fees and keeping diaries for the barristers would also be your responsibility.

There are 12 stables of advocates in Edinburgh, each with a clerk and at least one deputy. Their remit includes organising members' diaries, scheduling court commitments, arranging consultations, liaising with instructing solicitors, distributing work and negotiating fees.

Opportunities for Training

There is no quick route to becoming a successful clerk to chambers. Training is 'on the job', learning through observation and helping the more senior clerks. When you become a practising Junior Clerk working in London, chambers may offer training associated with the Institute of Barristers' Clerks (IBC). This leads to a BTEC Advanced Award at level 3 in chambers administration. Much of the work for this is undertaken in chambers under the guidance of a mentor.

On becoming an associate member of the IBC and completing five years service in chambers, you could apply for qualified membership. To enable clerks to keep abreast of current legal issues, market changes and administration needs, the Institute organises regular seminars.

In Scotland, there is no formal training or resulting qualification, although there are short courses run by the Faculty Services Ltd and junior clerks are encouraged to attend.

Requirements for Entry

While there are no official entry requirements specified in England, the majority of new barristers' clerk entrants start after completing their GCSE, A level or equivalent qualifications. The IBC recommends to chambers a minimum qualification of four GCSE grades A-C in academic subjects, including maths and English.

In Scotland, advocates' clerks need Higher English and must be computer literate and numerate.

Kind of Person

This is still a very small and in some ways old-fashioned profession and in many respects this aspect of the legal profession is still very hierarchical. You would need to be prepared to tackle menial jobs and to respect the established pecking order that exists within the system. Good manners and a smart appearance are important attributes. You would be expected to be loyal to the members of your set or stable.

You must have the confidence to deal with enquiries and problems that arise without having to bother the barristers/advocates. You would have to be tactful, discreet, honest and reliable. At times, you would be expected to think on your feet to solve a problem. To be involved in negotiating the fees, you would have to be reasonably competent at maths. As there is a lot of administration and paperwork, you need to be well organised.

Broad Outlook

There are limited opportunities for work as this is a small and close-knit profession but the Institute does run a scheme whereby, for a small fee, you can receive notification of vacancies. Most jobs for barristers' clerks are in London, although there are some openings in chambers in towns on the court circuits. *In Scotland, there are very few advocates' clerks and deputies and turnover is low.*

The role of barristers' clerk has changed significantly with the advent of legislation allowing barristers to advertise their services rather than wait for work to come to them. Clerks can now be much more proactive in seeking work for chambers and in promoting the expertise of both the chambers and individual barristers.

There is no scope for progressing to professional qualification as a barrister/advocate.

Related Occupations

You might be interested in other law-related work such as a legal executive; alternatively, you might consider administrative work in local government or the civil service.

Impact on Lifestyle

The hours worked can be long and can include evenings and weekends. *In Scotland, deputy clerks are paid overtime but this is unlikely to be the case for junior clerks in England and Wales.*

Earnings Potential

Starting salaries are generally low, starting from £12,000 to £15,000 in London for a school leaver or university graduate. This can rise with experience to £30,000 to £60,000. Some senior clerks are paid a salary or a percentage of the fee due to each barrister; alternatively, they may combine a small salary with a percentage of the earnings. This gives senior clerks the potential for very high earnings - over £100,000 in some cases - if they are in a large and successful set of chambers.

Advocates' clerks, all employed by the company responsible for the administration of the advocates' library, earn from £24,000 upwards once fully qualified.

Further Information

England and Wales: Institute of Barristers' Clerks, London WC1 7HZ
Website: www.ibc.org.uk

Scotland: Faculty Services Ltd., Edinburgh EH1 1RF
Website: www.advocates.org.uk

Alternative/equivalent entrance requirements can include: ILC, IB, EB, NC/ND and many other similar international systems. For further details see the Equivalent Qualifications section in the Introduction.

Biochemist

What is Involved?

Working as a biochemist, you would be a scientist applying the principles of chemistry to the structure and functioning of living things. This is a science at the heart of all areas of biological or life sciences. You might be concerned with organisms from viruses and bacteria to plants and humans; you might find employment in the food, brewing or pharmaceutical industries, where you could help to develop new products or monitor the quality of existing ones; you might work in the agricultural industry, developing high-yielding, disease-free crops; you could be involved in monitoring the environment and advising on pollution or water quality. There are also opportunities for biochemists to work in hospitals. (See Clinical Biochemist)

Opportunities for Training

Although it is possible to start a career as a biochemist straight from school, a degree is now becoming the more normal requirement. There are degree courses in biochemistry at most universities and it is possible to study for joint honours degrees with a range of other subjects. It is important to read the prospectuses carefully, as the content and emphasis of the degrees can differ enormously. Some universities offer four-year sandwich courses, which give the chance to work in industry or even abroad for a year.

It is also possible to start work as a technician straight from school, taking part-time study leading to a Higher National Diploma and occasionally converting to a shortened two-year degree course.

Requirements for Entry

Universities differ widely in their entrance requirements for biochemistry. Most would be looking for an A level/Advanced Higher/Higher or equivalent qualification in chemistry and some would want at least another science at A level or equivalent. Some universities or colleges will accept an AS or Higher in chemistry together with another science or maths and some will specify GCSE/S Grade passes in maths or the sciences at particular levels of achievement. It is best to check directly with the universities to find out what they expect. At some universities, it is possible for candidates without science A level/Advanced Higher, Higher or equivalent qualifications to take a year-long conversion course before they start a degree course. You would need GCSE/S Grade passes at A-C/1-3 in science if you wish to do this. In order to work towards a Higher National Diploma, you are likely to need at least four GCSE/S Grade passes at A-C/1-3, together with one or two A level/Advanced Higher, two or three Higher or equivalent qualifications in appropriate subjects. Some colleges specify that the GCSE/S Grade passes must include maths, English and a science.

Kind of Person

You would need to have a strong interest in science and in laboratory techniques. If you do not enjoy your practical science sessions at school, this may not be right choice for you. You will be expected to show a logical and analytical approach to problem solving. At times you may need to show persistence in order to solve particular problems. Some problems may need to be approached with creative thinking and imagination. In addition to your scientific skills, you should be able to communicate well with others. You are likely to be working as part of a team and may have to explain your findings to others, some of whom may not have your scientific background.

Broad Outlook

The largest proportion of new graduates move on to further biochemical study or training, mainly registering for MSc and PhD degrees. The majority of these will eventually make a career in scientific research.

Job prospects are generally very good, with a particularly low unemployment rate for biochemistry graduates compared with other life sciences. Although it is very much a laboratory-based science, there are also openings for biochemists in areas such as technical sales or information and management.

Related Occupations

You might be interested in other careers in a scientific field such as clinical biochemist, pharmacist, microbiologist, or forensic scientist.

There are close links with other specialist life sciences, such as cell biology, genetics, microbiology, molecular biology, physiology and pharmacology. In fact, in many cases the distinctions between these disciplines are becoming increasingly blurred.

Impact on Lifestyle

You are likely to be working regular hours without working at weekends or late into the evenings, although there may be occasions when you are required to work late and under pressure in order to meet deadlines. In the laboratory, you may need to wear protective clothing and to take scrupulous care over hygiene; at times you may need to work in sterile conditions. You may need to move around the country in order to find the right job for you.

Earnings Potential

Graduate trainees should earn in the range of £24,000 to £26,000 a year, rising with experience to £36,000 to £44,000. Higher earners can make £60,000 to £90,000 a year, depending on their employer, role and responsibilities.

In the National Health Service, qualified biochemists are generally in Band 7 of the pay scales, earning from £29,789 to £39,273 a year.

Further Information

Biochemical Society, London WC1V 6NX
Website: www.biochemistry.org

Biomedical Engineer

What is Involved?

Working as a biomedical engineer, you would be using your engineering knowledge and skills to help with the treatment and rehabilitation of patients with serious diseases or disabilities. You would work with medical consultants to develop the instruments necessary for diagnosing or monitoring patients. You could be concerned with designing new equipment, such as that used in keyhole surgery, aids for the handicapped, such as replacement joints and limbs, or implants like pacemakers. Your work might be said to harness the techniques of electrical, electronic and mechanical engineering to supplement the mechanics of the human body.

Opportunities for Training

Your first step in training to become a biomedical engineer would probably be to take an accredited degree in mechanical, electrical or electronic engineering. Some degree courses in these subjects include medical engineering options, so it is worth looking carefully at prospectuses when you are researching your university application. There are also postgraduate qualifications in medical engineering, with some training places funded directly by the National Health Service or by a hospital trust.

In order to become a chartered engineer, you would normally need to take a four-year MEng degree and reach a recognised standard on an accredited training programme incorporating suitable periods of practical experience. A three-year BEng degree would normally take you to Incorporated Engineer status, although there is special provision to switch to the chartered route if you wish. (See the separate article on engineering qualifications in the introduction)

Requirements for Entry

In order to be accepted on a suitable engineering degree course, you would need at least three A level/Advanced Higher, four Higher or equivalent qualifications, normally including maths and physics, together with five GCSE/S Grade passes at A-C/1-3. These should include maths, another science subject and English. Some universities run foundation courses for candidates who do not have the appropriate A level/Advanced Higher, Higher or equivalent. A course of this sort would prepare you for the first year of an engineering degree.

Kind of Person

You would need to be interested in discovering practical solutions to the problems experienced by patients. You would therefore need a logical but creative approach to problem solving. In addition to your technical and engineering skills and knowledge, you would have to be able to work as part of a medical health team providing care for your patients. You could find yourself dealing with fellow professionals, patients and their carers as well as with technical and administrative staff. You would need to keep abreast of developments in your field and to share your own specialist knowledge with other professionals at meetings, courses and seminars.

*B*road Outlook

The medical engineering industry is currently valued at approximately £50 billion worldwide and it is growing. This sector offers a great opportunity for graduates with entrepreneurial ideas to carve out lucrative careers. Students with enthusiasm and a sound engineering background can use medical engineering to make a difference to healthcare and can have a direct influence on the health of people around the world.

There is a need for engineers in companies that research and manufacture medical products, such as artificial heart valves, replacement joints and monitoring equipment. Some private sector manufacturers operate internationally and may offer scope to work in mainland Europe and beyond.

*R*elated Occupations

You might be interested in one of the related engineering professions, such as electronic, electrical, mechanical or telecommunications engineer. Alternatively, you might like to consider another of the professions allied to medicine, such as biotechnologist or medical physicist.

*I*mpact on Lifestyle

You are likely to be able to work regular hours but may need to work overtime if there are tight deadlines to meet. As this is a field that depends extensively on research and new technology, you may find that you have to travel to conferences and meetings in order to exchange ideas with other experts or clients.

*E*arnings Potential

Starting salaries for clinical scientists in the NHS Band 6 are currently £24,831 to £33,436, rising in Band 7 to £29,789 to £39,273. Senior manager or consultant posts can offer salaries ranging from £53,256 to £95,333. Additional payments are made for employment in and around London. Work in the industrial sector is, in general, better paid than research and development positions in university and government medical research departments.

*F*urther Information

Institute of Physics and Engineering in Medicine, York YO24 1ES
Website: www.ipem.ac.uk

Association of Clinical Scientists, London SE1 2TU
Website: www.assclinsci.org

Institution of Mechanical Engineers, London SW1 9JJ
Website: www.imeche.org.uk

Engineering Council UK, London WC2R 3ER
Website: www.engc.org.uk

Biomedical Engineering Society
Website: www.bmes.org

Royal Academy of Engineering UK Focus for Biomedical Engineering
Website: www.raeng.org.uk/policy/ukfocus

Alternative/equivalent entrance requirements can include: ILC, IB, EB, NC/ND and many other similar international systems. For further details see the Equivalent Qualifications section in the Introduction.

Biomedical Scientist

What is Involved?

As a biomedical scientist (sometimes known as a medical laboratory scientific officer or MLSO), you would carry out tests on samples of tissue and body fluids to support doctors, nurses and other healthcare professionals in diagnosing disease and monitoring the treatment of patients. Your work would usually involve specialisation in one of the following areas:

- **Medical Microbiology** - isolating disease-causing micro-organisms by culturing specimens on suitable media or in susceptible living cells.

- **Clinical Chemistry** - analysing blood and other biological materials to help with the diagnosis of metabolic diseases, toxicological studies and the monitoring of therapy.

- **Transfusion science** - working in hospital blood banks and the blood transfusion service to identify individual blood groups and test for compatibility of donors' blood with that of patients.

- **Haematology** - studying the morphology and physiology of blood.

- **Histopathology** - processing samples of tissue from surgical operations and autopsies.

- **Virology** - detecting viruses such as herpes simplex, influenza and human immunodeficiency virus (HIV).

- **Immunology** - investigating abnormalities and disturbances of the immune system.

Opportunities for Training

You would need to complete a university degree course to acquire a detailed scientific knowledge of anatomy, physiology and pathology. The most appropriate science degrees are those designed specifically for the profession and accredited by the Institute of Biomedical Science. Other honours degrees may also be accepted or may be 'topped up' with an accredited postgraduate certificate or diploma. After obtaining your honours degree, you would need a period of in-service training of at least one year. The practical experience needed for State Registration is often incorporated into relevant sandwich degree courses.

Requirements for Entry

University entry qualifications would normally include A level/Advanced Higher/Higher biology and chemistry and GCSE/S grade passes at A-C/1-3 in mathematics and English. You must be state registered with the Health Professions Council before you can be employed in a qualified grade of biomedical scientist in a pathology or biomedical laboratory in or serving the National Health Service.

Kind of Person

Your work must be accurate and efficient because patients' lives could often depend on your skills. You would be using sophisticated automated equipment, microscopes and other hi-tech laboratory equipment, but you would need to control and understand the technology in order to recognise false signals. You would have to be prepared to update your skills as laboratory techniques develop and as research paves the way for new applications of science and medicine. You would normally work with other professionals as part of a healthcare team.

Broad Outlook

Biomedical science is a continually changing profession with long-term prospects including management, research, education and specialised laboratory posts. UK biomedical scientists work mainly in National Health Service or private sector laboratories but are also involved in organisations such as the National Blood Authority (which provides support to hospital blood banks) and the Blood Transfusion Service. If you work for the Medical Research Council, you could carry out research to help preserve health and combat and control disease.

Biomedical scientists are also employed in a variety of roles including the veterinary service, the Health and Safety Executive, university and forensic laboratories, pharmaceutical and product manufacturers, the Armed Services and various government departments. There could be opportunities to use your training and skills in healthcare posts and projects around the world, and you might consider undertaking a period of voluntary work in a developing country.

Related Occupations

You might also consider: pharmacist, pharmacologist, clinical biochemist, forensic scientist, food scientist or research biologist/chemist.

Impact on Lifestyle

You would normally work a 37.5-hour week, with some shift working on a rota basis to provide 24-hour cover to support clinical services. Working conditions try to ensure that, while biomedical scientists may sometimes work unsocial hours, they are not working excessive hours.

Earnings Potential

Qualified biomedical scientists in the NHS usually start in Band 5, on a scale currently ranging from £20,710 to £26,839. Earnings can rise to £33,436 for a specialist biomedical scientist at the top of the scale and to £39,273 at the top of the advanced scale. Additional allowances are paid for appointments in and around London, ranging from 20% of basic salary for Inner London, to 15% for Outer London and 5% for the London Fringe. Earnings in the private sector are generally likely to be higher, depending on where you live and the hours you are prepared to work.

As a new entrant to the profession, you will find that a professional portfolio will assume major significance. You will need it to provide evidence of specialist and higher specialist training to support any claims for promotion to a higher pay band.

Further Information

Institute of Biomedical Science, London EC1R 5HL
Website: www.ibms.org

Alternative/equivalent entrance requirements can include: ILC, IB, EB, NC/ND and many other similar international systems. For further details see the Equivalent Qualifications section in the Introduction.

Biotechnologist

What is Involved?

Working as a biotechnologist, you would be involved with using tiny living organisms such as bacteria or yeasts in industrial processes. You might find yourself, for example, working in the food or drinks industry; developing fertilizers or animal foodstuffs; or manufacturing pharmaceuticals. There are also opportunities to work with pollution control and the management of environmental waste.

You might become involved with the production of complex molecules, such as hormones or enzymes, which could be particularly useful in the medical field. One area of biotechnology that is expanding at the moment is that of harnessing genetic engineering.

Opportunities for Training

There are several courses in Biotechnology at undergraduate level, but degrees in biological sciences, molecular biology, genetics or biochemistry could also provide a good foundation for postgraduate work in this area. The main recruitment for work in the biotechnological field is from scientists with two to three years' postgraduate experience. To obtain this you would need a first class or upper second class degree, followed by specialist research in the area.

Pure research in biotechnology is concerned with subjects such as: proteomics - the structure and function of proteins, including the way they work and interact with each other inside cells, body fluids and tissues; functional genomics - the function of individual genes and interactions amongst groups of genes; structural genomics - the three-dimensional structure of proteins.

Requirements for Entry

To gain admission to a degree course, you would need three good A level/Advanced Higher, four Higher or equivalent qualifications, including biology and usually chemistry, together with five GCSE/S Grade passes at A-C/1-3 including English and maths.

Kind of Person

You would need a keen interest in biology and chemistry and in the application of specialised techniques. Attention to detail and a logical approach to problem solving would be essential. If you were involved in research, you would need to be persistent in the face of setbacks because it can take a long time to make headway in solving scientific problems. In return, you could be breaking new ground in an ever-changing world of discovery.

Some of the work would be routine testing and you should enjoy your current laboratory practical work. You would need a facility with statistics as well as good communication skills, as you would be called on to explain your experiments, results and conclusions to others, some of who may not have your technical knowledge. The internet is being used increasingly as a research tool and as a means of communicating by scientists, so you should be happy in using computers. You are also likely to be working as part of a team of scientists and, as you become more senior, would need to direct the work of other members of the team.

Broad Outlook

Once qualified, there would be a range of career options available to you. Not only is there choice in the area in which you could work but also in the type of job that you could do. You could, for example, continue with research or move into technical sales and marketing in your particular field. It is often possible to move between industries and so apply your knowledge and expertise in different fields as your career and interests develop. There is normally a shortage of qualified specialised scientists of this nature, although you may need to move to find the job that you really want.

Related Occupations

You might be interested in working in another area of scientific research by becoming a biochemist, microbiologist, biologist, pharmacist or pharmacologist. You could consider the broad areas of biomedical/clinical sciences.

Impact on Lifestyle

You are likely to be based in a laboratory, although you may also be working in an office attached to a factory, university or hospital. You may need to travel to other laboratories or to meet other scientists or attend conferences or lectures. At times you may have to work late when you have an important deadline to meet or when you are coming close to a breakthrough with a particular experiment.

Earnings Potential

Your salary when you first start working as a graduate biotechnologist is likely to be around £21,000 to £25,000. This should rise with experience to £35,000 to £50,000 and could exceed £55,000 if you were working in industry and had a particular specialism that is in short supply.

Further Information

Biotechnology and Biological Sciences Research Council, Swindon SN2 1UH
Website: www.bbsrc.ac.uk

Institute of Biology, London EC4A 3EF
Website: www.iob.org

Biotechnology Young Entrepreneurs Scheme
Website: www.biotechnologyyes.co.uk

Bioindustry Association
Website: www.bioindustry.org

Biotechnology Ireland
Website: www.biotechnologyireland.com

Institute of Food Research
Website: www.ifr.ac.uk

Alternative/equivalent entrance requirements can include: ILC, IB, EB, NC/ND and many other similar international systems. For further details see the Equivalent Qualifications section in the Introduction.

Broadcasting/Media Researcher

What is Involved?

As a researcher working in the broadcast media, you would generate new and original ideas for programmes, source information, contacts and contributors and turn ideas into actual broadcasts. As the person responsible for making first contact with potential contributors to programmes, you would have to ensure that they are good speakers and that the stories they provide are accurate and fair. All your sources must be thoroughly corroborated.

On the day of the programme, you would meet the guests you have booked and brief them about what to expect. You may be researching something topical and currently in the news or something more human interest led,. and you could spend some time delving into archives, combing newspapers or surfing the internet for background information.

You would have to keep meticulous records of the work you do, notes of interviews with people, copyright details, where permissions to use material have to be obtained and so on. You would also have to work strictly within the constraints of time and budget.

Opportunities for Training

There is no single way to train to become a researcher. It is likely but in no way essential that you would have a degree or bring to the industry transferable skills from another area such as print journalism. Much more important than qualifications would be to prove you have the talent, commitment and knowledge of the industry to make a positive contribution to production research.

Skillset, the Sector Skills Council for the audio visual industries, is the central information point for relevant training courses.

Requirements for Entry

You would need two or three A level/Advanced Higher, three or four Higher or equivalent qualifications for degree course entry. The subject of your degree is not important, although you could consider a course in journalism or media studies. Three or four years at university would be an opportunity to build experience in student journalism or broadcasting. You should take every opportunity to gain relevant work experience because that is often more highly valued than academic qualifications.

Kind of Person

You must be a team worker, with constant energy, a passion for programming and the ability to generate a variety of ideas for a range of programmes. You must be able to get on with people, particularly contributors, and able to make them feel at ease. You would need a high level of literacy and numeracy skills, together with intellectual rigour. You should be able to work independently and under pressure, to extract relevant details and write detailed notes or reports.

Wide general knowledge would be useful, together with good organisation and accuracy, and a high degree of computer literacy. As important as anything would be excellent intellectual and analytical skills. You would have to be very organised and have good communication skills, as you would be dealing with a wide variety of people. You would need mental and physical toughness, to cope with frustration as well as success, and probable long hours. Knowledge of and an ability to analyse different types of programmes would be essential.

Broad Outlook

Competition for contracts is intense. Most researchers work on freelance contracts, either directly for broadcasters or for independent production companies. Factual programmes regularly employ researchers, and sometimes drama and light entertainment programmes will too (particularly specialist researchers in, say, music or stills research).

Much of the work is in London and the south east, although major cities such as Belfast, Cardiff, Dublin, Edinburgh, Leeds and Manchester are strong centres.

Related Occupations

You might also consider: producer, director, programme editor or presenter, journalist, advertising copywriter or scriptwriter.

Impact on Lifestyle

You should be prepared for short-term contracts, unpredictable hours and tight deadlines. You may have to supplement your income with other work between contracts, especially in the early days as you build up your network of contacts. Your work would probably involve you in a good deal of travel, so a driving licence would be a virtual necessity.

Earnings Potential

It is virtually impossible to define annual earnings for a freelance researcher. Rates vary considerably, from around £150 to £400 per day. Experienced researchers may earn £20,000 to £24,000 a year, while specialist researchers can earn over £50,000.

You would normally be paid expenses for travel, accommodation and subsistence when you spend time away from home.

Further Information

British Broadcasting Corporation, London W12 8GJ
Website: www.bbc.co.uk

Ft2-Film and Television Freelance Training, London SE1 1TJ
Website: www.ft2.org.uk

Skillset Sector Skills Council for the Audio Visual industries, London N1 9GB
Website: www.skillset.org

Your Creative Future
Website: www.yourcreativefuture.org

Broadcasting Entertainment Cinematographic and Theatre Union (BECTU), London SW9 9BT
Website: www.bectu.org.uk

Broadcast Journalism Training Council (BJTC), Lincolnshire PE10 0TH
Website: www.bjtc.org.uk

Dublin Media Centre, Dublin 6
Website: www.dublinmediacentre.com

Alternative/equivalent entrance requirements can include: ILC, IB, EB, NC/ND and many other similar international systems. For further details see the Equivalent Qualifications section in the Introduction.

Building Services Engineer

What is Involved?

As a building services engineer, you could be involved with the design of energy efficient buildings, renewable energy, green architecture, ventilation, lighting, acoustics, electricity and control, many or all of which are necessary in modern buildings. You might also use your skills to meet demands for building energy management systems, fire/smoke control, indoor air quality standards and environmental pollution control. You could design the sophisticated systems that are required and draw up the necessary plans on paper or computer. You would also be expected to supervise the installation of all of these services and ensure they meet the correct specifications and safety regulations. You would often work alongside architects, allowing you to input your creative expertise at the concept stage in the design process.

Opportunities for Training

To qualify as a chartered engineer, responsible for research, development and senior management, the simplest route would be to complete a four-year accredited MEng degree, followed by about four years of structured training with an employer. To qualify as an incorporated engineer, responsible more for the day-to-day management of projects, you could take a three-year accredited BEng degree, followed by a similar period of structured training. There are alternative routes to both chartered and incorporated engineer status and you should consult the Chartered Institution of Building Services Engineers (CIBSE) for more information. Graduates who specialise in IT or acoustics are particularly sought after.

Requirements for Entry

Entry requirements vary for different degrees and at different universities. Generally speaking, you would need three A level/Advanced Higher, four Higher or equivalent qualifications for the MEng route, including maths and physics, and two A level/Advanced Higher, three Higher or equivalent qualifications for the BEng route. In either case, you should also have a broad platform of GCSE/S Grade passes at A-C/1-3. Some universities offer a one-year foundation course for students who do not have the necessary maths or physics passes.

Kind of Person

You would need to be able to display initiative and enterprise in planning and executing a programme for the development of an engineering project and able to work effectively both as an individual and as a member of a team. You should have excellent numeracy and problem solving skills and the ability to communicate ideas verbally, in written reports and by means of presentations to groups.

You would also need good awareness of management methods and of the financial environment in which you would be working. This is a rapidly changing work environment, so you would need to keep up to date with new developments and technology. Computer skills would be essential in your design work - using computer-aided design (CAD) software packages. You would find yourself analysing and solving practical problems and taking responsibility for your decisions and possibly for large projects. You would need to make site visits during the construction phases, which would require agility and physical fitness.

Broad Outlook

Building services engineering is recognised as an important discipline and for many years demand for graduates in this area has outstripped supply. There was, before the current recession, a nationwide shortage of building services engineers, which meant that you were in an extremely good position to find a job, with potential employers including large building contractors, architectural or design practices and equipment manufacturers. Large companies with a buildings portfolio also need building services engineers and there are jobs in companies responsible for the maintenance and servicing of buildings. There are also opportunities to work overseas.

Employment forecasts suggest that construction and engineering opportunities will pick up again - especially with regeneration schemes and projects in preparation for the 2012 London Olympics.

Related Occupations

You might also consider: quantity surveyor, building surveyor, civil, electrical or mechanical engineer, architect or town planner.

Impact on Lifestyle

If you were office based, you would expect to work regular hours, probably a 36- hour week Monday to Friday. However, you might need to work longer hours when there were important deadlines to meet. If you were working on site, you could expect to work longer and less regular hours than this, including evenings and weekends.

You might need to travel a long distance to reach the site or even to stay away from home whilst you were working. You would also be expected to work all around the site, which could involve climbing ladders or scaffolding. You would need to be prepared to get wet, cold and dirty and probably to wear protective clothing

Earnings Potential

Once the economic downturn of 2009 is behind us, the shortage of building services engineers should indicate attractive salaries, secure employment and good promotion prospects. You could expect to start earning around £20,000 to £25,000 when you first graduate and should be able to increase your earnings fairly rapidly, to around £35,000 to £55,000, within a few years, rising to £70,000 plus for an experienced manager.

Further Information

Chartered Institution of Building Services Engineers, London SW12 9BS
Website: www.cibse.org

Building Engineering Services Training, Slough SL2 5DA
Website: www.best-ltd.co.uk

Alternative/equivalent entrance requirements can include: ILC, IB, EB, NC/ND and many other similar international systems. For further details see the Equivalent Qualifications section in the Introduction.

Building Surveying Technician

What is Involved?

As a building surveying technician, you would carry out a number of tasks that would provide important technical support to a building surveyor. See our separate article on this work. You might find yourself carrying out detailed surveys of buildings, preparing accurate plans and specifications for work, costing work and handling tender documents or dealing with contractors.

You might be required to offer advice to clients on the suitability of buildings for particular purposes, the feasibility of proposed building work or on the soundness of a building. You should be able to advise on relevant legislation and the availability of grants, on the choice of contractors in your area and on maintenance or repair requirements. Another area of work in which you might become involved is that of on-site supervision.

Opportunities for Training

To become a building surveying technician, you would usually be training whilst working towards qualifying membership of one of three organisations: the Faculty of Architecture and Surveying, the Association of Building Engineers or the Royal Institution of Chartered Surveyors.

Whichever you choose, you could study full- or part-time for a foundation degree or higher national certificate or diploma (HNC/D) in building surveying, or work towards National or Scottish Vocational Qualifications (N/SVQ) at levels three/four. You would normally follow a structured training programme for at least two years and you would need to attain a series of competence levels.

You may be able to study for further qualifications to become a chartered surveyor.

From 2010 workers on construction sites will have to hold a Construction Skills Certification Scheme (CSCS) card or equivalent, to prove their competence to do the job. You will need to pass a health and safety test to qualify for this scheme. Many construction firms already require a relevant CSCS card to allow workers to work on site.

Requirements for Entry

For the HNC/D route, you would need at least one A level/Advanced Higher, two Higher or equivalent qualifications, together with three GCSE/S Grade passes at A-C/1-3, including English and maths. There are no minimum entry requirements for the foundation degree or N/SVQ route, although individual employers or training providers may set their own standards.

You would almost certainly need a driving licence, as you would be required to visit sites on a regular basis.

Kind of Person

You would be working in a technical field and as such would need to have a methodical and logical approach to solving practical problems. You would have to enjoy working with figures and have some mathematical ability. You may find yourself using quite complicated measuring equipment, so would need some technical skills.

In addition to your practical nature, you would need to be able to communicate with a wide range of people. You might need to read and write reports and convey the information in them to other professionals. You could be talking directly to clients, who may not have your knowledge of buildings. Alternatively, you might be on site dealing with the work force, giving them instructions and organising their work.

Broad Outlook

Job prospects for building surveying technicians are generally good, although the state of the housing market in early 2009 is far from encouraging. A more positive picture will undoubtedly appear once the current downturn is over. In large companies there is often a recognised career structure and opportunities for promotion are readily available if you are prepared to work hard.

However, promotion can be more difficult in smaller companies and you may need to change jobs and move around to gain experience. It is also possible for experienced technicians to become self-employed or consultants and there are opportunities to work abroad.

Related Occupations

You might also consider: building services engineer, estate agent, technician engineer, town planner or architectural technologist.

Impact on Lifestyle

If you are working in an office-based role then you are likely to work regular hours, mainly Monday to Friday. However, you are also likely to work on sites when you may have to work in wet, cold and dirty conditions. You may need to climb ladders or go up scaffolding and would need to be reasonably fit to cope with the demands of the job. You may need to walk some distance and scramble around sites in order to take accurate measurements. At times you may have to wear protective clothing such as a hard hat.

Earnings Potential

If you start as a school leaver studying part-time, you could earn around £14,000 to £16,000 a year. This is likely to rise to around £22,000 to £25,000 when you qualify and should increase with experience to £30,000 plus. Salaries for surveying technicians can vary enormously, depending on demand for staff and also on the particular expertise that you can offer.

Further Information

Faculty of Architecture and Surveying, Chartered Institute of Building
Website: www.ciob.org.uk/topics/foaas

Royal Institution of Chartered Surveyors, Coventry CV4 8JE
Website: www.rics.org

Association of Building Engineers, Northampton NN3 8NW
Website: www.abe.org.uk

Alternative/equivalent entrance requirements can include: ILC, IB, EB, NC/ND and many other similar international systems. For further details see the Equivalent Qualifications section in the Introduction.

Building Surveyor

What is Involved?

As a building surveyor, you would provide detailed advice on the design, construction, maintenance, management or repair of proposed or existing buildings. You would be looking for defects in, or ways to improve, all types in existing buildings. You would also advise on the feasibility and possible costs of repair to the building, of conversion and the suitability of the building for particular purposes.

Your clients would include prospective purchasers, vendors, building societies and property owners. You might find yourself drawing up detailed plans, advising on government or health and safety regulations and on whether a grant might be available for the work. You could also be involved with instructing an architect to prepare detailed plans and with obtaining estimates for carrying out the work.

Opportunities for Training

In order to become a member of the Royal Institution of Chartered Surveyors (RICS) or the Chartered Institute of Building (CIOB), you would need an accredited degree (or equivalent), together with a minimum of two years training whilst you are employed. This on-the-job training must normally be approved before you start. There are full-time degree courses, which take three years to complete. There are also sandwich courses, which include a year of practical work experience that can count towards the required two years training.

If you want to 'earn whilst you learn' there are part-time degree courses available, which you take whilst you are employed. In addition, there are some accredited distance learning degree or diploma correspondence courses, which can be taken whilst you work, and relevant postgraduate courses.

Requirements for Entry

Degree courses in surveying normally ask for a minimum of two A level/Advanced Higher, three Higher or equivalent qualifications, together with least four or five GCSE/S Grade passes at A-C/1-3, often specifying English and maths.

Kind of Person

You would need a practical approach to problem solving. There is likely to be quite a lot of paperwork involved. You would be drawing up and interpreting plans and for this you need to be accurate. You might be involved with reading and evaluating both tender documents and documents relating to the law. You could be involved with making decisions relating to deadlines and budgets for work for which you will need to have a good grasp of maths.

Above all, you would need to bring common sense and logic to your decision making. In addition to this, you are likely to be working with a large number of different people. These can include your employers, who you may need to persuade to your point of view, and the site workers, who you may need to instruct and lead. At times you would be imparting complex technical information to people without your specialist knowledge. You are also likely to be working as part of a team of building professionals, with whom you may need to negotiate the best solution to a problem.

Broad Outlook

Although the entire construction industry has been severely affected by the economic downturn in early 2009, the demand for the building surveyor's expertise has generally growing in line with the refurbishment of urban areas, rural sites and older properties. The largest employer is the private sector, which ranges from very small practices to large companies with overseas operations. Your qualification would be recognised in many countries if you wanted to work abroad. Local authorities also employ a number of building surveyors, as do major companies with a large amount of property, such as major retailers or hotel chains. There are also opportunities to work with large historical buildings for the trusts or charities that manage them and are concerned with their maintenance.

Related Occupations

You might consider: town and country planner, architect, estate agent, civil engineer, valuer or auctioneer.

Impact on Lifestyle

You are likely to be involved in inspecting buildings very thoroughly; this can involve going into dirty, damp and dark areas such as attics and cellars. You would need to be reasonably fit and agile in order to carry out your surveys effectively. At times you may need to climb ladders or scramble around on scaffolding. Your work could involve you being outside in all kinds of weather and you could need to walk for quite long distances.

A driving licence is likely to be essential to get you to the sites and you may be expected to travel quite long distances within the UK and in some cases to spend time abroad.

Earnings Potential

Graduate starting salaries are generally around £19,000 to £22,000, slightly higher in the London area. The average salary for chartered surveyors is around £37,000, and for a partner around £70,000. Top-end salaries can be over £100,000. Most surveyors receive additional benefits as part of their salary package. These may include a performance related bonus and a company car.

Further Information

Royal Institution of Chartered Surveyors, Coventry CV4 8JE
Website: www.rics.org

Chartered Institute of Building, Ascot SL5 7TB
Website: www.ciob.org.uk

Association of Building Engineers, Northampton NN3 8NW
Website: www.abe.org.uk

Alternative/equivalent entrance requirements can include: ILC, IB, EB, NC/ND and many other similar international systems. For further details see the Equivalent Qualifications section in the Introduction.

Building Technician

What is Involved?

As a building technician, you are likely to find yourself specialising in one or more of the areas of work involved in managing a construction site. For example, you could be working from an architect's or engineer's drawings to estimate the costs of a project or plan the stages of construction. Taking account of the materials and manpower needed, you would calculate the time and costs involved. You might be involved with buying the materials needed and working out how to store the equipment and materials on site. Alternatively, your work could take you on to the site itself where you would check the progress and standard of the work being carried out.

Opportunities for Training

There are several possible training routes. You could, for example, take a part- or full-time higher national certificate/diploma (HNC/D) at a college or training centre; you could take a lower level construction course at a local college or you could train in a craft skill - such as bricklaying or plastering - before taking a National or Scottish Vocational Qualification (NVQ/SVQ) at technician level. Another way of training would be to take a construction apprenticeship, in which you could study part-time up to NVQ/SVQ level 3 while in paid employment. This would probably take three or four years to complete.

Requirements for Entry

Practical experience of working on a building site or in a construction environment is usually the most important requirement. For the HNC/D route, you would normally need at least one A level/Advanced Higher, two Higher or equivalent qualifications, together with four GCSE/S Grade passes at A-C/1-3, including English, maths and a science. Similar GCSE/S Grade requirements would apply to most apprenticeships and college courses for this type of work. You would often be able to enter a craft level course by passing a selection test.

Kind of Person

You would need to be a practical person with a logical and sensible approach to problem solving. In order to be successful you would need to learn a considerable amount of technical information about the building industry and also gain some knowledge of law and health and safety issues. Your job is likely to involve computers, so you would need to be computer literate. Your job would involve dealing with large variety of people and you would need to have good communication skills. You might, for example, be negotiating with other professionals or supervising workers on a building site.

In either case you would need to make yourself clearly understood. You are also likely to be involved with interpreting plans and with making calculations based on the information you are given. You may need to organise your own work and that of others and should be able to work on your own initiative.

Broad Outlook

There are opportunities to work for local and central government, for large building contractors and for large organisations that have property portfolios such as hotel chains or major retailers. The demand for technicians depends to a great extent on the state of the building trade and it must be said that the picture in early 2009 is far from encouraging, as the housing market continues to weaken and demand for industrial, office, retail and leisure facilities declines considerably. Forecasts suggest, however, that construction will pick up again in 2010. You may choose to change employers and job roles over time in order to gain the experience necessary to develop your career and perhaps set up your own business.

Related Occupations

You might consider other construction-related careers, such as: surveying technician, architectural technologist, town planning support worker, building manager, surveyor or estate agent.

Impact on Lifestyle

If you are working in an office-based job, the hours of work are likely to be around 40 hours a week. However, you would also be expected to work overtime in the evenings and at weekend, particularly if you have a contract deadline to meet. The hours of work on building sites can be long, especially in the summer to make maximum use of daylight hours. You could also get dirty, wet and cold at times on a building site and would need to wear protective clothing such as a hard hat, boots and a reflective coat.

Earnings Potential

Salaries for building technicians vary between companies and different parts of the country. A trainee could expect to earn around £14,000, rising on qualification to £20,000 or more. Some technicians earn around £30,000 as they become more experienced. There are also allowances for working on site and sometimes travel expenses are reimbursed.

Further Information

Construction Skills
Website: www.constructionskills.net

Association of Building Engineers, Northampton NN3 8NW
Website: www.abe.org.uk

Chartered Institute of Building, Berkshire SL5 7TB
Website: www.ciob.org.uk

Alternative/equivalent entrance requirements can include: ILC, IB, EB, NC/ND and many other similar international systems. For further details see the Equivalent Qualifications section in the Introduction.

Business Executive

What is Involved?

As a business executive, you might be working for a large multinational organisation with a turnover bigger than the economy of a small country or you might be part of a small, family-run concern with no more than a handful of staff. Whatever the size or type of the organisation, you would soon play a key role in helping it achieve its goals, through managing resources - such as people, money, materials - and work activities.

Your precise responsibilities would vary according to the type of organisation and your position within it. At the first level of management, for example, you may have responsibility for only a small team and are likely to have limited influence on the organisation's policies. As a more senior person, on the other hand, you may be responsible for a specific function - such as finance, human resources, IT/management services, marketing/sales or production - and could have a high degree of responsibility for, and influence on, the organisation's policies and future development. Frequently, you would be seen by clients as the 'face' of the company for their purposes.

Opportunities for Training

Most business executives undertake training on the job. This can be supported by a wide range of management qualifications at business schools and colleges. NVQ/SVQ courses and other vocationally-related qualifications include levels 3 and 4 in management and level 5 in operational or strategic management. Details of accredited courses are available from the Chartered Management Institute (CMI) and the Institute of Leadership and Management (ILM).

An alternative route is to progress to higher education and continue your studies with a degree or HNC/HND. Useful subjects would include business studies, management science, business information systems, accountancy, economics, law and modern foreign languages, but most good degree subjects would be acceptable for new entrants. You might even undertake a postgraduate Master in Business Administration (MBA), usually after several years of business experience.

Requirements for Entry

There are no set academic entry requirements for business executives. Most people do not go directly into a key executive role, as it is important to start by building considerable experience of relevant work. If you do want an executive role as early as possible in your career, you might consider a trainee post as offered by some of the larger organisations, particularly in the retail industry. Entry requirements vary, but for school leavers are usually a minimum of five GCSEs/S grades (A-C/1-3) including English and maths, plus either two A levels/three H grades or equivalent. Employers may also ask for specific skills, such as communication, problem-solving or teamworking.

Kind of Person

It goes without saying that you will be motivated by achieving set goals or targets. You should also be decisive, willing to take responsibility, and able to work well in a team under pressure, to delegate when appropriate and to motivate and encourage others. Excellent communication and number skills should make you effective at planning, monitoring and reviewing, and able to analyse and interpret information. You should also possess effective presentation and public speaking skills.

You must be persuasive in order to influence people, able to command respect and trust and be good at problem solving. It would help if you can speak at least one major foreign language.

*B*road Outlook

Depending on the size of your organisation, there may be opportunities for internal promotion to a more senior management level, or it may be necessary to move elsewhere. With the right experience and a proven track record of success, you may be promoted to company director level. With even more experience, you may progress to the role of chief executive and subsequently chair of an organisation. There may also be opportunities to become a non-executive director, usually on a part-time basis, for one or more organisations. Another option could be to set up your own business for which your training would provide invaluable experience.

*R*elated Occupations

You might consider: chartered secretary, marketing executive, human resources manager, sales executive, health service manager, retail manager, civil service administrator or accountant.

*I*mpact on Lifestyle

You may nominally work office hours, which are usually 9am to 5.30pm, Monday to Friday. However, many executives work additional hours in order to meet the demands of the job. You would be largely office based, but may be required to travel to visit clients or attend meetings at other sites within the organisation. This may be within the UK or overseas.

*E*arnings Potential

Salaries for executives vary considerably according to the size of the organisation, the nature of the business, its location and function. You might start on, say, £18,000 to £25,000, rising with experience to £45,000 to £65,000. As a director, you might earn anything from £80,000 a year to over £2,000,000! In addition, you may receive bonus payments and share options.

*F*urther Information

Association of Business Schools, London NW1 2AA
Website: www.the-abs.org.uk

Chartered Management Institute, Corby, Northamptonshire NN17 1TT
Website: www.managers.org.uk

Institute of Directors, London SW1Y 5ED
Website: www.iod.com

Institute of Leadership & Management, London EC1A 9DD
Website: www.i-l-m.com

Chartered Quality Institute, London SW1X 7EE
Website: www.thecqi.org

Alternative/equivalent entrance requirements can include: ILC, IB, EB, NC/ND and many other similar international systems. For further details see the Equivalent Qualifications section in the Introduction.

Buying Executive

Also called Buyer or Purchasing Officer

What is Involved?

As a buying executive, you would be responsible for obtaining the products and services needed by your organisation to support its key activities. This could include, for example, purchasing the raw materials or components for a manufacturing process, sourcing spare parts for machinery maintenance, ordering the merchandise for a retail outlet or updating the IT facilities in an office environment. You would be expected to negotiate competitive prices at the same time as building relationships with suppliers who understand your needs, can meet your quality specifications and can deliver the right quantity of materials on a reliable basis.

You would have to maintain adequate reserve stock levels to cope with fluctuations in demand and ensure that supplies reach their intended destination on time. You would probably set up automated systems to cope with some of these functions but you would need to discuss contracts with suppliers, monitor deliveries and stock levels, challenge price changes, check sources of new materials and keep pace with technological and design improvements. You could work in almost any sort of manufacturing or service organisation, although you would need special skills to act as a buyer in, say, the retail fashion business or a technical background before you could purchase engineering components.

Opportunities for Training

Most employers would expect you to work towards Chartered Institute of Purchasing and Supply (CIPS) qualifications. These are available on a full- or part-time basis or by distance learning and range from the clerical level Certificate in Purchasing and Supply to the CIPS Graduate Diploma. You could also work towards National or Scottish Vocational Qualifications (N/SVQ) in Procurement or take an accredited degree or higher national diploma (HND). The CIPS qualifications would usually be supported in many companies by an internal training scheme. With appropriate qualifications and experience, you could become a member and then a fellow of CIPS.

There is now a wide variety of UK universities offering purchasing and supply related degree courses. General business degrees also often include some core elements of purchasing and supply disciplines in their syllabus.

Requirements for Entry

While there are no specific entry requirements, most employers look for a degree, HND or equivalent qualification. This could be in any subject, although business studies, management science, computing or logistics could be useful. In the engineering/manufacturing industries, a technological qualification would be an advantage, as would chemistry in the chemical industry or computing in IT. For degree entry, you would normally be expected to have at least two A level/Advanced Higher, three Higher or equivalent qualifications, together with four or five GCSE/S Grade passes at A-C/1-3, including English and maths.

Kind of Person

As an essential link in the supply chain, you would be in a very demanding and responsible position. You would need to understand the overall requirements of your own organisation and to be able to assess the relative merits of suppliers' goods or services. A logical and analytical mind would be essential, together with good powers of judgement and the ability to negotiate contracts. You should have strong numerical skills and a grasp of finance and accounting, since you would often be handling large sums of money. In addition to these technical qualities, you would need excellent written and verbal communication skills, a liking for others and a sense of fairness and integrity.

Broad Outlook

You might achieve promotion - to senior management or even to board level - within your existing organisation. Alternatively, you could develop your career by moving elsewhere. All kinds of organisation throughout the country need buying executives, so many opportunities to move should be possible. There may be scope to specialise in a particular field calling for special expertise, such as buying art at auction, next season's designs for a fashion store or lorries and vans for a freight company.

Related Occupations

You might also consider: logistics manager, sales executive, retail manager, freight forwarder, or shipbroker .

Impact on Lifestyle

You would work normal office hours but would occasionally need to take work home at night or over weekends, so that you could formulate your strategic plans and analyse your departmental performance, check levels of stock or write a monthly report for directors. You may need to travel fairly extensively, including making trips overseas, in order to check suppliers' procedures, transport systems and quality controls.

Earnings Potential

You could expect to start at around £21,000 to £25,000 as a graduate trainee, with your income rising after five years to £30,000 to £35,000. Once you reach middle or senior management levels, say after ten years in the business, you could expect a salary of £55,000 to £65,000. If you can demonstrate that your buying skills lead to savings in costs and improvements in efficiency, you could earn significant performance-related bonuses.

According to the CIPS/Croner Reward 2007 Salary Survey, purchasing directors received an average salary of £76,000 a year and senior managers averaged an annual salary of £60,000. The survey also claims that senior and middle-ranking purchasing managers are now commanding higher salaries than their colleagues in marketing, sales, human resources, IT and finance.

Further Information

Chartered Institute of Purchasing and Supply, Stamford PE9 3NZ
Website: www.cips.org

Chartered Institute of Logistics and Transport, Northants NN17 4XQ
Website: www.ciltuk.org.uk

Alternative/equivalent entrance requirements can include: ILC, IB, EB, NC/ND and many other similar international systems. For further details see the Equivalent Qualifications section in the Introduction.

Careers Adviser/Guidance Counsellor

What is Involved?

As a careers adviser or guidance counsellor, you would provide information, advice and guidance (IAG) to help people make decisions about their future. You might work in a careers centre, in schools and colleges, a university or an adult guidance centre, and your clients might need guidance on, for example, their long-term career goals or help with decisions related to their education and training. You would usually work with people individually, although you may occasionally lead groups, using your counselling skills and your knowledge of education, training and employment to help them decide on next steps. You may use psychometric and other interest and ability tests to support the guidance process. After your interview or group work session, you would provide a written report summarising the outcomes of the guidance interview and the implications in terms of career plans. In an educational establishment, your work may involve preparing education programmes related to careers and personal development, taking classes and leading group discussions. You would also be expected to have close, regular contact with employers and other opportunity providers.

In England at present, guidance provision for young people is in a state of flux. IAG must be offered by local authorities, who may run their own in-house service or contract out to other organisations. Provision is more settled in Scotland, Wales and Northern Ireland.

Opportunities for Training

Many entrants hold the Qualification in Careers Guidance (QCG), which is available full- or part-time at 15 institutions. You might follow this with an N/SVQ Level 4 in Advice and Guidance or Learning Development and Support Services (LDSS) for children, young people and those who care for them. Both of these qualifications are gained on the job.

Alternatively, you could start work as a trainee or administrator in a careers organisation, then take the N/SVQ Level 4 as part of your career development. A few foundation degrees in guidance and related areas are available, but may not be recognised for entry to the profession. In Northern Ireland, careers advisers are often experienced civil service employees who have been promoted or moved sideways.

Training preferences vary from one employer to another, so you should research information carefully. Advisers working in higher education have their own qualification organised by the Association of Graduate Careers Advisory Services.

Requirements for Entry

There are no specific entry requirements for the QCG or the N/SVQ, although you would have to demonstrate your ability to cope with the academic aspects of the training. Many new entrants are graduates, with a degree in any subject, but employers also value a broad range of life and work experiences.

Kind of Person

You would need enthusiasm, flexibility and a real interest in helping people to make the most of the opportunities available. Depending on the client group that you were working with, you would also need a wide range of counselling and guidance skills, an understanding of educational systems and knowledge of local, national and international labour markets.

You would need to be able to plan and organise your own time and to be able to work as part of a team. Computer systems are widely used for record keeping, maintaining occupational databases and administering tests, so you would need good IT skills. If your clients are facing difficulties in obtaining employment, you may need advocacy skills as well as the ability to network with relevant agencies.

Broad Outlook

With considerable uncertainty about guidance provision in England, many posts are being offered on a temporary or fixed-term contract basis. This is far from encouraging for potential new entrants to the profession but it is hoped that a more settled picture will soon emerge.

Outside England, the main national employing organisations are Careers Scotland, Careers Wales and the Northern Ireland Department for Employment and Learning. Other employers include higher education institutions, voluntary organisations and private careers consultancies, providing services on a fee-paying basis.

Related Occupations

You might also consider: teacher, social worker, probation officer or youth worker.

Impact on Lifestyle

The work has traditionally been based on normal Monday to Friday hours, with occasional evening and weekend events and some time spent away from home on training courses.

Earnings Potential

You would probably start as a trainee on around £19,000 to £21,000, rising to £22,000 to £27,000 on full qualification. With experience and increased responsibility, your earnings should increase to £30,000 to £45,000. Some senior posts offer £55,000 plus.

Further Information

Institute of Career Guidance, Stourbridge DY8 1TA
Website: www.icg-uk.org

Association of Graduate Careers Advisory Services, Sheffield S3 7QX
Website: www.agcas.org.uk

Careers Scotland
Website: www.careers-scotland.org.uk

Careers Wales
Website: www.careerswales.com

Careers Service Northern Ireland
Website: www.careersserviceni.com

Institute of Guidance Counsellors, Dublin 2
Website: www.igc.ie

Alternative/equivalent entrance requirements can include: ILC, IB, EB, NC/ND and many other similar international systems. For further details see the Equivalent Qualifications section in the Introduction.

Cartographer

What is Involved?

As a cartographer you would be dealing with the making of maps. You must be careful not to confuse the work of the cartographer with that of the surveyor, nor expect employment to involve strenuous outdoor activity and travel to remote places. With very few exceptions, you would normally be found seated at a desk or graphics workstation, processing original survey data collected and recorded by specialists in the field. The work falls into two areas: the **editorial** side, where the contents of the map are chosen and its appearance is designed, or the **drafting** side, where the map is actually produced.

Cartography has been revolutionised by information technology and traditional methods of map-making continue to change. For example, information is now obtained by photography from satellites. Unlike earlier mapmakers, whose challenge was to obtain the relevant information, today there is so much information available that the problem has become how to select what is required. What we are able to map has also changed and will continue to do so. We can now map the seabed with great accuracy and our increasing exploration of space will bring with it new demands for maps and charts.

Opportunities for Training

The degree courses with content of most direct relevance to working in cartography are Surveying and Mapping Sciences or Geographical Information Science (GIS) at the Universities of East London, Newcastle upon Tyne and Portsmouth.

GIS courses tend to place great emphasis on practical mapmaking and you would gain a lot of 'hands on' experience, either designing on paper or creating maps on a computer screen.

Many other universities offer courses or modules in cartography, usually as part of a geography or GIS degree.

At postgraduate level, the main course with a substantial element of cartography (map design and visualisation) is the MSc in Geoinformation Technology and Cartography at Glasgow University.

Requirements for Entry

Degree entry would require a minimum of two A level/Advanced Higher, three Higher or equivalent qualifications, ideally including geography, together with five GCSE/S Grade passes A-C/1-3, including English and maths.

Kind of Person

You should have a genuine feeling for maps, combined with the patience and powers of concentration necessary to undertake work which may be both mentally and physically demanding, as the preparation of a single sheet may take several weeks or even months. Artistic flair and a sense of design are valuable assets, as is an ability to work with precision and sometimes against the clock. This is very precise work using complex equipment and techniques.

Cartographers have to be experts in communication: in real life roads are not red, nor motorways blue, and there are no dotted lines marking the borders between countries, but we see these things on a map and immediately know what they mean.

In short, you need to love maps, be interested in design, like geography and enjoy designing on a computer screen.

Broad Outlook

The IT revolution has meant that far fewer cartographers are needed than before and there is enormous competition for the comparatively few employment openings which occur. Potential employers include government departments and national organisations like the Ordnance Survey, Met Office and Civil Aviation Authority; local, district and regional authorities; and the private sector such as map publishers, the AA or RAC. There are also opportunities to work abroad, for example for oil companies.

Employers with vacancies tend to approach the universities that offer cartography- or surveying-related degrees. Membership of the two main professional groups, the Society of Cartographers and the British Cartographic Society, is useful for making contacts and keeping up with developments.

Related Occupations

You might wish to consider: town planner, surveyor, graphic designer or illustrator.

Impact on Lifestyle

This is an office-based job and you could expect to work regular office hours. Many cartographers work freelance on a contract basis and enjoy the freedom of being their own boss. If you have the right qualifications, you can progress from being a map drafter to a map editor and gradually assume responsibility for whole projects.

Earnings Potential

Cartographers themselves will tell you that their rewards are more often aesthetic, or come from knowledge that the end product will be of use to another person, than they are financial. Few, if any, have been known to make their fortune. As a graduate trainee, you could expect a starting salary between £18,000 and £20,000, progressing over three to five years to about £22,000 to £30,000, and rising with experience and responsibility to £35,000 to £45,000.

Further Information

British Cartographic Society, Somerset TA21 9AT
Website: www.cartography.org.uk
*(click on **publications** to take you to **careers in cartography**)*

Society of Cartographers, Glasgow G12 8QQ
Website: www.soc.org.uk

Ordnance Survey, Southampton SO16 4GU
Website: www.ordnancesurvey.co.uk

Go-Geo!
Website: www.gogeo.ac.uk

Alternative/equivalent entrance requirements can include: ILC, IB, EB, NC/ND and many other similar international systems. For further details see the Equivalent Qualifications section in the Introduction.

Catering Manager

What is Involved?

As a catering manager, you would most likely work in the rapidly expanding food service management, or contract catering sectors of British industry. This is made up of companies of all sizes, who win contracts to manage the catering needs and related services of a whole range of organisations. It can involve feeding people at work, catering in schools, colleges and universities, hospitals and healthcare or any other companies who prefer to call upon the experts, so that they can get on with taking care of their core business. Food service management companies are now developing their services to include catering for members of the public in such outlets as leisure centres, department stores, airports, railways stations, public events and places of entertainment. Alternatively, you could work in one specific restaurant, hotel or other food outlet, in which case you might be termed a restaurant manager.

In either case, you would be expected to ensure satisfaction with the quality of food and service, manage the whole operation efficiently and profitably and know how to deal with people, both staff and public. The bigger the organisation, the less likely it is that you would be required to cope with front-line welcoming and table organisation; you would concentrate your energies on recruitment, motivation, training, the arrangement and supervision of shifts, quality control, hygiene, health and safety and controlling budgets. Whatever the context, standards would feature high on your priorities.

Opportunities for Training

Opportunities exist at every level, with a range of training routes for school leavers or university graduates. Relevant previous experience or qualifications usually ensure that you are able to join the profession a few rungs higher on the career ladder.

You could go into the business straight from school, perhaps via an Apprenticeship or a craft course, and develop your career up to a managerial position. Alternatively, you could continue your studies to higher national diploma (HND), foundation degree or degree level or you could join a company management training scheme.

Requirements for Entry

For degree entry, you would need at least two A level/Advanced Higher, three Higher or equivalent qualifications, together with a good spread of GCSE/S Grade passes A-C/1-3. The HND route usually requires one A level/Advanced Higher, two Higher or equivalent qualifications. A foreign language would be very useful. You may be able to join a company scheme with A level/Advanced Higher, Higher or equivalent, but a degree or HND would be more usual.

Experience in the industry, at however humble a level, would always be proof of your interest and commitment.

Kind of Person

Above all, you should be highly motivated, with a keen interest in food and drink. You would need a smart personal appearance, the ability to communicate effectively with customers and staff and the confidence to operate in a very public setting. You would have to remain calm under pressure and have the flexibility to cope with the occasional crisis in the kitchen. Physical fitness and the stamina to keep going for many hours a day would be important.

Broad Outlook

As the catering sector grows, so do the career opportunities available. It is not just about preparing and serving food, although these are vital jobs for the success of the sector. Areas that you could work in include: catering services, corporate events and functions, domestic services, facilities management, food production, human resources, marketing, residential services, sales, service development and support services.

Once you have sufficient experience, you could open your own restaurant or set up a contract catering business.

Related Occupations

You might also consider: restaurant manager, hotel manager, conferences and events manager, chef, or leisure services manager.

Impact on Lifestyle

In contract catering, your working hours could be reasonably regular; as a restaurant manager, however, you would have to work late into the evening and could expect to be busiest at weekends and during public holidays. You may work on a split shift system and you may find that, rather than having fixed hours, you have to keep working until the last customer leaves.

Earnings Potential

Junior managers usually earn between £16,000 and £23,000, while more experienced managers could expect £25,000 to £35,000. Some senior managers would receive in the region of £50,000 to £70,000. You may be offered live-in accommodation in some restaurant manager posts. If you can set up and run a successful restaurant or catering business, you should be able to achieve higher financial rewards.

Further Information

Institute of Hospitality, Surrey SM1 1SH
Website: www.instituteofhospitality.org

People 1st for Skills, Uxbridge UB8 1LH
Website: www.people1st.co.uk

Springboard, London WC2H 8LP
Website: www.springboarduk.org.uk

British Hospitality Association, London WC2A 3BH
Website: www.bha.org.uk

Irish Hospitality Institute
Website: www.ihi.ie

Alternative/equivalent entrance requirements can include: ILC, IB, EB, NC/ND and many other similar international systems. For further details see the Equivalent Qualifications section in the Introduction.

What is Involved?

This is not secretarial work in the normally accepted sense. As a chartered secretary, you would play a central role in the administration and management of an organisation. Your work would include advising the directors/trustees of their legal obligations, administering finances, communicating with stakeholders, preparing agendas, taking minutes of meetings and maintaining the statutory records. You would need a wide knowledge of the law, accounting and business organisations.

As a bridge between the management board, stakeholders and other organisations, you would need to be fully aware of every aspect of your organisation, including the nature of the business and its overall direction, the functions of employees and the current finances.

Opportunities for Training

While it is not essential for you to become a member of the Institute of Chartered Secretaries and Administrators (ICSA), you would find this valuable, especially if you were working as a company secretary. You would, for example, be legally qualified to file the annual report with Companies House and you would be able to supply financial information to the Stock Exchange.

The ICSA training programme takes two or three years (less for graduates with relevant first degrees) and provides a structured course of modules and exams: ICSA Certificate; ICSA Diploma; Professional Programme Part 1; and Professional Programme Part 2. If you already hold previous qualifications, you may be eligible for exemptions at the certificate and diploma level. Graduates can usually begin the scheme at Professional Programme Part 1. With a related degree or professional qualification, you may be able to begin at Part 2. No formal qualifications are required to register for the Certificate.

Requirements for Entry

While this area of work is open to graduates of all subjects, or even non-graduates, specialisms in law, business/management or accountancy/finance in may be preferred and may offer some exemptions from the professional examinations.

As most company secretary positions demand a professional qualification or significant professional experience, it is very unlikely that a recent graduate would have direct entry into the role. Pre-entry experience is therefore desirable and also strongly recommended.

You might, for example, first qualify as a lawyer or accountant with the aim of becoming a company secretary later; you might consider a full-time diploma course leading to a full or partial ICSA qualification. For most people, formal training in company secretarial work starts after a few years of administrative work experience. Suitable experience could include areas such as pensions, personnel, accounts, credit control, purchasing, insurance, sales administration or office management.

Kind of Person

You would need to be good at administration as this is the core of the work. You would be co-ordinating departments and would therefore need to be good at prioritising and seeing the overall picture. Your management responsibilities would require you to be tactful and discreet. You would also be dealing with financial and legal matters, requiring you to be numerate and also able to work under pressure to comply with legal deadlines.

Minute-taking would require the ability to write clearly and accurately, while explaining technical matters to a non-expert audience would demand excellent speaking skills. This is a very responsible job demanding the highest standards in professional integrity.

Broad Outlook

Given that there is a legal requirement for every company in the UK to have a company secretary, there should be plenty of scope to work in this area. Not all company secretaries are chartered - they could have a legal or accountancy qualification instead - but the ICSA qualification is a broad one and can be adapted to a wide variety of administrative work in charities, local government, educational institutions and health organisations. You could go on to become a company director or chief executive.

Related Occupations

You may wish to consider: accountant, solicitor, barrister/advocate, civil service administrator or human resources officer.

Impact on Lifestyle

This is an office-based job and you could expect to work usual office hours unless there is a deadline to meet, which could mean working unsocial hours. There may be some evening meetings to attend. You would be expected to observe a strict code of personal and professional conduct.

Earnings Potential

There are no fixed national scales, and actual rates of pay may vary, depending on the employer and where you live. Typical starting salaries range from £25,000 to £30,000, rising to £40,000 to £60,000 or higher with five years' experience. At senior level, salaries generally range from £70,000 to £180,000. A survey published in April 2008 found that the average salary of company secretaries working in FTSE 100 companies was in excess of £200,000.

Further Information

Institute of Chartered Secretaries and Administrators, London W1B 1AH
Website: www.icsa.org.uk

Worshipful Company of Chartered Secretaries and Administrators, London EC2V 6BR
Website: www.wccsa.org.uk

Companies House, Cardiff CF4 3UZ
Website: www.companieshouse.gov.uk

Alternative/equivalent entrance requirements can include: ILC, IB, EB, NC/ND and many other similar international systems. For further details see the Equivalent Qualifications section in the Introduction.

Chemical Engineer

What is Involved?

As a chemical engineer you would apply mainly engineering principles to produce and control the chemical plant and machinery needed to manufacture chemicals, plastics, synthetic fibres, pharmaceuticals, petroleum products, certain food and drink products and medical gases. You would need considerable skill to control reactions which can be highly unstable and where factors such as temperature, pressure, flow rate, heat removal and concentration of reactants must all be taken into account. Your work would often revolve around turning a small-scale laboratory project into a large-scale, economically viable, safe and reliable industrial process.

Apart from this area of new product development, you might work in plant design and construction, in production management or in more general management, technical sales or exports.

Opportunities for Training

Several UK universities offer degrees in chemical engineering. These can last three years for a BEng or four years for an MEng (or a year longer in either case for a sandwich course giving practical experience in industry). In order to become a chartered chemical engineer, you would need to complete at least four years of academic study. The MEng would meet this requirement, whereas you would need to add another year of more specialised study, known as a 'matching section', to top up a BEng qualification.

You would then need, in either case, to follow your degree with a number of years of approved work experience known as the period of Initial Professional Development (IPD). The BEng degree can take you to incorporated engineer status (see our separate article on engineering qualifications).

Requirements for Entry

You are likely to need two or three A level/Advanced Higher, three or four Higher or equivalent qualifications. These should include chemistry and maths and preferably another science subject, together with at least five GCSE/S Grade passes at A-C/1-3 to include maths, English and a science. Some universities run a foundation course for students who do not have the required science qualifications.

Kind of Person

You would need a strong practical interest in science, with meticulous attention to detail and a logical and methodical approach to problem solving. You would need good communication skills, as you would be required to discuss detailed proposals with other chemists and technologists and to explain technical issues to people who do not have your knowledge and expertise.

You are likely to need good IT skills as computers are used extensively in the design of chemical plants. You would need to work both under your own initiative and as part of a team. You are likely to be working in some sort of industrial, research or business environment and so would need to have relevant management and business skills.

Broad Outlook

There are normally very good job opportunities for chemical engineers and there is every expectation that steady growth in demand will continue across the world once the 2009 recession is behind us. According to Cogent, the Sector Skills Council for this industry, a recent skills need assessment identified one in four vacancies as hard to fill, with not enough young people entering the profession. This has led to a situation in which self-employment and consultancy are common, particularly in the design and commissioning of new plant.

Related Occupations

You might like to consider another specialism as an engineer, such as mechanical, electrical or civil. Alternatively, you may prefer to work in the scientific field as a pharmacologist, pharmacist, metallurgist or biochemist.

Impact on Lifestyle

Whilst you may have set hours of work, you are likely to be required to work irregular hours, should you be asked for example to manage 24-hour petroleum or chemical production processes or to meet a tight deadline. You may find yourself working under pressure from time to time. If you are working in a laboratory or a chemical plant, you may sometimes need to wear protective clothing. You may need to relocate in order to find the job that you really want and you could be expected to travel, for example to negotiate construction contracts, act as a consultant or attend conferences and meetings.

Earnings Potential

Salaries vary according to location, sector, size and the nature of the organisation's business, and are dependent on chartered status. As a new graduate, you would normally start on around £22,000 to £33,000, rising with experience. According to the most recent salary survey conducted by the Institution of Chemical Engineers, chartered engineers working in oil and gas are the best paid, with average annual earnings of £70,000; contracting comes second with average earnings of £59,000.

The average annual earnings for engineers designing and managing plant construction are £47,000.

Further Information

Institution of Chemical Engineers, Rugby CV21 3HQ
Website: http://cms.icheme.org

Engineering Council UK, London WC2R 3ER
Website: www.engc.org.uk

Cogent: the Sector Skills Council for Chemicals, Pharmaceuticals, Nuclear, Oil and Gas, Petroleum and Polymers, Cheshire WA1 1GG
Website: www.cogent-ssc.com

British Chemical Engineering Contractors Association, London SW1Y 4NR
Website: www.bceca.org.uk

Alternative/equivalent entrance requirements can include: ILC, IB, EB, NC/ND and many other similar international systems. For further details see the Equivalent Qualifications section in the Introduction.

Chiropractor

What is Involved?

As a chiropractor, you would be working in a complementary healthcare profession that specialises in the diagnosis, treatment and overall management of conditions related to mechanical dysfunction of the joints, particularly those of the spine, and their effects on the nervous system. Treatment consists of a wide range of manipulative techniques designed to improve the function of the joints, relieving pain and muscle spasm. Your manipulation would have to be highly skilled and very specific, directed at individual joints in order to reduce strains and improve mobility in one area without disturbing another. You would support this treatment with individual counselling and advice about each patient's lifestyle, work and exercise, in order to help in managing the condition and preventing a recurrence of the problem. The work is similar in some ways to that of an osteopath or physiotherapist but with much greater emphasis on manual treatment, including spinal manipulation or adjustment. Your work may involve taking x-rays as part of the diagnostic process.

Opportunities for Training

You must be registered with the General Chiropractic Council (GCC) before you can call yourself a chiropractor. The GCC training standard means that you must graduate from an accredited institution before being accepted onto the register. There are currently two institutions offering suitable courses: the Anglo-European College of Chiropractic in Bournemouth and the University of Glamorgan. Both offer four-year full-time chiropractic degree courses. Both institutions also offer one-year full-time preliminary courses designed for candidates who do not meet the normal entry requirements for the full courses.

The four-year BSc in Chiropractic Sciences covers in-depth training in a variety of subjects, including life sciences, biomechanics, clinical medicine and differential diagnosis. You would also undergo practical training in adjustment and supervised clinical training, where you would have hands-on practice in treating patients. After qualifying, you would have to undertake a year's structured training with a qualified practitioner in order to gain the diploma in chiropractic. Finally, you must undertake continuing professional development as a requirement for re-registration on an annual basis.

Requirements for Entry

For entry to an accredited course, you would normally need at least two or three A level/Advanced Higher, three to four Higher or equivalent qualifications, preferably including biology and chemistry. Some courses may require GCSE/S Grade passes A-C/1-3 in English and maths plus science subjects. You must be at least 18 before you can start a course.

Kind of Person

You would need a keen interest in human biology and in chemistry, together with a certain amount of physical endurance, as the manipulative skills required can be hard work at times. Good communication and problem-solving skills would be essential when dealing with a wide range of patients, all expecting a high standard of professional care from you. This would involve you in listening to each patient and then explaining your diagnosis. You would probably be working as a self-employed practitioner, so would need to be approachable and someone in whom patients could have confidence. In addition, you would need to be well organised and to have sufficient commercial skill to run your own business.

Broad Outlook

Employment prospects have improved recently as this is an area of medicine that is growing and there should be room for more practitioners to establish themselves. Most chiropractors set up as independent consultants, or possibly as part of a group with other practitioners of complementary medicine. You would have to work for at least a year as an assistant to an established chiropractor before you could set up your own practice. You would not be directly employed in the NHS.

Related Occupations

You may be interested in investigating other options in complementary medicine, such as osteopath, homoeopath, reflexologist or aromatherapist. Alternatively, you might be interested in other therapy-based professional roles in the medical field, such as physiotherapist, occupational therapist, radiographer or speech and language therapist.

Impact on Lifestyle

Being self-employed means that you would have to work hard to get yourself established and to build a reputation. This may include working long hours in the evenings and at weekends.

Earnings Potential

As a newly qualified practitioner working as an associate in private practice, you might be paid a percentage of the fees that you generate for the practice, along with a small retainer while your client list increases. Typical starting salaries range from £22,000 to £25,000.

Predicting salaries later in a career can be difficult as most practitioners are self-employed. Earnings will depend on the number of patients seen and the size, location and length of time the practice has been established. Financial rewards can be very good. Salaries in the region of £50,000 to £70,000 are not uncommon, with the potential for even higher earnings. The British Chiropractic Association quotes a recent survey suggesting that earnings within five years of graduation can be as high as £100,000 per year.

Further Information

British Chiropractic Association, Reading RG1 7SN
Website: www.chiropractic-uk.co.uk

General Chiropractic Council, London WC1X 9HL
Website: www.gcc-uk.org

College of Chiropractors, Reading RG4 7DH
Website: www.colchiro.org.uk

Alternative/equivalent entrance requirements can include: ILC, IB, EB, NC/ND and many other similar international systems. For further details see the Equivalent Qualifications section in the Introduction.

Civil Engineer

What is Involved?

As a civil engineer, you would design and manage the construction of bridges, roads, tunnels, pipelines, dams, sewage plants, railways, power stations and major buildings. You would be involved with aspects of the national infrastructure, including transport networks and energy and water supply systems. You would use your knowledge of the properties and behaviour of materials to create imaginative and aesthetically pleasing designs, which meet all relevant safety and durability requirements within specified budgetary constraints.

You would oversee construction projects and this would involve detailed planning and co-ordination with other professionals, including surveyors and architects, together with checking that the actual construction work is being carried out according to specifications. You would liaise in particular with site engineers, who are concerned with the day-to-day activity on site, monitoring such issues as construction methods, delivery of materials, supply pipes and cables and the marking out of the foundations.

Opportunities for Training

In order to become a chartered civil engineer, responsible for research, design and development, you would need to spend at least four years in undergraduate study, followed by postgraduate study and supervised experience. The initial requirement can be achieved by taking a four-year degree course that leads directly to an MEng. Alternatively, you could take a three-year degree course leading to a BEng and follow this with a year of more specialised post-graduate study. To become an incorporated engineer, responsible more for the efficient day-to-day management of projects, you could take the BEng route and follow this with further study and on-the-job training. Another route to incorporated engineer status would be a two- or three-year Higher National Diploma (HND), followed again by further study and relevant experience.

A number of construction companies sponsor undergraduates for some of their time at university, offering work experience and/or sandwich placements.

Requirements for Entry

In order to be accepted for an MEng in civil engineering, you are likely to need three A level/Advanced Higher, four Higher or equivalent qualifications, including maths and physics, together with at least five GCSE/S Grade passes at A-C/1-3. Entry requirements for the BEng are usually slightly lower but would still normally include maths and physics at A level/Advanced Higher, Higher or equivalent. HND entry usually requires study of maths and physics to A level/Advanced Higher/Higher, with a pass in at least one of these subjects.

Kind of Person

As a civil engineer, you would need to be creative as well as practical and good at problem solving. You should have a good grasp of both maths and the principles of design. You would need to be a team player. On site, you could find yourself in charge of many people and your leadership skills would be very important. Good communication skills would also be needed, as you would be dealing with a wide variety of people who would need to be very clear about your instructions.

Broad Outlook

Civil engineers can take advantage of work opportunities in both the private and public sectors, often changing jobs to gain more professional experience. They tend to specialise in areas such as roads and bridges, oil and gas rigs and pipelines, power stations, docks and harbours or public health and sewerage. There are courses run by the Institution of Civil Engineers for on-going professional development. UK civil engineering qualifications are internationally recognised and there are many opportunities to work on projects abroad. You could eventually become a director or partner in a civil engineering firm. Alternatively, you could join the armed services, become a university lecturer or set up as a consultant.

Civil engineering projects have been severely affected by the economic downturn in 2009. However, forecasts indicate that the industry should pick up again in 2010.

Related Occupations

You might also consider: structural engineer, architect, construction manager, surveyor or town planner.

Impact on Lifestyle

When working in the office, you would tend to keep to normal office hours. When working on site or abroad, the hours can be much more unsocial if deadlines need to be met and you could be on 24-hour call in case of problems. Most civil engineers work both in an office and on site. The work on site can be dirty, cold and wet and involve working at heights.

Earnings Potential

As a newly qualified graduate, you could expect to earn about £20,000 to £24,000. This could rise to £45,000 to £65,000 as you gain experience, although this would depend on your employer. As a partner, you would have a share in the firm's profits. The average annual earnings for experienced chartered engineers are around £50,000 and for incorporated engineers around £41,000.

Further Information

Institution of Civil Engineers, London SW1P 3AA
Website: www.ice.org.uk

Construction Skills, King's Lynn PE31 6RH
Website: www.bconstructive.co.uk

Association for Consultancy and Engineering, London SW1H 0QL
Website: www.acenet.co.uk

Alternative/equivalent entrance requirements can include: ILC, IB, EB, NC/ND and many other similar international systems. For further details see the Equivalent Qualifications section in the Introduction.

Civil Service Administrator

What is Involved?

As a civil servant, you would be one of approximately half a million people in a multi-million pound business. You would most likely work in a department or agency - such as Defence or Health - or in a linked smaller organisation. Whatever your particular role, you would have to work in a non-political capacity for the elected government of the day. The different parts of the Civil Service have two main functions: to advise Government Ministers on the pros and cons of particular decisions; and to manage and deliver a range of services to the public, such as issuing driving licences, running jobcentres or paying benefits. There is such a wide range of administrative jobs across the departments and agencies that it is impossible to describe the work in detail here. Within the scope of this Careers Directory, you would probably start as a junior manager (sometimes called executive officer) or fast stream graduate trainee. The fast stream is an accelerated development programme for graduates, preparing you for careers at the highest levels of the Civil Service. Fast streamers are exposed to a range of placements in government departments and agencies, usually lasting around 12 to 18 months but occasionally up to two years.

Opportunities for Training

There are opportunities for on-the-job training within the departments or agencies and sometimes there are further tests to be passed before promotion is secured. Your training might be linked to the department in which you work, focusing for example on investigating benefit fraud or carrying out immigration checks. Your initial training as a fast streamer would focus on your immediate development needs and on the competencies expected of you at senior management level. This would begin with an induction course at the National School of Government to introduce you to the Civil Service and possible future roles and responsibilities.

Requirements for Entry

Each department and agency sets its own entry requirements, depending on the type and level of work available. You would normally need a minimum of two A level/Advanced Higher, three Higher or equivalent qualifications for a junior manager position. In practice, around half the junior managers recruited are graduates. The majority of fast streamers are recruited from any degree discipline (the exceptions being those entering the streams for statisticians, economists, technology in business and science and engineering). A 2.2 honours degree is the minimum entry requirement (2.1 for economists and the technology in business stream). The recruitment process is extremely thorough and places greater emphasis on future potential than past achievement. In addition, you must hold a UK passport or be a citizen of a Commonwealth or European Economic Area country. Applications for the fast stream are normally open only to UK nationals. Recruitment procedures often involve a number of tests.

Kind of Person

At all levels, you would need to be able to work as part of a team, relate well to others and have a calm, reliable personality. You would also need good organisational skills and the ability to work quickly and accurately under pressure. You would need to show leadership potential for junior manager or higher appointments, together with the ability to use your initiative, analyse problems and deliver results. The fast stream would demand all these qualities and more, especially outstanding intelligence, creative thinking and sound judgement.

Broad Outlook

With so many different departments and agencies, there are opportunities to work all over the country or even change departments. Most civil servants, however, tend to stay within the fields where they have expertise. For those with two years' service, there may be the opportunity to progress through the in-service nomination scheme into the fast stream.

Competition is very keen. Last year, there were over 17,000 applicants for 500 vacancies across the general and specialist fast stream programmes.

Before applying, you are advised to work through the online self-assessment tests on the website.

Related Occupations

You might also wish to consider: press/information officer, tax inspector, economist, surveyor, health service manager, or local government administrator.

Impact on Lifestyle

Many civil servants work a basic 37-hour week, which may revolve around flexible start and finish times or even shift work. As you become more senior, you may have to work longer hours to complete reports for Ministers if they are needed at short notice.

Earnings Potential

Salaries vary according to department and the location of the post. Salaries for senior civil servants also depend on job performance and bands set by the government. As a guideline, typical starting salaries range from £19,387 to £22,386, rising after four to five years in post to £22,995 to £38,688. Posts in London often command a higher salary.

The average fast stream starting salary is £24,500, rising after promotion, usually after four or five years, to around £39,000, and eventually climbing to around £51,000. These salary ranges apply to London-based posts because this is where most fast streamers work.

Further Information

Civil Service Careers, Bristol BS1 8DG
Website: www.careers.civil-service.gov.uk

Fast Stream Development Programme, Basingstoke RG21 7JP
Website: www.faststream.gov.uk

National School of Government
Website: www.nationalschool.gov.uk

Alternative/equivalent entrance requirements can include: ILC, IB, EB, NC/ND and many other similar international systems. For further details see the Equivalent Qualifications section in the Introduction.

Clinical Biochemist

What is Involved?

As a clinical biochemist (or chemical pathologist), you would be largely concerned with the use of biochemical investigations to diagnose diseases in which the body's chemistry goes wrong: diabetes, for example, or kidney failure. A major part of your work would be to provide scientific leadership in the pathology laboratory, through the direction of scientific services and the interpretation of test results for the doctor in the clinic or at the bedside. You could attain equivalent status to a medical consultant and become head of a laboratory. Although your expertise would contribute to the management of patients, you would not be medically trained and so could not take clinical responsibility for patients. In other words, you would not be able to treat them.

You might specialise in a particular area, such as toxicology or endocrinology, using sophisticated equipment to carry out tests on body tissues. Like the majority of clinical biochemists, you would most likely work within the National Health Service, the National Blood Service (blood transfusion) or the Public Health Laboratory Service.

Opportunities for Training

Clinical biochemists are graduates, usually with a first or upper second honours degree in a subject like biochemistry or chemistry, and often with a PhD. They would then undertake a three-year programme of pre-registration training, leading to further experience and state registration with the Health Professions Council.

Virtually every university in the country offers a degree course in biochemistry or one in which biochemistry is a major component. It is important to read the prospectuses carefully to find out what each course involves. Many universities offer sandwich courses, which give the opportunity to spend a year working in industry. Because biochemistry is a research-based discipline, many graduates continue into postgraduate training. The universities of London, Birmingham, Manchester and Surrey currently offer MSc courses in Clinical Biochemistry. The training of medical graduates wishing to specialise in clinical biochemistry is coordinated through the Royal College of Pathologists.

Requirements for Entry

To gain entry to a degree course in this field, you would need A level/Advanced Higher/Higher or equivalent passes in biology and chemistry, together sometimes with maths or physics. At some universities it is possible for applicants without such science qualifications to take a 'conversion course' before starting their degree. You would also need a broad platform of GCSE/S Grade passes at A-C/1-3, including English and science subjects.

Kind of Person

You would need to have a strong interest in science and in laboratory procedures. If you do not enjoy your practical science lessons at school, this is probably not the career for you. Patients' lives could depend on your accuracy and efficiency in carrying out tests and interpreting results. You would need to have a logical and methodical approach to your work. Although you would be primarily based in a laboratory, you would be working as part of a team of professionals. You would need to make clear explanations of your findings and opinions, which would demand good communication skills.

Broad Outlook

There are good prospects for employment in this field, particularly in some specialised fields. Opportunities vary across the country, so you may need to move to gain promotion. It is possible to advance your career by taking on more responsibility and by gaining wider or more detailed experience. Senior clinical biochemists often have managerial responsibilities by taking charge of a department or section or by moving to production, sales or marketing departments in the pharmaceutical industry. These opportunities can arise quite early in your career.

Related Occupations

You might be interested working in other science-based fields particularly those involving biology or chemistry. Such careers as research chemist or biologist, doctor, pharmacologist, pharmacist, or forensic scientist could be of interest. In researching this career, you need to be clear about the distinction between a clinical biochemist, a medically qualified doctor and a biomedical scientist. Each has a different and essential role and requires different qualifications and training.

Impact on Lifestyle

You are likely to be working regular hours and a 37-hour week, which should not normally include weekend or evening work. However, you may be expected to be on call at times in cases of emergency.

Earnings Potential

Starting salaries for clinical scientists in the NHS Band 6 are currently £24,831 to £33,436, rising in Band 7 to £29,789 to £39,273. Senior manager or consultant posts can offer salaries ranging from £53,256 to £95,333. Additional payments are made for employment in and around London.

Further Information

Association for Clinical Biochemistry, London SE1 2TU
Website: www.acb.org.uk

Biochemical Society, London W1N 3AJ
Website: www.biochemistry.org

Royal College of Pathologists, London SW1Y 5AF
Website: www.rcpath.org

Health Professions Council, London SE11 4BU
Website: www.hpc-uk.org

NHS Careers
Website: www.nhscareers.nhs.uk

Alternative/equivalent entrance requirements can include: ILC, IB, EB, NC/ND and many other similar international systems. For further details see the Equivalent Qualifications section in the Introduction.

Construction Manager

What is Involved?

As a construction manager, you would be responsible for running a construction site or a section of a large project. You might also be known as a site manager, site agent or building manager. Your work would include developing a strategy for the construction of the project, planning ahead to anticipate problems and solve them before they happen, making sure all processes are carried out safely, reporting on the progress of the project and motivating the workforce to get the best out of them. You would be responsible for liaising with the architects and planners, for carefully assessing the specifications and site plans. You would consult engineers, surveyors, quantity surveyors and estimators, checking costs of labour, supervision and materials before producing time schedules, agreeing labour force requirements and placing orders. You would be in control of the site throughout the construction process.

Opportunities for Training

There are several possible training routes. You could, for example, take a three- or four-year degree in a relevant subject such as construction, building, construction or building management, building studies or technology; you could take a full- or part-time higher national certificate or diploma (HNC/D) in a similar subject; or you could start as a technician with a national certificate or diploma. Sandwich courses are available, which give the opportunity for practical paid experience during your degree. There are also opportunities for sponsorship during your degree course, usually with the larger construction companies. Following your academic training, you could work towards professional qualifications awarded by the Chartered Institute of Building or the Association of Building Engineers.

The professional qualification 'Chartered Builder' is increasingly important for career progression. Details are available on the Chartered Institute of Building website.

Requirements for Entry

The degree route would normally require two or three A level/Advanced Higher, four Higher or equivalent qualifications often including passes in maths and/or physics, together with at least five GCSE/S Grade passes A-C/1-3, including English, maths and a science subject. For the HNC/D, one or two A level/Advanced Higher, three Higher or equivalent qualifications, or a national certificate/diploma would be necessary.

Kind of Person

You would need to apply all your knowledge of construction techniques to ensure that each project is completed to time, on budget and safely. You would have to be able to motivate people and would need excellent communication skills. You would also have to be able to stay calm when things don't go quite as planned. Other people would expect to rely on your judgement. Your decisions would need to be based on your knowledge of technical, legal and health and safety factors but above all on practical common sense and experience. You may find yourself working under pressure when, for example, schedules are slipping or materials fail to arrive.

Broad Outlook

The demand for construction managers depends to a great extent on the state of the building trade and it must be said that the picture in early 2009 is far from encouraging, as the housing market continues to weaken and demand for industrial, office, retail and leisure facilities declines considerably. Forecasts suggest, however, that construction will pick up again in 2010.

Related Occupations

You might also consider: civil engineer, architect, building services engineer, quantity surveyor, town planner or estate agent.

Impact on Lifestyle

Whilst your basic hours of work are likely to be around 40 hours a week, you could expect to be working longer hours than this when you are on site. The hours of work on building sites tend to be particularly long during the summer, when there are a lot of daylight hours, but much shorter in the winter. At times, you may be expected to work in the evenings and at weekends. In addition you can expect to be working outside in all kinds of weather, and would need to wear protective clothing such as a hard hat when on site. Most of your working day would be spent on site or even travelling from site to site. Some managers move from one location to another as projects are completed and new ones start. Some are able to reach the site by travelling every day; others live away from home during the week and return home at weekends.

Earnings Potential

You would expect to start on a salary of about £19,000 to £23,000, depending to some extent on where in the country you are working. This can be raised by allowances for being on site or for travelling. Experienced construction managers can expect to earn between £33,000 and £45,000. Salaries are higher in London.

Further Information

Construction Skills
Website: www.constructionskills.net

Association of Building Engineers, Northampton NN3 8NW
Website: www.abe.org.uk

Chartered Institute of Building, Berkshire SL5 7TB
Website: www.ciob.org.uk

Alternative/equivalent entrance requirements can include: ILC, IB, EB, NC/ND and many other similar international systems. For further details see the Equivalent Qualifications section in the Introduction.

Countryside/Nature Conservation Officer

What is Involved?

As a countryside/nature conservation officer, you would be an environmental specialist responsible for advising on issues concerned with protecting and conserving the countryside. You would ensure that conservation laws are being observed and would take steps to enforce them if necessary; you could be responsible for managing a site of special scientific interest or for designating a new one; or you may assess the environmental impact of proposed major construction developments. While you might spend some time outside on site surveys, you would be largely office-based, reading and writing reports, consulting maps and charts, preparing talks or checking details of legislation.

Opportunities for Training

Although there is no set training route, you would be unlikely to secure a post without a relevant degree and even a postgraduate qualification. Possible degree subjects would include ecology, environmental science, geology, geography, conservation and countryside management, biology or estate management. There is fierce competition for jobs, so part-time and voluntary experience is very important. You should take every opportunity to show your commitment by undertaking voluntary projects and you should check degree courses for the amount of fieldwork and other practical experience they offer. A postgraduate qualification at MSc or PhD level in conservation, ecology or land management would also be advisable.

Requirements for Entry

Degree entry requirements would vary depending on your choice of both subject and university. However, you would normally need a minimum of two A level/Advanced Higher, three Higher or equivalent qualifications and five GCSE/S Grade passes at A-C/1-3. In order to be accepted for postgraduate study, you are likely to need first class or upper second honours in your first degree.

A full driving licence would almost always be essential.

Kind of Person

You may find yourself having to negotiate with people who are opposed to your ideas, so you would need to show diplomacy and tact in your approach to them. At the same time, you would have to have confidence in your point of view and powers of persuasion to make your case clear. This may involve communicating complex scientific or technical information to non-specialists. You could be required to write reports and to speak at public meetings. You would need to be prepared for criticism of your work from people who do not understand your point of view or your recommendations. You would find yourself working as part of a team but you would need to be able to work unsupervised and to manage your own time. A real commitment to, and knowledge of, preserving the environment would be essential.

Broad Outlook

There are jobs for countryside conservation officers with government agencies such as Natural England or Scottish National Heritage, with local government and with organisations such as The National Trust. However, there is very strong competition for jobs and each advertised post often has a large number of applicants. You may well need to move around the country and to apply for a large number of jobs in order to secure a suitable post. Some positions are on short-term contracts or are purely seasonal, and you may have to gain experience with one or more of these before finding a full-time position. There would be opportunities to progress to managing a team of conservation officers or to pursue a specific interest, which could lead you into research, lecturing or specialist consultancy work.

Related Occupations

You might also consider: countryside ranger, forest manager, town planner, landscape architect, rural practice surveyor, research biologist, cartographer, geologist, microbiologist or zoologist.

Impact on Lifestyle

You would nominally work a normal week of around 40 hours, Monday to Friday. You may, however, have to attend evening and weekend meetings and you would have to work whatever hours it takes to write up a report in the required time.

Earnings Potential

As a countryside conservation officer working for a government agency, you would be likely to have a starting salary of around £20,000, rising to around £26,000. Senior positions may command salaries of around £34,000. Local government salaries are likely to be similar but charitable organisations often start at lower levels, perhaps around £13,000.

Further Information

British Trust for Conservation Volunteers, Doncaster DN4 0RH
Website: www.btcv.org

Natural England, Sheffield S1 2ET
Website: www.naturalengland.org.uk

Countryside Council for Wales, Bangor LL57 2LQ
Website: www.ccw.gov.uk

Scottish Natural Heritage, Edinburgh EH9 2AS
Website: www.snh.org.uk

Northern Ireland Environment Agency, Belfast BT1 1FY
Website: www.ni-environment.gov.uk

Department of Community, Rural and Gaeltacht Affairs, Dublin 4
Website: www.pobail.ie

Field Studies Council
Website: www.field-studies-council.org

Alternative/equivalent entrance requirements can include: ILC, IB, EB, NC/ND and many other similar international systems. For further details see the Equivalent Qualifications section in the Introduction.

Countryside Ranger/Warden

What is Involved?

As a countryside ranger or warden, your job would be to protect, manage and develop a particular area of countryside. This might be something like a wildlife habitat or a site of special scientific interest. Your role would also involve helping the public to enjoy that particular area of countryside. You are likely to be working somewhere like a national park, an area of outstanding beauty or a nature reserve.

Your job might include patrolling the area to look for repairs that need doing or developments that could be achieved to enhance the site. You may carry out the necessary work yourself or organise teams of people. You could become a specialist in a particular area relevant to your area of work. In addition to the outdoor activities, you might also work in an information centre or an office, producing information booklets or planning exhibitions and site visits to explain the flora and fauna and geographical features of your site.

Opportunities for Training

Countryside management is a high-qualification, training-conscious industry, with nearly two-thirds of employed workers having degrees, Higher National Certificates/Diplomas or equivalent professional qualifications. While opportunities are available for non-graduates through routes such as Apprenticeships and National Diplomas, there is a tendency for graduates to apply for jobs at all levels, including the most basic.

Requirements for Entry

While there are no specific entry requirements for many of the training schemes, competition for places is strong and you should have a good standard of education. You would probably need at least four GCSE/S Grade passes at A-C/1-3 or equivalent, including English, maths a science subject and another academic subject.

Many applicants, as noted above, have a degree or HND in a relevant subject such as ecology, biology, environmental science, land management, agriculture, leisure and recreation, geography or geology. You would need to show evidence of part-time or voluntary work in a countryside or conservation field and you would probably need to be able to drive.

Kind of Person

You would need to be physically fit and prepared for hard practical work. Your employers would be looking for evidence of a genuine interest in the countryside. You would probably be dealing with the public, who may need you to explain aspects of the site or the work. For this you would need a pleasant and tactful manner.

You may be expected to speak in public, giving presentations to publicise your area of work. Depending on where you work, you may need to have knowledge of the law relating to countryside rights and to health and safety issues. Your personal, practical skills and willingness to learn are likely to be as important as your academic achievements.

Broad Outlook

The environmental conservation industry is expected to continue expanding in the future but it is estimated that there are 200,000 volunteers and a mere 49,000 paid staff. Included in this number are some 5,000 countryside rangers or wardens. Competition for full-time jobs is intense and there is almost always an expectation of considerable voluntary or part-time experience before you apply. There are limited opportunities for promotion, although it is possible - depending on your qualifications and experience - to move into some of the related occupations listed below. You may need to be prepared to move around the country in order to find a suitable vacancy.

Related Occupations

You might like a job in a related field such as countryside conservation officer, conservationist, land agent, forest manager, amenity horticultural manager, microbiologist or marine biologist.

Impact on Lifestyle

Your job as a countryside ranger is likely to involve working in the evenings and at weekends. You might be working in a fairly remote countryside area, which could be quite isolated. You may find the work tiring, as it can include walking many miles or handling heavy equipment. You will be exposed to the elements at all times of the year.

Earnings Potential

Countryside rangers are usually paid between £13,000 and £20,000, with senior rangers or site managers earning up to £25,000. A vehicle is usually provided for use at work but you would also need your own transport.

Further Information

Lantra, Coventry CV8 2LG
Website: www.lantra.co.uk

Growing Careers Partnership
Website: www.growing-careers.com

British Trust for Conservation Volunteers, Doncaster DN4 0RH
Website: www.btcv.org.uk

Natural England, Sheffield S1 2ET
Website: www.naturalengland.org.uk

National Trust, London SW1H 9AS
Website: www.nationaltrust.org.uk

Forestry Commission, Edinburgh EH12 7AT
Website: www.forestry.gov.uk

Alternative/equivalent entrance requirements can include: ILC, IB, EB, NC/ND and many other similar international systems. For further details see the Equivalent Qualifications section in the Introduction.

Dental Technician/Technologist

What is Involved?

As a dental technician/technologist, you would be involved in the design and construction of appliances prescribed for their patients by dental surgeons. These would include dentures, crowns and bridges and orthodontic appliances such as braces designed to correct misalignment of the teeth.   You would most likely work in a commercial dental laboratory, using a wide range of materials - metal alloys, gold or porcelain for crown and bridge work, acrylic or metal for braces, plastic or chrome cobalt for dentures - to meet the specific requirements of each prescription. The work requires great precision and technical skill but only rarely involves actually meeting the patient for whom you are ultimately working.

You might carry out work for a number of local dentists or even offer a postal service for dentists from a wider area. Alternatively, you might work in a hospital, supporting oral and maxillofacial surgeons in restructuring patients' faces and mouths.

Opportunities for Training

A registered dental technician (RDT) must undertake education and training to a minimum standard as indicated by the General Dental Council's Curricula for Dental Technicians. The following qualifications are recognised in the UK for registration purposes: Foundation Degree/EdExcel/BTEC National Diploma in Dental Technology/Scotvec Higher National Certificate in Dental Technology/ BSc Hons.

There is a Foundation degree at De Montfort University, and there are honours degrees at Manchester Metropolitan University and the University of Wales Institute, Cardiff.

Requirements for Entry

One A level is required for direct entry on to the Foundation Degree in Dental Technology, which will normally take 2 years full-time or 3 years part-time.

Four GCSE passes at grade C or above or the equivalent are required for entry on to a bridging qualification, such as the BTEC National Award in Dental Technology, which will take approximately one year to complete.

To enrol for the SQA National Certificate in Dental Technology in Scotland, you must have five Standard grades or equivalent at level 1, 2 or 3, including English and science. To enrol for the SQA Higher National Certificate in Dental Technology, satisfactory completion of the National Certificate or accredited prior learning, plus interview.

Kind of Person

The work you would be involved in is highly skilled and you would need to be practical, with a high level of manual dexterity and some artistic flair. You would need a keen eye for detail; the ability to concentrate on what is often very precise work and sufficient scientific understanding to follow detailed technical instructions. You may work alone or as part of a team. Good eyesight with or without glasses and good colour vision are important.

Broad Outlook

There is a shortage of skilled dental technicians, which should mean that finding a job is relatively straightforward. Most of the 8,000 dental technicians in the UK work in commercial laboratories but there is also scope in the NHS, in individual dental practices or in the armed services. There may be opportunities to work abroad or to set up your own laboratory once you have the required experience.

Related Occupations

You might also consider: dental nurse, medical technical officer, or orthotist/prosthetist.

Impact on Lifestyle

You would probably have a normal working week of 37 to 39 hours in the NHS, slightly longer in a commercial laboratory. If you specialise in maxillofacial work, you may expect to be called out at any time in cases of emergency.

You may have to be reasonably flexible about where you work, for many laboratories are concentrated in the larger population areas.

Earnings Potential

As a newly qualified dental technician in the NHS, you would be paid in Band 5 on a scale ranging from £20,710 to £26,839. Promotion to the specialist grade could take your earnings to £32,653 at the top of the scale, while a further appointment as an advanced dental technician could increase your salary to a maximum of £39,273. Additional allowances are paid for appointments in and around London, ranging from 20% of basic salary for Inner London, to 15% for Outer London and 5% for the London Fringe. Earnings in the private sector are generally likely to be higher, depending on where you live and the hours you are prepared to work.

Further Information

Dental Laboratories Association Ltd, Nottinghamshire NG9 2NR
Website: www.dla.org.uk

Dental Technologists Association, Northampton NN3 9ZX
Website: www.dta-uk.org

General Dental Council, London W1G 8DQ
Website: www.gdc-uk.org

Inspiring Dental Education and Advice
Website: www.ideacareers.co.uk

Alternative/equivalent entrance requirements can include: ILC, IB, EB, NC/ND and many other similar international systems. For further details see the Equivalent Qualifications section in the Introduction.

Dentist

What is Involved?

As a dentist, you would be responsible for the dental health of a group of clients, examining, diagnosing and treating patients in line with your professional judgement. Your work would include fillings, removing teeth and fitting bridges or crowns. When necessary, you may refer patients for specialist treatment such as orthodontics.

Alternatively, you might choose to work in a hospital and specialise in a particular area such as oral surgery - which could include repairing damage to the jaw caused by accident or disease and also corrective surgery to repair birth defects. This could also include carrying out more complicated bridgework or surgery to gums that cannot be performed by a general dentist. Another area is orthodontics, which is concerned with straightening teeth. In hospital there is a hierarchy of dentists that works up to a consultant level as with doctors. The majority of dentists work in general practice, on their own or as part of a group. You could also work in the armed forces, as a company dentist in a large organisation or as a community dentist in a clinic. There is some scope for specialising in work with animals, including dogs, cats and horses.

Opportunities for Training

You would have to take a degree (BDS or BChD) before you could register with the General Dental Council and start to work as a dentist. This is a five-year course, which combines theoretical subjects such as anatomy, physiology and dental materials science with the practical and clinical skills needed to treat patients. In addition, you would need to learn about anaesthesia and radiology, how to design and fit dental aids as well as relevant aspects of dental law and ethics. Most dental students start practical work on patients in the second or third year of study, although some courses offer integrated courses with clinical work in the first year.

Requirements for Entry

Competition for places at dental schools is very fierce and you would have to offer three very good A level/Advanced Higher, five Higher or equivalent qualifications to get in. While some schools require three A level/Advanced Higher, Higher or equivalent qualifications to be in science subjects, the minimum is usually chemistry plus another science subject or maths. A few dental schools allow students without the right subjects to take a pre-dental year, although this would severely limit your choice of school. In addition to academic success, you should have a strong interest in the subject and should arrange some work experience with a dentist before you apply.

You may also have to take the UK Clinical Aptitude Test (UKCAT), which is used in the selection process by a consortium of UK university Medical and Dental Schools.

The test helps universities to make more informed choices from amongst the many highly-qualified applicants who apply for their medical and dental degree programmes.

Kind of Person

Dentists need to have good interpersonal skills, to be interested in people and able to communicate with all types of people. Patients may be worried about the visit and it is important that the dentist is friendly and can help them to relax. All dentists need to be able to work as part of a team with a number of different people - dental nurses, receptionists, hygienists or other medical staff in hospital. Dentistry requires an interest in science, good eyesight and manual dexterity. Working in general practice also involves some business and marketing skills.

Broad Outlook

Most dentists choose to work as family general dental practitioners (GDPs). The first step is to undertake vocational training (VT), which is supervised training, working in an approved practice. Following satisfactory completion of the VT period, dentists usually enter an established practice as an associate, that is as a self-employed dentist, responsible for the treatment that they provide, but working in a practice owned by someone else. Later on, a dentist may often become a practice owner (principal), either becoming a partner, buying a practice or establishing a new practice. There is no formal GDP career structure, so you can further your knowledge at your own pace and follow the particular dental specialties that are of interest to you. An increasing number of dentists are providing general dental care independently of the NHS. This may be under a private contract between dentist and patient where the dentist's fees are determined by things such as the time spent, materials used and the complexity of the procedure. Alternatively dentists may offer their patients treatment under dental insurance and capitation schemes.

Related Occupations

You might consider: doctor, medical laboratory scientific officer, chiropractor or osteopath. Look at dental hygienist or dental nurse if you want to specialise in oral care.

Impact on Lifestyle

In general practice, you could be quite flexible about the hours you work, although NHS dentists often have to offer emergency cover on a rota basis. Dentists in hospital may have to work anti-social hours and be prepared to be on call. The work can be physically very tiring as it involves a lot of standing and bending of the spine.

Earnings Potential

GDPs can choose where they work and the hours they keep. They may practise under the NHS or privately - most dentists see a mixture of NHS and private patients. In the NHS, patient charges are set depending on the treatment, and the dentist is paid for a set number of 'units of dental activity.' Private fees are set by each dentist individually and vary according to individual practice circumstances.

NHS dentists, mostly self-employed contractors, can typically expect to earn between £60,000 and £120,000 depending on their working arrangements. Salaried dentists, who work mainly with community dental services, earn between £40,000 and £78,000. Consultants in dental specialities are paid on the same scales as other hospital consultants and earn between £73,403 and £173,638 dependent on length of service and payment of additional performance-related supplements.

Further Information

Inspiring Dental Education and Advice
Website: www.ideacareers.co.uk

British Dental Association, London W1G 8YSL
Website: www.bda-dentistry.org.uk

General Dental Council, London W1G 8DQ
Website: www.gdc-uk.org

Equine Dentistry
Website: www.equinedentistry.info

Alternative/equivalent entrance requirements can include: ILC, IB, EB, NC/ND and many other similar international systems. For further details see the Equivalent Qualifications section in the Introduction

Dietitian

What is Involved?

As a dietitian, you would need a fascination with food and health, together with the ability to translate medical advice and scientific findings about food into practical diets that people can understand. You may work as part of a healthcare team in a hospital or in the community, offering advice on a well-balanced diet to ensure healthy living. In a hospital or GP's clinic, you may be helping patients with problems such as difficulty in swallowing or checking that the meals provided are nutritionally balanced and appropriate for each individual. You may run clinics in outpatients departments for people who are overweight, people with eating disorders or those who have to live with diabetes, food allergies or other conditions. You might also be involved in health promotion activities or talking to groups such as pregnant women or those with young children.

In the food industry, you might provide specialist advice to manufacturers or trade associations. You would analyse food products and check information leaflets to ensure that the content is correct and nutritionally sound.

Opportunities for Training

To become a state registered dietitian, you must take an approved degree or post-graduate diploma. Degree courses are generally full-time and take four years. All courses include practical training in a hospital or community setting. In addition to nutrition and dietetics, you would study physiology and biochemistry, medicine and pharmacology, psychology and social science, some microbiology and food science, with statistics and research methods to help with your final Honours project.

The postgraduate courses are for students with a relevant first degree in a science subject.

Requirements for Entry

You would need a sound base in science to gain entry to an honours degree course. You would need chemistry and another science A level/Advanced Higher, Higher or equivalent qualification, as well as five GCSE/S Grade passes at A-C/1-3 including English and maths. Some universities run foundation courses, which can give access to the degree if you do not have the required A level/Advanced Higher, Higher or equivalent qualifications.

Kind of Person

Your role as a dietitian would require tact and perseverance to convince people who are ill that, by changing their diet, they can reduce their symptoms and put themselves more in control of their illness.

You would need to be able to interpret scientific and medical information so that your patient can understand it. In order to give advice, you must be aware of how a person's personal circumstances can affect their lives and how your dietary recommendations might need to be adjusted to make them workable. You would have to accept your patients' lifestyles and religious or cultural beliefs without passing judgement.

Broad Outlook

With increased interest in healthy living and growing awareness of the importance of well balanced diets, the prospects for dietitians look extremely promising. There are lots of jobs at the moment in the NHS but, if you want to do research, you'll need to look around and be prepared to move. Other opportunities include work in the food industry, in retail chains such as supermarkets, acting as a nutrition adviser, or in product development and marketing for food companies producing specialist dietary products.

Related Occupations

If your main interest is in food and nutrition, you might also consider: food scientist or technologist or hotel and catering manager. If you want to work with people on health-related issues, you might prefer to explore alternative careers such as nurse, pharmacist, radiographer, speech therapist or occupational therapist.

Impact on Lifestyle

An NHS dietitian works a 36.5-hour week, which can include some weekend work or hours on call.

Your job may require you to work with vulnerable groups of people and, as a result, you would need to declare any criminal record. You would also need to complete a health declaration. Problems in either of these areas may not stop you from completing a university course but they may not allow you to become State Registered, which means that you would not be able to practise at the end of your course.

Earnings Potential

As a newly qualified dietitian in the NHS, you would be paid in Band 5 on a scale ranging from £20,710 to £26,839. Promotion to the specialist grade could take your earnings to £33,436 at the top of Band 6, while a further appointment to dietetic team manager could increase your salary to a maximum of £39,273. Additional allowances are paid for appointments in and around London, ranging from 20% of basic salary for Inner London, to 15% for Outer London and 5% for the London Fringe. Earnings in the private sector are generally likely to be higher, depending on where you live and the hours you are prepared to work.

Further Information

British Dietetic Association, Birmingham, B3 3HT
Website: www.bda.uk.com

Health Professions Council
Website: www.hpc-uk.org

Alternative/equivalent entrance requirements can include: ILC, IB, EB, NC/ND and many other similar international systems. For further details see the Equivalent Qualifications section in the Introduction.

# Diplomat

What is Involved?

As a member of the diplomatic service, you would be working for one of the major departments of the civil service. You would be primarily involved with representing British interests abroad and advising government ministers on aspects of foreign policy. The service is based in London, with high commissions in Commonwealth countries and embassies in other countries around the world, together with missions to international organisations such as the European Commission and United Nations. During the course of your career, you might work in several different areas of the service, including commercial, information, consular, immigration, political assessment and liaison and general administrative or managerial duties. You would normally spend much of your career working abroad, with tours of duty of two to four years.

Opportunities for Training

The first three years of your career in the service would normally be spent at the Foreign and Commonwealth Office in London, initially learning the broad outline of diplomatic work and then acquiring the knowledge and skills for the specialisation in which you are going to work. For some postings, full-time language training would be provided as part of a continuous programme of preparation for working in a particular country. All staff would have the opportunity to learn the local language before taking up an appointment.

As a graduate with at least a second class honours degree, you could compete for selection to the Fast Stream Development Programme.

Requirements for Entry

You must be a British citizen and have been resident in the UK (apart from temporary periods of travel, or study abroad) for at least two of the ten years preceding your application. Competition for places is intense and the majority of successful applicants are graduates with good honours degrees. In the past, arts graduates have predominated but science, business, economics and technological degrees are increasingly welcome.

It is not essential to speak a foreign language, but knowledge of certain 'hard' languages such as Arabic, Cantonese, Farsi, Japanese, Korean, Mandarin or Russian, or having a general aptitude for languages, can be useful.

Because of the security vetting procedures, the recruitment process may take up to nine months.

Kind of Person

Because of the nature of the work, you would be expected to have a keen interest in international issues and recognise Britain's unique role in world affairs. You should be a natural team player; confident, friendly, calm and reliable in your dealings with others, particularly with those you do not know. You should be keen to travel and prepared to visit and live in some of the less developed parts of the world. Much of your work would require a good organisational approach and the ability to work to precise and demanding standards as well as to think on your feet.

Broad Outlook

The traditional view of the civil service offering a job for life with good promotion prospects is less true today than it might once have been. The diplomatic service could be said to have been less vulnerable to this change, with prospects remaining very bright for those with the right qualities and attitudes. There may be opportunities to work in related government departments, such as the Department for International Development.

Regular appraisal of your work and detailed assessment of your performance would give you a clear picture of your progress and of the prospects for your future career development.

Related Occupations

If you have the qualities demanded by the diplomatic service, with high levels of integrity and excellent communication and organisational skills, you could aspire to high level positions elsewhere in the civil service, in industry or in export/import organisations. You might also find a role in the media.

Impact on Lifestyle

The majority of your service would be in overseas locations and you would need to uproot your family, adjust to new climates and cultural systems, make new friends and leave others behind. You would need to be adaptable, to see changes as exciting challenges and to build up your contacts within and outside the service. If you have children, you would need to help them cope with an interrupted family life and adjust their education to your travels.

Earnings Potential

Typical starting salaries, inclusive of a £3,000 London location allowance, are £21,653 at operational officer grade and £23,742 at policy officer grade. The average starting salary for a fast-streamer is £24,500.

When stationed abroad, you would be entitled to a range of payments on top of your basic salary to cover the local cost of living, in addition to rent-free accommodation, educational allowances for your children and various fare paid allowances for travel to and from the UK. Your salary would compare very favourably with the main professions and would rise with promotion and the relative importance of your work.

Further Information

Civil Service Careers, Bristol BS11 8DG
Website: www.careers.civil-service.gov.uk/

Fast Stream Development Programme, Basingstoke RG21 7JP
Website: www.faststream.gov.uk

Foreign and Commonwealth Office, London SW1A 2AH
Website: www.fco.gov.uk

Alternative/equivalent entrance requirements can include: ILC, IB, EB, NC/ND and many other similar international systems. For further details see the Equivalent Qualifications section in the Introduction.

Dispensing Optician

What is Involved?

As a dispensing optician, you would supply and fit glasses and other optical aids but you would not be trained to carry out eye tests or treat disorders of the eyes. You would be qualified to interpret the prescriptions you are given by an optometrist or ophthalmic surgeon and then make an order for the glasses to be made up by a prescription house. You could also fit contact lenses after additional training.

You would most likely work in private practice in a high street retail outlet, ensuring that clients get the correct glasses or lenses for their needs and lifestyle. You would need to spend time with each patient, taking precise facial measurements and discussing with them the optimal balance between the prescription requirements and their own feelings about appearance, comfort and the conditions in which the glasses or contact lenses are to be used. You would also ensure that the final choice fits securely and matches the prescription.

Opportunities for Training

You must pass the Fellowship exams of the Association of British Dispensing Opticians (ABDO) and register with the General Optical Council. You can do this in several different ways: by taking a full-time honours degree or foundation degree in a subject such as optical management, ophthalmic dispensing or ophthalmic dispensing with management; taking a full- or part-time diploma in ophthalmic dispensing; or by completing the ABDO distance learning course while working with a qualified optometrist.

Whichever route you choose, you would have to follow your course with a pre-registration year of paid work supervised by a registered optometrist. The ABDO final examination then has to be passed.

Requirements for Entry

You would need at least five GCSE/S Grade passes at A-C/1-3, to include English, maths or physics and another science based subject. The degree courses offered at universities or colleges require two A level/Advanced Higher, three or four Higher or equivalent qualifications and some specify science subjects such as biology, physics, chemistry and/or maths. It is essential to check prospectuses before you apply. Some diploma courses call for one or two A level/Advanced Higher, three to four Higher or equivalent qualifications but others may specify GSCE/S Grade passes in maths and science subjects.

Kind of Person

You must like people and you must be able to deal with them tactfully and confidently. In addition, you would be required to understand the information contained in prescriptions and to operate a number of scientific instruments. You would be to some extent selling frames and accessories, so you would need to know which styles are in fashion and which colours are available. A smart appearance, patience and a sense of humour would all be helpful.

Broad Outlook

Most dispensing opticians work in general practice either for an independent optometrist or for one of the big chains. There are also some openings in hospital clinics and in prescription houses (lens manufacturers), together with opportunities to be self-employed or to work in partnership. The job market is becoming more competitive but there are still lots of opportunities for work, especially if you are prepared to move and are confident enough to take on management responsibilities. There are opportunities for job sharing and part-time employment.

Related Occupations

You might be interested in other professions concerned with visual problems or disorders, such as optometrist or orthoptist. You might also consider therapeutic professions in the medical field, such as occupational therapist, speech and language therapist or dietitian.

Impact on Lifestyle

Most dispensing opticians work a five-day week, but in a high street shop you would certainly find yourself working on Saturdays and possibly one or two evenings a week.

Earnings Potential

Trainees working full-time can earn about £12,000 to £17,000. On registration, dispensing opticians earn from £18,000 to £30,000 and this can rise according to experience and responsibility to as high as £50,000 for a manager in partnership with an optometrist.

Further Information

General Optical Council, London W1G 8DJ
Website: www.optical.org

Federation of Ophthalmic and Dispensing Opticians, London W2 6LD
Website: www.fodo.com

Association of British Dispensing Opticians, London W2 6LD
Website: www.abdo.org.uk

Alternative/equivalent entrance requirements can include: ILC, IB, EB, NC/ND and many other similar international systems. For further details see the Equivalent Qualifications section in the Introduction.

Doctor

What is Involved?

As a doctor you would be responsible for promoting good health to try to prevent illness or working to restore patients' well being after an illness or an accident. You would work either as a General Practitioner (GP), dealing with a wide range of patients with many different problems, or as a hospital doctor specialising in a particular field of medicine.

Opportunities for Training

All medical students in the UK must initially take an undergraduate course leading to a Bachelor of Medicine and Surgery, normally referred to as a 'first MB.' Courses tend to fall into three different categories: <I>traditional</I>, <I>integrated</I> and <I>problem-based</I>. The main differences between them lie in the way they organise 'pre-clinical' and 'clinical' teaching, although the 'clinical' element - based in hospitals or in primary care with teaching carried out by clinicians leading small groups - is ultimately similar for all three types of course. The categories are not rigid and there is some overlap between, for example, integrated and problem-based courses. What is vital is that you research the full range of courses on offer before you draw up a shortlist for your UCAS application.

Two-year foundation schools (known as F1 and F2) then require you to demonstrate your abilities and competence against set standards. After the foundation years, you would be able to compete for entry to specific vocational training for general practice or to specialist training in one, or occasionally two, of 55 different specialist medical training programmes. At this stage, you would be legally eligible for entry to the Specialist or GP Register and able to apply for an appropriate senior medical appointment.

Requirements for Entry

Individual medical schools set their own requirements, making it essential that you consult prospectuses and/or contact the schools directly to seek clarification where needed. The majority require A level or equivalent in chemistry, whilst others will accept AS level or equivalent in chemistry, depending upon the other qualifications being offered. Some require biology at A level or equivalent. If you do not have these subjects, it is possible to undertake an additional pre-medical year at some universities. This is essentially a preliminary course in chemistry, physics and biology.

In addition to exceptionally demanding academic entry standards, most schools have adopted the UK Clinical Aptitude Test (UKCAT) to help them select the best candidates. A much smaller group uses the Bio Medical Admissions Test (BMAT). Competition for places to read medicine is very intense. You would need to show that you have a genuine interest in the subject and if possible demonstrate relevant paid or voluntary work experience.

Kind of Person

You must be dedicated and prepared for an enormous amount of hard work, absorbing vast amounts of technical information while developing highly tuned listening and communication skills. Practical ability and manual dexterity are also important. You would need to deal with a wide range of people, to be tolerant of their weaknesses, pain and fear and to help them when they are at their most vulnerable. At times you would need to show emotional resilience as you may be faced with making rational and objective decisions in difficult and distressing circumstances. Others must be able to trust you and depend on you to keep calm in a crisis.

Broad Outlook

Major reform of the ways in which junior doctors develop their careers (Modernising Medical Careers), has been causing concern among members of the British Medical Association (BMA). You may find it useful to check on the latest developments via the BMA website or that of the doctors' pressure group Remedy UK.

Related Occupations

You may be interested in other medical based professions such as dentist, physiotherapist, radiographer, pharmacist, pharmacologist, osteopath or chiropractor.

Impact on Lifestyle

The hours can be very long and anti-social, particularly in the early years. The training takes a long time, which means that you would be working hard for little financial reward for much longer than in many other careers. You need to be prepared for shift work and to have the determination to continue even when you are tired and over worked. On the positive side, doctors are generally among the most valued, highly regarded and trusted members of any community.

Earnings Potential

Junior doctors earn a basic salary and are usually paid a supplement based on the extra hours worked above a standard working week and the intensity of the work. The most common banding supplement is 50% of basic salary. In the most junior hospital doctor post (F1), a doctor on a 50% supplement would earn £32,793. This increases in the second year (F2) to £40,674. A doctor in specialist training on a 50% supplement could earn from £43,464 to £68,343.

Consultants can earn between £73,403 and £173,638, dependent on length of service and payments of additional performance related supplements.

Many GPs are self-employed and hold contracts, either on their own or as part of a partnership, with their local primary care trust (PCT). Most GPs would expect to earn between £80,000 and £120,000. Salaried GPs employed directly by PCTs earn approximately £52,462 to £79,167, dependent on, among other factors, length of service and experience.

Further Information

British Medical Association, London WC1H 9JP
Website: www.bma.org.uk

General Medical Council, London NW1 3JN
Website: www.gmc-uk.org

Biomedical Admissions Test
Website: www.bmat.org.uk

UK Clinical Aptitude Test
Website: www.ukcat.ac.uk

Remedy UK
Website: www.remedyuk.net

Alternative/equivalent entrance requirements can include: ILC, IB, EB, NC/ND and many other similar international systems. For further details see the Equivalent Qualifications section in the Introduction.

Dramatherapist

What is Involved?

As a dramatherapist, you would use improvisation, mime and other dramatic techniques to support people who are experiencing physical, psychological, psychiatric or social problems. You could be working with people of any age, including those with autistic tendencies, those with mental health problems, those living with HIV or AIDS, those in prison or children who have been abused. You would be applying your knowledge and experience of drama to promote healing, open up new experiences and improve the quality of life for each individual.

Opportunities for Training

You could become a dramatherapist either through a part-time course undertaken while working in the health or community services or through one of four postgraduate courses run across the UK. The courses, based in Derby, Exeter, London and Roehampton, combine a strong practical element with theoretical and academic study. You would normally go out on clinical placements in addition to studying core subject areas such as drama and improvisation, myth, analytical psychology, human development, movement with touch and sound and group therapy in training.

These courses lead to a qualification approved by the Health Professions Council (HPC), accredited by the British Association of Dramatherapists (BADth), and recognised by the Department of Health

Only successful completion of courses with HPC approval and BADth accreditation can lead to full membership of the British Association of Dramatherapists. To become a full BADth member, proof of registration with the HPC is needed. Student membership is available whilst training.

Derby, Exeter, Roehampton and Sesame also offer a one-year MA upgrade for those with the postgraduate diploma (Pgdip) in Dramatherapy. Sesame, Roehampton and Manchester offer short courses for prospective students.

Requirements for Entry

The entry criteria to any of the courses would normally include a first degree in drama or a psychological health related subject or appropriate professional qualification/degree, equivalent of one year's full time experience working, paid or voluntarily, with people with specific needs, for example mental ill health, learning disabilities, experience of practical drama work and good interpersonal skills. Selection is usually by interview and audition, with applicants coming from all over the world.

Kind of Person

As a drama and movement therapist you would be working with a wide range of clients, some of whom could have very difficult and deep-seated problems. Respect for each individual would be vital. You would have to be strong - mentally, emotionally and physically - since you could be working in a variety of demanding environments. You would need to be totally committed to your work, able to enthuse your clients and talented enough to demonstrate dramatic techniques. Resilience would be another valuable quality, together with the ability to cope with both success and apparent failure.

Broad Outlook

You could work as a dramatherapist in hospitals, schools, connexions or careers companies, prisons, community centres and in private practice. You could work full-time or part-time. You might decide to specialise in one particular area of work or go on to train as a course leader. You may work on a freelance basis, building up your reputation through effective practice over a period of several years.

Related Occupations

Other occupations which might interest you could include: art therapist, music therapist, actor, occupational therapist, psychiatric nurse, psychotherapist, social worker, speech and language therapist or teacher.

Impact on Lifestyle

Given the very demanding nature of drama therapy, you would have to be totally committed to your work. You would almost certainly be expected to work within a wide variety of work environments. You should be prepared to give up time in the evenings and at weekends for some sessions.

Earnings Potential

Payment would vary widely, according to the type of work and whether the sessions were with individuals or with groups. As a freelance drama therapist, you might charge £35 to £40 per hour. Detailed advice on a suitable fee structure can be obtained from the British Association of Dramatherapists. Within the NHS, you would normally start in Band 6, on a scale ranging from £24,831 to £33,436. This could rise to £39,273 at the top of Band 7. Additional allowances are paid for NHS appointments in and around London, ranging from 20% of basic salary for Inner London, to 15% for Outer London and 5% for the London Fringe.

Further Information

British Association of Dramatherapists, London SW6 3DP
Website: www.badth.org.uk

Dramatherapy Network
Website: www.dramatherapy.net

Dramatherapy Northern Ireland
Website: www.dramatherapynorthernireland.org.uk

Sesame Institute
Website: www.sesame-institute.org

Scottish Arts Therapies Forum
Website: www.satf.org.uk

Alternative/equivalent entrance requirements can include: ILC, IB, EB, NC/ND and many other similar international systems. For further details see the Equivalent Qualifications section in the Introduction.

Economist

What is Involved?

As a professional economist, you would be one of a small group of advisers working for the government, a financial institution or a very large organisation. Alternatively, you might be part of a specialist consultancy. Your work would involve analysing information about what is happening in world financial and employment markets in order to identify significant trends or other points that might influence future policy or strategy. You might study, for example, the ways in which labour markets determine wages and unemployment, why some countries take a bigger share of the world market than others or the role of government in providing goods and services.

Your work might vary considerably according to the sector in which you are working but certain tasks would be similar in any employing organisation:

• You would research data from every relevant source and analyse it using mathematical, statistical and logical tools, particularly computer-based simulations

• You may focus on macro-economic - concerned with large economic units such as nation states - or micro-economic issues - concerned with the financial characteristics of firms, industries or individual households, and the way individual elements in an economy (such as consumers or commodities) behave. A typical macro-economic task might be to forecast the GDP (gross domestic product) of the USA in the coming year, whilst at the micro-economic level you could be concerned with predicting the demand for furniture in South East England over the next quarter

• You would produce a report based on your research and analysis.

Opportunities for Training

To work as a professional economist, you would need a good (first or upper second class) honours degree, usually in economics although a joint degree may be acceptable as long as economics forms the major part. You may find it useful or even essential to continue your studies with a postgraduate award before seeking employment. Similarly, you should consider joining a professional organisation such as the Society of Business Economists or the Royal Economic Society in order to receive their journals and attend their programme of events. The Government Economic Service (GES), the largest single employer of economists in the UK with 600 economists in 30 departments and agencies, runs a 'fast track' programme for selected graduates and also a Diplomatic Service scheme through the Foreign and Commonwealth Office.

Requirements for Entry

To take an honours degree in economics you would need two or three A level/Advanced Higher, four Higher or equivalent qualifications, usually including maths. You would also need a minimum of five GCSE/S Grade passes at A-C/1-3, including maths and English. A good honours degree would be essential for admission to a relevant postgraduate course.

Kind of Person

You would need to enjoy analysing data, to be comfortable with figures and able to communicate your findings to non-specialists. Logic and accuracy are also very important, as are advanced computing skills. You would need to work as part of a team, to meet deadlines for producing reports and to be quick thinking during meetings. As your role would usually be that of an adviser, you must be prepared to accept that your recommendations might not always be acted upon.

Broad Outlook

Economics is a relatively small profession and competition for jobs can be fierce. It is estimated that fewer than 10% of economics graduates go on to work as professional economists and you would have to be both exceptionally able and determined to succeed. You could join the GES as an assistant economist, rising to economic adviser usually within four or five years. The Bank of England is another major employer, followed by other banks and financial institutions, large companies, consultancies and other organisations.

Related Occupations

You might also consider: accountant, actuary, chartered secretary, civil service administrator, financial adviser, investment analyst or statistician.

Impact on Lifestyle

Economists are office based and tend to work regular office hours, although deadlines can mean evening and weekend work from time to time. You may be involved in travel abroad depending on your employer.

Earnings Potential

Salaries vary between employers and even between civil service departments but, as an example, the average GES starting salary in London is about £25,000 for someone with a first degree. More is available to reflect relevant experience or qualifications. The average starting pay in London for someone with a relevant Masters degree is around £27,500. Successful senior economists can expect to earn around £60,000, although a few earn considerably more. Economists working in banking, financial services, industry and consulting sectors are usually better paid, with reported salaries up to £350,000 alongside good benefits packages.

Further Information

Society of Business Economists, Andover SP11 0JZ
Website: www.sbe.co.uk

Government Economic Service, London SW1A 2HQ
Website: www.ges.gov.uk

Royal Statistical Society
Website: www.rss.org.uk

Bank of England
Website: www.bankofengland.co.uk

Civil Service Fast Stream Development Programme
Website: www.faststream.gov.uk

Royal Economic Society
Website: www.res.org.uk

Alternative/equivalent entrance requirements can include: ILC, IB, EB, NC/ND and many other similar international systems. For further details see the Equivalent Qualifications section in the Introduction.

Electrical Engineer

What is Involved?

As an electrical engineer, you would be largely concerned with generating and supplying electrical power, although you might branch into the closely related field of electronic engineering, where you would be more involved with designing and making machines that use electricity. Electrical engineers work mainly with large power applications, generating and harnessing electrical power. You could be researching more efficient power generation systems, developing alternative energy sources or planning the future development of the electricity supply network.

In the move away from burning fossil fuels to generate electricity, your work might involve designing an improved wind turbine, re-examining the advantages and disadvantages of nuclear reactors or exploring ways of harnessing the power of the oceans.

Opportunities for Training

There are a number of universities offering degrees in electrical engineering either as a single subject or in combination with electronic or manufacturing engineering, management, languages or other subjects. It is important to read prospectuses carefully and to ensure that your final choice is accredited by the Institution of Engineering and Technology. In order to become a chartered engineer, focusing on research, design, development and management, you would need to complete four years of academic study. Your degree should be an accredited four-year Master of Engineering (MEng) or three-year Bachelor of Engineering (BEng) qualification. You would have to follow the BEng with an extra year of specialised study, known as a matching section, in order to progress to chartered status. In either case, you could take a sandwich course, which would include a year working on an industrial placement. After graduating, you would need to complete a period of approved work experience in order to achieve chartered status. If you want to be more involved with the day-to-day management of production processes as an incorporated engineer, you could take the BEng route and follow it with a period of formal training.

Requirements for Entry

For degree entry, you would need at least two A level/Advanced Higher, three Higher or equivalent qualifications, usually including maths and physics, together with a broad platform of GCSE/S Grade passes at A-C/1-3. There are foundation courses available at some universities for students who do not have the required passes in maths and physics.

The MEng route usually requires higher grades (or more UCAS points) than the BEng.

Kind of Person

Electrical engineers work in a rapidly developing environment and you would need to be creative, imaginative and prepared to keep up to date with changes in your field. You should have a logical and practical approach to solving complex scientific problems. A useful indicator at this stage could be how much you enjoy maths, design and technology and science (especially experiments with wires and batteries) at school. In addition to your scientific skills, you are likely to need good communication skills. You would probably be working as a member of a team and may need to communicate with a wide range of people, not all of whom would have your technical knowledge and skills. You may be involved in some form of cost management, so some awareness of financial or business management would be helpful.

Broad Outlook

The UK engineering and technology sector has been affected by the global recession in 2009 but, when the predicted recovery comes in 2010, companies driven by innovation and the creation of technological advantage should find that prospects are extremely good. Strong growth is likely, for example, in the area known as 'cleantech' - a term used to describe knowledge-based products or services that improve operational performance, productivity or efficiency while reducing costs, inputs, energy consumption, waste or pollution.

Chartered engineer status is recognised throughout Europe and there are other chances to work all over the world.

Related Occupations

You might also consider: electronic, manufacturing or aeronautical engineer, materials scientist, metallurgist, physicist or medical physicist.

Impact on Lifestyle

You may be working set hours and a five-day week. However, you are also likely to work overtime and under some pressure when you have a tight deadline to meet. There might be occasions when you are rushing to solve a problem or finish a product ahead of a competitor. You may need to wear protective clothing in some environments. You could be required to travel for your job, both in the UK and overseas.

Earnings Potential

The overall shortage of qualified electrical engineers means that you are likely to be quite well paid and could expect to earn around £22,000 to £28,000 straight after you graduate. Once you are chartered, your salary is likely to rise considerably and should exceed £55,000. Average earnings for incorporated engineers are around £41,000.

Further Information

Institution of Engineering and Technology, London W2CR 0BL
Website: www.theiet.org

Engineering Council UK, London WC2R 3ER
Website: www.engc.org.uk

Alternative/equivalent entrance requirements can include: ILC, IB, EB, NC/ND and many other similar international systems. For further details see the Equivalent Qualifications section in the Introduction.

Electronic Engineer

What is Involved?

As an electronic engineer, you would be concerned with designing or making equipment that uses low power electric current. Your work would be likely to have a large impact on the way that people live their lives in the modern world, and could range from communications satellites through to the smallest calculator or digital camera. As society demands ever more sophisticated technological development, you could be among the team of people exploring new possibilities in robotics, artificial intelligence and the information superhighway. There is considerable overlap with electrical engineering (see our separate article on this subject) or you might specialise in areas such as communications, computing, software, control, informatics or manufacturing.

Opportunities for Training

There are a number of universities offering degrees in electronic engineering either as a single subject or in combination with electrical or manufacturing engineering, management, languages or other subjects. It is important to read prospectuses carefully and to ensure that your final choice is accredited by the Institution of Engineering and Technology. In order to become a chartered engineer, focusing on research, design, development and management, you would need to complete four years of academic study. Your degree should be an accredited four-year Master of Engineering (MEng) or three-year Bachelor of Engineering (BEng) qualification. You would have to follow the BEng with an extra year of specialised study, known as a matching section, in order to progress to chartered status. In either case, you could take a sandwich course, which would include a year working on an industrial placement. After graduating, you would need to complete a period of approved work experience in order to achieve chartered status. If you want to be more involved with the day-to-day management of production processes as an incorporated engineer, you could take the BEng route and follow it with a period of formal training.

Requirements for Entry

For degree entry, you would need at least two A level/Advanced Higher, three Higher or equivalent qualifications, usually including maths and physics, together with a broad platform of GCSE/S Grade passes at A-C/1-3. There are foundation courses available at some universities for students who do not have the required passes in maths and physics. The MEng route usually requires higher grades (or more UCAS points) than the BEng.

Kind of Person

You would be working in an area of rapid change and advance and would need to keep up to date with the latest developments, and indeed to be one step ahead of the opposition. You are likely to be continually learning and solving problems in new and creative ways. You would need to have good analytic and logical skills to apply to problems. You should enjoy maths, physics and design and technology lessons at school, as these point towards the types of problems that you would be working on. In addition to your technological skills, you would also need to be able to work on a project as a member of a team. You would need good communication skills as you may be required to make presentations to people who do not share your technical knowledge. You could require a sound business sense, as you might be involved with feasibility studies to assess whether a project is worth starting or completing.

Broad Outlook

The UK engineering and technology sector has been affected by the global recession in 2009 but, when the predicted recovery comes in 2010, companies driven by innovation and the creation of technological advantage should find that prospects are extremely good. Strong growth is likely, for example, in the area known as 'cleantech' - a term used to describe knowledge-based products or services that improve operational performance, productivity or efficiency while reducing costs, inputs, energy consumption, waste or pollution. The medical technology, wireless, consumer and transport sectors also look very promising.

Related Occupations

You might also consider: electrical, manufacturing or aeronautical engineer, materials scientist, metallurgist, physicist, medical physicist or computer scientist.

Impact on Lifestyle

Although you may have specified hours, you are likely to have occasions when you are working under considerable pressure to meet a tight deadline or to keep ahead of the opposition and this may require you to work overtime. In addition, you are likely to need to read a lot and to keep up to date with developments in this field. You may be required to travel to conferences or meetings in order to liaise with other specialists or to advise or solve the problems of clients.

Earnings Potential

Salaries vary from company to company, with some sectors attracting higher salaries due to demand. Your starting salary as a newly graduated electronic engineer is likely to be in the range £19,000 to £30,000. With qualifications and experience, this should rise to between £35,000 and £45,000. As a highly experienced electronic engineer, you could earn in excess of £65,000 per annum.

Further Information

Institution of Engineering and Technology, London W2CR 0BL
Website: www.theiet.org

Engineering Council UK, London WC2R 3ER
Website: www.engc.org.uk

Alternative/equivalent entrance requirements can include: ILC, IB, EB, NC/ND and many other similar international systems. For further details see the Equivalent Qualifications section in the Introduction.

Environmental Health Practitioner

What is Involved?

As an environmental health practitioner, your job would be to ensure that the food we eat is safe and of good quality, to improve housing conditions, to safeguard standards of workplace health and safety, and to create a better environment. You can choose to be a generalist or to specialise in a particular area. You might be employed by a major supermarket chain to manage food safety and hygiene, by a housing association to advise on housing standards, or by a local authority to deal with noise nuisance or environmental pollution. In the public sector, you would be empowered to make unannounced visits to such places as shops, factories and offices, leisure facilities, abattoirs, restaurants and hospitals; you could issue warnings, give advice on how to correct matters or even serve notices of closure if you were to find a situation which contravened the law.

Opportunities for Training

You would need to complete a first degree or postgraduate course accredited by the Chartered Institute of Environmental Health (CIEH).   There are currently several universities offering accredited courses, on a full- or part-time basis.

Many of these courses include the statutory 48 weeks' practical work experience necessary for qualification, but it would be possible for you to do your work experience after graduation. You would need to register with the Environmental Health Registration Board (EHRB) and pass the professional exams set by the CIEH in order to obtain the Certificate of Registration of the EHRB. The training is similar in Scotland but you would register with the Royal Environmental Health Institute of Scotland and would need to be accepted on the accredited environmental health course at the University of Strathclyde. In Ireland, the Dublin Institute of Technology runs a degree in Environmental Health, together with an MSc in Environmental Health and Safety Management MSc

Although they may vary slightly, all accredited courses cover essentially the same ground, including the five key areas of environmental health - food safety, housing, environmental protection, occupational health and public health. Just as important is the emphasis placed on developing your skills in general management, communication, negotiating, analysis and evaluation. You'll learn how to intervene and how to go about ensuring legal compliance.

Requirements for Entry

The minimum entry requirements for an undergraduate degree course in environmental health or science (BSc) would be 160 UCAS points with science at AS/A2 or equivalent, or 200 UCAS points without science. The course would last three or four years. Alternatively, you could qualify for entry to a two-year postgraduate course in environmental health (MSc) after completing a first degree in a relevant science subject.

Kind of Person

A concern for the environment and for the welfare of your fellow citizens would be very important. You would need excellent communication skills, balancing sympathetic understanding with the need to explain your findings and decisions clearly and firmly, since you would be talking to people of widely differing backgrounds, sometimes in difficult situations. You would also have to be able to express yourself very clearly in your written reports. You might not always be welcome (or at least your findings might not be), so you would need to be resilient, scrupulously fair, and willing to back your judgment. You should be able to assimilate and understand a large amount of scientific, technical and legal detail and, while you would be working on your own quite a lot, you should also be a willing member of a team.

Broad Outlook

A clearly defined promotion structure within a local authority leads to senior, principal and chief officer posts in environmental health. It may be necessary to move to other councils to gain more experience, breadth of work and promotion. There are increasing opportunities for experienced environmental health practitioners to diversify into other fields in central government, consultancies and the private sector.

Related Occupations

You might also consider: food technologist, forensic scientist, health and safety inspector and trading standards officer.

Impact on Lifestyle

You would normally work a standard five-day week, but you should be prepared to put in extra hours in the evening or at weekends in an emergency. The work would involve a good deal of travelling and you might well have to move to another area of the country for promotion. Some of the places you would have to visit might be unpleasant, such as abattoirs, and you might encounter some hostility, so you would have to be mentally and physically tough. It is not a job for those of a squeamish disposition.

Earnings Potential

A newly qualified environmental health practitioner could expect to earn around £25,000 to £35,000. With experience and promotion, you could earn around £70,000 as a director of public health. Pay scales in the private sector would be generally higher, particularly if you reached managerial status, and could rise to well above £90,000 in the oil, gas and chemical industries.

Further Information

Chartered Institute of Environmental Health, London SE1 8DJ
Website: www.cieh.org

Royal Environmental Health Institute of Scotland, Edinburgh EH3 7DH
Website: www.rehis.org

Environmental Health Careers
Website: www.ehcareers.org

Environmental Health Officers' Association, County Wicklow, Ireland
Website: www.ehoa.ie

Alternative/equivalent entrance requirements can include: ILC, IB, EB, NC/ND and many other similar international systems. For further details see the Equivalent Qualifications section in the Introduction.

Estate Agent

What is Involved?

As an estate agent, you would specialise in the buying and selling of property, including house, commercial, industrial and land sales. You would normally act for the seller (vendor), taking a percentage of the selling price as commission when you have completed a successful sale. You might also deal with the letting and management of properties. As an agent involved with buying and selling houses, you would be known as a negotiator. In this capacity, you would visit the client's house, advise on a suitable selling price and then try to find a suitable buyer by marketing the property and contacting your database of potential buyers. If a buyer is not willing to pay the full purchase price, you would negotiate with both sides to reach an acceptable agreement. Often more than one prospective buyer could become involved and you would have to negotiate on your client's behalf.

Opportunities for Training

Much training is in-house and on-the-job. You may be able to work towards qualifications awarded by the National Federation of Property Professionals (NFOPP), a body brought about by the recent merger of the National Association of Estate Agents with the National Association of Valuers and Auctioneers, the Association of Residential Letting Agents, and the Institution of Commercial and Business Agents.

The NFOPP Technical Award in Sale of Residential Property is a nationally recognised level 3 qualification, which shows that you have the knowledge to undertake your job successfully. You can progress to the level 5 Diploma in Residential Estate Agency.

Some estate agents are qualified chartered surveyors. In order to qualify, you would need to complete a degree or diploma accredited by the Royal Institute of Chartered Surveyors (RICS). It is also possible to take a degree course in a relevant subject, such as estate management or building and land surveying and valuation.

Requirements for Entry

There are no specific qualification requirements to become an estate agent, although you would normally need three A level/Advanced Higher, four Higher or equivalent qualifications for admission to a RICS-approved degree course.

Whilst academic qualifications are always helpful and applicable, personal qualities and abilities are the most important aspect. Increasing legislation means that estate agents require a good knowledge of relevant law and it can help to be able to show clients or potential employers that you are a professional with a good knowledge of the business.

Kind of Person

You would have to like meeting all sorts of people and be good at negotiating and communicating. Buying or selling a house is often the single most important financial transaction that people make. The housing market is complicated, often involving 'chains' of buyers and sellers, deals often fall through and as a consequence feelings can run high. You would need to be a tactful and sympathetic person to cope with this. You would also need to be a good salesperson.

Broad Outlook

The housing market has suffered a devastating year between April 2008 and March 2009, with a massive drop in sales, widespread redundancies, falling house prices and potential buyers finding great difficulty in securing mortgage finance. For a number of years before that, however, the market had been extremely buoyant and all the indicators suggest that it will be again in the near future. If you pursue a career in estate agency, you must accept that this is a field that fluctuates and that your prospects and your pay will rise or fall in relation to the volume of sales you generate.

Related Occupations

You might also consider: surveyor, auctioneer/valuer or estate manager/land agent.

Impact on Lifestyle

You would probably be expected to work during some evenings and on Saturdays at weekends. You would be out of the office a great deal, going to see clients and showing them around houses, other property or land. The workload tends, however, to be seasonal and to fluctuate.

Earnings Potential

This can be up to you. Starting pay is usually around £17,000 to £20,000 but you would often receive commission, so the more houses you sell the more you would make. At senior level, salaries range from £25,000 to £50,000 plus. Working hard, networking and getting your name and face known would all be important here. You would be dealing closely with solicitors, banks and other lending organisations and it would be to your advantage to build up personal contacts. If you progress to become a partner, you could earn significantly more depending on the success of the agency and the state of the economy at the time.

Further Information

National Association of Estate Agents, Warwick CV34 4EH
Website: www.naea.co.uk

Royal Institution of Chartered Surveyors, Coventry CV4 8JE
Website: www.rics.org

National Federation of Property Professionals
Website: www.nfopp.co.uk

Alternative/equivalent entrance requirements can include: ILC, IB, EB, NC/ND and many other similar international systems. For further details see the Equivalent Qualifications section in the Introduction.

Events Manager

What is Involved?

In the ever more competitive world of business and commerce, events, conferences and corporate hospitality days are being used to promote and increase awareness of products, stimulate customer loyalty and reward staff. As an events or conference manager, you would be in charge of the overall organisation of an event, including the venue, the catering, the staffing and the reception arrangements. You might be employed by a large organisation or company, or by a particular venue, or by a specialist company brought in to do the job. Your work could involve a good deal of travel and would certainly mean that you had contact with a wide variety of people, both clients and your own staff. You would discuss and agree what the organisation wanted and what size budget would be at your disposal.

You would need to be aware of all the facilities required to ensure that delegates gain the maximum benefit from each event under your control.

Opportunities for Training

There is no single route into events or conference management but many entrants would have experience of working in hotels or restaurants, or perhaps in a managerial position in such areas as personnel (human resources), leisure, marketing or tourism. You could also work your way up through the ranks. Training would usually be carried out on-the-job. The Association for Conferences and Events runs short courses and can provide lists of companies and venues, together with other useful information.

Requirements for Entry

While there are no particular educational qualifications required, increasing numbers of graduates are being employed. Almost any subject would be acceptable, although you might give particular consideration to courses in hospitality management or leisure and tourism, or to others including elements of business studies, marketing or modern languages.

For entry to a degree course, you would normally need a minimum of two A level/Advanced Higher, three Higher or equivalent qualifications, together with five GCSE/S Grade passes at A-C/1-3, or equivalent. Courses usually last three or four years and many would be described as 'sandwich courses', which means that they incorporate periods of industrial experience. There are also Higher National Diploma (HND) courses, which are usually a year shorter than corresponding degrees. For HND entry, you would need one or two A level/Advanced Higher, two or three Higher or equivalent qualifications, together with five GCSE/S Grade passes A-C/1-3.

Kind of Person

You would need excellent communication skills to deal with a wide variety of people. The ability to persuade others to your point of view would be particularly valuable. A good head for business and an understanding of how particular companies work would stand you in good stead. You would need to be tough, both mentally and physically, as the work would probably involve you in long hours, weekend and evening work. You would need to be a good organiser, concerned with getting all the details right while juggling several priorities at any time. You would be on show, so a smart appearance would be important.

Broad Outlook

Events and conference management is being seen more and more within the hospitality industry as an important tool for commercial and business success. It is, however, very much at the mercy of the national economic climate. Competition for the top jobs is intense but the rewards can be substantial. As a successful manager, you could progress to setting up your own company or go on to a senior managerial position.

Related Occupations

You might also consider: advertising executive, hotel manager, catering manager, leisure services manager, marketing executive or public relations officer.

Impact on Lifestyle

You would have to be prepared to work long hours, at the weekends and in the evenings, sometimes in order to meet deadlines and sometimes to conduct actual events or conferences. There would almost certainly be quite a lot of travel involved.

Earnings Potential

There is a considerable range in earnings, since the type of work involved varies so widely. As a graduate trainee, you might expect to start on a salary of around £18,000 to £25,000, increasing to £27,000 to £40,000 once you gain experience and can demonstrate success. At a more senior level, you might earn £50,000 to £70,000 per annum. You may receive additional income through commission payments.

Further Information

Association for Conferences and Events, Huntingdon PE18 6SG
Website: www.martex.co.uk/ace

People 1st: The Sector Skills Council for the Hospitality, Leisure, Travel and Tourism Industries, Middlesex UB8 1LH
Website: www.people1st.co.uk

Springboard, London WC2H 8LP
Website: www.springboarduk.org.uk

Association of British Professional Conference Organisers, Birmingham B3 3HT
Website: www.abpco.org

Business Visits and Events Partnership
Website: www.businesstourismpartnership.com

Alternative/equivalent entrance requirements can include: ILC, IB, EB, NC/ND and many other similar international systems. For further details see the Equivalent Qualifications section in the Introduction.

Farm Manager

What is Involved?

As a farm manager, you would oversee the running of a farm as an efficient and profitable business. You might work for the owner of a large estate or for a big commercial organisation and the exact nature of your work would depend on the size of the business and the type of farming involved. Broadly speaking, you would be likely to work in one of three areas:

• An **arable enterprise** would see you producing crops such as wheat, potatoes, sugar beet, linseed, flax, lavender or turf. You might choose to specialise in the rapidly expanding business of organic production, avoiding the use of artificial fertilisers and pesticides on your land.

• The **livestock sector** would involve you in the production of pigs, beef, dairy cattle, sheep and poultry or, more rarely, deer and ostrich. Here you would have the opportunity to work with animals both outdoors and indoors and to plan breeding programmes.

• A **mixed farm** would offer you a combination of both arable and livestock elements.

While your work may involve you being outside in all weathers, you would spend at least some of your time in an office, planning ahead, dealing with staffing issues, keeping records and managing the accounts. You would be responsible for the financial success of the farm, making sure that whatever you produce arrives at the right market at the right time and sells for the best possible price.

Opportunities for Training

You would normally have a degree, a (Scottish) Higher National Diploma in agriculture or agricultural business management from university or agricultural college, or a national/Scottish vocational qualification at level 3 or 4, as well as considerable relevant experience. Courses usually last three or four years and may include work placements or opportunities for work or study abroad.

Course content varies enormously and is often specifically geared to arable or livestock farming as outlined above. Other relevant courses could range from wildlife conservation to soil science.

Requirements for Entry

At least two A level/Advanced Higher, three Higher or equivalent qualifications are required for entry to degree courses. Chemistry is often specified; biology and geography are regularly mentioned. For diploma courses, you should have at least one A level/Advanced Higher, two Higher or equivalent qualifications, together with three or four GCSE/S Grade passes at A-C/1-3 including English, maths and a science subject. You would need considerable work experience and you would find it difficult to survive without a driving licence.

Kind of Person

In the rapidly changing world of modern agriculture, you may find that business management and IT skills are even more important than a thorough grounding in farmyard skills and a love of the countryside. Farming can be highly unpredictable as weather conditions change, crops lose their market value or animals become sick. As a manager, you would need to be adaptable, unflappable and able to rearrange plans at very short notice. Good communication skills would be essential for working with staff, advisers, suppliers and customers.

Broad Outlook

Farming has been going through difficult times in recent years and this could affect the number of managerial jobs available. As they diversify into less traditional activities to 'add value' and increase profitability, farm businesses will be looking to use traditional resources, such as land, labour, buildings and equipment, for uses over and above livestock, milk and crop production. You could improve your overall prospects by trying to apply innovative thinking to the process of moving away from intensive production towards such areas as leisure pursuits, organic farming and conservation.

Related Occupations

You may wish to consider: horticultural manager, conservationist, estate manager, forest manager, countryside ranger or fish farmer. You could move into other commercial aspects of agriculture, such as technical sales or contracting. With the increase of tourism in the countryside, you could specialise in the management of tourist facilities.

Impact on Lifestyle

Many people view agriculture as an industry that offers long hours for poor reward. You should find in reality that, while there are rarely any set hours and you are expected to vary your workload according to the changing demands of the seasons, farming is becoming increasingly "market aware", calling for flexible, innovative and enthusiastic people who are well rewarded for their commitment. Running a farm tends to become a way of life and early mornings, late evenings and weekend commitments can often be part of the lifestyle.

Earnings Potential

There is no official salary scale for farm managers. An assistant or trainee farm manager can expect to start on around £20,000. This should rise fairly quickly to around £26,000. As an experienced farm manager, you might earn in the region of £50,000. Senior posts, including those in a consultancy or advisory role, can pay in excess of £70,000. You could have a car and a house on the farm as part of your employment package and you may even be able to participate in a profit-sharing scheme.

Further Information

Lantra, Kenilworth CV8 2LG
Website: www.lantra.co.uk

Growing Careers, Essex CM1 3RR
Website: www.growing-careers.com

Department for Environment, Food and Rural Affairs, London SW1P 3JR
Website: www.defra.gov.uk

Institute of Agricultural Management, Bristol BS20 7TE
Website: www.iagrm.org.uk

Alternative/equivalent entrance requirements can include: ILC, IB, EB, NC/ND and many other similar international systems. For further details see the Equivalent Qualifications section in the Introduction.

Fashion Designer

What is Involved?

As a fashion designer, you would work with others in designing and making clothes and accessories. There are three areas of fashion design: 'haute couture', 'designer ready-to-wear' and 'high street fashions'. Haute couture is the top end of the market, where individually designed clothes are made for exclusive clients. The fashion houses involved - Armani, Dior, Calvin Klein, Chloe, for example - all display their latest collections at glitzy shows and it is often these designs that influence what the rest of us wear over the next season. Designer ready-to-wear clothes are produced by the haute couture fashion houses and are emblazoned with their all-important designer label or logo. These are usually limited runs of the design, sold in specialist boutiques. Most fashion garments are sold in high street stores, including French Connection, Marks and Spencer, Debenhams and TopShop. Fashion is one of the largest industries in the UK, employing more than 165,000 people and contributing significantly to British exports.

You could work in the dominant womenswear market or you could choose to focus on the growing menswear and childrenswear segments. Other possible areas include accessory design, millinery, shoe and sportswear design or you could even specialise in costume design for film, TV and theatre work.

Opportunities for Training

With over 250 fashion degrees and higher national diplomas (HNDs) currently available in the UK, you would need to research training courses carefully before making a final choice. A good starting point could be a one- or two-year foundation course in art and design, allowing you time after school to explore a range of options in creative design and to develop a suitable portfolio of your work. Courses should take you through all the stages from an initial design idea to a prototype garment.

You may find an on-the-job training place with a design studio but you would need to be sure that you would focus on design rather than on manufacturing garments.

Requirements for Entry

Most institutions offering degree and HND courses require five GCSE/S Grade passes at A-C/1-3 or equivalent, preferably with maths and English, together with relevant AS/A level/Advanced Higher/Higher or equivalent qualifications including an art related subject, and/or the completion of an art foundation course. You must be able to present a portfolio of work, with evidence of good drawing skills and a lively interest in fashion. Work experience is important and it would be helpful to demonstrate that you have made up a garment, taken photographs or assembled your own fashion scrapbook.

Kind of Person

You would need a real passion for fashion, with a love of clothes, textiles, colour, texture and pattern. Good drawing skills would be essential, together with the ability to communicate your ideas to buyers or manufacturers and the practical ability to make up sample garments. You would need to work as part of a team, to be able to use fashion-specific IT packages and to have some knowledge of the business constraints of budgeting and costing. For haute couture, in particular, you would need to be exceptionally creative and determined to succeed.

Broad Outlook

Competition in fashion design is intense and success can be as dependent on getting a lucky break as on having talent, drive and irrepressible determination. You may want to gain experience by working in the UK or abroad, possibly for low pay in a very junior position, in the fashion centres of London, Paris, Milan and New York. The majority of actual jobs in the UK are at the high street end of the market and may be somewhat removed from the glamour associated with stars such as Galliano, Westwood and McQueen. You should ask about career destinations of previous students before selecting a degree or HND course.

Related Occupations

You may wish to consider other designer areas such as: textile, interior, industrial product, jewellery or graphic. Alternatively, you might wish to consider other fashion options such as: photographer, buyer, or journalist.

Impact on Lifestyle

Fashion design could well become dominant in your life as you work through the night to meet deadlines for fashion shows and rearrange holidays to fit work schedules. Inspiration can come at any time and you would need to capture ideas before they disappear again.

Earnings Potential

You could expect to start on about £16,000 to £23,000 a year, probably based in London. Depending on your talent and opportunities, you could be earning in the region of £40,000 to £60,000 after ten years and, if you become a top design director, you might earn £100,000 or more.

You may choose to work on a freelance basis, in which case your earnings would depend totally on how hard you work and how successful you are in selling your designs.

Further Information

Skillfast-UK, Leeds LS28 6BN
Website: www.skillfast-uk.org

Chartered Society of Designers, London SE1 3GA
Website: www.csd.org.uk

Your Creative Future
Website: www.yourcreativefuture.org

UK Fashion Exports, London W1B 1PW
Website: www.5portlandplace.org.uk

Alternative/equivalent entrance requirements can include: ILC, IB, EB, NC/ND and many other similar international systems. For further details see the Equivalent Qualifications section in the Introduction.

Financial Adviser

What is Involved?

As a financial adviser, you could work in one of two major areas: you may be tied to an individual bank, building society or insurance company, advising solely on the financial products of your organisation; you may have a broader role as an independent adviser, recommending suitable investments, mortgages, pensions and insurance policies on an impartial basis. In either case, you would need a detailed knowledge of investment opportunities, insurance policies, pension plans, mortgages and savings schemes. You would analyse each client's financial position and draw up plans to help meet his or her future requirements and commitments. For example, in addition to house purchase and retirement planning, a client might wish to educate their children privately and you would advise how they could best achieve this through structuring their savings and investments. You could work as a completely independent financial adviser, charging clients by the hour in the same way as an accountant, or you could offer your advice free of charge, earning commission on the financial products you promote and sell.

Opportunities for Training

As a trainee, you would have to undertake industry-recognised training that meets standards set by the Financial Services Skills Council and is regulated by the Financial Services Authority. This is likely to take between two and three years and it is necessary to pass examinations in order to become fully qualified. Various professional qualifications are available, including the Chartered Insurance Institute Certificate, Diploma and Advanced Diploma in Financial Planning; the Institute of Financial Services Certificate for Financial Advisers; the Securities and Investment Institute Certificate in Investment Management; the Institute of Financial Planning Certified Financial Planner; the UK Society of Investment Professionals Investment Management Certificate; and the Chartered Institute of Bankers in Scotland Certificate and Diploma in Financial Services.

Most employers provide training and pay for exams, but you would usually be expected to study outside working hours, with many courses offering distance learning opportunities.

Requirements for Entry

While there are no formal academic entry requirements, the most prestigious employers would require a degree or at least A level/Advanced Higher, Higher or equivalent qualifications, together with evidence of numeracy. Many people starting as financial advisers are graduates in business studies, accountancy or similar subjects, although this is not an essential requirement. Some people become financial advisers after gaining experience in clerical positions, although this could take some time because of the level of maturity expected by clients.

Kind of Person

This is a job for a 'people' person. You would have to be good at communicating - both listening carefully to your client's requirements and being able to explain your proposed solutions to their financial needs. You would meet all sorts of people and you would need to inspire confidence in them. You would need to be numerate and have an understanding of financial products and the legal or taxation implications of making certain investment decisions. Good IT skills are essential. If working on commission for a company, you would have to be good at selling. Honesty is vital here, both in terms of explaining the extent of your independence and of treating personal information confidentially. You would normally be expected to dress smartly and conventionally for this type of work.

Broad Outlook

Financial advice is an area undergoing rapid change and considerable growth. As more and more people change jobs throughout their working lives, they need financial planning advice. The financial services sector has had some bad publicity in recent years but its image is changing with tighter regulation and the introduction of compulsory training. You could progress into management or training or you could start your own business.

Related Occupations

You may consider: accountant, banker, insurance broker or investment analyst.

Impact on Lifestyle

Generally financial advisers are office based, working normal office hours. However, you might be expected to visit clients in their homes and this could involve having to see them in the evening or at weekends.

Earnings Potential

This can vary considerably. Your method of payment could range from a full salary to a salary with bonuses for achieved targets, to commission only or fees only. So, to a certain extent, what you earn would be up to you. As a graduate, you could expect to earn £22,000 to £30,000 in your first year and considerably more later if you exceed your targets. You could achieve very high earnings as an experienced and successful independent adviser.

Further Information

Financial Services Skills Council, London EC2V 7HQ
Website: www.fssc.org.uk

Personal Finance Society
Website: www.thepfs.org

Association of Independent Financial Advisers, London EC2N 2HD
Website: www.aifa.net

Institute of Financial Planning, Bristol BS1 2NT
Website: www.financialplanning.org.uk

Chartered Institute of Bankers in Scotland, Edinburgh EH3 7SW
Website: www.ciobs.org.uk

Chartered Insurance Institute, London E18 2JP
Website: www.cii.co.uk

Institute of Financial Services, Kent CT1 2XJ
Website: www.ifslearning.com

Securities and Investment Institute, London EC3R 8AQ
Website: www.sii.org.uk

UK Society of Investment Professionals, London EC2V 5AY
Website: www.uksip.org

Alternative/equivalent entrance requirements can include: ILC, IB, EB, NC/ND and many other similar international systems. For further details see the Equivalent Qualifications section in the Introduction.

What is Involved?

As a fire officer or firefighter, you would be working as part of a team to reduce deaths and losses from fire. While you would certainly be involved in the often dangerous and stressful process of actually fighting fires, you would also be responsible for making the general public aware of fire hazards, visiting public and commercial premises to advise on fire regulations and safety standards and responding to other emergency calls. These may range from floods to road, rail and air crashes or working with other emergency services at sites of major disasters. You would be trained in first aid so that you could administer immediate help before the arrival of the emergency medical services.

As a more senior officer, you might organise the response of your service to call-outs and you might attend major incidents to co-ordinate the work. At other times, you could be reviewing the operating policies of your brigade or organising the training of the firefighters under your command.

Opportunities for Training

As a new recruit, you would train for a minimum of 80 working days at a training school. Initial training is tough, with an emphasis on strict discipline and high standards of physical fitness. You would cover both the theory and practice of all aspects of the firefighter's role, including the use of ladders and hoses, wearing protective clothing and breathing apparatus and learning about fire regulations. On leaving training school, you would join an operational station and enter the Phase 2 scheme. During this period you undertake on-the-job training and development, and undergo final assessment of competence when you are deemed ready. This takes between 18 months and three years and varies between individual fire and rescue services.

Training continues throughout your career, including refresher courses, training in new techniques and specialist qualifications. You may be encouraged to study for membership of the Institution of Fire Engineers or to gain management qualifications. Various leadership courses run by the Fire Service College are also available for junior and senior officers. A number of services and the Fire Service College now have links with higher education institutions, through which academic qualifications up to Masters level are awarded.

Requirements for Entry

There are no formal entry requirements, although some brigades may require specific GCSE/S Grade passes, and you would have to pass a series of initiative and fitness tests. There is no separate entry scheme for candidates with higher level qualifications but you should be able to pass training and promotion exams relatively more quickly.

You must be at least 18 before you can join the Fire Service, fully fit and able to meet national fitness standards in lung capacity and upper body strength. Good vision in both eyes is essential and you should have normal colour vision.

Kind of Person

You must be able to work as part of a highly disciplined team but with the capacity to respond to challenges by showing initiative when required. You would be required to accept the brigade dress code and restrictions on your personal appearance.

Handling specialist equipment calls for a variety of practical skills and you must be able to react calmly but quickly in dangerous situations. Good communication and interpersonal skills are vital. You would need to be physically strong to carry your equipment and mentally resilient in view of the sometimes harrowing situations you would encounter.

Broad Outlook

There is fierce competition for Fire Service positions and there are always many more applicants than vacancies, although there is scope in rural areas to work as a part-time 'retained' firefighter.

All new entrants start on the same grade and promotion is strictly on merit. You could rise to the rank of station commander through internal promotion but would need to move to different areas to obtain more senior appointments.

Related Occupations

You might also consider: army, RAF, Royal Navy, merchant navy, police or security officer or ambulance technician/paramedic.

Impact on Lifestyle

Firefighters work a shift system, which means both day and night time working and work at weekends. Occasionally, you may be expected to work overtime but can expect on average to have two days off each week. Because of the nature of the job you may be called out on emergency work at short notice and would have to see the job through however long it takes for you to be relieved.

Earnings Potential

As a trainee firefighter, you would start on a salary of £20,896, rising to £27,851 when competent. A watch manager earns up to £34,529 and an Area Manager up to £53,268. There is also a London weighting allowance and there are agreed overtime rates for all grades.

Further Information

Contact the recruitment department of your local fire service.

UK Fire Service Resources
Website: www.fireservice.co.uk

Chief Fire Officers Association
Website: www.cfoa.org.uk

Fire Officers' Association, Gloucestershire GL56 0RH
Website: www.fireofficers.org.uk

Fire Brigades Union, Surrey KT2 7AE
Website: www.fbu.org.uk

Fire and Rescue Service Online
Website: www.frsonline.fire.gov.uk

Fire Service College, Gloucestershire GL56 0RH
Website: www.fireservicecollege.ac.uk

Institution of Fire Engineers, Gloucestershire GL56 0RH
Website: www.ife.org.uk

Alternative/equivalent entrance requirements can include: ILC, IB, EB, NC/ND and many other similar international systems. For further details see the Equivalent Qualifications section in the Introduction.

Food Scientist or Technologist

What is Involved?

As a food scientist, you would examine the chemistry and biology of manufactured foods from the raw materials through to the final product. As a food technologist, you would use food science and other technological expertise to turn raw materials into finished products for the consumer, often with the aid of sophisticated equipment. You might work for a food processing company, for a large supermarket chain, for the civil service or for the environmental health service, ensuring that food products are safe to eat and economical to produce, that they taste good and look inviting. You could be testing products in a laboratory to monitor chemical and microbiological changes during cooking and storage; you could be developing new products to meet changing consumer demands; you may be creating low-fat, ready-to-eat meals for airlines; you may be experimenting with new ways of preventing fruit from rotting. While there is considerable overlap between the two types of work, you would be more likely to work in a laboratory as a food scientist and in a food production establishment as a food technologist.

Opportunities for Training

There are over 30 institutions in the UK offering Food Science, Food Technology or closely related subjects at degree or higher national diploma (HND) level or N/SVQ level 4. Some of the courses are sandwich-based, giving you a chance to combine your academic study with practical experience in the industry. It is also possible to train on the job, without a higher education qualification, possibly starting on an Apprenticeship. There may be opportunities to specialise in areas such as meat and poultry processing, baking technology or brewing.

If you are interested in working abroad, some degrees and HNDs offer study in Europe as part of the course. You would be expected to continue to study throughout your working life in order to keep up to date with new developments in the food market.

Requirements for Entry

You should be thinking of studying chemistry plus at least one subject from food science, maths, biology or physics as a grounding for a degree or HND. Most universities require three good A level/Advanced Higher, four Higher or equivalent qualifications for degree entry, including chemistry. The HND route would normally require one A level, two Higher or equivalent qualifications.

It is possible to work as a technician in food and drink production if you have four GCSE/S Grade passes A-C/1-3 in English, maths, biology and chemistry or an equivalent qualification.

Kind of Person

You would need a genuine interest in food and drink, coupled with a meticulous approach to detail and hygiene when you are conducting trials or laboratory tests on food. You would also need good communication skills and the ability to work as part of a team. Knowledge of food safety law is required, to ensure that you work within relevant health and safety regulations.

Broad Outlook

Food and drink is a large, expanding and changing industry, with new jobs being created all the time. There is wide range of possible employers, from food or drink manufacturers, large retailers or supermarket chains to Government research establishments, local authorities or universities.

To gain promotion in a large organisation, you would need to develop specialised skills relevant to the company and to demonstrate the broad qualities sought for management responsibility. You may find it necessary to change employers a few times in order to develop your career. There is currently a shortage of new graduates joining the industry.

Related Occupations

You may be interested in working in the food industry as a dietitian/nutritionist, biochemist, biotechnologist, microbiologist, environmental health officer or chef.

Impact on Lifestyle

You would most likely work a typical 35- to 40-hour week. Some manufacturing companies may have a 24-hour production programme, in which case you would work shifts in order to supervise and test the quality of the food during production. This may include some weekend work.

Meticulous hygiene requirements would mean that you would at times have to wear special clothing, including a hat or hairnet, gloves and even a mask.

Earnings Potential

As a graduate food scientist or technologist, you should start earning in the region of £25,000 to £28,000. This should rise to £35,000 with experience and to £65,000 or more for a senior managerial position, depending on the size of the organisation, your responsibilities and your qualifications.

Further Information

Food Science and Technology Careers
Website: www.foodtechcareers.org

Department for Environment, Food and Rural Affairs, London SE1 7TL
Website: www.defra.gov.uk

Food and Drink Federation, London WC2B 5JJ
Website: www.fdf.org.uk

Institute of Food Science and Technology, London W6 7NL
Website: www.ifst.org

Alternative/equivalent entrance requirements can include: ILC, IB, EB, NC/ND and many other similar international systems. For further details see the Equivalent Qualifications section in the Introduction.

Forensic Scientist

What is Involved?

As a forensic scientist, you would be working at the meeting point between science and the law, examining and analysing minute traces of materials in the search for physical traces which might be useful for establishing or excluding an association between someone suspected of committing a crime and the scene of the crime or victim. Such traces commonly include blood and other body fluids, hairs, textile fibres from clothing, materials used in buildings such as paint and glass, footwear, tool and tyre marks, flammable substances used to start fires and so on. Much of your work would be carried out in close co-operation with the police and would make a very valuable, at times critical, contribution to the process of the law. You are likely to be involved with cases of arson, burglary and fire and murder investigations. You might also be concerned with car accidents or cases involving drugs. You would work in a laboratory, possibly analysing samples of DNA, and occasionally visiting the scenes of crimes.

Opportunities for Training

There are two main elements in the training required to become a general forensic scientist. The first involves academic courses, and the second on-the-job training, usually with one of the main suppliers of primary services to police. Most of the training, for example, for the Forensic Science Service in England and Wales or the police laboratories in Scotland would be carried out once you have started working. You would need a good honours degree in a relevant subject in order to become a forensic scientist and progress to senior level. There are some universities offering degrees in Forensic Science either as single or joint honours but it is possible to start training with a good degree in a subject such as chemistry, biochemistry, pharmaceutical chemistry, biology or metallurgy, followed by a one- or two-year postgraduate course in forensic science. This is the route currently recommended by the Forensic Science Society. However, there is no route that will guarantee you a job in this oversubscribed field.

Requirements for Entry

For entry to a relevant science degree, you would need A level/Advanced Higher, Higher or equivalent qualifications in chemistry and another science subject, with some universities specifying maths or biology. If the university does not specify maths as an A level/Advanced Higher, Higher or equivalent subject, you are likely to need at least a B/2 in maths at GCSE/S Grade. There is a rapidly growing number of forensic science degree courses available and admission offers can be higher than for other chemistry- or biology-based courses.

Kind of Person

You would need a strong interest in science and a methodical and analytic approach to problem solving. At times you would be required to make very detailed examinations of the scene of an incident. The tests that you carry out would call for accuracy and a sound understanding of maths. In addition to your scientific and analytical skills you would need to express yourself clearly both verbally and in written reports. You may be required to stand up in court and give evidence, in which case you may have to face cross examination. You are likely to become an expert in one particular area of forensic science and would, therefore, work fairly independently but always as a team member. Finally, you would have to cope with crime scenes, which can be very unpleasant.

Broad Outlook

This is a fiercely competitive area of work, with many well-qualified candidates chasing every vacancy. You may have to move around the country in order to secure a post.

The majority of forensic scientists in the United Kingdom are employed by the Forensic Science Service (in England and Wales), by specific police forces (in Scotland) and by regional government (in Northern Ireland). There are also private companies, which specialise in providing primary forensic science services to the police, together with organisations which focus on specific areas of forensic science such as fire investigation.

It is possible to move into a managerial position, but your career progress could depend on developing an area of expertise. Recent scientific developments and the creation of the national DNA database have led to an increased demand for DNA analysts.

Related Occupations

You might be interested in other careers with a scientific base such as research chemist, pharmacologist, chemical engineer, metallurgist, biochemist or pathologist.

Impact on Lifestyle

You may be called out to a crime scene at night or at weekends, and this could clearly have an impact on your social life. Apart from being available on an on-call rota of this sort, you could expect your normal working week to be around 40 hours spread over five days. Some of the scenes of crime you attend may be distressing, so this is not a career for the faint-hearted!

Earnings Potential

As a general guide, bearing in mind that actual rates of pay may vary, depending on your employer and where you live, starting salaries for trainee forensic scientists typically range from £16,000 to £18,000. An MSc or PhD in a relevant subject may enable you to start higher on the salary scale. With two to three years' experience, salaries increase to £25,000 to £30,000. Typical salaries at senior levels are around £50,000 plus.

Further Information

Forensic Science Society, Harrogate HG1 1BX
Website: www.forensic-science-society.org.uk

Forensic Science Service, Birmingham B37 7YN
Website: www.forensic.gov.uk

Forensic Science Northern Ireland, County Antrim BT38 8PL
Website: www.fsni.gov.uk

Alternative/equivalent entrance requirements can include: ILC, IB, EB, NC/ND and many other similar international systems. For further details see the Equivalent Qualifications section in the Introduction.

Forest Manager

What is Involved?

Forestry is defined as the science and practice of managing forests and woodlands but modern multi-purpose forestry is about far more than just growing trees for timber. Your work as a forest manager could embrace everything from planting and managing large coniferous forests to creating and tending small broadleaved woodlands; from raising young trees in nurseries to felling and delivering timber to wood-using industries. Timber production still underpins the work but your remit would be much broader, including managing woods and forests to offer multiple benefits for people, wildlife and the environment in general. Forests can provide havens for wildlife, can screen and enhance the landscape, filter the air and cater for many types of recreation.

You would usually commence your career as a technical manager or supervisor, known in the industry as a forester. You would plan and control forest operations and ensure that the forest environment is protected and enhanced. You might also manage public recreation and access. There are chances to specialise in wildlife conservation, recreation, training, research, harvesting, marketing and processing. You would probably spend about three days a week out in the forest and the rest of the time in an office.

Opportunities for Training

There are several possible training routes. You would normally need a degree, postgraduate qualification or a higher or national diploma in forestry (ND/HND). An Apprenticeship could also enable you to progress to a similar level. A degree would take three or four years to complete and ND/HND two or three years. You should obtain relevant work experience before starting any of these courses. You may find it useful to work towards full membership of the Institute of Chartered Foresters, which carries with it recognition of your experience and success in passing their examinations.

Requirements for Entry

For entry to a forestry degree, you should have at least two A level/Advanced Higher, three Higher or equivalent qualifications in science subjects and five GCSE/S Grade passes A-C/1-3. The HND would require at least one A level/Advanced Higher, two Higher or equivalent qualifications and GCSE/S Grade passes A-C/1-3 in maths, English and a science subject; for the ND you would need similar GCSE/S Grade passes. A full driving licence would be essential.

Kind of Person

You would need to be interested in the successful development and economic viability of forests, in their conservation and their environmental roles. You would have to be fit and to enjoy working outdoors. You would need good team skills, the ability to organise the schedules of those working for you and to communicate effectively with colleagues and members of the public.

Broad Outlook

The UK is one of the few places in the world where the tree cover is actually expanding as more and more trees are planted with the advent of community forests and the National Forest. Recent government initiatives in the expansion of leisure facilities in both private and public forests, coupled with grants to encourage the use of more land for forestry, have increased employment possibilities. Nevertheless, competition is keen and gaining work experience is vitally important. The Forestry Commission employs about 20% of people in forestry, private estates and the wood-processing industry account for about 60%, with the balance working for forest management and timber harvesting companies.

Openings exist with national and local government agencies, forest management companies, private estates, land agency firms, timber companies and independent consultants. There are forestry opportunities in New Zealand, Canada and the USA. Volunteer forestry workers can also be employed by charities working in underdeveloped countries. There are opportunities for postgraduate work and research in forestry with universities and the Forestry Commission.

The increase in environmental awareness and outdoor recreation has highlighted the need for professionally trained foresters and arboriculturists capable of managing Britain's woodlands and trees.

Related Occupations

You might also consider: countryside ranger/warden, conservationist, horticultural manager, landscape architect, chartered surveyor or land agent.

Impact on Lifestyle

You may have to work long hours, especially in commercial forests to meet contract deadlines. The Forestry Commission has an official 42-hour week, although that may include evening and weekend work. You are likely to be based in a very rural and possibly quite remote environment.

Earnings Potential

As a graduate you could expect to start earning between £16,000 and £20,000, rising to £30,000 to £50,000, depending on your experience and qualifications. The commercial forests tend to pay rather less than the Forestry Commission but there may be additional benefits.

Further Information

Forestry Commission, Edinburgh EH12 7AT
Website: www.forestry.gov.uk

Institute of Chartered Foresters, Edinburgh EH3 6AA
Website: www.charteredforesters.org

Royal Forestry Society, Hertfordshire HP23 4AF
Website: www.rfs.org.uk

Alternative/equivalent entrance requirements can include: ILC, IB, EB, NC/ND and many other similar international systems. For further details see the Equivalent Qualifications section in the Introduction.

Freight Forwarder

What is Involved?

In today's global economy, we buy our everyday needs from all around the world: mobile phones from Finland, furniture from Sweden, televisions from Japan and computers from the USA. We also sell our own goods all over the world. As a freight forwarder, you would be part of the international industry that uses ships, planes, trucks and railways to transport these goods to their markets around the globe.

You might work as a freight forwarding agent, assisting exporters or importers by collecting and delivering between them and the shipping line or airline, buying space on sailings or flights, handling documentation and dealing with HM Customs. Alternatively, you might work for an airline, a shipping company, a road transport operator or a courier, dealing in high volumes of small and urgent packages. See also our separate article on 'Logistics Manager.'

You would need a clear knowledge of the advantages and disadvantages of all types of transport and of the handling techniques at ports, railway stations, road transport terminals and airports worldwide.

Opportunities for Training

While there is no single recommended training route, there are many relevant higher national diploma (HND) and degree courses in international trade, business and logistics management. These can lead to a fast-track development programme within some of the larger freight organisations. The British International Freight Association (BIFA) provides training leading to a professional qualification recognised both inside and outside the industry: Understanding the Freight Business and International Trade, offering progression from certificate to diploma to advanced diploma. This covers key areas such as dealing with customer disputes, dangerous goods awareness, rate negotiation and agreement, and the role of customs authorities.

Continuing professional development is offered to individual members of BIFA by distance learning. Other relevant qualifications are offered by the Chartered Institute of Logistics and Transport and the Institute of Export.

Requirements for Entry

For degree course entry, you would normally need two or three A level/Advanced Higher, three or four Highers or equivalent qualifications, together with a good platform of GCSE/S Grade passes A-C/1-3. HND entry would normally require one A level/Advanced Higher, two Higher or equivalent qualifications. There are no specific subject requirements but subjects such as economics, foreign languages and geography could be useful. You should try to spend some time on a relevant work experience placement before making an application.

Kind of Person

The main qualities required would include an analytical mind with a practical side to it, as you could be constantly called upon to unravel problems such as goods going astray, suffering damage or failing to connect with a container ship or cargo plane. You would need to examine the fine detail without losing sight of the wider picture. You must be willing to assume independent responsibility, to communicate clearly and decisively, to insist on getting the facts, to negotiate and be adaptable and to cope with all these stresses and frequent changes. Excellent communication skills, both verbal and written, would be vital to carrying out your tasks, in which efficiency of operation, speed of turn-around time and the availability of return freights would be essential.

Broad Outlook

The world is coping, in the first quarter of 2009, with the first global decline in international trade for many decades, with particular attention being focused on the reluctance of banks to finance large contracts. Falling exports inevitably have an impact on career opportunities in freight forwarding, especially in the rather bleak short term. However, there is still a great demand for the movement of goods around the world, and this is predicted to increase in line with economic recovery from 2010 onwards.

Many people come into the freight industry by accident but then stay for a life-long career. There are several thousand freight-forwarding offices in the UK, from large companies (with 30 or more branches) down to single-outlet operators. All the pointers suggest that this is an industry facing significant change but one in which there remains considerable room for optimism and growth when world trade starts to pick up again.

Related Occupations

You might also consider: logistics manager, shipbroker, marketing executive, insurance broker, insurance underwriter or tour operator.

Impact on Lifestyle

The freight industry operates 24 hours a day, seven days a week. It could make major demands on your time, especially if you are in regular contact with people living on the other side of the world. Your hours of work could be long and irregular and you may be expected to travel extensively.

Earnings Potential

A typical starting salary for a graduate management trainee is around £18,000 to £22,000, although this can vary according to company size, location and so on. Other salaries are difficult to gauge but many experienced freight forwarders earn around £33,000 to £45,000.

Further Information

Chartered Institute of Logistics & Transport, Corby NN17 4XQ
Website: www.ciltuk.org.uk

Institute of Chartered Shipbrokers, London EC3V 0AA
Website: www.ics.org.uk

British International Freight Association, Middlesex TW13 7EP
Website: www.bifa.org

Careers in Logistics
Website: www.careersinlogistics.co.uk

Institute of Export, Peterborough PE2 6FT
Website: www.export.org.uk

Alternative/equivalent entrance requirements can include: ILC, IB, EB, NC/ND and many other similar international systems. For further details see the Equivalent Qualifications section in the Introduction.

Geologist/Geoscientist

What is Involved?

As a geologist or geoscientist, you would study the structure, evolution and dynamics of the planet Earth and its natural mineral and energy resources. You would investigate the processes that have shaped the Earth through its 4600 million year history in order to unravel that history and reveal its direct relevance to modern society. By mapping the distribution of rocks exposed at the Earth's surface, looking at how they are folded, fractured and altered by geological processes and determining their ages and field relations, you could produce the geological maps and databases which are the basic tools underpinning the use of all geological resources. You might analyse how energy resources such as oil and gas, coal and uranium are formed and where they may be found, or you might be involved in the search for sources of geothermal energy. You may be employed in exploration and surveying on land and sea, using aerial or satellite photography and electro-magnetic measurements (remote sensing). If you were to specialise in engineering, you might advise on the best locations for the construction of mines, roads, buildings and bridges. As an *environmental geologist*, you would give advice on contaminated sites and sites used for waste disposal. You might also advise on the effects of past activities, such as subsidence resulting from earlier mining, or on ongoing processes such as coastal erosion.

Opportunities for Training

To pursue a professional career, you would need an MSc or MGeol degree in geology or geoscience. Most students follow a broadly based course, although you could concentrate on a particular aspect such as environmental geology or geophysics. Fieldwork plays a vital part in most courses and you should be prepared to spend time out of doors to undertake group expeditions lasting from a few days to one or two weeks. Increasingly, students wishing to become geoscientists go on to take a postgraduate qualification, such as a PhD, concentrating on a particular area of interest to employers (e.g. petroleum geology, geophysics or hydrogeology). The Geological Society runs an accreditation scheme for geoscience degrees and successful completion of an accredited course can be the first stage of becoming a chartered geologist (CGeol).

Requirements for Entry

For degree entry, you would normally need two or three A level/Advanced Higher, three or four Higher or equivalent qualifications. Science and technological subjects, especially chemistry, physics, biology, mathematics and engineering, are preferred and a foreign language can be useful. As geology is not available in the majority of UK schools, it is not a university entrance requirement.

Kind of Person

You would need good spatial awareness and practical skills to use sophisticated instruments and you would have to possess good IT skills. You would sometimes work alone and sometimes as part of a team; you would need to be fit and healthy, since you may be working in physically challenging environments anywhere in the world. Any colour blindness could be a serious problem. Good communication skills would be essential for writing reports, making presentations and participating in discussion with professional colleagues.

Broad Outlook

Many geology graduates enter professions directly related to their degree. Popular roles include exploration and production, water supply, environmental engineering and geological surveying. Typical employers include the oil, gas and petroleum sector and environmental consultancies and civil engineering companies. Overseas work can be a common feature, while some experienced professionals may also become self-employed consultants.

Statistics collected from geology students graduating in 2007 show that just over half of those surveyed were in full-time paid work six months after graduation. The majority of these were employed as scientific research, analysis and development professionals (26%) with a further 15% in engineering and 13% employed as other professionals and in associate professional and technical occupations.

A high percentage of geology graduates choose to undertake further study. For example, of those who graduated in 2007, around 30% went on to full- or part-time further study. The majority opt for a vocational MSc such as Petroleum Geology, Engineering Geology or Geochemistry whilst others choose to do a PhD.

Related Occupations

You might also consider: engineering geologist, exploration geologist, marine geologist, geochemist, geophysicist, land surveyor (geomatics), surveyor, petroleum, civil, structural or mining engineer, hydrographic surveyor or cartographer.

Impact on Lifestyle

Most professional geologists spend at least part of their working career doing fieldwork, sometimes in remote areas in difficult conditions. You could be land-based, in mining operations or take part in underwater drilling operations. Temperatures can be extremely high in desert areas in the day and very low at night. In locations like Alaska you would experience sub-zero conditions and very short daylight hours. You would need a wide range of safety equipment and protective clothing to cope with each situation.

Earnings Potential

Typical starting salaries range from £22,000 to £30,000, depending on level of qualification on entry. Earnings usually increase significantly following completion of necessary training. At senior level, salaries are rarely less than £50,000 and may climb to more than £70,000 to £80,000 plus benefits. Salaries vary considerably by sector, employer's business and location, and level of qualification (graduates will generally have either an MSc or PhD). Positions based offshore or in risky or remote locations are often compensated in their salary. The highest salaries are in major oil companies, but some consultancies pay well too.

Further Information

British Geological Survey, Nottingham NG12 5GG
Website: www.bgs.ac.uk

Geological Society, London WIJ 0BG
Website: www.geolsoc.org.uk

Geologists' Association
Website: www.geologists.org.uk

Rockwatch
Website: www.rockwatch.org.uk

Petroleum Exploration Society of Great Britain, London W1J 8DW
Website: www.pesgb.org.uk

Alternative/equivalent entrance requirements can include: ILC, IB, EB, NC/ND and many other similar international systems. For further details see the Equivalent Qualifications section in the Introduction.

Golf Course Designer

What is Involved?

As a golf course designer, you would be commissioned by a client or golf club to work on a new project or to make alterations to an existing course. Your work is likely to fall under four headings: conceptual design, covering the ideas and development of the concept of the project; detailed design, focusing on the engineering detail and associated documentation of the architecture to greens, tees, bunkers, drainage, irrigation and so on; design management, involving inspections and supervisory visits during the construction and irrigation phases; establishment management, in which final visits and inspections would be made.

Opportunities for Training

There is no direct career path within what is a relatively small profession, though it has now been given a European dimension by the creation of the European Institute of Golf Course Architects (EIGCA). The Institute runs its own postgraduate diploma in golf course architecture, comprising part-time attendance and distance learning opportunities. The five centres offering the course are: Merrist Wood College, Surrey;

Myerscough College, Lancashire; Elmwood College, Fife; Deula, Kempen, Germany; and Boavista, Algarve, Portugal.

Each centre offers the opportunity to visit nearby noted and historic golf courses, playing from time to time and taking advantage of presentations by officials.

The diploma consists of five modules, each lasting two weeks, with tuition each day, run over a 24-month period. Approximately half of the module periods are devoted to design studies and practice. During the course, you would have to hand in a number of assignments covering the taught topics.

Requirements for Entry

Specific entry requirements for the postgraduate course should be discussed with EIGCA. Account would be taken of any relevant vocational training and prior practical experience.

Kind of Person

You must possess and be able to display a feeling for shape and form in design terms, coupled particularly with an appreciation of nature. Although you may well be based in an office, your essential work would be out on site. With the worldwide expansion of golf, opportunities for travel and for meeting clients from different countries with differing customs and cultures are numerous. The ability to enjoy and cope with this aspect of the job would, therefore, be vitally important.

You would need good communication and presentation skills to convince golf club officials and members that your plans meet all of their specifications, and you would need to be aware of legislation relevant to protecting and preserving the environment. In the context of developing existing course, you would need the ability to analyse, identify and select the strengths and weaknesses of any course and then recommend ways to improve it. You would probably arrive at this specialism as a result of a keen interest in playing golf.

Broad Outlook

You would find that this is a small and very specialised profession, with approximately 100 practising architects in Europe. However, golf is an expanding game, which has undergone amazing growth in the last 50 years. There are still countries with no golf courses at all, so there is considerable potential in areas like central Eastern Europe, Mid-Asia and the Middle East. The EIGCA is currently structuring a positive education programme and career path, even though many golf course design practices are owned and run by individuals.

It remains, however, a difficult career to enter, unless you can secure employment, internship or a studentship with one of the larger, more dynamic practices. Some 150 golf course architects run practices in the USA and are members of the American Society of Golf Course Architects, but you would have to obtain a green card if you wish to find employment in America as an intern.

Related Occupations

You might also consider: landscape architect, chartered surveyor, rural practice surveyor or countryside conservation officer.

Impact on Lifestyle

This is not a job with regular office hours from Monday to Friday. With the frequent travel necessitated, it would be common for golf course designers to put in many additional hours per week, which may be unsociable but could also be enjoyable. Projects may well not be close to hand, so some disruption of your social and domestic life would be inevitable.

Earnings Potential

As a student or intern, you could expect a relatively low salary, whereas you should earn in excess of £25,000 once qualified. Those who run their own practices would earn considerably more, dependent on the value of projects in hand at any time.

Further Information

European Institute of Golf Course Architects, Surrey GU5 0AJ
Website: www.eigca.org

British Association of Golf Course Constructors
Website: www.bagcc.org.uk

British Association of Landscape Industries, Warwickshire CV8 2LG
Website: www.bali.org.uk

Alternative/equivalent entrance requirements can include: ILC, IB, EB, NC/ND and many other similar international systems. For further details see the Equivalent Qualifications section in the Introduction.

Graphic Designer

What is Involved?

As a graphic designer, you would add a dimension of visual flair to the words and pictures making up magazine and newspaper layouts and covers, advertisements, posters, book jackets, sales brochures, catalogues, websites and product packaging. Graphic design is about drawing and presentation skills and about the ability to handle colours, lettering and patterns. Increasingly too, because of the development of design software, it is about a high degree of computer literacy. You might work on a wide range of projects or you could become a specialist in, for example, typography (print), illustration, packaging, corporate identity or magazine design.

You would often be expected to suggest a number of designs and colour combinations for consideration, possibly modifying layouts, typestyles and overall emphasis according to the wishes of your client or art director. Branding and house style, costing/budgeting, delivery dates and media to be used would all need to be agreed before your design work is finalised and handed over for printing or publication.

Opportunities for Training

There are no required qualifications but a good starting point would normally be to take an art foundation course before going on to a further course of training at an art school or university. A foundation course would give you a broad introduction to working in different areas of design and would provide the opportunity to build up a portfolio of your best work before you choose a specialised degree or higher national diploma (HND) course. In Scotland, the foundation would be the first year of a four-year course.

As a graphic designer, you will need to be skilled in using a variety of software packages, such as Quark Xpress, FreeHand, Illustrator, Photoshop, 3D Studio Max, Acrobat, Director, Dreamweaver and Flash. If you are involved in media design, you may be required to learn about TV special effects systems. Some employers will fund participation on training courses, but many freelance and self-employed designers have to fund their own development.

Requirements for Entry

Entry to foundation courses can be from GCSE/S or A level/Advanced Higher, Higher or equivalent qualifications, with great importance placed on a current portfolio of your own artistic work. The courses last one or two years full-time and can be found at sixth form colleges, further and higher education colleges, art colleges and some universities.

Entry to an HND course would normally require a minimum of four GCSE/S Grade passes and one or two A level/Advanced Higher, Higher or equivalent qualifications. The course would usually last two years, with the possibility of conversion to a degree course.

Kind of Person

You would need to be artistically creative and imaginative. You would also need to have good technical and drawing skills and the ability to visualise a design concept. You would need to be able to understand the technical aspects of printing and, if applicable, multimedia systems. Computer skills would be essential, as graphic design is almost always based on specialist design software. You would need to communicate well with your clients, to listen carefully to their ideas and suggestions and be able to explain your own design concepts. In addition, you would need some understanding of budgeting and costing when preparing your plans.

Broad Outlook

Britain has the largest number of higher education courses in graphic design in Europe, which means that entry to the profession is competitive. However, there are more openings in graphic design than in any other area of design - in advertising agencies, design studios, in-house company departments and consultancies as well as in the freelance sector. Most agencies and studios are based in the larger cities, with a particular concentration in the London area. There is growing demand for designers specialising in television and video graphics and in website design.

Related Occupations

You might also consider: advertising art director, photographer, artist/illustrator, exhibition designer or webmaster.

Impact on Lifestyle

You may have a contract that states your hours will be nine to five, Monday to Friday. At times, however, you would be expected to be flexible and work longer than this if there is a tight deadline to meet. You may find yourself travelling to visit clients and having to meet them at times that are convenient to the client rather than to you. As a junior designer, you are likely to find yourself working in an open plan environment with other designers.

Earnings Potential

There is a wide range of starting salaries depending on your age and experience, but you can expect to earn around £16,000 to £19,000 when you first start. This can rise with experience to around £25,000 to £50,000, and to £60,000 and above for a senior designer. There are good opportunities for experienced designers to work freelance, in which case your salary would depend on your skills, your ability to market yourself and the hours you are prepared to work.

Further Information

Chartered Society of Designers, London SE1 3GA
Website: www.csd.org.uk

Your Creative Future
Website: www.yourcreativefuture.org

D&AD, London SE11 5EE
Website: www.dandad.org

Alternative/equivalent entrance requirements can include: ILC, IB, EB, NC/ND and many other similar international systems. For further details see the Equivalent Qualifications section in the Introduction.

Health and Safety Inspector

What is Involved?

As a health and safety inspector, you would visit a wide variety of workplaces and other sites, including building sites, farms, factories, fairgrounds, schools and hospitals, to ensure that all aspects of relevant health and safety law are being upheld.

You would most likely be a civil servant, working for the Field Operations Directorate of the Health and Safety Executive (HSE). In seeking to protect the welfare of the workforce and the general public, you would have the power to arrive at premises, unannounced, to examine equipment and machinery, manufacturing processes and working methods, and write up a full report. Local authorities are responsible for enforcement in offices, shops and other parts of the services sector.

If you find evidence of unsafe practice, you would make recommendations for change to the employer and you would have the sanction, in extreme cases, of issuing a prohibition order - closing the premises until the required improvements are made - or even taking the employer to court. You would work alone for much of the time, although you would be part of a small team of six to eight inspectors, and you would have a fair degree of freedom to organise your own work within the overall limits set by your principal inspector.

Opportunities for Training

The HSE training programme offers a clearly defined, two-year training period, including practical training on the job. You would attend short, in-house courses as well as studying for an NVQ/SVQ Level 5 in Occupational Health and Safety Regulation and in most cases a postgraduate diploma (PgDip) in Occupational Health.

Health and safety inspectors within local authorities usually undergo a similar period of training. Irrespective of the setting, all inspectors must attend frequent courses in order to update their knowledge on new developments in health and safety.

Requirements for Entry

Although it is not actually laid down as an educational requirement, you would in practice be expected to come into the profession with a degree or equivalent qualification. You should have completed a year or two of work experience.

The subject of your degree would not be crucial, although agricultural inspectors might be expected to have studied a related subject and other specialist inspectors might enter via industrial experience and professional qualification in an area such as engineering. Entry to a degree course would normally require two or three A level/Advanced Higher, three or four Higher or equivalent qualifications. A full driving licence would be essential.

Kind of Person

An interest in people's welfare would be important. This is a very responsible job and you would need to be confident and tough enough to back your own judgment in potentially awkward situations. Good communication skills would be vital (particularly in the realms of tact and diplomacy), as you would be dealing with a wide variety of people at all levels of employment, and you would need to write clear and detailed reports.

You might have to present your findings in a court of law. You would need to be able to assimilate large amounts of knowledge (some of it quite technical) and apply this in practical situations. You would need good powers of observation and would have to pay great attention to detail.

Broad Outlook

There is always a demand for health and safety inspectors, although the overall number employed by the Health and Safety Executive is not very large and there is fierce competition to fill vacancies, with approximately 3,000 applicants for 60 places in a typical year. You might like to specialise in one particular area or branch out into the field of policy making.

Inspectors are also employed by large organisations to advise on health and safety matters, while some experienced inspectors start up their own advisory consultancies or work on a freelance basis. Promotion can be gained into management positions.

Related Occupations

You might also consider: environmental health officer, operational researcher/work study officer, human resources (personnel) manager or trading standards officer.

Impact on Lifestyle

You would normally work a standard five-day week, but you should be prepared to put in extra hours in the evening or at the weekend in cases of emergency. As well as being involved in a fair amount of travel, you might have to move around the country in order to gain further experience and/or promotion. You would also have to be prepared to visit some rather unsavoury places - possibly cold, wet, dangerous or noisy - and sometimes wear protective clothing.

Earnings Potential

Salaries for trainee inspectors based in the HSE begin at £23,730, while salaries for HSE inspectors who have completed their training and have three to five years' experience is around £36,000. At senior levels, those with either increased responsibility or knowledge of a particular specialist area can earn up to £65,000. Annual increments are dependent upon performance.

Further Information

Health and Safety Executive, London SE1 9HS
Website: www.hse.gov.uk

British Safety Council, London W6 9RS
Website: www.britishsafetycouncil.co.uk

Department for Work and Pensions, London WC2N 6HT
Website: www.dwp.gov.uk/

Institution of Occupational Safety and Health, Leicestershire LE18 1NN
Website: www.iosh.co.uk

European Agency for Safety and Health at Work
Website: http://osha.europa.eu/fop/united-kingdom/en

Alternative/equivalent entrance requirements can include: ILC, IB, EB, NC/ND and many other similar international systems. For further details see the Equivalent Qualifications section in the Introduction.

Health Service Manager

What is Involved?

As a health service manager, you could work in the private or public sector, although you would be more likely to operate within the public National Health Service (NHS). Depending on your qualifications and experience, your post may be operational or based around policy-setting, planning or strategic development. Health service management is such a large and varied sector that your role could be that of an administrator running a doctor's surgery or that of a chief executive controlling a large hospital with a budget of many millions of pounds.

Opportunities for Training

It is possible to enter healthcare management at all the major stages: post-16, post-18 and post-college/university. Alternatively, you could enter after gaining experience in the voluntary or social care sectors. However, most managers are experienced healthcare professionals who move into managerial positions after achieving state registration in their specialised area. As a new graduate in England, you could join the NHS Future Leaders Management Training Scheme. Split into general, financial, informatics and human resources management, the scheme offers a two- to three-year structured training programme. If you already have at least four years' management experience and a good Honours degree, you can apply for the 18-month fast-track Gateway to Leadership programme. Scotland, Wales and Northern Ireland administer their own management training schemes.

Requirements for Entry

You could join the NHS at a clerical level without any formal qualifications and work your way up. For the NHS Future Leaders management training scheme, you would need a degree in any subject or an equivalent professional qualification in a health or management-related discipline. A good way of checking that you meet the requirements is to try the NHS online self-assessment questionnaire.

Kind of Person

You would need excellent communication skills, the ability to lead through example and to influence others through persuasion and negotiation. Other qualities listed by the NHS include: conceptual skills - seeing the implications of actions and decisions; analytical skills - using and interpreting data and facts; impact and influence - making informed decisions, justifying your position and persuading others; taking action - planning your work, setting priorities and dealing with problems in a flexible and proactive way; numerical skills - understanding and applying figures.

Broad Outlook

Entry to the NHS management training scheme is very competitive but successful completion should mark you out as a high flyer with considerable potential. The skills you gain could take you to a senior position in the NHS or on to other executive roles in the public and private sectors.

Related Occupations

You might also consider: civil service administrator, local government administrator, accountant or human resources/personnel manager. Alternatively, you could begin by qualifying as a nurse, radiographer, physiotherapist, speech and language therapist or other healthcare professional.

Impact on Lifestyle

Advances in medical technology, tough expenditure targets, a high political profile and rising public expectations mean that, at the higher levels, this can be a very demanding job. You may need to move around the country to broaden your experience and seek promotion.

Earnings Potential

As a management trainee, you should start on around £20,500, with the prospect of future earnings of £70,000 - £90,000 as an executive director or £120,000+ as a chief executive. If you are already working as a healthcare professional, you may be able to retain your existing salary while working through the management training programme. A project manager would currently earn from £24,831 to £33,436, a human resources team manager £29,789 to £39,273 and a professional manager (clinical) from £37,996 to £95,333. Additional allowances are paid for appointments in and around London, ranging from 20% of basic salary for Inner London, to 15% for Outer London and 5% for the London Fringe. Earnings in the private sector are generally likely to be higher.

Further Information

Institute of Healthcare Management, London SE1 7QZ
Website: www.ihm.org.uk

NHS Management Training
Website: www.futureleaders.nhs.uk

NHS Education for Scotland
Website: www.nes.scot.nhs.uk

National Leadership and Innovation Agency for Healthcare
Website: www.nliah.wales.nhs.uk

Management Training Scheme, NHS Northern Ireland
Website: www.beeches-mc.co.uk

Gateway to Leadership
Website: www.come2life.nhs.uk

Skills for Health
Website: www.skillsforhealth.org.uk

Alternative/equivalent entrance requirements can include: ILC, IB, EB, NC/ND and many other similar international systems. For further details see the Equivalent Qualifications section in the Introduction.

What is Involved?

As a homoeopath, you would be working in a branch of complementary medicine based on the 'like cures like' concept, in which minute doses of a medicine that could produce similar symptoms in a healthy person are used to stimulate the body's own natural healing powers. You would examine a patient's whole physical, emotional and social state and look closely at those aspects of their lifestyle, including diet, posture, exercise and relationships, which could be contributing to their symptoms. The idea is that you would develop a clear picture of your patients and would match your remedy to each individual, encouraging them to take a major role in helping themselves. You could choose to specialise in homoeopathic treatment of animals.

Opportunities for Training

There are several bodies offering different training routes for homoeopaths. The Society of Homoeopaths, for example, lists 18 training centres in the UK offering courses lasting three years full-time and four years part-time. The courses are structured in four main ways:

- Part-time courses - four years, usually meeting for 10-15 weekends each year or for a similar number of two-day blocks mid-week

- Part-time courses with initial correspondence course - four years, with the first one or two years available through a correspondence course. The clinical education aspect would make your physical presence essential in the later stages

- Full-time courses - three years, with attendance typically for three days each week, during three terms each year

- Degree courses - similar to diploma courses but with additional academic components, often in the wider field of health studies

All routes would take you to the same status as a licensed homoeopath. You could become a registered member by completing a course successfully, practising for at least a year and presenting cases for inspection by the society. The Faculty of Homoeopathy, on the other hand, promotes training at five centres but only if you are already a qualified healthcare professional, such as a doctor, dentist, vet, pharmacist, podiatrist or nurse.

Requirements for Entry

You would normally need five GCSE/S Grade passes A-C/1-3 and three A level/Advanced Higher, four Higher or equivalent qualifications, preferably including biology or human biology, chemistry and physics, for entry to a course accredited by the Society. However, life and work experience are as important and may be acceptable in place of examination passes.

Late entry is common, especially if you have already met the registration requirements of a conventional healthcare profession and wish to join the faculty as outlined above.

Kind of Person

You would need excellent interpersonal skills, particularly when it comes to listening and explaining. You should have a genuine desire to help people (or animals), be confident and emotionally stable yourself and able to treat your patients with objectivity. You would need to assess conditions, offer clear advice and be able to recognise when a patient needs referral to a conventional practitioner. As you are likely to be self-employed, you would need sufficient commercial awareness to run your own business.

Broad Outlook

Complementary medicine has expanded rapidly in the last twenty years and homoeopathy has steadily acquired respect and recognition by the NHS. You may work in private hospitals or clinics or in the NHS with patients recommended to you by their GPs.

Demand continues to increase, with opportunities throughout the UK.

Related Occupations

You may choose to qualify first as a conventional healthcare professional such as, doctor, dentist, vet, pharmacist, podiatrist, nurse or health visitor. Alternatively, you may wish to consider other specialisms in complementary medicine such as aromatherapist, osteopath, chiropractor, herbalist or naturopath.

Impact on Lifestyle

As most homoeopaths are self-employed, you could enjoy considerable flexibility both in the hours you choose to work and the places you work in. On the other hand, there are few promotion prospects, fluctuations in demand for treatment and the costs to consider of maintaining a therapy room and associated expenses.

You may find that patients are most keen to see you when they are not themselves at work, keeping you busy in the evening and at weekends.

Earnings Potential

Your income would depend on how many people you see and how much you charge. Earnings vary considerably, usually based on charges of between £40 and £250 per hour. Fees in London and the South East of England are likely to be higher than in most other parts of the UK. Many homoeopaths work part-time and may earn around £5,000 a year in the early stages, rising to around £30,000 when established.

Further Information

Society of Homoeopaths, Northampton, NN3 6WL
Website: www.homeopathy-soh.org

Homoeopathic Medical Association, Kent, DA12 5DZ
Website: www.the-hma.org

Alliance of Registered Homeopaths, East Sussex TN22 3PJ
Website: www.a-r-h.org

British Homeopathic Association/Faculty of Homeopathy, Luton LU1 3BE
Website: www.trusthomeopathy.org

Council of Organisations Registering Homeopaths, West Sussex RH15 9HR
Website: www.corh.org.uk

Faculty of Homoeopathy
Website: www.facultyofhomeopathy.org

Alternative/equivalent entrance requirements can include: ILC, IB, EB, NC/ND and many other similar international systems. For further details see the Equivalent Qualifications section in the Introduction.

Horticultural Manager

What is Involved?

There are two main branches of horticulture: commercial and amenity, sometimes referred to as production and non-production horticulture respectively.

As a commercial horticultural manager, you would be involved in the production for sale of fruit, vegetables, glasshouse crops, mushrooms, herbs, pot plants, shrubs, trees, bulbs and flowers. Your role as a manager would include deciding what to grow, bearing in mind the land available, local growing conditions and your knowledge of the market. You would also have to ensure that you recruit the right staff, buy the seeds, plants and other materials needed for the next crop cycle, keep detailed planting and cropping records, control your finances and deliver consistent product quality to your customers at competitive prices. All this would usually be in addition to the day-to-day practical necessities of planting, weeding, pruning, spraying, harvesting and so on.

As an amenity horticultural manager, you would be responsible for planning and maintaining large public parks, sports grounds, private estates and green spaces in towns and cities. Your role as a manager might include determining how to make your park or garden attractive and accessible, supervising the work of gardening staff, controlling the budget for park maintenance, publicising your amenity and keeping abreast of plants that are currently in vogue. You would also normally want to be actively involved with the practicalities of digging, sowing, lopping, grass-cutting and so on.

Opportunities for Training

There are many possible training routes, ranging from degree and postgraduate courses through specialist qualifications offered by the Royal Horticultural Society or the Royal Botanic Gardens to part-time National/Scottish Vocational Qualifications.

Degree courses in horticulture normally take three years full-time or four years if they include a 'sandwich' of industrial experience. They may specialise in commercial or amenity horticulture, so it is important to read prospectuses carefully before you apply. All courses would normally include the underlying science of horticulture, crop characteristics, growing techniques and marketing and finance. Higher national diploma (HND) courses cover similar ground at a more practical level and over a shorter period of time.

Requirements for Entry

For a degree course, you would normally need two or three A level/Advanced Higher, four Higher or equivalent qualifications in one or two sciences, especially chemistry and biology; for the HND route, one or two A level/Advanced Higher, two to three Higher or equivalent, would be required. For either route, your application should ideally be supported by periods of work experience in horticultural or agricultural organisations. There are no entry requirements for some of the specialist qualifications.

Kind of Person

You would need to be physically robust, very interested in the cultivation of plants, good at teamwork and willing put up with irregular hours depending on the seasons of the year and the weather. You would need a strong sense of priorities in meeting essential deadlines and a firm grasp of production costing, aided by good numeracy and book-keeping/accounting skills and a reasonable level of computer literacy. Communication skills would be essential in dealing with clients and suppliers and in clearly explaining your requirements to staff.

Broad Outlook

Opportunities are forecast to increase in commercial horticulture. Ever-growing technological demands are creating an ongoing requirement for higher-level skills in information and production technologies as well as the ability to understand and operate complex production systems. There is also a demand for business management and marketing abilities.

The amenity side is slightly less positive, with local authorities in particular cutting back staffing levels. Specialised skills associated with historic gardens, restoration and environmental conservation are, however, in increasing demand. In the economic gloom of spring 2009, the National Trust has published a survey report showing that parks and gardens are widely seen as the ideal antidote to recession, with 84% of those surveyed saying that the simple pleasures of a walk in the park or visiting a beautiful garden are important to them.

Related Occupations

You might also consider: landscape architect, forest manager, countryside conservation officer or countryside ranger/warden.

Impact on Lifestyle

You would normally work a theoretical 39-hour week but you might at times have to tailor your hours to fit the demands of particular growing seasons. Many people in horticulture like to start work early in the morning to make the most of daylight hours. Sports grounds and public gardens are often busiest at the weekend. In setting-up your own nursery or garden centre, enormous efforts and sacrifices would be essential, with often a seven-day week, in order to meet strong weekend demand.

Earnings Potential

As a junior manager, you would start at between £15,000 and £20,000, rising to £25,000 to £55,000 as a senior manager within a well-established company. The rewards for owner managers can be considerably greater.

Further Information

Lantra, Warwickshire CV8 2LG
Website: www.lantra.co.uk

Royal Botanic Garden, Kew, Richmond TW9 3AB
Website: www.rbgkew.org.uk

Royal Botanic Garden, Edinburgh EH3 5LR
Website: www.rbge.org.uk

Institute of Horticulture, London SW1X 8PS
Website: www.horticulture.org.uk

Royal Horticultural Society, Wisley GU23 6QB
Website: www.rhs.org.uk

Horticultural Development Company
Website: www.hdc.org.uk

Grow Careers
Website: www.growcareers.info

Alternative/equivalent entrance requirements can include: ILC, IB, EB, NC/ND and many other similar international systems. For further details see the Equivalent Qualifications section in the Introduction.

Hospitality/Hotel Manager

What is Involved?

Hotels vary enormously in size and scope but your job as a manager would include ensuring that the day-to-day running of the establishment is well organised and efficient and that guests enjoy using your services. You might have responsibility for accommodation, food and drink, conferences, special events and leisure facilities, hence the use in the business of the broader term hospitality. You could be in overall control of every department, with a number of assistants, or you might have to manage several of these responsibilities yourself, especially in a smaller hotel.

Opportunities for Training

There is no single training route for hospitality management and you do not always need academic qualifications. You may decide, for example, to gain experience at a lower level and work your way up, or you may enter the industry from an allied occupation such as human resources, accountancy or restaurant management. If, however, you want to obtain direct entry to a management trainee scheme, you would do well to consider a relevant higher national diploma (HND) or degree course.

The HND in Hospitality Management would take two or three years, while a similar degree would take three or four years to complete. Alternatively, you could consider the two-year professional certificate offered by the Institute of Hospitality. Look out also for foundation degrees, which are similar to HNDs covering the hospitality framework.

Requirements for Entry

To enter a hospitality/hotel management degree course, you would need two or three A level/Advanced Higher, three or four Higher or equivalent qualifications, together with a minimum of five GCSE/S Grade passes A-C/1-3. Entry to an HND course would require a minimum one A level/Advanced Higher, two Higher or equivalent qualification, together with four GCSE/S Grade passes A-C/1-3. It is vital to check each institution's entry requirements and it would help to obtain work experience before applying. (A relevant A level/Higher: hospitality/catering)

Kind of Person

You should be able to communicate effectively with other people, both staff and guests, and take a keen interest in their welfare and comfort. You would need to be tough, both physically and mentally, to cope with long hours and the need to be constantly available for decision making and problem solving. You should also be well versed in IT, with acute business awareness, good organisational skills and the ability to deal with financial matters. A smart appearance would be essential and knowledge of foreign languages would certainly be an asset.

Broad Outlook

Although competition for hospitality manager positions is intense, the industry usually has no shortage of opportunities on offer. Much importance is placed on experience and proven performance. Managers of small hotels can be promoted to jobs in larger or more prestigious establishments, or to responsible jobs in the administration of chains of hotels. Working for a hotel chain could lead to travel or work abroad. You may need to move several times to develop your career, while there is always the prospect of using your experience to set up your own guest house or hotel.

Related Occupations

You might also consider: events and conferences organiser, leisure services manager, marketing executive, personnel (human resources) manager, public relations officer, restaurant manager or travel and tourism clerk.

Impact on Lifestyle

As a hotel manager you would be expected to work long hours, including regular evening and weekend commitments. If you worked in a small hotel or owned your own establishment, you would probably have to accept that the work could sometimes even spread over 24 hours, with considerable implications for your family and social life. Accommodation is often provided as part of the job but that can make it difficult for you ever to be completely off duty.

Earnings Potential

There is a wide range of salaries, according to the size and type of hotel you would be working in and the level of management responsibility you achieve. Some managers can receive profits or performance bonuses, and there could be financial advantages to living in (although there could be obvious disadvantages as well). You might start as a trainee manager on about £16,000 to £22,000. This could rise to around £25,000 as a deputy manager and £60,000 to £100,000 plus for an experienced manager in a top international establishment.

Further Information

People 1st - Sector Skills Council for the Hospitality, Leisure, Travel and Tourism industries, Uxbridge UB8 1LH
Website: www.people1st.co.uk

Institute of Hospitality, Sutton SM1 1SH
Website: www.instituteofhospitality.org

Springboard, London WC2H 8LP
Website: www.springboarduk.org.uk

British Institute of Innkeeping, Camberley GU15 3PT
Website: www.bii.org.uk

British Hospitality Association, London WC2A 3BH
Website: www.bha.org.uk

Irish Hospitality Institute
Website: www.ihi.ie

Alternative/equivalent entrance requirements can include: ILC, IB, EB, NC/ND and many other similar international systems. For further details see the Equivalent Qualifications section in the Introduction.

Human Resources Manager

What is Involved?

Your job as a human resources (HR) or personnel manager would focus on getting the best from the people who work in your organisation, from selecting the right people in the first place to managing them effectively when they are in post. The exact nature of your work would depend on what your organisation does, whether it is in the private or public sector, how large it is and whether it has strong union representation.

However, common issues would include understanding what your organisation needs in terms of workforce skills and experience, planning future recruitment and training and devising policies for health and safety, equal opportunities, communication, training and development, pay and conditions of employment. You might also design procedures to measure performance, handle complaints, maintain discipline and keep employee records.

You could operate as a generalist across all of these areas or you could choose to specialise in a topic such as health and safety, employee relations or recruitment and selection.

Opportunities for Training

There is no single route into HR management but a degree or higher national diploma (HND) would be a good starting point. Any subject would be acceptable but business studies, law or psychology could be particularly relevant and may give some exemption from the professional qualifications awarded by the Chartered Institute of Personnel and Development (CIPD). Your goal, whether achieved by exemption or by full- or part-time study, would be Practitioner level qualification through the CIPD professional development scheme. Many large organisations also offer their own in-house training schemes.

Requirements for Entry

You would normally need two or three A level/Advanced Higher, three or four Higher or equivalent qualifications, together with five GCSE/S Grade passes A-C/1-3, for degree course entry. HND entry would require at least one A level/Advanced Higher, two Higher or equivalent qualifications, together with similar GCSE/S Grade passes.

Relevant experience is always regarded as important, and a postgraduate qualification could be useful.

Kind of Person

You should be genuinely interested in the way people work and behave. In order to succeed, you would have to be able to deal with many different situations in a fair and even-handed way, balancing the needs of each individual employee against the overall interests of the organisation. Tackling issues such as discipline or redundancy can be extremely stressful.

Excellent communication skills, both oral and written, would be necessary, together with willingness to work in a team, both as a leader and member. Tact, discretion and an understanding of the need for complete confidentiality when dealing with people's personal details would be essential.

Broad Outlook

Competition for the available vacancies, especially for inexperienced graduates, continues to be very keen. Indeed, some employers indicate that they have a higher percentage of applications for HR work than any other function.

All kinds of organisations employ HR professionals, including banks, local government, health services, further and higher education institutions, airlines, hotels, retail organisations and manufacturing industries. The nature of the HR profession has undergone some change during recent years, with movement away from staff welfare and administration-centred activities towards strategy and planning. HR departments are now expected to add value to the organisation they support.

You might start out as a trainee manager and work your way up the ladder in one organisation or move to a larger one with more scope. With sufficient experience, you might set up your own business, offering specialist recruitment, training or other services. You could have the opportunity to travel, if you work for a multi-national organisation.

Related Occupations

You might also consider: personal or careers adviser, occupational psychologist, office manager, or recruitment consultant.

Impact on Lifestyle

You would normally work the usual office hours from Monday to Friday, though you might have to work overtime at certain times, for interviewing or attending meetings. Weekend work would be unusual.

Earnings Potential

According to the annual pay survey conducted by the CIPD, the average HR salary across all sectors in autumn 2008 was £30,270. Rewards were highest in manufacturing and lowest in the voluntary sector. The average salary for a senior manager in HR is currently £45,000. Starting salaries paid to graduates entering HR traineeships immediately after a first degree are very similar to those entering other trainee posts. Graduates with relevant postgraduate qualifications or experience may be able to command slightly higher starting salaries.

Further Information

Chartered Institute of Personnel and Development, London SW19 1JQ
Website: www.cipd.co.uk

Recruitment and Employment Confederation
Website: www.rec.uk.com

Alternative/equivalent entrance requirements can include: ILC, IB, EB, NC/ND and many other similar international systems. For further details see the Equivalent Qualifications section in the Introduction.

Hydrographic Surveyor

What is Involved?

Working as a hydrographic or marine surveyor, you would be concerned with mapping the vast expanse of the earth's surface that is underwater. You might measure and chart the seabed or survey underwater for mineral resources, gas and oil deposits. You could get involved with land reclamation schemes, with dredging or with defining international boundaries. You might also survey ports, oceans, channels and inland waterways.

Another area in which you could become involved is the search for hazards to shipping, such as rocks or wrecks, strong currents and tides. You would be likely to use advanced technological equipment, including sonar scanning, to obtain information about the seabed and aerial or satellite photography for mapping and charting. In common with all measurement at sea, precise positioning is essential and you would use a range of systems, from lasers for short-range, very high accuracy work to global satellite navigation systems for positioning throughout the world's oceans.

Most of the processing and presentation of the data collected at sea is undertaken using computers. In many cases survey data can be processed on board ship, providing immediate access to the end product charts and maps. Certain types of survey data processing would require access to large computing resources and very elaborate processing software.

Opportunities for Training

For chartered membership of the Royal Institution of Chartered Surveyors (RICS), completion of an accredited degree or postgraduate qualification and a minimum of two years' planned training and experience are required for the Assessment of Professional Competence (APC). Graduates with non RICS-accredited degrees need to complete an additional period of training and experience to meet the requirements of the APC.

If you follow the Royal Navy entry route, training is available via basic and long hydrographic courses at the Royal Naval Hydrographic School. These courses are accredited by the International Hydrographic Organisation (IHO).

Requirements for Entry

You would normally need three A level/Advanced Higher, four Higher or equivalent qualifications to enter an accredited degree in a surveying discipline, together with five GCSE/S Grade passes A-C/1-3, including English and maths.

You would find it helpful to have a driving licence and RYA powerboat qualifications.

Kind of Person

You would need to be quite technically minded in order to operate and understand all the sophisticated equipment involved. The use of computers is also an important aspect of this work. You would need to be physically robust and able to cope with being at sea in all kinds of weather. You may be out on a boat for extended periods of time.

Whilst some of your time would be spent out on location, you would also need to be prepared to work in an office, usually with a computer, analysing data and writing up and explaining the results of your surveys. You are likely to be part of a team and at times this could be an international team of professionals. As you may be working in confined conditions on a boat for several days at a time, you would need to be tolerant of others.

Broad Outlook

Career opportunities are generally good in both the private and public sector, and should pick up again once the 2009 recession is over. Many of the opportunities in the private sector are associated with the offshore oil and gas industry, which is exploring ever-deeper waters for hydrocarbon reserves, and there are a number of specialist marine survey companies. Many of the companies and organisations concerned with marine survey operate on a worldwide basis and hence offer careers with considerable opportunity for overseas travel. The Royal Navy also employs quite a number of hydrographic surveyors as naval officers.

Related Occupations

You might be interested in another specialist career in surveying, such as mining or land surveyor, or in another career involving the sea, such as oceanographer or marine biologist.

Alternatively, you might consider a career as a Royal Navy/Royal Marines Officer, cartographer or meteorologist.

Impact on Lifestyle

You would need to be prepared to work at sea in hostile environments when the weather is rough, or even when it is extremely hot. You are likely to have to spend extended periods of time away from home, which could sometimes make family and social life difficult.

Earnings Potential

A typical graduate starting salary would be around £16,000, plus an allowance of £70 a day for each day spent offshore. In a full year, you would spend between 140 and 180 days at sea, earning an additional £9,000 - £12,000. The base salary for a party chief is around £40,000, with £100 per day for every day offshore, which is usually around 150 days per year, so earning potential could reach around £55,000. If you choose to join the Royal Navy as a hydrographic surveyor, your salary would be set by the normal officer pay scales. Sub-lieutenants currently receive £28,216 to £31,188, rising to £36,160 to £43,002 for lieutenants. Salaries rise significantly on further promotion and officers receive additional allowances for such things as flying, serving in submarines or being at sea. A Captain currently earns £77,545 to £85,268.

Further Information

Royal Institution of Chartered Surveyors, Coventry CV4 8JE
Website: www.rics.org

Society for Underwater Technology, London EC2R 5BJ
Website: www.sut.org.uk

International Federation of Hydrographic Societies, Plymouth PL4 7YP
Website: www.hydrographicsociety.org

International Hydrographic Organisation, BP 445, MC 98011 Monaco
Website: www.iho.shom.fr

Alternative/equivalent entrance requirements can include: ILC, IB, EB, NC/ND and many other similar international systems. For further details see the Equivalent Qualifications section in the Introduction.

Industrial Chemist

What is Involved?

As a newly qualified chemistry graduate, you could decide to work in such industries as chemicals and pharmaceuticals, food and drinks, oil refining or agricultural chemicals and polymers. Alternatively, you could become an analyst in the water industry, join one of the environmental protection agencies or enter the general graduate employment market.

You could go into research and development in industry. Research is normally carried out in teams with other scientists, seeking to discover new chemical entities such as a new enzyme, drug or a plastic. Development is more about turning research knowledge into commercially valuable products to meet customers' needs. This requires skills beyond chemical knowledge, such as marketing, economics, safety and management.

You could go into production management, ensuring that the manufacturing process is run efficiently and cost effectively, and that chemical plant operatives are given suitable leadership and that production schedules are maintained.

Alternatively, you could opt for UK or export sales or you could provide techno-commercial support for a range of your company's products. In most of these cases, your insight and understanding of chemistry would be of great advantage.

Opportunities for Training

Many universities have degree courses in chemistry, biochemistry, pharmacology and similar subjects and these usually take between three and four years of full-time study. It is also possible to read chemistry as a joint honours degree with a range of different subjects. For example, it might be useful to read chemistry and a foreign language, which could be beneficial for working on chemical exports, or perhaps chemistry and law for organising legal agreements to make sure new discoveries are protected by patent and are economically viable. You will see some degrees described as MChem or MSci. These are extended programmes that last four years, whilst BSc courses last three years. The first two years are usually identical to those of the Chemistry BSc course at the same institution. Students then take different routes in year 3 or 4.

Courses vary immensely, but a basic stipulation is that the additional year included in MChem/MSci courses must contain more advanced material than the BSc, rather than just a greater quantity. The extended programmes are designed to prepare students for direct entry into professional practice or provide a basis for progression to a PhD.

Requirements for Entry

A level/Advanced Higher or Higher qualifications in chemistry and ideally in maths or another science are likely to be required for entry to a chemistry degree. However, if you choose to combine chemistry with a very popular subject, such as law, you may need to obtain higher grades than are required for chemistry alone. It is possible for students without these qualifications to take a foundation course before starting their degree, either at a university or a college of further education. The entry requirements for the MChem/MSci courses are generally a little higher than those for the corresponding BSc courses.

Kind of Person

In order to be successful as a chemist, you would need to have a technically enquiring mind. You would want to know why chemical reactions occur and what the effects of these changes might be. Chemistry is an investigative science, so you would need to have an analytical approach to problem solving. You would be required to be extremely accurate in measuring and recording your results.

In addition to such scientific and intellectual abilities, you would need to communicate with a wide range of other people. You are likely to be working as part of a team and may find yourself supervising production workers, technicians or sales staff. You would need to communicate in technical or sales discussions and requests for further information and samples in written reports to your colleagues.

Broad Outlook

There are generally good prospects of employment for chemists, although all of industry is affected by the economic downturn in early 2009. As a graduating chemical scientist, you could choose to work in a field vital to the future, such as addressing climate change, providing energy, securing food and water or developing new technologies in healthcare, communication and security.

Should you decide that you want to continue with postgraduate study, it is sometimes possible to get your research funded by your company once you start. Depending on the type of career you choose to pursue, you could find yourself working in a chemical production plant, a laboratory or an office.

Chemistry graduates also work in professions such as financial services, where their proven skills - not only data analysis and numeracy but an understanding of the physical world and providing robust intellectual challenge - are highly valued and well rewarded.

Related Occupations

You might consider other careers in the field of chemistry, such as dietitian, pharmacologist, forensic scientist, biochemist, geochemist, microbiologist or pathologist.

Impact on Lifestyle

Although you are likely to work office hours mainly during the week, you may at times need to work late and in production management to cover shift work. You may have tight deadlines to meet, a report may be needed to brief a senior director or a piece of research may require you to work extra hours to complete it. In addition, you would be expected to keep up to date with the numerous developments in your subject, which would involve reading scientific and technical literature in your own time.

Earnings Potential

As a scientist who has recently graduated, you might expect to earn £21,000 to £30,000 initially, rising with experience to £30,000 to £45,000. This could increase to £60,000 and beyond in some industries when you start to take on managerial responsibilities.

Further Information

Royal Society of Chemistry, London W1J 0BA
Website: www.rsc.org

Society of Chemical Industry, London SW1X 8PS
Website: www.soci.org

Chemistry and Industry magazine, London WC2E 7HR
Website: www.chemind.org

SEMTA - Science, Engineering & Manufacturing Technologies Alliance, Watford WD18 0JT
Website: www.semta.org.uk

Alternative/equivalent entrance requirements can include: ILC, IB, EB, NC/ND and many other similar international systems. For further details see the Equivalent Qualifications section in the Introduction.

Industrial or Product Designer

What is Involved?

As an industrial or product designer, you could design almost any sort of product from toys, toasters, television sets or washing machines to bicycles, cars and even spacecraft. You would be given a design brief and would have to consider not only the aesthetic appeal of the product but also its viability in terms of cost, materials used, ease of manufacture, safety and marketability. You would quite often be working in a team of designers but, even if you were working alone, you would be in constant consultation with other professionals, such as engineers, manufacturers, computer experts and marketing managers, as well as with your client.

You would prepare plans (often computer-generated) with models for inspection and discussion, and would have to be prepared to modify them as necessary. You would normally be based in a design studio or workshop. Some industrial or product designers have extensive knowledge of engineering and manufacturing techniques, and many tend to concentrate on particular technical areas of design work.

You may also be involved in packaging design, specialising in finding ways of making products look attractive while you protect them until they are safely in the hands of the consumer.

Opportunities for Training

While it is not essential, the best-established training route is a degree or higher national diploma (HND) in a design-based subject. The usual way into this is via a foundation course in art and design (general year in Scotland). Universities and art colleges offer many relevant courses, with varying titles but usually classified under a heading such as 'three-dimensional design'.

Requirements for Entry

For entry to a one-year art foundation course in England or Wales, you would need a good portfolio of work, relevant A level/Advanced Higher, Higher or equivalent qualifications, together with five GCSE/S Grade passes A-C/1-3. You could then progress to your chosen HND or degree course. In Scotland, the first year of a four-year degree is broadly similar to the foundation course.

Some universities and colleges place a greater emphasis on the technological aspects of industrial/product design and may require passes in maths or physics, so you must check prospectuses very carefully. Equally, some admissions staff for art and design courses could accept you purely on the strength of an exceptionally good portfolio of work.

Kind of Person

You would need a high degree of artistic, creative talent but this would have to be matched with an appreciation of the various constraints, particularly those of attractive appearance and good function versus cost of production and materials. You should be able to persuade others of your point of view, but you should also be able to take criticism and suggestions for improvement, and be happy working as part of a team.

You should have a good grounding in maths and an understanding of basic engineering principles and properties of engineering materials. A high level of computer proficiency would be essential to take advantage of the design software tailor-made for this field. Poor colour vision would limit your potential in industrial/product design but would not necessarily be a complete barrier.

Broad Outlook

As manufacturers have become more conscious of the marketability of good design, so the demand for industrial and product designers has increased, particularly for those with specialised knowledge of technology. Some large companies have their own design departments, while others employ design consultancies. Experienced designers also work on a freelance basis, having set up their own businesses. UK industry has been severely affected by the economic downturn in early 2009 but recovery is predicted from 2010 onwards.

Related Occupations

You might also consider: architect, mechanical engineer, graphic designer, interior designer, television/theatre set or stage designer and film set designer.

Impact on Lifestyle

Designers employed by a company usually work normal office hours, but you would need to be prepared to work in the evenings and at the weekend if there were deadlines to be met. If you work as a freelance you would have to face the possibility of financial insecurity until you become established.

Earnings Potential

Earnings vary a great deal, depending on the nature of the work, location and type of employer. Trainees working in-house could start at around £20,000 to £25,000, with those in consultancies getting more. Experienced designers and freelancers can typically earn around £33,000 to £55,000, while a senior consultant could earn in excess of £70,000.

Further Information

Your Creative Future
Website: www.yourcreativefuture.org

Institution of Engineering Designers, Westbury BA13 3TA
Website: www.ied.org.uk

Design Council, London WC2E 7DL
Website: www.design-council.org.uk

Chartered Society of Designers, London SE1 3UW
Website: www.csd.org.uk

Design Business Association, London EC1V 9HX
Website: www.dba.org.uk

Alternative/equivalent entrance requirements can include: ILC, IB, EB, NC/ND and many other similar international systems. For further details see the Equivalent Qualifications section in the Introduction.

Insurance Broker

What is Involved?

As an insurance broker, you would be an independent expert helping clients decide what sort of insurance cover they need, where to look for it and how much they should pay for it. You would use your knowledge and experience to assess risks thoroughly and accurately, and to find the appropriate policy or policies. You must put the interests of your client first, even though it is the insurance companies who pay you commission for the business you put in their direction. The range of insurance products is expanding all the time and it is possible to insure virtually anything, from cars, ships and aeroplanes to pets, pianists' hands and even the risks associated with a country's politics. You would have to know who to contact among over 700 insurance companies. This could include Lloyd's, a London market consisting of individuals or syndicates offering insurance cover, but not all brokers are authorised to do this.

You would normally be able to deal instantly with straightforward cases, such as motor insurance, but more complex risks would involve you in compiling a detailed report to present to the underwriters. You would use the report to negotiate cover with the insurers and obtain a quotation for your client. For very large risks, such as ships and aircraft, the risk is spread among a number of insurers, with each underwriter accepting only a small percentage of the risk. You would then have to contact many different insurers to obtain full cover for your client.

Opportunities for Training

Training for insurance brokers is generally provided in-house, under the supervision of experienced staff. In order to gain promotion, you would find it useful to take examinations set by the British Insurance Brokers Association (BIBA) or the Chartered Insurance Institute (CII). The CII has recently launched the Broker Academy, which is essentially a 'one stop shop' training and development facility for insurance brokers, offering qualifications, learning and revision materials, access to face-to-face training, online learning and assessment facilities, membership of the CII and its dedicated Faculty of Broking. If you work for a Lloyd's brokers, you would have to sit the Lloyd's and London Market Introductory Test within 15 months of starting. The development of regulation under the Financial Services Authority has greatly increased the importance of appropriate qualifications and continuing professional development.

Requirements for Entry

Whilst there are no specific educational requirements, many organisations prefer graduates or A level/Advanced Higher, Higher or equivalent students for their trainee broker positions. However, a great deal of emphasis is placed on personal characteristics, making it possible to join a broking firm as a 16 year-old school leaver and progress to a post with quite considerable responsibility. For entry to a degree course, you would need two or three A level/Advanced Higher, three or four Higher or equivalent qualifications.

Kind of Person

You would need good communication skills, both oral and written, since you would be dealing with a wide variety of people and often explaining complex matters. The information in a report must be presented to the underwriter logically and clearly, with great attention to detail. When approaching underwriters, you would require confidence and good negotiating skills. Numeracy would also be important. Another essential quality would be honesty, together with discretion, since you could be dealing with confidential and sensitive issues. You would benefit from an outgoing personality and business flair. In particular, you would need an analytical mind and the ability to assimilate large amounts of information. Much of your work would be on computer, so good IT skills would be essential.

Broad Outlook

Opportunities for brokers are increasing in line with the overall growth of the insurance market. You could develop your career by taking on greater responsibility as your experience increases, or you might choose to specialise in particular insurance fields, such as marine and aviation or life and pension. You could eventually set up your own business or act as a consultant.

Related Occupations

You might also consider: insurance underwriter, accountant, actuary, loss adjuster, stockbroker, banking executive or financial adviser.

Impact on Lifestyle

Broking can be very demanding and at times frustrating when things go wrong and, despite hard work, a deal is lost. You would have to be persistent and calm even when underwriters are being uncooperative or clients impatient. You would usually work normal office hours during a five-day week, but you would need to be prepared to work in the evenings or at the weekend to meet particular clients.

Earnings Potential

You could expect to earn around £18,000 to £25,000 as a graduate trainee. Salaries may be performance-related and can vary significantly depending on the size and nature of the firm. With a few years' experience, you should be earning in the range £30,000 to £60,000. At the top end of the scale, a top broker in the City of London could earn well over £100,000. Additional benefits can include company car, private medical insurance and pension scheme, often non-contributory. The graduate training scheme at Lloyd's offers a starting salary of £26,000, rising to £30,000 on successful completion.

Further Information

Chartered Insurance Institute, London E18 2JP
Website: www.cii.co.uk

British Insurance Brokers Association, London EC3A 7NT
Website: www.biba.org.uk

Financial Services Authority, London E14 5HS
Website: www.fsa.gov.uk

Lloyd's of London, London EC3M 7HA
Website: www.lloyds.com

Alternative/equivalent entrance requirements can include: ILC, IB, EB, NC/ND and many other similar international systems. For further details see the Equivalent Qualifications section in the Introduction.

Insurance Underwriter

What is Involved?

As an insurance underwriter, you would work for one of the major insurance companies or Lloyd's of London, assessing the extent of any given risk and deciding whether your organisation should accept it and on what terms. You would have to determine the appropriate premium for the risk, setting an amount high enough to reflect the potential loss that could result but low enough to attract the business away from any competitors.

In order to carry out these tasks, you would have to build up a thorough understanding of the risks you handle. In the early stages of your career, the risks you underwrite would be those for which there are well-established statistical data and for which rating guides are available. However, with more complex or more unusual risks, you would rely on your skill and the experience to assess and rate risks appropriately.

You could specialise in, for example, large-scale risks in marine or aviation insurance or you could focus on smaller-scale but hugely valuable sectors such as motor car, life or property insurance. Lloyd's itself is an insurance marketplace, where underwriters and brokers meet to agree terms on what might be very straightforward or highly unusual or complicated risks.

Opportunities for Training

Training for insurance underwriters is usually in-house, under the supervision of experienced underwriters, or by moving from department to department to learn how premiums are charged, and claims checked and paid out. You can study by day release, evening classes or distance learning for the Associate examination of the Chartered Insurance Institute (CII), which is not essential but could be valuable when seeking promotion. If you work for a Lloyd's brokers, you would have to sit the Lloyd's and London Market Introductory Test within 15 months of starting. The development of regulation under the Financial Services Authority has greatly increased the importance of appropriate qualifications and continuing professional development.

Requirements for Entry

Most underwriting trainees are school and college leavers with two A level/Advanced Higher, three Higher or equivalent qualifications, but increasing numbers of graduates are joining the insurance industry. As there is no school or degree subject which would fully equip you for an underwriting career, employers are unlikely to specify any particular course of study. However, subjects such as business studies, economics, law, science and engineering can be helpful, as can some interest in biology, physiology or medical matters for life underwriting. Some universities offer degrees in insurance, business studies or financial services with modules giving partial exemption from the CII Associate examinations. You could, on the other hand, enter a clerical post in an underwriting department with GCSE/S Grade passes at A-C/1-3, including English and mathematics, and work your way up, with experience, training and study for further academic or vocational examinations, to an underwriting position.

Kind of Person

You would need to be decisive and capable of justifying your decisions with logical and sound argument. Given that you would often be dealing with extremely confidential information about an individual or organisation seeking insurance protection, you must be able to handle these details with the utmost discretion. For the more unusual risks, the ability to think and solve problems creatively could be extremely valuable. You would need a logical, analytical and retentive mind and the ability to take into account many different factors before making decisions. You would need to feel confident when dealing with numerical and statistical data, and would need to communicate clearly with actuaries, insurance technicians and other members of your team. It would be vital to be able to write up contracts covering the terms and conditions of your underwriting agreements.

Broad Outlook

The insurance industry is changing and many companies now have call centres and websites to deal with straightforward risks, cutting out some of the traditional work of the underwriting department. There are still, however, good career opportunities in over 700 insurance companies, including household name groups, small specialist insurers and Lloyd's of London.

Related Occupations

You might also consider: insurance broker, actuary, accountant, banking executive, loss adjuster, stockbroker, surveyor or financial adviser.

Impact on Lifestyle

Underwriting can be a very intense way of life, with a huge responsibility to get your quotations right and avoid unacceptable levels of loss. This calls for courage and confidence and the ability to accept worry and stress when large claims are made. Otherwise normal office hours should apply with very little disruption of your family and social life, although you may have to work unsocial hours if you need to be available to answer the more unusual call centre enquiries.

Earnings Potential

A typical starting salary for a graduate trainee would range from £20,000 to £25,000. This should increase with experience, increased responsibility and successful performance to £40,000 to £100,000. Professional underwriters at Lloyd's of London, who are different from 'underwriter members', can earn over £300,000.

Salaries can vary between employers and regions, and may include benefits such as subsidised mortgages and discounted insurance.

Further Information

Chartered Insurance Institute, London E18 2JP
Website: www.pathways.cii.co.uk

International Underwriting Association, London EC3R 7DD
Website: www.iua.co.uk

Lloyd's of London, London EC3M 7HA
Website: www.lloyds.com

Financial Services Authority, London E14 5HS
Website: www.fsa.gov.uk

Association of British Insurers, London EC2V 7HQ
Website: www.abi.org.uk

Institute of Risk Management
Website: www.theirm.org

Alternative/equivalent entrance requirements can include: ILC, IB, EB, NC/ND and many other similar international systems. For further details see the Equivalent Qualifications section in the Introduction.

Interior Designer

What is Involved?

Interiors are big business. As an interior designer, you could be hired to create a desirable ambiance in a pub, club or restaurant to attract big-spending customers. You could be working with a chain of DIY stores to market a new range of wallcoverings, paint effects or soft furnishings. You could be adding a touch of designer style to private homes. In work that is often highly technical, you would liaise with your clients (or their architects) about design schemes to take account of the purpose of the space involved, the needs of the people using it, their budgets and timescales. Your brief may include curtains, carpets, furniture, lighting, fixtures and fittings.

This would involve design sketches, mock-ups, samples of fabrics and colour schemes and sourcing items such as light fittings. You would then oversee your projects, which would involve liaising with contractors. Closely associated specialist design work is also available in film, television and theatre set design; exhibition and display design; and any other interior space, from an aeroplane to a department store. You could work freelance, for an interior design consultancy, within an architectural practice or for a large hotel or store group or furniture manufacturer.

Opportunities for Training

Most entrants have a formal qualification in art and design. There are numerous degree courses in interior design, which are available either as specialist courses or as an element in other art and design courses. There are also Higher National Certificates/Diplomas and postgraduate courses.

Requirements for Entry

To obtain entry to an art and design course, you would usually have completed a foundation course in art and design (general year in Scotland). The foundation courses in England and Wales take two years for students aged 16 with five GCSE/S Grade passes A-C/1-3, or one year for students aged 17, who might also have an A level/Advanced Higher, Higher or equivalent qualification in a relevant subject. In most cases, a good portfolio of your best artistic work is more important than exam passes. Progression to a degree course would then be via interview, at which your portfolio would be carefully examined by the staff and questions asked.

Kind of Person

As a designer you would not have as much of a free hand as you would as an artist. You would have to meet your clients' needs and wishes, which can sometimes be difficult for creative people, and you would need to be tactful and persuasive but be prepared to compromise when it is wise to do so. You would need good drawing skills and must be able to communicate your ideas to the client. Team working skills would also be important, together with a willingness to meet deadlines.

You would need to be practical as well as creative, have a technical understanding of the materials you are working with and the sensitivity to assess their suitability for use. You would need a keen interest in fashion and an eye for colour, texture and pattern.

Broad Outlook

Interior design is seen as a glamorous profession and demand for jobs outstrips supply, although there is always a place for good creative talent. Most entrants start as an assistant in order to learn the practical aspects of the work, which can be for the company sector or for private clients. Self-employment is an option for experienced and established designers.

Related Occupations

You might also consider: architect, artist/illustrator, fashion designer, graphic designer or industrial product designer.

Impact on Lifestyle

As an interior designer, you would be working both in a studio and on site as well as visiting clients in their homes. Designs have to be prepared, discussed and changed; furniture, fittings, fabrics and colour schemes have to be agreed...which is all very time consuming and calls for much patience, charm and diplomacy.

Although the work tends to be done in regular office hours, there are always deadlines to meet and contractors to engage and supervise, which could involve working evenings and weekends. Then there is the problem of finding time to assess work, produce written quotations, compete for prestigious contracts with hotels, restaurants, new housing estates, time-shares, property, land developments, holiday chalets and furnished flats, without which business would grind to a halt.

Earnings Potential

Earnings would vary widely, depending on your talent, your location and who you are working for. Starting as an assistant designer, you could expect to earn between £20,000 and £26,000. This should rise with experience to £30,000 to £70,000, and you could earn considerably more if you manage to make a name for yourself. Freelance designers charge anything from around £35 per hour upwards.

Further Information

British Interior Design Association, London SW10 0XE
Website: www.bida.org

Your creative future
Website: www.yourcreativefuture.org.uk

Chartered Society of Designers, London SE1 3GA
Website: www.csd.org.uk

Design Nation, London E1 1LA
Website: www.designnation.co.uk

Alternative/equivalent entrance requirements can include: ILC, IB, EB, NC/ND and many other similar international systems. For further details see the Equivalent Qualifications section in the Introduction.

What is Involved?

As an interpreter, you would be a highly skilled linguist specialising in the spoken word. You could be involved in simultaneous or consecutive interpreting, usually translating into your mother tongue from one or several other languages. Simultaneous interpreters generally work from a soundproof booth at multi-language conferences, listening to speeches through headphones and relaying an instant translation into a microphone; at smaller meetings, for one or two people and certain court proceedings, direct whispering may replace the technology. Consecutive interpreting occurs when the speaker pauses at intervals to allow you to translate what has been said into the target language. You might need to take notes in order not to forget anything that the speaker has said.

You would be expected to have a broad understanding of the cultural, technical, professional or practical issues under discussion, with the requisite vocabulary in the target language to convey what is necessary. Linguistic skills alone would not be enough.

Opportunities for Training

You would normally need a degree in interpreting or in languages followed by a postgraduate course. Your training should give you language laboratory practice in interpreting techniques, experience of technical vocabulary, note-taking and memorising exercises and practical work experience. You may be expected to work towards the National/Scottish Vocational Qualifications (N/SVQ) in interpreting and you would usually need to join and pass the examinations of professional organisations such as the International Association of Conference Interpreters (AIIC), the Chartered Institute of Linguists (IOL) and/or the Institute of Translation and Interpreting (ITI).

Requirements for Entry

You would need two or three A level/Advanced Higher or three or four Higher passes (or equivalent) for degree entry, including one or more foreign languages. At least a year of your course should be spent in another country. The N/SVQ route does not require any formal academic qualifications and could prove attractive if you have advanced linguistic skills, cultural awareness or technical knowledge but do not want to go to university. You would have to provide evidence of your ability in the form of recordings and simulated performance.

Kind of Person

Interpreting would require you to be alert, confident, capable of spontaneous reactions and articulate enough to communicate ideas rather than exact translations. You must have total mastery of your mother tongue and of one but preferably more foreign languages, together with a thorough knowledge of the institutions, culture, attitudes and practices in the countries where your languages are spoken, normally acquired through residence there. You would also need, for much of the work, a flair for technical subjects and a readiness to keep up to date with new developments. A good memory, the ability to concentrate for extended periods and a clear speaking voice would all be essential.

Broad Outlook

Starting up as an interpreter is not easy. The competition is intense and only the really skilled succeed. Few organisations employ full-time interpreters and, if they do, it is normally on short contracts. It is much more common for interpreters to be freelance. This would give you a great deal of freedom but it could take several years to establish your reputation and build up a network of contacts.

You could operate in international organisations such as the European Union, the United Nations and its agencies, NATO or aid agencies; you could work in law courts and conferences as well as in multinational corporations and companies. Public services employ interpreters for liaising with ethnic communities, or in legal work in court when a person does not understand the English language adequately.

Related Occupations

You might also consider: translator, teacher, secretary linguist, tour operator, journalist, solicitor or diplomat.

Impact on Lifestyle

The implications for your domestic life are considerable, since you would be expected to travel extensively, sometimes at short notice. Conferences often take place in the evenings or at weekends and the work can be extremely tiring. Given the unpredictable nature of the work, you may need to supplement your income with other activities, such as teaching or translating.

Earnings Potential

Typical starting salaries are usually in the range of £20,000 to £25,000. Freelance rates, currently around £250 to £700 per day, plus expenses, depend on location and level of demand for the languages. At a more senior level, the salary range goes up to £26,500 to £54,000. Senior positions often include management responsibility. The highest paid jobs tend to be outside Britain. It is often difficult to sustain a steady income from interpreting, unless employed by one organisation as a conference interpreter. Most interpreters are also involved in translation, teaching or training.

Further Information

Institute of Translation and Interpreting, Milton Keynes MK9 2EU
Website: www.iti.org.uk

CILT, the National Centre for Languages, London WC2N 4LB
Website: www.cilt.org.uk

Chartered Institute of Linguists, London SE1 1UN
Website: www.iol.org.uk

International Association of Conference Interpreters, CH-1202 Geneva, Switzerland
Website: www.aiic.net

European Commission Traineeships Office, B-1049 Brussels, Belgium
Website: http://ec.europa.eu/stages

European Commission Directorate General for Interpretation, B-1049 Brussels, Belgium
Website: http://scic.ec.europa.eu/europa/jcms/j_8/home

Alternative/equivalent entrance requirements can include: ILC, IB, EB, NC/ND and many other similar international systems. For further details see the Equivalent Qualifications section in the Introduction.

Investment Analyst

What is Involved?

As an investment analyst, you would study the performance of companies on the stock markets of the world in order to advise your clients or employers on good new investment opportunities, or to warn them of any growing weaknesses in performance, which could undermine their existing investments. You would initially work in a team under the supervision of a qualified senior analyst. Typically, you would study company accounts, relevant newspaper articles or announcements, information on the Internet and statistical data on past performance. You would also visit companies to discuss their profit forecasts and the development of their trading activities.

This information would then be collated and written up in report format for your clients or managers, with your recommendations to buy, hold or sell the stocks concerned. You could advise investment banks or fund managers of pension funds or you could deal directly with companies needing advice on investment, including stockbrokers who wish to help their own clients. The roles of investment analyst and fund manager are quite similar but the fund manager would make buying decisions after considering the research/advice of the investment analyst.

Opportunities for Training

Almost all entrants are graduates, often with a professional qualification in a related field and with experience of a specialist market sector. You would normally train on the job and would be expected - after at least six months' experience - to obtain the Investment Management Certificate (IMC), which is assessed by the CFA Society of the UK. The syllabus would cover financial regulations, investment in equities, commodities, currencies, accountancy, portfolio management, economics and taxation (including capital gains tax). The IMC is a requirement of the Financial Services Authority (FSA) but it is also in your employer's interest to encourage you to develop your skills and knowledge. You may decide to continue your training to obtain the Chartered Financial Analyst (CFA) qualification.

Requirements for Entry

You would normally need a degree or professional qualification for which typically two or three A level/Advanced Higher, three or four Higher or equivalent qualifications would be required in the first place. Postgraduate qualifications are not necessary, although some firms may favour applicants with an MBA. Pre-entry experience can be highly beneficial, for example work experience or vacation work in a financial institution.

Kind of Person

You would need to be strongly interested in the stock market and financial news and prepared to keep up to date with trends and developments. Numerical and statistical skills would be vital to deal with the huge amount of financial data you would have to analyse, summarise and assess for future trends. You would need reasonable IT skills, as you would be using computers for much of your work. Sound judgement would be essential, with the ability to see behind the headlines and not to be swept into recommending excessively speculative investments.

A grasp of international politics and geography would be necessary to recognise the possible impact of war, conflict or other economic and financial problems on levels of world trade. It would also be helpful to earn the trust and respect of managers whose company results you are analysing, given that your recommendations could have a huge impact on their future trading. You would be expected to dress smartly and conventionally.

Broad Outlook

The global economic crisis of 2009 is blamed by most commentators on reckless investment in high-risk sectors by professionals who should have known better. In its most pessimistic forecast, the International Labour Organisation estimates that the downturn could lead to the loss of 51 million jobs worldwide by the end of the year, and the world's richest countries are pumping trillions of dollars into the markets in an effort to pull the world economy out of recession. Consequently, investment analysis, normally one of the most sought-after careers by the most ambitious graduates, has suddenly lost most of its allure. There is even a fear that many talented junior level professionals will leave the financial services sector altogether. However, mindful of the predicted recovery in market confidence in 2010, many firms are looking to maintain their recruitment levels and continue to offer opportunities for young people.

Related Occupations

You might also consider: insurance underwriter, actuary, accountant, statistician, merchant banker, stockbroker or financial adviser.

Impact on Lifestyle

Although this is an office-based career, stock markets are global and financial news arrives on a 24-hour basis. This can mean working irregular hours at times and keeping in touch with clients and colleagues around the world by telephone, fax and email every day.

Your performance would be continuously assessed, so you would need to be alert to significant news and to move fast in channelling this to clients. You would need to travel abroad to assess the soundness of some overseas companies and to hold meetings with overseas clients. Considerable disruption of your social and family life could occur at times in keeping pace in this highly demanding career field.

Earnings Potential

A typical starting salary for an entry-level graduate position in London is £35,000, although the addition of guaranteed bonuses is almost certainly now a thing of the past. Earnings would be lower in other parts of the UK. After five to eight years, salaries would normally rise to £65,000 to £100,000. Typical salaries at senior levels can be £120,000 to £150,000.

Further Information

CFA Society of the UK, London EC2V 5AY
Website: www.uksip.org

London Stock Exchange, London, EC2N 1HP
Website: www.londonstockexchange.com

Securities and Investment Institute, London EC3R 8AQ
Website: www.sii.org.uk

London Investment Banking Association, London EC2R 8BT
Website: www.liba.org.uk

Financial Services Authority, London E14 5HS
Website: www.fsa.gov.uk

Alternative/equivalent entrance requirements can include: ILC, IB, EB, NC/ND and many other similar international systems. For further details see the Equivalent Qualifications section in the Introduction.

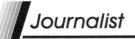

Journalist

What is Involved?

As a newspaper journalist working for a local or national newspaper you would gather information about relevant people, places, events, politics, sport or crime. If you are reporting a football match, for example, you would describe the match, interview the coaches and goal scorers to find their reactions to the game and do any research necessary before writing your 'copy'.

As a magazine journalist working for the ever-increasing number of magazines from the world of business, computing, sport, fashion, art and leisure, you would find many similarities with your newspaper journalist colleagues. You would, however, be less likely to spend your time chasing news stories and more likely to write specialised feature articles. The process of recording interviews, researching information, writing up copy and sub-editing is largely the same, although deadlines can be measured in weeks rather than minutes!

As a broadcast journalist working for national and local radio and television companies, you may benefit from earlier experience as a magazine or newspaper journalist. You would be involved in researching, writing and presenting programmes and you may also have to operate studio equipment.

As an agency journalist you would supply news, stories and photographs to magazines, newspapers and television stations.

Opportunities for Training

There is no standard entry route into journalism. The National Council for the Training of Journalists (NCTJ) regulates training for newspaper work, offering possibilities linked to 'direct entry' or 'pre-entry.' Direct entrants usually follow a two-year training contract, working as journalists while studying part-time; pre-entry means following an accredited full-time course before finding a job. If you are sure that you want to make a career in journalism, you can take an NCTJ-approved post-A level/Advanced Higher, Higher, degree or postgraduate course.

While the NCTJ is also involved with training for magazine journalism, you should be aware of courses accredited by the Periodicals Training Council. Training for broadcast journalism focuses rather more on ad hoc provision organised by individual companies, although there are courses accredited by the Broadcast Journalism Training Council.

Requirements for Entry

The majority of journalists enter as graduates but not necessarily with a degree in journalism. You need to have a strong command of English, good communication skills and to be interested in people and news. Previous experience can often prove to be as valuable as academic achievement. Being on the editorial staff of your school/college magazine or undergraduate newspaper can show this, as can working as a volunteer on your local hospital or campus radio station or work-shadowing a journalist. It is important to build up a portfolio of your writing and any published articles to give evidence of your work.

Kind of Person

You would need to be familiar with computers and modern methods of communication and to meet deadlines. If you struggle to hand in your homework on time, consider whether you're really likely to succeed in the heat of the newsroom! You would need to be self-confident and persistent, to relate well to others and to be willing to work hard, often at unsocial hours. Any interests you have such as sport, fashion or a hobby may also be useful.

Broad Outlook

Despite the number and range of newspapers and magazines, competition for jobs and promotion is fierce and success is achieved solely on merit. There are always more candidates than places available and a constant stream of fresh young graduates serves to remind even experienced journalists that they are only as good as their last story.

Some freelance journalists become well established before embarking on their own and selling articles to newspapers and magazines. Others only write the occasional article and are not dependent on journalism for their income.

Related Occupations

You may be interested in other jobs in this field such as press and information officer, advertising copywriter, public relations officer, media researcher.

Impact on Lifestyle

You may work irregular hours, often at weekends and evenings, and when a story breaks you have to be there. It is a job many people would like to do, and those in it have to be dedicated. Magazine journalists are more likely to work regular hours, although deadlines can still require staying on the job until your material is ready to print.

Earnings Potential

The starting salary for a trainee reporter on a local/regional paper may be as low as £12,000, but you can expect rises of £2,000 to £3,000 as you progress through the training period. Starting salaries for postgraduate trainees on a national paper are higher and range from £16,000 to £19,000. The average salary for all journalists is £23,000 but there is wide variation - from £17,500 for staff on regional papers to £40,000 on national newspapers. Salaries for senior reporters, feature writers and sub-editors on local/regional papers can range from £16,000 to £40,000, although salary levels are linked to the size and type of paper rather than level of the post. The range of salaries for senior editors on regional daily papers is £50,000 to £80,000. On the national papers, salaries are usually higher. Different rates apply for broadcast and magazine journalism.

Further Information

National Council for the Training of Journalists, Saffron Walden CB11 3PL
(Send a stamped addressed envelope)
Website: www.nctj.com

Periodicals Training Council, London WC2B 6JR
Website: www.ppa.co.uk

Broadcast Journalism Training Council, Lincolnshire PE10 0TH
Website: www.bjtc.org.uk

National Union of Journalists, London WC1X 8DP
Website: www.nuj.org.uk

Alternative/equivalent entrance requirements can include: ILC, IB, EB, NC/ND and many other similar international systems. For further details see the Equivalent Qualifications section in the Introduction.

Land/Geomatics Surveyor

What is Involved?

As a land/geomatics surveyor, you would be primarily concerned with the accurate measurement of the natural and built environment, the description and classification of features, the analysis and collation of relevant data and the presentation of data in forms required by users such as architects, civil engineers, property developers, planners, solicitors, environmentalists, geologists, archaeologists, geographers and map makers. Your work would be an essential preliminary to virtually all planning, property development and construction, major engineering and other projects relating to the natural environment and urban infrastructure.

You would learn about the traditional survey methods of triangulation and traversing, and would use them when appropriate, but you would come to rely more and more on satellite geodesy and computerised mapping and Geographic and Land Information Systems. Your detailed surveys would often be based on plotting from aerial photography and the use of sophisticated computer driven plotting equipment.

Opportunities for Training

Land surveying is part of the geomatics faculty of the Royal Institution of Chartered Surveyors (RICS). There are various routes to full RICS membership but the most likely in this case would to take an accredited degree or postgraduate course in land surveying or a similar subject with a land or geomatics option. Your course should introduce you to the major methods of measuring and recording data, from levels, theodolites and simple maps to techniques involving the modern technology outlined above. An introduction to positioning and navigation using the Global Positioning System (GPS) would also be given and a residential field course would ensure that you could apply your knowledge to real-world tasks. On completion of your accredited course, you would be eligible to move to the two-year RICS structured training stage with an employer, concluding with an interview known as the Assessment of Professional Competence (APC).

Postgraduate courses in more specialist areas are also available, including subjects such as geodetic surveying, environmental management and earth observation, hydroinformatics and geographical information science.

Requirements for Entry

You would normally need three A level/Advanced Higher, four Higher or equivalent qualifications to enter an accredited degree in a surveying discipline, together with five GCSE/S Grade passes at A-C/1-3, including English and maths.

Kind of Person

Your job would involve the interpretation and analysis of data, requiring you to be observant and comfortable with numerical work. There would be extensive use of computers, so you would need to be confident in using the relevant software packages. You would need to be well organised and ordered in your approach to work as you would be collecting data from a number of different sources, often at enormous expense. You would usually work as a member of a team, particularly on larger projects. This might involve you in managing and coordinating the work of members of your team. In addition to liaising with fellow professionals, you might have to explain quite complicated and technical information to clients with little previous knowledge. You would need to be physically fit, as you are likely to spend a lot of time out on site or in open countryside.

Broad Outlook

The demand for land surveyors depends to a great extent on developments in construction and civil engineering and it must be said that the picture in early 2009 is far from encouraging, as the housing market continues to weaken and demand for industrial, office, retail and leisure facilities declines considerably. Forecasts suggest, however, that construction will pick up again in 2010.

There are opportunities to work abroad, or to branch out into areas such as archaeological surveying. Land surveyors are employed in certain government departments, large construction and civil engineering companies and local authorities. There are also increasing opportunities to work in private practice or as an independent consultant.

Related Occupations

You might also consider: hydrographic, quantity, rural practice or building surveyor, town planner, architect, cartographer or civil engineer.

Impact on Lifestyle

This is unlikely to be a nine to five job. Whilst there would be times when you are based in an office with regular hours, you would also be expected to go out to sites. When on location, you could be in a remote area, which might take a long time to reach.

Earnings Potential

The average graduate salary is £24,000, rising to around £30,000 on reaching chartered status. With seniority and experience, you should be able to earn over £50,000 a year. Salaries in the commercial fields tend to be greater than those in the public sector and surveyors working in cities earn more than their rural counterparts.

Further Information

Royal Institution of Chartered Surveyors, Coventry CV4 8JE
Website: www.rics.org

Faculty of Architecture and Surveying, Chartered Institute of Building
Website: www.ciob.org.uk

Institution of Civil Engineering Surveyors, Cheshire M33 7PP
Website: www.ices.org.uk

Alternative/equivalent entrance requirements can include: ILC, IB, EB, NC/ND and many other similar international systems. For further details see the Equivalent Qualifications section in the Introduction.

Landscape Architect

What is Involved?

As a landscape architect, you would work to preserve the natural scenery and ecology of an area while creating attractive settings for construction projects such as housing developments, roads, parks, play areas, offices or industrial buildings. You might also work on preserving parts of the coastline, rescuing derelict factory sites or restoring disused pits and quarries. You could specialise in countryside issues or you could focus on urban projects. Whatever the particular project, you would hold discussions with your clients to find out what the job is about, make visits to the site to carry out surveys and then draw up plans and projected costs.

Once these have been agreed, you would visit the site from time to time to check that the landscaping work is progressing smoothly. In order to produce workable design solutions, you would need an understanding of topics such as civil engineering, surveying, geology, horticulture and earth-moving techniques. Indeed, you would usually be part of a team including architects, civil engineers, town planners and construction technicians.

Opportunities for Training

There are two possible routes to qualification: a degree in landscape architecture or postgraduate study after taking a degree in a related subject, such as architecture, horticulture or botany accredited by the Landscape Institute. The higher degree can be taken straight away or, on a full- or part-time basis, after you have spent some time in related work.

Being a full Member of the Landscape Institute (MLI) is the recognised professional qualification in landscape architecture. To achieve this chartered status, you must first attain associate membership by completing your first degree or postgraduate course and then gain at least two years' approved practical experience on the Pathway to Chartership before taking the Institute's professional practice examination.

Requirements for Entry

The minimum requirements for degree entry would normally be two A level/Advanced Higher, three Higher or equivalent qualifications, plus supporting GCSE/S Grade passes at A-C/1-3, which should include English and either maths or a science. The Landscape Institute regards subjects such as art, biology, botany and geography as particularly relevant, although you should check with university prospectuses to be sure of exact entry requirements. You would also be expected to show a portfolio of artwork, including landscape designs, to provide evidence of your creative potential. For entry to a postgraduate course, you would need a good first degree.

Kind of Person

You would need a genuine concern for the environment, an understanding of conservation issues, creative vision, good drawing ability and excellent communication skills. You would almost certainly use a computer for your design work and would need a reasonable standard of IT literacy. Good organisational and negotiating skills would be very important for working as part of a team. Inspecting construction sites can be demanding physically, so you would need to be reasonably fit.

Broad Outlook

Like the construction industry generally, landscape architecture has highs and lows reflecting the state of the national economy. In the recession at the start of 2009, building has slowed down considerably and with it opportunities for architects. When the economy picks up again, there should be more than enough work for everyone.

About half of all landscape architects work in private practice for small firms or consultancies, with the rest employed by large organisations such as major building companies, the forestry commission or local government.

There is a formal career structure in the public sector, with corresponding security, but many landscape architects prefer to move to private practice when they have some experience, in order to develop their ideas more freely.

Related Occupations

You might also consider: chartered surveyor, forest manager, horticultural manager, town planner, civil engineer or architect.

Impact on Lifestyle

You would need to be prepared to go on site in all weathers but you would usually spend less than a quarter of your time outdoors. Far more of your time would be taken up with deskwork and meetings. Landscape architects working in private practice are likely to spend quite a lot of time travelling, undertaking commissions around the country.

In the public sector, you would normally work a basic 37-hour week, whereas private practice is more likely to include long and irregular hours, often involving evening and weekend meetings with clients.

Earnings Potential

Your salary once you have graduated and are gaining professional experience is likely to be around £21,000 to £22,000. When you are fully qualified, this can rise to around £25,000 to £45,000, depending on the amount of work you can attract and the number of hours you are prepared to put in.

Further Information

Landscape Institute, London W1W 8QG
Website: www.landscapeinstitute.org

British Association of Landscape Industries, Warwickshire CV8 2LG
Website: www.bali.co.uk

Landscape Design Trust, Surrey RH1 1LY
Website: www.landscape.co.uk

Society of Garden Designers, Herefordshire HR9 5AX
Website: www.sgd.org.uk

Alternative/equivalent entrance requirements can include: ILC, IB, EB, NC/ND and many other similar international systems. For further details see the Equivalent Qualifications section in the Introduction.

Legal Executive

What is Involved?

As a legal executive in England and Wales (there is no direct equivalent in Scotland), you would be a qualified lawyer, working alongside solicitors and barristers, and would be involved in a specialist area of the law. For example you could choose to specialise in family law, probate, criminal or civil cases or conveyancing.

You may well find yourself as the main point of contact for clients concerned about their legal affairs and may have an administrative or managerial role within a legal practice. Your day-to-day work would be similar to that of many solicitors and you could continue to train, should you wish to do so, until you qualify as a solicitor.

Opportunities for Training

Most trainee legal executives work in a solicitor's office and study part-time to gain qualification as a Fellow of the Institute of Legal Executives (ILEX). The examinations are in two stages:

- **Part I**, set at A level standard, can either be studied 'academically'- in which case you sit four papers on aspects of law and the legal system - or 'vocationally', where you compile case studies and a portfolio before taking a test on elements of the legal system.

- **Part II**, set at degree standard, involves four specialist exams, three of which are in specialist areas of law and one in related legal procedure.

Having passed both levels, which usually takes three to four years, you are eligible to apply for Membership of ILEX. To achieve the Fellowship, you must have had at least five years' experience of working in a legal office. At least two of these years must be after becoming a member of ILEX.

Some law degrees incorporate ILEX Membership on graduation.

Requirements for Entry

You would need at least four GCSE/S Grade passes at A-C/1-3 or equivalent. These must include English and at least another two academic subjects. However, there is strong competition for places in legal practices, so you may need more that these minimum stated requirements. Many successful applicants are graduates, including Law graduates. You can make valuable contacts by doing holiday work in a solicitor's office or in a local court. This should show that you have a genuine interest in and knowledge of this sort of legal career.

Kind of Person

You would meet a wide range of people in your job, so you would need the ability to communicate effectively at all levels. You would be required to express yourself fluently and persuasively, both verbally and in writing, with a clear understanding of technical legal terms.

At times you would have to work under pressure and you would have to analyse and solve problems as and when they arise. It would be important that you have good attention to detail. You would be working in an office, possibly dealing with several different cases at the same time, and would need to have good organisational and administrative abilities.

Broad Outlook

Although it can be difficult to find a place in a legal practice, becoming a legal executive offers the chance to earn money at the same time as studying for a professional qualification. It also provides an alternative route to becoming a solicitor and you will already be an experienced lawyer by the time you qualify.

Once qualified as a Fellow, you could act as a Commissioner for Oaths and administer oaths, declarations and affidavits. You would also have extended rights of audience in the County Court and Magistrates Court and could become a fully qualified Legal Executive Advocate, allowing you to manage clients' cases from start to finish.

Related Occupations

You may be interested in other careers in the legal field such as barristers' clerk, solicitor or shorthand writer.

Impact on Lifestyle

Although you would be working in an office, your hours may at times be long when you have a deadline to meet or when there is a large volume of work to complete. In addition, you would need to be prepared to use your free time in the early years to study for your exams.

Earnings Potential

There is no recommended minimum salary for trainee legal executives but starting salaries typically range from £18,000 to £25,000. Your salary is likely to rise with experience and increasing responsibility to £25,000 to £50,000, and even more for a senior Fellow of ILEX. Salaries vary greatly depending on employer, location and type of work, with those in the city, particularly in commercial litigation, normally very high. This salary diversification looks set to continue increasing.

Many employers help out with course or examination fees while you are working for them.

Further Information

Institute of Legal Executives, Bedford MK42 7AB
Website: www.ilex.org.uk

Law Careers Net in association with the Law Society
Website: www.lawcareers.net

Alternative/equivalent entrance requirements can include: ILC, IB, EB, NC/ND and many other similar international systems. For further details see the Equivalent Qualifications section in the Introduction.

Leisure Services Manager

What is Involved?

As a leisure services manager, you would be responsible for the efficient operation of a leisure and sports complex or centre. You would ensure that the whole organisation runs smoothly on a day-to-day basis, that there are sufficient suitably-trained staff on the premises, that safety procedures are in place and that the customers are enjoying themselves. You would be in charge of the sports coaches and instructors, together with office, catering and maintenance staff, and you would be dealing with every aspect of running the centre, including financial control and book-keeping, the recruitment of staff and the organisation of timetables and special activities (such as school holiday courses and tournaments).

You might have some face-to-face involvement with customers, dealing with complaints and possibly doing some sports coaching yourself, if you are suitably qualified. Leisure and sports centres vary widely in size and scope, with the largest quite possibly encompassing indoor and outdoor facilities, such as swimming pools, gymnasia and fitness centres, badminton, squash, tennis and basketball courts, football and cricket pitches. They may also include dance floors, saunas, and children's activity centres, and there will almost always be cafés, usually with bars too. Some centres specialise in outdoor and adventure pursuits, such as rock-climbing and canoeing.

Opportunities for Training

While there are several possible routes to a responsible position of this kind, employers are increasingly looking to appoint graduates with professional qualifications and relevant experience. A good starting point would therefore be a degree in sports and leisure studies or sports science or a degree in another subject followed by a postgraduate course.

You could then study on a part-time basis for the certificates and diplomas of the Institute of Sport and Recreation Management or the Institute of Sport, Parks and Leisure. An alternative would be to start at a lower level and study part-time for degree and professional qualifications.

Requirements for Entry

Degree course entry would normally require two or three A level/Advanced Higher, three or four Higher or equivalent qualifications, together with five GCSE/S Grade passes at A-C/1-3. You should check course details carefully because they vary a great deal and may not contain the right elements for you. A talent for sport, and proven success, would be an advantage and the ability to drive could be useful. Lifeguard qualifications and first aid training might also be looked for.

Kind of Person

You should be well-motivated, organised and efficient, in order to make sure that the centre functions smoothly at all times. If there is a problem, you should be able to deal with it or delegate someone else to do so. You should have a good sense of business, in order to promote the centre and attract new customers, and you should be able to cope with financial matters where necessary.

Good communication skills, both verbal and written, would be extremely important and you should enjoy being both a leader and member of a team, so that your staff will respect you and enjoy working with you. You should also be enthusiastic and knowledgeable about sport, enjoying the contact with the customers, and helping them to enjoy what the centre has to offer.

Broad Outlook

Leisure and sports centres have proliferated over the past few years, all over the country, and are usually very popular. Opportunities to progress to senior management positions have generally kept pace with the growth in leisure provision. There is scope for managers to be promoted to bigger centres, or to take up administrative and managerial posts with local authorities in their sports and recreation departments.

Related Occupations

You might also consider: marketing manager, PE teacher, public relations officer, retail manager or sports coach.

Impact on Lifestyle

By the very nature of the industry, you would have to expect to work some weekends and in the evenings, as well as normal office hours. Usually a rota would be worked, in order to share out the unsocial hours. You should also be prepared to work additional hours whenever necessary. You may have to move around the country to find a new post as you develop your career.

Earnings Potential

Salaries vary widely, according to the size and location of the centre (with higher pay in London), and between the public and private sector. There are national pay scales for those employed by local authorities. In general, starting salaries range from £15,000 to £27,000, rising with promotion and increased responsibility to around £29,000 to £43,000.

Further Information

Institute of Sport and Recreation Management, Loughborough LE11 3TU
Website: www.isrm.co.uk

Institute for Sport, Parks and Leisure, Reading RG8 9NE
Website: www.ispal.org.uk

Central Council for Physical Recreation, London SW1P 1DE
Website: www.ccpr.org.uk

SkillsActive - Sector Skills Council for Active Leisure and Learning, London WC1A 1PX
Website: www.skillsactive.com

Fitness Industry Association, London WC1A 1PX
Website: www.fia.org.uk

Alternative/equivalent entrance requirements can include: ILC, IB, EB, NC/ND and many other similar international systems. For further details see the Equivalent Qualifications section in the Introduction.

What is Involved?

As a librarian, you might just as likely be known as an information manager or scientist, since the management, storage, retrieval and presentation of information would be at the core of your job, and the amount and variety of information, both in content and form, would be absolutely huge. Gone are the days of the stereotypical librarian, surrounded by mounds of dusty or dog-eared volumes, fussily telling readers to "shush"! Books, periodicals and printed catalogues are still of vital importance but information now comes via a great many other media, including the internet, CD-ROM, video and DVD, making your work as a librarian increasingly diverse.

You might be based in a public library, with plenty of contact with readers and responsibility for a wide variety of topics; you might specialise in a particular field (possibly medical or legal) and work for a learned or professional organisation; you might like the idea of working in an academic library in a university or other institution of higher education.

Whatever type of library you chose, the basic principles of your work would be the same: to make sure that your acquisitions are up to date and meet the needs of your clients; to organise the material in the most accessible way; to help users find the information they require, if necessary researching and acquiring new material for them. You might also, in a public library, organise events to promote the library and encourage new readers.

Opportunities for Training

A pre-entry postgraduate qualification accredited by the Chartered Institute of Library and Information Professionals (CILIP) is essential. A postgraduate diploma or MA/MSc in librarianship, information science, or information management is required unless your first degree is in librarianship or information studies. Some universities will take experienced library professionals without a degree on to their postgraduate courses after an interview or enter you on to a postgraduate diploma course. Early application for postgraduate courses is advised.

In order to qualify for chartered membership of CILIP, you must undertake further training as part of a continuing professional development (CPD) programme, and demonstrate evidence of appropriate skills gained through professional practice. Most members gain chartered membership two or three years after graduating.

Requirements for Entry

The minimum entry requirement for undergraduate degree courses is two A level/Advanced Higher, three Higher or equivalent qualifications, together with five GCSE/S Grade passes A-C/1-3, though in practice many courses will be looking for more than this. The courses usually take three or four years full-time or four or five years part-time. Postgraduate courses take one year full-time or two or three years part-time. Up to one year of library experience is normally required for entry to postgraduate courses.

Kind of Person

You should have excellent communication skills, since you would be dealing with a wide variety of people and would need to understand what they want and how to direct them to the information they require. In any library, a high level of computer literacy would be important, together with a methodical approach and excellent record keeping. Wide-ranging general knowledge and active intellectual curiosity would be clear assets in this type of work, together with specialised knowledge if you are working in an academic library.

*B*road Outlook

As a librarian/information professional, you would be at the heart of the information revolution. This does not necessarily indicate a huge shortage of suitably qualified people but it does acknowledge that library work is changing rapidly. Indeed, your career development may depend on how willing you are to embrace new methods of storing and accessing information and to move between different employment sectors in order to broaden your experience. There is a particular shortage of librarians with scientific or technical backgrounds.

*R*elated Occupations

If you like the sound of librarianship/information management, you might also be interested in: archivist, museum curator, or teacher.

*I*mpact on Lifestyle

Your working hours as a librarian would depend very much on where you are based. You might well have to work on a shift basis, including evenings and weekends, particularly in the public library service or in university libraries. On the other hand, you might have a term-time only contract in a school library. There is considerable potential for part-time working or job-sharing. You may have to move around the country to develop your career.

*E*arnings Potential

Earnings vary massively from job to job and you are advised to consult CILIP for detailed salary guides. In public libraries, for example, the current salary scale for a paraprofessional is £15,990 to £18,100, rising to £19,145 to £23,300 for a newly qualified librarian. The minimum rate for a chartered librarian is £23,300, an assistant head £33,000 and head librarian £47,000.

*F*urther Information

Chartered Institute of Library and Information Professionals, London WC1E 7AE
Website: www.cilip.org.uk

Society of College, National and University Libraries (SCONUL)
Website: www.sconul.ac.uk

Association for Information Management (Aslib), London EC2A 4PS
Website: www.aslib.co.uk

Alternative/equivalent entrance requirements can include: ILC, IB, EB, NC/ND and many other similar international systems. For further details see the Equivalent Qualifications section in the Introduction.

Licensed Conveyancer

What is Involved?

As a licensed conveyancer, you would be a specialist property lawyer, trained and qualified in all aspects of the law dealing with property transfer. You could act for buyers, sellers and lenders in the process of transferring the ownership of a house, flat, commercial property or piece of land from one person to another, otherwise known as conveyancing.

Your work would be office-based and would involve conducting searches into the ownership of properties, their leasehold or freehold status, likely planning changes, rights of way, checking the new owner's liability for unsound building structures and repairs, planned changes to roads and highways and local factory and property developments. You might work for a licensed conveyancer, solicitor, local authority, bank or building society, provided that an appropriately qualified conveyancer or solicitor is head of the legal department.

Opportunities for Training

In order to qualify, you would need to work for at least two years in a legal environment, gaining practical experience of conveyancing. At the same time, you would have to pass the foundation and final examinations of the Council for Licensed Conveyancers (CLC). You could study for these by part-time attendance at a college or university or through distance learning. The topics covered would include all aspects of conveyancing law and practice, law of contract, land law, landlord and tenant agreements and accounts.

Having successfully completed the examinations and practical training, you would be eligible to apply for a limited licence, allowing you to offer conveyancing services through your employer. After a minimum period of three years at this level, you could apply for a full licence and become a partner in a firm or even set up your own business as a sole practitioner.

Requirements for Entry

You would need to have at least four GCSE/S Grade passes A-C/1-3 or equivalent which must include English and three other approved subjects. However, many applicants have A level/Advanced Higher, Higher or equivalent qualifications as well. A degree in law would give you exemption from many of the qualifying examinations. Most trainees in Scotland have a degree in law or a diploma/certificate in legal studies.

Kind of Person

You would need to be well organised in order to deal efficiently with the large amount of paperwork involved. Attention to detail would be important to avoid potentially costly errors in the documents you are preparing. At times these documents could be quite complex, so you would need to have the patience and perseverance necessary to work your way through them. In addition, you would need good communication skills to explain legal matters to your clients. If you establish yourself as an independent practitioner, you would need the relevant commercial skills to run your own business. The CLC will not approve your licence until it is satisfied that you are a 'fit and proper person' to practise as a licensed conveyancer.

Broad Outlook

This is a relatively new profession, which started in 1987 after the law was changed to end the effective conveyancing monopoly held by solicitors. The number of practising conveyancers is now growing and the qualification is becoming increasingly sought after, both by people wishing to practise on their own account and by employers responsible for providing legal services.

The housing market has suffered a devastating year between April 2008 and March 2009, with a massive drop in sales, widespread redundancies, falling house prices and potential buyers finding great difficulty in securing mortgage finance. For a number of years before that, however, the market had been extremely buoyant and all the indicators suggest that it will be again in the near future. If you pursue a career in conveyancing, you must accept that this is a field that fluctuates and that your prospects and your pay will rise or fall in relation to the volume of property transfers.

Related Occupations

You might also consider: legal executive, solicitor, civil service administrator, accountant or insurance underwriter or broker.

Impact on Lifestyle

You would be working office hours but may well need to work into the evenings and at weekends to meet deadlines. This would be particularly true if you were trying to establish a business and develop your own customer base. You might need to offer a faster, cheaper, more efficient service in order to entice clients away from traditional providers of conveyancing services. The initial training can be expensive and you may wish to seek financial support from your employer to help you through this phase of your professional development.

Earnings Potential

In general, salaries for trainees without experience tend to be around £15,000 to £20,000, while those for qualified licensed conveyancers with three years' experience range from £30,000 to £40,000. Employed conveyancers may be salaried or paid on a commission basis. A partner or owner of a conveyancing firm could earn around £60,000.

Further Information

Council for Licensed Conveyancers, Chelmsford CM1 1QG
Website: www.conveyancers.gov.uk

Alternative/equivalent entrance requirements can include: ILC, IB, EB, NC/ND and many other similar international systems. For further details see the Equivalent Qualifications section in the Introduction.

Local Government Administrator

What is Involved?

As a local government administrator, you would be part of a huge workforce of some two and a half million people employed by a network of unitary authorities, county and district councils and London Boroughs. Your work would address the needs, conflicts and concerns of the local population in a variety of services ranging from education, leisure and environmental protection to trading standards, social services and waste collection. You could be engaged in a range of management challenges relating to any one of these services, working alongside specialist professionals such as architects, surveyors, social workers, teachers and environmental health officers.

Local authorities are led by elected councillors and you would have to implement their policies. You might advise on the initial decision-making process and you would certainly be involved in setting up procedures to carry out decisions, manage systems efficiently and ensure that public money is being spent wisely. You would be expected to report back to councillors on a regular basis. You might work from a large public building such as a county hall or from a smaller office in the area covered by your authority.

Opportunities for Training

There are several different training routes. You could, for example, join as a clerical or administrative assistant and work your way up to administrator level by achieving a relevant National or Scottish Vocational Qualification (N/SVQ). Alternatively, you could take a degree in any subject and apply for the National Graduate Development Programme (NGDP), which is specifically designed to create a new generation of managers with the ability to take on senior roles.

Though recruited at a national level, you would join a local authority and would spend two years there, taking on strategic project work, obtaining a postgraduate management qualification and participating in short-term placements with other public and private sector partners. As you progress through the programme, you would gain the capabilities and experience to make an impact on the direction local government might take in the future.

Requirements for Entry

The NGDP aims to attract high calibre graduates with a wide range of abilities and knowledge. You would therefore need at least an upper second class honours degree in any subject. There are no formal requirements for the N/SVQ route, although most employers would stipulate A level/Advanced Higher, Higher or equivalent qualifications.

Kind of Person

According to the NGDP, you would need to demonstrate the following range of skills and personal characteristics to respond to the challenges of local government administration: teamwork - using your skills to complement others and sharing your talents to achieve a common goal; leadership - inspiring, directing and influencing staff at every level with enthusiasm, energy and assertiveness; analysis - identifying, analysing and interpreting relevant information from a range of sources to develop well-informed solutions; communication - talking, writing and presenting your ideas clearly and logically; organisation - managing your time and priorities to deliver to deadline-driven objectives; IT awareness - understanding the benefits and pitfalls of computer applications within local government; motivation - personal and career drive to achieve success through continued learning, perseverance and proactivity.

Broad Outlook

You might be expected to move around the country to broaden your experience as you seek to develop your career. Administrators are needed in every department of every local authority and you should be able to progress to middle or senior management if you have the necessary talent, ambition and commitment.

Many traditional local government services have been privatised or contracted out in recent years, leading to increased opportunities for switching between the public and private sectors. Once you have gained sufficient experience, you could set up your own consultancy specialising in areas such as drawing up service specifications, negotiating contracts and monitoring contractor performance.

Related Occupations

You might also consider: civil service administrator, health service manager, human resources/personnel manager or chartered secretary.

Impact on Lifestyle

You would normally work a fairly standard 37-hour week, Monday to Friday, although you may be expected to attend some evening meetings. Local government employers often make provision for very flexible working patterns, including flexitime, job sharing and term-time only contracts.

Earnings Potential

As a graduate recruit to the NGDP, you would receive a starting salary of £22,122 or £25,309 in London. If you start as an administrative assistant, you would be paid on a scale ranging from around £12,500 to £19,500. Your entry point would depend on such factors as the grade of the job and your level of responsibility.

Further Information

Local Government Talent
Website: www.lgtalent.com

National Graduate Development Programme, Newbury RG14 1AF
Website: www.ngdp.co.uk

Institute of Administrative Management, London WC1V 6DX
Website: www.instam.org

Convention of Scottish Local Authorities, Edinburgh EH12 5XZ
Website: www.cosla.gov.uk

Alternative/equivalent entrance requirements can include: ILC, IB, EB, NC/ND and many other similar international systems. For further details see the Equivalent Qualifications section in the Introduction.

Logistics Manager

What is Involved?

As a logistics manager, you would specialise in organising and improving the supply chain, the complex sequence of events and decisions which connects sourcing raw materials with manufacturing and the end consumer. You may work for a large organisation, such as a manufacturer or retail company, aiming to get the right quantity of a product to the right place, at the right time, in the right condition and at an acceptable cost.

You might be responsible for the smooth operation of a manufacturing process or for managing a distribution centre. Equally, you may plan a new supply strategy or be involved in production scheduling or vehicle routing. Getting the supply chain exactly right is vital, as late deliveries, over-ordering of stock or miscalculating delivery times could cost your company their competitive edge. You would aim to make things happen 'just-in-time', which means being involved with buying, manufacturing, movement of goods by say road or rail, warehousing and general distribution. All of these areas are inter-dependent and you would have to co-ordinate them efficiently, making considerable use of IT to process data.

Opportunities for Training

Entry into the industry is usually via a graduate training scheme. There are industrial placements available both for sandwich course students and also summer internships for undergraduates. Once in employment, you would receive in-house training and have the opportunity to study for a professional qualification in logistics.

The Chartered Institute of Logistics and Transport offers professional qualifications at junior, middle and senior management levels, with courses covering the development of general management skills, key personal abilities, professional standards, road freight regulations, operations and administration, transport economics, inventory management, movement of people, government transport policy and resource management. Companies may offer full-or part-time training or distance learning, including postgraduate study to MSc level.

Requirements for Entry

The minimum requirements for degree course entry would be two or more A level/Advanced Higher, three Higher or equivalent qualifications, together with five GCSE/S Grade passes A-C/1-3 including English and maths. There are some degree courses in logistics management but many employers would accept a good quality degree in other subjects.

Kind of Person

To manage, co-ordinate and improve the total supply chain demands high-level managerial skills and the capacity to play a key part in meeting your company's longer-term strategic objectives. You would need to be numerate and able to solve problems, think on your feet and manage people. The ability to use IT packages and electronic communication methods would be vital, not least because, with the growing use of Internet shopping, the supply chain is at the heart of developments in telecommunications and e-commerce. Foreign language skills would be a great advantage, since you could be in contact with suppliers or buyers all over the world.

Broad Outlook

Career opportunities in logistics continue to grow. Even during downturns in the business cycle, when companies are cutting costs, the demand for able and experienced supply chain managers tends to remain high. You could expect to achieve managerial level after about five years and could go on to be a director. There should be many opportunities to move to other companies wishing to develop their logistics expertise or you could consider setting up your own consultancy business.

Environmental concerns are creating new areas of opportunity. For example, the supply chain no longer ends with the consumer but includes consideration of how goods can be recycled; you might be involved in ensuring that a distribution centre is energy efficient or in minimising the pollution impact of a large fleet of lorries.

Related Occupations

You might also consider: marketing manager, shipbroker or freight forwarder.

Impact on Lifestyle

As this job is all about deadlines, you would be expected to work extra hours when the occasion demands, especially during emergencies such as transport delays. Logistics management often operates 24 hours a day, seven days a week. It could make major demands on your time, especially if you are in regular contact with people living on the other side of the world. Your hours of work could be long and irregular and you may be expected to travel extensively.

Earnings Potential

The range of typical starting salaries for new graduates is £18,000 to £27,000. Larger companies may pay more, especially on completion of training. It is common for graduates to double their starting salary after five years. On promotion to middle to senior management level, salaries range from £45,000 to £120,000. The Chartered Institute of Logistics and Transport website lists current vacancies together with details of remuneration offered.

Further Information

Chartered Institute of Logistics and Transport (UK), Northants NN17 4XQ
Website: www.ciltuk.org.uk

Alternative/equivalent entrance requirements can include: ILC, IB, EB, NC/ND and many other similar international systems. For further details see the Equivalent Qualifications section in the Introduction.

Management Consultant

What is Involved?

As a management consultant, your job would be to help companies and organisations improve their success rate by investigating their current structure and work practices, searching out any weaknesses and suggesting or implementing appropriate remedies. This would involve in-depth research, including the consideration of staffing, marketing strategies, growth potential, financial controls and the strength of the competition where appropriate.

In a time of technological change, as now, you might also be called upon to advise on and often oversee the implementation of new methods of working, bearing in mind the implications this would have on existing staffing and traditional work patterns.

Opportunities for Training

There is no single route of training to become a management consultant. Many practitioners come into the work after successful management experience in industry or commerce and, quite often, with a postgraduate qualification such as the MBA (Master of Business Administration).

However, some very large management consultancies do recruit recent graduates and give them intensive in-house training. You can become a member of the Institute of Business Consulting, the professional body which regulates standards of qualifications and competence.

Requirements for Entry

Although there is no educational requirement actually laid down for entry into the profession, it is virtually all graduate. The subject of your first degree could be drawn from a wide variety, followed by management training. There are, however, plenty of degrees in management and related fields or a combination of, say, a modern language and management/business, financial or engineering studies, which could provide a good introduction.

If you like the idea of studying for a degree in management, you should look very carefully at the subjects required at A level/Advanced Higher, Higher or equivalent for entry. Some courses might specify maths beyond GCSE/S Grade levels.

Kind of Person

You would need excellent communication skills, both spoken and written, as you would be dealing with a wide variety of people, at all levels of seniority, and would have to write clear, cogent reports on your findings and recommendations. Some of these would not necessarily be very popular, and you would need tact, resilience and understanding to deal with this. You would almost certainly be working as a member of a team, but should also have considerable independence of mind and the confidence to make decisions based on your own judgment.

You should enjoy problem solving and analysing situations and you should have plenty of stamina, both physical and emotional, as you might be working long hours in order to meet deadlines and you would be making far-reaching decisions. You should be able to work comfortably with a variety of IT systems.

Broad Outlook

Given the ever-increasing pace of change, management consultants often find it necessary or desirable to specialise in different aspects of the work, such as finance, marketing or IT, or in particular types of organisation, such as manufacturing, commercial sales/exporting, retailing or even charities. Competition for places in the best-known management consultancies is very great but, if you make the grade, the potential for promotion is good, particularly with the growth of multi-national companies, and increasing competition and mergers. Some experienced consultants set up their own agencies. The UK consulting market is the largest outside the US, with a current value of around £8bn.

In common with most other sectors, management consultancy is facing tough trading conditions in the economic downturn of 2009. While not all current practitioners will emerge from the present crisis unscathed, career prospects look much brighter from 2010 onwards.

Related Occupations

If you think you have the skills and qualities to be a management consultant, you might also like to consider: accountant; economist; information technology specialist; operational research/work study specialist; human resources (personnel) manager; recruitment consultant.

Impact on Lifestyle

Management consultants are generally called in to do a particular job, and are given a budget and a timescale. This means that you would have to be prepared to work long hours, possibly at the weekend, in order to fulfil your contract. You could also be expected to travel anywhere in the world.

If you were employed by a firm of consultants, your income would be steady but, if you were on a fixed-term contract, you might have to face a certain amount of insecurity from job to job. You would also have to be sure that you could handle the knowledge that your recommendations, based on your professional judgment, could result in people facing unemployment.

Earnings Potential

Earnings vary a great deal but are generally well above average for graduates, depending upon the size and nature of the contract. For senior management consultants the rewards can be very high. As with many competitive professions, it is getting the first job that can be the hardest. Typically, a new graduate would receive a base salary of £25,000 to £35,000, depending on the type of consulting. On progression to a more senior level, the pay rise percentages become considerably higher, ranging from £50,000 with a few years' experience to £250,000 at partner or director level.

Further Information

Institute of Business Consulting, London EC1R 0EQ
Website: www.ibconsulting.org.uk

Management Consultancies Association, London WC2N 5DS
Website: www.mca.org.uk

International Council of Management Consulting Institutes
Website: http://static.icmci.org

Alternative/equivalent entrance requirements can include: ILC, IB, EB, NC/ND and many other similar international systems. For further details see the Equivalent Qualifications section in the Introduction.

Manufacturing Engineer

What is Involved?

As a manufacturing engineer (sometimes known as a production engineer), you would be concerned with all stages of the conversion of raw materials into usable products either for the general public or for other industries. In some instances, your job would be very similar to that of a mechanical engineer but you would be more concerned with broad manufacturing technology. You could be involved with overseeing the production processes and systems involved in making any sort of manufactured goods. As a result, your job is likely to include designing or maintaining complex machinery. You could be using robotics or involved with other computer driven equipment. Your main concern could be with designing, testing and maintaining the equipment itself or you could be involved with the design and layout of the plant in a factory. In order to present your product(s) to the marketplace at the time, price and quality that the customer expects, you would need a wide range of knowledge and skills, from product design, marketing and accounting to management, economics and finance. You would also need to appreciate the blend of people, machines and materials necessary to impart quality to the manufacturing process.

Opportunities for Training

There are a number of universities offering degrees in manufacturing engineering, sometimes combined with product design or with mechanical engineering. In order to become a chartered engineer, primarily concerned with research, design and development, you would need to complete at least four years of academic study and would usually achieve this via an MEng degree. If you want to be more involved with the day-to-day management of production processes as an incorporated engineer, you could take a three-year BEng degree. You don't always have to choose your specific training route from the start, so you should read prospectuses carefully. See also our separate article on engineering qualifications. There are sandwich courses available for both types of degree; these add an extra year but give the opportunity for a period of work experience, which can be very valuable when you are looking for a job. After graduating, you would need to complete a period of industrial training and responsible work experience before you achieve chartered or incorporated engineer status.

Requirements for Entry

For degree entry, you are likely to need maths at A level/Advanced Higher, Higher or equivalent and usually physics plus another one or two subjects. If maths and physics are not required, they are certainly preferred by universities. In addition, you would need at least five GCSE/S Grade passes at A-C/1-3. You would normally need higher grades for MEng than for BEng admission.

Kind of Person

You would need the ability to learn and develop the multidisciplinary knowledge, competencies and skills relevant to manufacturing so that, on graduation, you would be able to undertake the diverse range of management functions found in industry. You would be involved with the application of computer technologies to integrate management and processes, requiring advanced IT skills, and you would find foreign language skills useful.

You might find yourself giving or taking orders, liaising with others and co-ordinating the work of fellow team members. In addition, you may need to give presentations to senior staff, to explain your ideas and discuss plans with people who do not always have your expertise.

Broad Outlook

UK manufacturing capacity has shrunk considerably, but it is certainly not dead and there are still around four million people who make a living from manufacturing, in big firms and small. There has in the past been strong demand for qualified manufacturing engineers, although UK industry has been severely hit by the economic downturn at the start of 2009.

You may choose to develop skills in emerging fields in order to stay ahead of the game or take advantage of skills gaps. Environmentally friendly processes and nanotechnology, for example, are currently the subject of intense interest within the manufacturing sector.

Related Occupations

You might consider: mechanical, automotive, electrical/electronic, telecommunications, civil, chemical, mining, petroleum, or marine engineer. Alternatively, you might be interested in robotics or cybernetics.

Impact on Lifestyle

Whilst you may have specific hours of work you are also likely to be asked to work overtime on occasion, when there is a deadline to meet or a problem with production. Some production lines run continuously, so you may be required to be on call when problems arise.

Depending on the area of production with which you are involved, you may need to spend at least some time working in a factory or manufacturing area. Occasionally this could be dirty or noisy and you may be required to wear protective clothing.

Earnings Potential

You are likely to earn around £23,000 to £25,000 when you first start work after graduating but this has the potential to rise sharply as you gain experience. Once you are chartered, your salary is likely to rise considerably and should range from £40,000 to £55,000. Average earnings for incorporated engineers are around £41,000.

Further Information

Institution of Mechanical Engineers, London SW1H 9JJ
Website: www.imeche.org.uk

Engineering Council UK, London WC1V 7EX
Website: www.engc.org.uk

Manufacturing Institute, Manchester M17 1HH
Website: www.manufacturinginstitute.co.uk

Alternative/equivalent entrance requirements can include: ILC, IB, EB, NC/ND and many other similar international systems. For further details see the Equivalent Qualifications section in the Introduction.

Marine Biologist/Marine Scientist

What is Involved?

Working as a marine biologist, you would be concerned with the astonishing diversity of plant and animal life in the world's oceans. Your area of study could include anything from microscopic bacteria to the largest whales. You could concentrate on a specific group of marine organisms or you could look more broadly at marine ecology and the interaction between groups of organisms. You might work in an area such as monitoring fish stocks and developing sustainable methods of harvesting food from the sea; you might be searching for new chemicals for the pharmaceutical industry; you might be measuring the effects of dumping waste in the oceans.

Opportunities for Training

There are about 25 universities offering degrees in marine biology, mostly organising their courses on a modular basis. This structure should give you experience of a range of biological disciplines, such as genetics, ecology, zoology, biochemistry, botany and microbiology. Other modules would be designed to give you a necessary background in marine chemistry, physics and geology and an understanding of how these disciplines interact to explain what is found in the ocean and why. You could also undertake more specialised postgraduate study in marine biology and you may find this essential before you enter the labour market.

You would find that most courses have a large fieldwork component, giving you plenty of opportunity to get your hands wet as you go to sea in a research vessel or collect samples on the shoreline. You may also have the opportunity to gain a diving qualification, which could prove highly useful.

It is possible to take a degree in any of the biological sciences (for example, molecular biology could enhance career prospects), and then go on to specialise in marine biology with a Masters or PhD.

Requirements for Entry

To gain admission to a degree course in marine biology, you would normally need three A level/Advanced Higher, four or five Higher or equivalent qualifications, together with at least five GCSE/S Grade passes A-C/1-3 or equivalent, including English and maths. Some universities specify A level/Advanced Higher, Higher or equivalent in biology and another science subject.

Kind of Person

You should have a keen interest in science generally, with a particular passion for the sea. You would probably be involved in research work and much of this would involve careful attention to accuracy and detail. You would be expected to communicate your results to others, some of whom may not have the same scientific background as you. You should therefore have good written and verbal communication skills. You would almost certainly make extensive use of computers for obtaining, processing and storing data and would therefore need excellent IT skills. Your work would involve you in being out of doors in all sorts of weather, sometimes at sea. For this you would need to be quite fit and robust.

Broad Outlook

Job prospects in this area are not good in the UK, where there are many more marine biology graduates than there are vacancies. There is only a limited amount of research being undertaken and this is often commissioned on short-term contracts.

There is some work in the commercial sector but marine departments tend to be small, with limited promotion prospects. You may find that a specialised postgraduate qualification is essential before you can get started in the labour market.

Related Occupations

You might wish to consider: biologist, biochemist, oceanographer, geologist, or conservationist.

Impact on Lifestyle

If you are working in a land-based, laboratory environment you are likely to be working normal office hours. However, you might at times have to go to sea, which would involve working longer hours, in harder conditions and could take you away from home for several weeks. Wherever you work as a marine biologist, you are very likely to get wet at times. Your lifestyle is likely to revolve around short-term contracts, much moving around and a lifetime of learning new skills.

Earnings Potential

Levels of pay are relatively low compared with other fields, certainly less than £20,000 a year for the majority of marine biologists, and perhaps only half that for some. With a PhD, you should command a starting salary of £21,000 or more, rising with experience to around £30,000. Typical salaries at senior level, such as head of department or leader of a large project, are £50,000 plus. Self-employment in environmental research probably provides the highest salary levels.

Further Information

Natural Environment Research Council, Swindon SN2 1EU
Website: www.nerc.ac.uk

Centre for Environment, Fisheries and Aquaculture Science, Lowestoft NR33 OHT.
Website: www.cefas.co.uk

Marine Conservation Society, Ross on Wye HR9 5NB
Website: www.mcsuk.org

Marine Biological Association, Devon PL1 2PB
Website: www.mba.ac.uk

Scottish Association for Marine Science, Argyll PA37 1QA
Website: www.sams.ac.uk

National Oceanography Centre, Southampton SO14 3ZH
Website: www.noc.soton.ac.uk

Alternative/equivalent entrance requirements can include: ILC, IB, EB, NC/ND and many other similar international systems. For further details see the Equivalent Qualifications section in the Introduction.

Marine Engineer

What is Involved?

As a marine engineer, you could be involved in the design, management and maintenance of many different sorts of systems and equipment used in a maritime environment, including:

- **Ocean engineering**, involving all aspects of the exploration and production of oil, gas and minerals found under the seabed. The range of activities includes oil and gas extraction, mining the seabed for minerals, and development of renewable energy resources.

- **Offshore engineering**, involving the design, construction, commissioning and operation of fixed and mobile offshore platforms and their associated systems. Designers and operators have to find ways of overcoming the problems presented by winds, waves, currents and the nature of the seabed, while dealing with high pressure, high temperature and corrosive fluids and gases.

- **Seagoing engineering**, involving the safe and efficient operation of a vessel's main propulsion machinery, associated equipment and systems. The traditional career path here would be to train with the Merchant or Royal Navy, gaining qualifications and experience at sea. See our separate articles for Royal Navy and Merchant Navy Officer.

Opportunities for Training

To become an Incorporated or Chartered Marine Engineer, you normally start by taking a BEng (Bachelor of Engineering) or MEng (Master of Engineering) degree accredited by the IMarEST in a relevant subject, such as marine engineering, marine technology or ship science. BEng courses usually last three years (four years in Scotland); MEng courses are a year longer. The MEng provides a broader engineering education than the BEng. On the other hand, the BEng would allow you to complete your academic studies more rapidly, and to enter industry a year earlier to continue your education in the workplace. See our separate article on engineering qualifications.

Your academic education would normally be followed by a period of structured training and experience known as Initial Professional Development.

Requirements for Entry

For degree entry, you would normally need at least two A level/Advanced Higher, three Higher or equivalent qualifications, including maths and usually physics or a subject which includes physics. You would also be expected to have supporting GCSE/S Grade passes A-C/1-3 or equivalent, usually including English. Other useful subjects would include technology and foreign languages. At many universities, students without the necessary background in science and mathematics can take a one-year foundation course.

Kind of Person

Maritime engineering is a practical subject, attracting people who are interested in science and technology and finding out how things work and who have an affinity with the sea. You should have an open and enquiring mind, with a creative approach to problem solving. Teamwork skills are important because co-operation is essential in maritime engineering, particularly for engineers who serve at sea. You would need to be good at numerical reasoning and at using computers for your work. You would also have to be able to explain your thoughts and ideas clearly to other members of the engineering team.

Broad Outlook

Research into the exploration and recovery of minerals from under the seabed is progressing rapidly and enormous engineering expertise will be required to carry out deep-sea operations in a sustainable and environmentally friendly way. Although the size of the UK shipbuilding industry has reduced dramatically over the past 20 years, market forces are beginning to work in favour of the remaining shipyards. The emphasis now is on building specialist vessels, particularly for the offshore industry and the Royal Navy, and there is a continuing demand for engineers in this area.

Related Occupations

You might also consider: naval architect, aeronautical, automotive, mechanical, civil or electrical engineer, oceanographer or hydrographic surveyor.

Impact on Lifestyle

Working hours vary from job to job. Your working environment might include an office, shipyard or boatyard, ship, submarine or offshore installation. Many jobs involve a combination of indoor and outdoor work

Traditionally, the engine room at sea is run on a continuous watchkeeping system, which involves working four hours on, eight hours off, round the clock. On more modern automated ships, the majority of engine room staff work during the day, with a single engineer on duty at night, although passenger vessels maintain continuous watchkeeping systems. Leave time is generous, to compensate for time spent on board and away from home. For example, after a voyage of around four months, you could get as much as two months or so off at home. Some jobs, eg in design or construction, are shore-based and would involve more normal working hours.

Earnings Potential

You are likely to start earning around £21,000 when you first graduate and this will rise quite rapidly as you gain experience and take on more responsibility. The average salary of an experienced chartered marine engineer is over £50,000.

Further Information

Institute of Marine Engineering, Science and Technology (IMarEST), London EC2R 5BJ
Website: www.imarest.org

Sea Vision UK, London EC1M 6EZ
Website: www.seavisionuk.org

British Marine Federation
Website: www.britishmarine.co.uk

Merchant Navy Careers at Sea, London ECIM 6EZ
Website: www.careersatsea.org.uk

Alternative/equivalent entrance requirements can include: ILC, IB, EB, NC/ND and many other similar international systems. For further details see the Equivalent Qualifications section in the Introduction.

Market Researcher

What is Involved?

As a market researcher, you might be employed by manufacturing companies or other organisations to find out what people think and what they want. Manufacturers, politicians, pressure groups and others need to know the public response to various products, advertising campaigns and initiatives. You might work as a freelance, for an independent agency or as a member of the research department of a large company.

It would be your job to target an appropriate sample of people, to ensure that the right questions are asked, to collate the results efficiently and to present them in the best possible way. Depending on your circumstances and seniority, you might be involved in interviewing and making presentations of your findings. Market research is increasingly being conducted on an international basis, and there might well be scope for travel.

Opportunities for Training

The Market Research Society (MRS) is an official awarding body in the UK for vocational qualifications in this field. As well as running short courses, the MRS offers the Advanced Certificate in Market and Social Research Practice and the Diploma of the Market Research Society. Many companies offer new graduates the opportunity to take part in the MRS professional development scheme.

Several business-related degree and higher national diploma (HND) courses offer options in market research and allied subjects, and there are some postgraduate courses available. Work experience or work shadowing would be an advantage when applying for courses or employment opportunities.

Requirements for Entry

While there are no particular educational requirements laid down for entry into market research, graduates are becoming increasingly in demand. The actual subject of your degree or HND would not be of critical importance, but business studies, economics or other subjects including evidence of numeracy would show that you have the aptitude for coping with numbers and statistics. Psychology or sociology could also be useful, and languages might give you an advantage in certain situations.

The minimum entry requirements for university degree courses are two A level/Advanced Higher, three Higher or equivalent qualifications, together with five GCSE/S Grade passes A-C/1-3. In practice, you should aim to offer more than the minimum. Courses last three or four years. For HND courses, you would need one or two A levels/Advanced Higher, two or three Higher or equivalent qualifications. The courses last for two or three years.

Kind of Person

In order to succeed in market research, you would need excellent communication skills, both spoken and written, as you would be in contact with a wide variety of people. Persuasive skills would also be an asset, and the ability to deal with disappointment in a highly competitive world.

A keen sense of business would be an advantage. You should be able to absorb and analyse data quickly and accurately, and you should have a high level of computer literacy. You should be able to work independently and also as part of a team, and be capable of working under pressure in order to meet deadlines. It would help if you were inquisitive and interested in how people think and behave.

Broad Outlook

In an increasingly competitive business world, the work of the market researcher is becoming extremely important, and agencies concerned with consumer research have proliferated over the past few years. Another growth area has been social research, with increased use of researchers by local and national government.

Competition to enter the profession is fierce but the rewards can be high, with good promotion prospects if you can demonstrate the right levels of drive and determination. Later on, you could set up your own agency or head a large department for a major employer.

Career progression can be very fast. Graduates would expect to be a Research Executive for 18 months, then a Senior Research Executive. Promotion is through merit, with many candidates managing accounts and teams by age 30.

Related Occupations

You might also consider: advertising executive, economist, marketing manager, personnel (human resources) manager, public relations officer, retail manager or statistician.

Impact on Lifestyle

Since many market research campaigns are linked to deadlines, you should be prepared for some long hours, together with working weekends and in the evenings. There would quite likely be travelling involved, maybe abroad. You would need to be tough and be prepared to fight your corner.

Earnings Potential

Salaries vary according to employment circumstances, since many market researchers are freelance. As a graduate, you could expect to start at around £20,000 to £24,000, rising after three to five years to £28,000 to £35,000. A senior executive might earn between £45,000 and £80,000 or more, depending on their track record and degree of managerial responsibility.

Further Information

Market Research Society, London EC1V 0JR
Website: www.mrs.org.uk

Social Research Association, London NW1 2HX
Website: www.the-sra.org.uk

Royal Statistical Society, London EC1Y 8LX
Website: www.rss.org.uk

British Market Research Bureau
Website: www.bmrb.co.uk

Alternative/equivalent entrance requirements can include: ILC, IB, EB, NC/ND and many other similar international systems. For further details see the Equivalent Qualifications section in the Introduction.

Marketing Executive

What is Involved?

Your role as a marketing executive would be to secure the best possible match between the goods or services produced by your organisation and the perceived needs of your actual or potential clients. This could mean conducting market research to find out what customers want and what they understand about the market. You might then use the results of your research to identify your own and your competitors' short-comings, decide on improvements needed, locate the main target markets in the UK and abroad and then put forward your proposals for the next steps. Typical approaches could include producing new promotional material, revamping your image, repositioning your products and upgrading your packaging. You might propose an advertising campaign, employ a public relations (PR) agency or department to enhance your public image, or introduce more effective distribution facilities. Your work might involve industrial products, consumer goods or services or the public sector.

Opportunities for Training

Although it is possible to start as a marketing assistant and progress through promotion, the majority of entrants join by direct entry on graduate trainee schemes. You could take a degree in marketing or a related subject but you would find that any degree subject is acceptable. You could also take a higher national diploma (HND) in business studies with a marketing specialism. Another method of entering this very competitive field is to start by gaining experience in a related area, such as customer service or market research, and then moving across. In most companies, you would train in-house by working alongside an experienced marketing executive. There are formal qualifications run by the Chartered Institute of Marketing (CIM) in association with the Communication Advertising and Marketing Education Foundation (CAM).

Requirements for Entry

For degree entry, you would need two or three A level/Advanced Higher, three or four Higher or equivalent qualifications, together with a supporting platform of GCSE/S Grade passes A-C/1-3. HND requirements are usually slightly less demanding. A similar level of achievement would be required for direct entry as a marketing assistant. In all cases, evidence of skills in English and maths would be important.

Kind of Person

Above all, you would need commercial flair to recognise and exploit market opportunities. You should have an analytical mind, capable of assessing the essentials of each situation, with a clear understanding of your organisation and the position of its products and services within an ever changing market place. Good communication skills, both written and verbal, would be essential, together with the ability to relay your enthusiasm to others and motivate them to meet your marketing targets.

You would frequently face deadlines and would have to produce marketing briefs for senior management or prepare for negotiations with important clients. Numeracy would play a key role in assessing and analysing costs and estimating the effects of changes in pricing policy. You would need writing skills to produce reports or promotional literature and good IT skills. The ability to speak one or more foreign languages would be valuable.

*B*road Outlook

Opportunities for promotion would usually exist within your own organisation if you can prove you are effective and produce good results, although competition for senior posts is likely to be fierce. Marketing is considered to be a good basis for moving into general management and promotion could eventually lead a post such as managing director or chief executive. Additional qualifications in marketing would enhance your chances. Marketing is recognised as one of the most important activities in manufacturing and service industries, and vacancies are widely available throughout the country. Marketing is closely linked with advertising and public relations and a great deal in interchange between these sectors is possible.

*R*elated Occupations

You might also consider: advertising executive, public relations officer, retail manager, market researcher, or logistics manager.

*I*mpact on Lifestyle

This is a high pressure careers field, with a constant need to keep in touch with other people and to achieve deadlines and objectives. You would be expected to produce information in reports, analyse new data or travel to clients, at home and abroad, often at short notice, especially when you reach more senior levels of management.

*E*arnings Potential

Typical starting salaries range from £20,000 to £26,000, rising with experience to £30,000 to £50,000 and considerably more for successful directors. Salaries tend to be higher in larger organisations in the professional services and financial and business sectors, compared with those in the public sector, charities and small independent companies.

*F*urther Information

Chartered Institute of Marketing, Maidenhead SL6 9QH
Website: www.cim.co.uk

Communication Advertising and Marketing Education Foundation, Maidenhead SL6 9QH
Website: www.camfoundation.com

Institute of Export, Peterborough PE2 6FT
Website: www.export.org.uk

Institute of Direct Marketing, Middlesex TW11 0AR
Website: www.theidm.co.uk

Alternative/equivalent entrance requirements can include: ILC, IB, EB, NC/ND and many other similar international systems. For further details see the Equivalent Qualifications section in the Introduction.

Materials Scientist/Engineer

What is Involved?

As a materials scientist, you would specialise in the physical and chemical properties of the materials used to manufacture products. You would be looking for the highest possible standards of performance and long-term reliability. You might, for example, work in the aerospace industry, developing stronger and lighter alloys for airframes or high temperature alloys for engines. Pressure for reductions in pollution and noise and increases in durability would drive your work forward. Other examples could include selecting the best combination of materials (plastics and metals) for a mobile phone, a replacement hip joint or the parts used in a domestic dishwasher. You would need to know the limitations and advantages of a variety of metal, plastic, ceramic, glass and carbon fibre resources and you would be expected to know how best to mould, extrude, shape and manufacture them. Thousands of different materials are available to deal with such problems as corrosion and rusting, high or low temperatures, vibration, bending, stretching, elasticity, resistance to chemical attack and simple daily wear and tear. The right combination of materials, allied to good design, can greatly enhance the performance, appearance, sales and profitability of a product.

Opportunities for Training

You would normally need a degree in materials science, metallurgy, materials engineering or similar. You should look carefully at the content of each course to find the right one for you, as they can vary widely. There is often the opportunity to include the study of a language and spend some time abroad, or to incorporate a management module; you might also consider a sandwich course, which would take a year longer but would offer a period of paid work placement. Some materials engineering courses are accredited for registration with the Engineering Council and could be the first step towards qualifying as a professional engineer. There is also the option of following a postgraduate materials science course, sometimes with sponsorship from an employer.

Requirements for Entry

For degree entry, you would need two or three A levels/Advanced Higher, three or four Higher or equivalent qualifications selected from physics, chemistry, maths or design and technology, together with at least five GCSE/S Grade passes A-C/1-3. Materials and metallurgy courses are often under-subscribed and at some universities it is possible for students without the right A levels/Advanced Higher, Higher or equivalent qualifications to take a foundation course before starting their degree. To be accepted for a postgraduate course, you would need a good honours degree in a relevant scientific or engineering subject.

Kind of Person

You should be interested and have reasonable ability in mathematics, physics and chemistry, but there is more to being a good materials scientist than that. You should enjoy applying scientific theory to practice, and be able to work accurately at all times. Good communication skills, both spoken and written, would be important, as you would be working as part of a team and would be expected to write up regular reports of your work. A logical approach would be required, although the ability to think laterally could be an asset in problem solving. You should also have a high level of computer skills. You may need good eyesight and colour vision for some aspects of the work.

Broad Outlook

The pace of scientific and technological change seems ever increasing, and you should have no difficulty in finding work in many areas of materials science once the UK economy recovers from the economic downturn of 2009. Opportunities arise with private employers, at home or abroad, in research and development, quality control, and management. You could also work for universities or government organisations such as the National Physical Laboratory. Promotion could be within an organisation to a senior position, while some experienced materials scientists establish their own private consultancies or diversify into technical writing, teaching or sales and marketing.

Related Occupations

You might also consider: biomedical scientist, aeronautical, chemical, civil, electrical, manufacturing or mechanical engineer, management consultant, metallurgist, industrial chemist or product designer.

Impact on Lifestyle

In most parts of industry, you would work a fairly typical nine to five week from Monday to Friday. In production or quality control, however, you may need to work on a rota basis as the production line is likely to be in 24-hour operation. You would need to wear protective clothing when dealing with some dangerous substances and at other times you might be required to wear anti-contamination clothing in a scrupulously clean environment.

Earnings Potential

Pay scales vary widely between companies but generally you might start at around £20,000 to £26,000, with progression as you became more experienced and undertake more responsibility to around £38,000 to £55,000. Some materials scientists can earn appreciably more than this, particularly if they go into management. Salaries tend to be higher in what are considered to be 'leading edge' technologies, such as telecommunications and biomedical engineering.

Further Information

Institute of Materials Minerals and Mining, London SW1Y 5DB
Website: www.iom3.org

UK Centre for Materials Education, Liverpool L69 3GQ
Website: www.materials.ac.uk and www.whystudymaterials.ac.uk

Alternative/equivalent entrance requirements can include: ILC, IB, EB, NC/ND and many other similar international systems. For further details see the Equivalent Qualifications section in the Introduction.

Mechanical Engineer

What is Involved?

As a mechanical engineer, you would be concerned with applying engineering principles and rules to all sorts of machines and their components. This means that you could be dealing with anything from the largest manufacturing equipment down to the nuts and bolts used in production. Depending on your interests and your level of qualification, you could become involved in design, manufacture, research, development, management or marketing or a combination of these.

Broadly speaking, you would focus more on research, design and development if you pursue your education, training and experience through to chartered status; you would be more involved with production processes as an incorporated engineer. See our separate article on engineering qualifications for a more detailed analysis of these issues.

Opportunities for Training

Training as a mechanical engineer would lead you into one of the broadest areas of engineering. There are many universities offering degrees in mechanical engineering and there is a wide variation in the types of courses and specialisms offered within these degrees, so it is a good idea to check the prospectuses carefully before applying. It is important to ensure that your degree is an accredited course recognised by the Institution of Mechanical Engineers. There are four-year courses, usually leading to an MEng qualification, which can take you to chartered engineer status.

Alternatively, there are three-year courses, usually leading to a BEng qualification, which can take you to incorporated engineer status. It is possible to add a further year of specialised study, known as a matching section, to enable you to progress to the chartered route. There are also sandwich courses, which include a year spent in industry gaining practical work experience, and you should find many opportunities for sponsorship.

Requirements for Entry

Most universities would either prefer or require you to have A level/Advanced Higher, Higher or equivalent in maths and physics, together with five GCSE/S Grade passes A-C/1-3, including maths and English.

Kind of Person

Your job would probably involve understanding and solving complex engineering problems. For this you would need a practical and logical mind that might need to show creative approaches to problems. You are likely to find yourself using maths and statistics in your work and you would make extensive use of computers, including specialised and sophisticated software packages.

You are likely to find yourself working as part of a multi-disciplinary team, which means that you would need to be able to communicate with a variety of people. These could be fellow engineers, who would share your technical expertise and understanding, or non-technical specialists in other fields, who would expect you to explain your ideas clearly to them. You could also find yourself managing a team of people working on a project. In addition, you may need to take into account the costs and budget of a project, so you would need some business skills.

Broad Outlook

UK manufacturing capacity has shrunk considerably, but it is certainly not dead and there are still around four million people who make a living from manufacturing, in big firms and small. There has in the past been strong demand for qualified mechanical engineers, although UK industry has been severely hit by the economic downturn at the start of 2009.

You may choose to develop skills in emerging fields in order to stay ahead of the game or take advantage of skills gaps. Environmentally friendly processes, lean manufacturing techniques and nanotechnology are, for example, currently the subject of intense interest within the sector.

Mechanical engineering can provide a good starting point for a career in management because it is a wide-ranging subject area that requires and develops a number of different technical, people management and business skills. There are opportunities for mechanical engineers in just about all areas of industry and in many other fields of employment. Many mechanical engineers decide to develop additional skills, for example in business, in order to become involved with larger projects and take on greater responsibility. Good commercial awareness is essential for career development, as well as developing people management skills, given that you may be required to lead teams or manage projects.

Related Occupations

You might be interested in working in another branch of engineering or in specialising to become an expert in a particular field such as CAD (computer-aided design). Alternatively, you might consider science-based options such as: medical physicist, metallurgist, geophysicist, oceanographer or biotechnologist.

Impact on Lifestyle

You might be working set office hours or you might be expected to work long hours or on a rota system if you are involved with industrial production. You are likely to have to work extra hours from time to time in order to meet deadlines, when you could find that you are working under some pressure. Working towards chartered status can involve several years of further study after you have completed your degree course.

Earnings Potential

You could expect to start earning around £20,000 to £25,000 when you first graduate and you should see your salary rise to around £40,000 to £50,000 within a few years. The average annual earnings for experienced chartered engineers are around £50,000 and for incorporated engineers around £41,000.

Further Information

Institution of Mechanical Engineers, London SW1H 9JJ
Website: www.imeche.org.uk

Engineering Council UK, London WC2R 3ER
Website: www.engc.org.uk

Alternative/equivalent entrance requirements can include: ILC, IB, EB, NC/ND and many other similar international systems. For further details see the Equivalent Qualifications section in the Introduction.

Medical Physicist

What is Involved?

As a medical physicist, you would be a specialist within a hospital clinical science group, applying science and technology for the benefit of the sick. Although your education and training would be different from that of a doctor, you could still be intimately involved in assessing and treating illness and disability. Close collaboration between a medical physicist and a doctor can achieve much more than either in isolation. You would work in many different medical fields, with a mixture of research, development and routine services to patients.

The main areas are nuclear medicine, radiotherapy, radiology and various aspects of physiological monitoring and investigation, but others specialities range from anaesthetics to urology. You could, for example, be responsible for establishing correct doses of radiation for treating malignant tumours, without causing unnecessary damage to other body tissues, and for ensuring that therapeutic and diagnostic radiographers use radiation equipment safely. You might also devise and erect special monitoring equipment, which can record patients' progress during or after surgery.

Opportunities for Training

With a good honours degree in physics or a closely related subject such as electronic engineering, you could join the two-year NHS training programme in an accredited department. Successful completion of the training programme, incorporating an accredited Master of Science (MSc) award, would result in the Diploma of the Institute of Physics and Engineering in Medicine (IPEM) and registration with the Association of Clinical Scientists.

You would be given time off and support for your studies during this training period. It would be possible to complete your MSc before starting the training period, although this is a less popular route. Having completed this stage, you would have the option of taking a further course of advanced training, which could lead to a doctorate (PhD). You cannot become state registered (with the Health Professions Council) until you have completed the MSc course and gained at least four years' practical experience.

Requirements for Entry

Entry to most relevant degree courses would require two to three A level/Advanced Higher, three to five Higher or equivalent qualifications, together with a good platform of GCSE/S Grade passes A-C/1-3. Since there is a shortage of applicants, grade requirements in some universities are not high but all departments would be looking for good grades in physics and maths. For postgraduate study, you would usually need a first degree passed with first or upper second class honours.

Kind of Person

You would be working in a field that is developing fast, so you would need to keep up to date with new discoveries and advances in technology and a very strong interest in physics, maths and technology. Getting your calculations and measurements right could be critical to the patient. You would need to have an interest in and be at ease with patients. You would be expected to work as part of a team of clinical science professionals, so you would need to communicate clearly and to explain your diagnoses or recommendations.

Broad Outlook

This is a small and very specialised field of medical science, but it is also one that is expanding rapidly. Within the NHS, you would follow a formal career structure, entering as a pre-registration trainee (formerly grade A). Once in possession of the IPEM diploma, you could compete for posts at practitioner level (formerly grade B), the main professional grade, covering a wide range of responsibilities.

Your career could develop to a point where you are in charge of a scientific department or a major departmental sub-division. The most senior medical physicists have equivalent status to medical consultants. You could also seek employment in the healthcare industry, where your career would be less structured than in the NHS.

Ongoing training and professional development would be an essential part of your career as a medical physicist. The IPEM provides a formal continuing professional development (CPD) programme for all its members, aimed to support and enhance your career progression. You may decide to specialise in an area such as magnetic resonance imaging, medical computing, ultrasound or physiological measurement.

Related Occupations

You might also consider: doctor, physicist, radiographer, electrical or electronic engineer, clinical biochemist, pharmacologist, optometrist or biomedical engineer.

Impact on Lifestyle

You would normally expect to work a 37-hour week in the NHS but might be expected to work extra hours to cover emergencies. You might need to attend lectures or conferences in order to complete your studies, which could be outside your normal working hours, as would keeping up to date on new developments in medical physics.

Earnings Potential

Starting salaries for clinical scientists in the NHS Band 6 are currently £24,831 to £33,436, rising in Band 7 to £29,789 to £39,273. Senior manager or consultant posts can offer salaries ranging up to £95,333. Additional payments are made for employment in and around London.

Further Information

Institute of Physics and Engineering in Medicine, York YO24 1ES
Website: www.ipem.ac.uk

Institute of Physics, London W1B 1NT
Website: www.iop.org

Association of Clinical Scientists, London SE1 2TU
Website: www.assclinsci.org

Health Professions Council, London SE11 4BU
Website: www.hpc-uk.org

Alternative/equivalent entrance requirements can include: ILC, IB, EB, NC/ND and many other similar international systems. For further details see the Equivalent Qualifications section in the Introduction.

Merchant Navy Officer

What is Involved?

As an officer in the merchant navy, you would work for a fleet which operates all over the world, consisting largely of ferries, container ships, passenger ships, survey ships and oil tankers. Additionally, some ships operate as auxiliary vessels for civilian and Royal Navy operations such as updating charts of shipping lanes. The person in charge of a ship is known as the master or captain. This post carries full responsibility for the ship, the crew, the cargo, passengers, the safety of the ship and everyone on board, and for navigating the ship to where it needs to go. The person in charge of a ship's engineering and technical systems is the chief engineer. This post carries full responsibility for the operation and maintenance of complex electrical and mechanical plant and associated control systems. As a ship's officer, you would have responsibility for a range of tasks in either the deck or the engine department. There are also some dual officer roles, covering both departments. You may also control the work of ratings, who perform a wide range of technical and non-technical jobs and have a lower level of responsibility.

Opportunities for Training

Training for deck and engineer officers follows a similar pattern of college- or university-based and shipboard training. The actual number and duration of these 'phases' differs depending on whether you train as a deck or engineer officer. A foundation degree/Scottish professional diploma sits at the heart of a three-year training programme that will qualify you as a junior officer, giving you Officer Of the Watch (OOW) certification, the first stage of your professional seafaring qualifications.

Individual shipping companies or training organisations will sponsor you to do the course. They may decide which college/university you attend and you will be placed on their ships for the sea-based part of the course. Your sponsoring company will pay your course fees and a salary or training allowance.

Requirements for Entry

You would need a total of 120 UCAS points in unspecified subjects at A level or equivalent, plus good grades at GCSE/S Grade or equivalent in mathematics, English and physics (or dual/combined science). This will generally mean having obtained passes at grades A or B/credit level. You will also need to satisfy the relevant statutory health and eyesight requirements for seafarers in the UK. The sponsoring companies will also give you guidance on any particular requirements they may have. You should be over age 18 to begin the foundation degree/Scottish professional diploma course.

If you have any doubt about your ability to pass the statutory health and/or eyesight requirements, you may find it worthwhile to take the appropriate examination before applying. You can ask the sponsoring companies or contact the Maritime and Coastguard Agency (MCA) to establish the details of the requirements and how they may affect you.

Kind of Person

You must be prepared to accept responsibility not only for making important decisions yourself but also for inspiring confidence in the crew. You would need the knowledge, leadership, communication and team-working skills to keep complex systems running in extremes of temperature and weather, to demanding schedules and within safety and efficiency requirements. You would need to be able to cope with living, possibly for several months at a time, in a confined space far from friends and family.

Broad Outlook

The merchant navy has in recent years had more vacancies (approximately 1000 per year) than it has applicants to fill them, so prospects are generally good. This is despite the fact that fewer crew will be required for the larger and more technically advanced ships of the future.

There are good opportunities for both men and women to obtain promotion but further training and examinations are involved, whilst length of service and personal characteristics also play an important part. After retirement from the service, there are civilian employers who look favourably on those with a successful merchant navy career behind them.

Related Occupations

You might also wish to consider: Marine Engineer, Royal Navy officer or the other uniformed services.

Impact on Lifestyle

Life on board a ship is a 24-hour a day operation, seven days a week, 52 weeks a year. The work is divided into shifts called watches, which are typically four hours on watch, followed by eight hours off watch. At busy times this may increase to six hours on watch and six hours off watch.

Leave time is generous, to compensate for time spent on board and away from home. For example, after a voyage of around four months, you could get as much as two months or so off at home. Most ships have excellent facilities for those living and working on them and some provide facilities for officers to be accompanied by their husband or wife.

Earnings Potential

Salaries vary from company to company and there is a small variation between salaries for engineering officers and for deck officers. Training salaries for cadets range from £8,000 to £9,500, with all tuition and on-board food and accommodation included. Shore-based accommodation costs are, however, deducted. Junior officers generally start on £21,000 to £25,000. Progression up to the rank of captain or chief engineer can lead to salaries within the range £36,000 to £60,000 depending upon the type and size of ship. Salaries on foreign-going ships, spending at least 183 days per year out of the UK, are tax-free.

Further Information

Merchant Navy Training Board, London ECIM 6EZ
Website: www.mntb.org.uk

Careers at Sea
Website: www.careersatsea.org

Maritime and Coastguard Agency
Website: www.mcga.gov.uk

Alternative/equivalent entrance requirements can include: ILC, IB, EB, NC/ND and many other similar international systems. For further details see the Equivalent Qualifications section in the Introduction.

Metallurgist

What is Involved?

As a metallurgist, you would be a specialist in the science and engineering of metals, concerned with examining how they behave during use, what we can make them do and how we can use them to our best advantage. There are literally thousands of different metal products with widely different physical and chemical properties. You could work in research to overcome problems of metal failure or corrosion in aeroplanes or motorcars, or on the formulation and quality control of new steels/alloys.

There is considerable overlap between the work of a metallurgist and that of a materials scientist, as more and more manufactured products use combinations of metals, plastics, ceramics and carbon fibre, which need to fit together and survive impacts, dampness and high or low temperatures whilst meeting the need for attractive product design and commercial viability.

You might specialise in the manufacturing processes of converting metals and alloys into products, or you might concentrate on the extraction of metals from ores or recovery from scrap.

Opportunities for Training

You would normally need a relevant degree and there are several universities offering suitable courses in metallurgy or materials science. Some courses cover a wide range of metals, plastics and ceramics, while others might concentrate on just one material, so it is important to examine prospectuses carefully to make sure that courses cover the areas you expect. Metallurgy can also be studied as a joint honours subject with languages, business, management or economics, for example. You could choose to continue your studies in metallurgy with a postgraduate course at MSc or PhD level.

Requirements for Entry

For degree entry, you would need two or three A level/Advanced Higher, three or four Higher or equivalent qualifications selected from physics, chemistry, maths or design and technology, together with at least five GCSE/S Grade passes A-C/1-3. Metallurgy courses are often under-subscribed and at some universities it is possible for students without the right A level/Advanced Higher, Higher or equivalent qualifications to take foundation courses before starting their degree. To be accepted for a postgraduate course, you would need a good honours degree in metallurgy or a related subject such as mechanical engineering.

Kind of Person

You would need to have a strong interest and proven ability in maths, physics and chemistry. You should enjoy the practical aspects of science, such as your practical laboratory work at school. You would need to have a methodical approach to your work and meticulous attention to precise detail.

You may need deep reserves of patience as you carry out repeated tests on particular metals before discovering an acceptable alloy. You are likely to use computers in analysing data from test equipment. You would also need to communicate well and to be prepared to seek advice from other experts when necessary. You may need to instruct technicians who are helping in your research, and to communicate clearly with others who do not have your scientific background. The ability to write clear, unambiguous reports would be essential if you work in scientific research.

Broad Outlook

The pace of scientific and technological change seems ever increasing, and you should have no difficulty in finding work in many areas of metallurgy once the UK economy recovers from the economic downturn of 2009. You might be employed by a steel producer or by an automotive, aeroplane, armaments, shipbuilding or railway engine manufacturer. There are opportunities to work in metallurgical research laboratories and for government science research centres, as well as in university research departments. Many other industries employ metallurgists at all stages of their production processes, including electricity and power companies and the oil and chemical industries. There are good opportunities to work abroad and also to work as an independent consultant.

Related Occupations

You might also consider: mechanical, aeronautical, civil, structural, mining or chemical engineer, materials scientist, physicist or geologist.

Impact on Lifestyle

In most parts of industry, you would work a fairly typical nine to five week from Monday to Friday. In production or quality control, however, you may need to work on a rota basis, as the production line is likely to be in 24-hour operation. You would need to wear protective clothing when dealing with some dangerous substances and at other times you might be required to wear anti-contamination clothing in a scrupulously clean environment.

Earnings Potential

Pay scales vary widely between companies but generally you might start at around £20,000 to £26,000, with progression as you became more experienced and undertake more responsibility to around £38,000 to £55,000. Some metallurgists can earn appreciably more than this, particularly if they go into management. Salaries tend to be higher in what are considered to be 'leading edge' technologies, such as telecommunications and biomedical engineering.

Further Information

Institute of Materials Minerals and Mining, London SW1Y 5DB
Website: www.iom3.org

UK Centre for Materials Education, Liverpool L69 3GQ
Websites: www.materials.ac.uk and www.whystudymaterials.ac.uk

Alternative/equivalent entrance requirements can include: ILC, IB, EB, NC/ND and many other similar international systems. For further details see the Equivalent Qualifications section in the Introduction.

Meteorologist

What is Involved?

As a meteorologist, you would be a specialist in the science and study of the earth's atmosphere and the interaction of the atmosphere with the earth itself. Meteorology seeks to understand and to predict the behaviour of weather, the climate and the atmosphere in general, from the surfaces of land and sea to the edge of space.

The Royal Meteorological Society, the professional body for meteorologists, lists 27 separate areas where meteorologists work. They range from weather forecasting to climatology and from horticulture to the planning and operation of great engineering undertakings. They include the development of complex mathematical representations of the way the atmosphere works and can be predicted, the manipulation of vast data resources, the design, development and testing of new instruments, and the use of modern communications and data- management systems. There are also close links with sister sciences such as hydrology and physical oceanography.

The Met (Meteorological) Office is the largest employer of meteorologists. It is a government institution involved in research, applied and operational meteorology.

Opportunities for Training

A university degree would be essential. This could be in meteorology but an alternative approach would be to enter meteorology at postgraduate level following a first degree in physics or maths or an associated subject such as computing, environmental studies, physical geography or electronics.

The Met Office has its own college in Devon providing training courses for new entrants and for continuing professional development. With a high level of knowledge and experience, you could become a chartered meteorologist. This professional qualification corresponds to others such as chartered accountant or chartered engineer. While it is not essential, accreditation can satisfy clients and employers that you have reached and continue to maintain a specified level of knowledge and experience and that you are conversant with current best practice.

Requirements for Entry

For a meteorology degree, you would need maths and physics at A level/Advanced Higher, Higher or equivalent level. You should research the exact entry requirements of individual universities. There are some Met Office opportunities for non-graduates, where you would need A level/Advanced Higher, Higher or equivalent passes including maths and/or physics.

Kind of Person

You would need a genuine and enthusiastic interest in the weather and climate phenomena, with a good working knowledge of maths and physics. You would also need to be observant, have good communication skills, enjoy problem solving and have a logical approach to collating data. You must be highly numerate and able to cope with sophisticated computer systems and software.

Broad Outlook

The Met Office is the main employer and has a promotion structure which operates on merit. There are jobs with the Natural Environment Research Council and Agricultural and Fisheries Institutes but, as they only employ a small number of meteorologists, there is less chance of internal promotion. There are some opportunities for working abroad with the Met Office, with British companies or with the United Nations.

There are opportunities for pure research, applied research, operational work, scientific and commercial management, entrepreneurial ventures, teaching and consultancy.

Staff employed in the Mobile Met Unit are attached to the Royal Air Force and may be deployed across the world on military exercises and operations. The Royal Navy's Flag Officer Sea Training group (FOST HM) trains specialist officers of the Royal Navy for a career in meteorology or hydrography. The training programme provides a thorough understanding of the complex physical environment in which the ships, aircraft, submarines and people of the Royal and Royal Marines operate.

Related Occupations

You may be interested in training as a physicist, oceanographer or hydrographic surveyor.

Impact on Lifestyle

You may be expected to move your work base from time to time in order to broaden your experience. Indeed, it is a condition of Met Office employment that you agree to work wherever required. Some weather stations are located in remote spots, carefully chosen for their extreme weather conditions! As the earth interacts with the atmosphere around the clock, you may have to work shifts, weekends and sometimes long hours.

Although a few meteorologists appear on television as weather forecasters, most of this work is carried out by professional broadcasters after a short course at the Met Office college.

Earnings Potential

The Met Office operates a pay banding system with five Job Levels (JL), starting with JL5 as the most junior. Graduates currently start on £21,000 to £24,500, before rising to JL3 and beyond. The top of JL1 is in excess of £70,000.

Further Information

Royal Meteorological Society, Reading RG1 7LL
Website: www.rmets.org

Meteorological Office, Exeter EX1 3PB
Website: www.metoffice.com

British Antarctic Survey, Cambridge CB3 0ET
Website: www.antarctica.ac.uk

World Meteorological Association
Website: www.wmo.int

Royal Navy Flag Officer Sea Training
Website: www.royal-navy.mod.uk

Alternative/equivalent entrance requirements can include: ILC, IB, EB, NC/ND and many other similar international systems. For further details see the Equivalent Qualifications section in the Introduction.

Microbiologist

What is Involved?

As a microbiologist, you would study micro-organisms such as fungi, bacteria, viruses or algae, investigating their growth conditions and sources. You would also consider the impact of microbes on the environment and the relationship between microbes and other living organisms. If you choose to specialise in the hospital service, you could practise as a clinical microbiologist, working alongside hospital doctors, general practitioners and environmental health officers in the diagnosis and prevention of disease. Alternatively, you could work as a biomedical scientist, dealing with samples from patients and isolating and identifying the microbes that cause illness (pathogens). See our separate article for biomedical scientist.

You may, on the other hand, choose to develop new products in the food industry or work in a public health laboratory, testing food, milk and water supplies for microbiological contamination. There are other openings in areas such as the pharmaceuticals, cosmetics and oil industries, where micro-organisms can be used to produce chemicals, hormones, antibiotics and enzymes, all of which can be of great benefit to society.

Opportunities for Training

To qualify as an NHS clinical microbiologist, you would undertake a programme of study and supervised experience that would normally include an MSc course, practical work and a research project. Successful completion would enable you to apply for more senior clinical scientist positions, and would lead, four years after entry, to certification of competence by the Association of Clinical Scientists and registration by the Health Professions Council as a clinical scientist.

Requirements for Entry

Most microbiologists are graduates and you would need a good honours degree, preferably in microbiology or in another life science such as biology, biochemistry or biomedical science. For degree entry, you would need A levels/Advanced Highers, Highers or equivalent passes in biology and one other science subject, together with five GCSE/S Grade passes at A-C/1-3 including maths, English and two sciences. Some universities may specify chemistry A or AS level/Higher, Advanced Higher or equivalent qualifications but offers are likely to vary considerably between institutions. It is best to check with admissions departments to be sure of their individual requirements. If you decide to take an HND, you are likely to need a science subject at A level/Advanced Higher or Higher, together with four GCSE/S Grade passes at A-C/1-3 including maths, English and a science subject.

Kind of Person

You would need a strong interest in science, particularly biology, although an interest in chemistry is also useful. You should enjoy the practical side of your science lessons at school and be able to work accurately and in a well organised way in the laboratory. Some types of work include following set procedures with rigorous attention to detail and this needs patience and persistence. You would have to show a responsible approach in carrying out your tests and analyses. Communication skills are very important since you would probably be working in a multi-disciplinary team and would need to explain your work to people who do not share your scientific background.

Broad Outlook

Clinical microbiologists work in diagnostic laboratories and pathology departments in large hospitals and medical schools. For example, the function of the Health Protection Agency (HPA) is 'to protect the community (or any part of the community) against infectious diseases and other dangers to health.' Through its Centre for Infections, the HPA is a major employer of clinical microbiologists and epidemiologists.

Beyond the health services, opportunities exist in food production, in the manufacture of all alcoholic beverages, cheeses, and yoghurt, and in the disposal of sewage or of harmful industrial waste.

Related Occupations

You might be interested in other scientific careers such as biochemist, pharmacist, biologist, food scientist, or forensic scientist.

Impact on Lifestyle

You are likely to work a 37-hour week. Shift or night work is sometimes necessary in manufacturing plants and on-call work is expected when providing a round the clock service, such as in the NHS. Occasionally you may have to work extra hours to meet deadlines. It is usual to wear protective clothing, which varies according to the work and includes laboratory coats, gloves and eye protection.

Earnings Potential

Pre-registration clinical microbiology trainees usually start in NHS Band 6 on £24,831 to £33,436, before moving to the main practitioner Bands. A consultant or senior manager can earn in excess of £95,000 a year. In all cases, additional allowances are paid for posts in and around London. Starting salaries in industry vary according to sector and employer but tend to be rather below average.

Further Information

Society for General Microbiology, Reading RG7 1AG
Website: www.biocareers.org.uk

Health Professions Council, London SE11 4BU
Website: www.hpc-uk.org

Institute of Biology, London EC4A 3EF
Website: www.iob.org

Society for Industrial Microbiology, Fairfax, VA 22030-2421 USA
Website: www.simhq.org

Association of Clinical Microbiologists
Website: www.aclinmicrobiol.org.uk

Institute of Biomedical Science
Website: www.ibms.org

Health Protection Agency, London NW9 5HT
Website: www.hpa.org.uk

Alternative/equivalent entrance requirements can include: ILC, IB, EB, NC/ND and many other similar international systems. For further details see the Equivalent Qualifications section in the Introduction.

Midwife

What is Involved?

As a midwife, you would work in the community or in healthcare settings such as hospital maternity units, providing care and support for expectant mothers both during pregnancy and throughout labour and the postnatal period. Apart from delivering babies, you would carry out clinical examinations, provide health education, help mothers and their partners prepare for their parental role and give them advice on feeding their baby. You would also work in partnership with other health and social care professionals to meet the particular needs of people such as teenage mothers, socially excluded mothers, disabled mothers and mothers from diverse ethnic backgrounds. Your priority would be to provide a "woman-centred" integrated care service, offering choice and continuity of support to mother and child.

Although you would be working as a healthcare professional, you would have a client group who are on the whole very healthy and in need of help and advice only because they are expecting a baby. The birth itself may be at the heart of the process, but midwives provide support to women, their babies, their partners and families, from conception to the first phase of postnatal care.

Opportunities for Training

You could enter the profession directly by undertaking a specialised three- or four-year degree course leading to a midwifery qualification. These courses are provided by a number of universities. You could also take a shortened (18 months) midwifery course after first qualifying as a nurse. Courses combine theory and practice, with periods of university-based study interspersed with supervised work in local hospitals, clinics and the community. The degree route generally includes free tuition and some means-tested bursaries.

Before you can practise, you must be registered with the Nursing and Midwifery Council and you must maintain a portfolio of evidence of your continuous professional development. This would mean updating your skills and knowledge on a regular basis.

Requirements for Entry

Entry to a degree course would require a minimum of two A level/Advanced Higher, three Higher passes or equivalent qualifications, plus supporting GCSE/S Grade passes. A pass in a science subject may be required. The NHS and universities encourage applications from people with a wide range of academic and vocational qualifications, so it is always worth checking with individual institutions before applying to see if your qualifications meet the required entry standard.

You must also pass a medical test.

Kind of Person

You would be providing professional support and reassurance to a huge diversity of women, during some of the most emotionally intense periods in their lives. You must be kind and caring, flexible and adaptable, prepared to look after all women regardless of their class, creed, economic status, race or age. You would need to be able to stay calm and alert in times of stress and enable women to feel confident and in control. On the rare occasions where something goes wrong, you would have to be ready to react quickly and effectively. Good organisation and record keeping are essential.

Broad Outlook

There should be no difficulty in getting work once you qualify. Your first job would probably be within the National Health Service but there are openings within the private sector and some midwives practise independently. There are also opportunities for work abroad, although some countries specify that midwives must have full nurse training. Promotion can come as, for example, head of midwifery services or you might like to take further qualifications and become a midwifery teacher.

Related Occupations

You might also wish to consider: nurse, nursery nurse, dietitian, doctor, health visitor, occupational therapist, physiotherapist, social worker or teacher.

Impact on Lifestyle

You must be prepared to work shifts, including nights, weekends and holiday periods. You would also have to respond to emergency calls and you would need your own transport in order to travel between the hospital or clinic and people's homes. You would wear a uniform all the time you are on duty.

Earnings Potential

A newly qualified midwife working in the NHS would start in Band 5, earning from £20,710 to £26,839 a year. After that, allowances are paid for additional skills, overtime, shift working, responsibilities and experience, rising to £39,273 at the top of the scale for a midwife team manager. A consultant midwife can currently earn up to £65,657. Additional allowances are paid for appointments in and around London, ranging from 20% of basic salary for Inner London, to 15% for Outer London and 5% for the London Fringe. Earnings in the private sector are generally likely to be higher, depending on where you live and the hours you are prepared to work.

Further Information

Royal College of Midwives, London W1G 9NH
Website: www.rcm.org.uk

NHS Careers, Bristol BS2 2ZX
Website: www.nhscareers.nhs.uk

Nursing and Midwifery Council, London W1B 1PZ
Website: www.nmc-uk.org

NHS Education for Scotland, Edinburgh EH12 5HE
Website: www.nes.scot.nhs.uk

Northern Ireland Practice and Educational Council for Nursing and Midwifery
Website: www.nipec.hscni.net

Alternative/equivalent entrance requirements can include: ILC, IB, EB, NC/ND and many other similar international systems. For further details see the Equivalent Qualifications section in the Introduction.

Mining Engineer

What is Involved?

The scale of industrial operations in mining can be immense, requiring teams of trained professional engineers. As a mining or quarrying engineer, you would design and manage systems used in the extraction of ores; as an environmental engineer, you would provide essential planning and monitoring services; as a minerals engineer, you would design and manage plants for processing the minerals into metals and saleable concentrates or for recycling metals and related minerals. You would be expected to apply environmental best practice in all of these activities and you may find increasing opportunities to work solely in cleaning up the environment and in conservation. This is a very technologically driven industry and one that tries to balance ever-increasing demands for raw material resources with environmental issues.

Opportunities for Training

You would need a degree in mining engineering from one of the small group of universities specialising in this area. In order to become a chartered engineer, primarily concerned with research, design and development, you would need to complete at least four years of academic study and would usually achieve this via an MEng degree. If you want to be more involved with the day-to-day management of production processes as an incorporated engineer, you could take a three-year BEng degree. You don't always have to choose your specific training route from the start, so you should read prospectuses carefully. See also our separate article on engineering qualifications. There are sandwich courses available for both types of degree; these add an extra year but give the opportunity for a period of work experience, which can be very valuable when you are looking for a job. After graduating, you would need to complete a period of industrial training and responsible work experience before you achieve chartered or incorporated engineer status.

Requirements for Entry

For a degree course, you are likely to need A level/Advanced Higher, Higher or equivalent passes in two or three subjects selected from maths, physics and chemistry. If the latter subjects are not actually required, they will be strongly preferred by universities. In addition, you would need five GCSE/S Grade passes (A-C/1-3), including English, maths and at least one science subject. You would also be expected to have visited some mines and to have an understanding of the key issues in the industry.

Kind of Person

You should be interested in technology and in keeping up to date with developments in your field. You would need a strong interest in maths and science and it might be helpful to have an interest in geology or physical geography. You would probably be expected to find practical solutions in your work, so you should have a logical and creative approach to problem solving. You are likely to be analysing complex information, and may be required to use computers so you would need IT skills. Some of your work is also likely to require you to show meticulous attention to detail. In addition to your technical skills you will need to communicate well with others. You are likely to be working as a member of a small team. In addition to talking to other engineers, you may be expected to direct the work of others and also to explain your ideas to people who may not have your technical expertise.

Broad Outlook

The major mining companies were riding high on the commodities boom, enjoying record metal prices and record profits. All this has come to a juddering halt with the world recession of 2009. Metal prices have plummeted and expansion plans have been put on hold. The major companies are no doubt big enough to survive without serious damage, although the immediate prospects for new graduates are not encouraging. The global outlook is predicted to improve again from 2010 onwards.

Potential employers range from large multinational organisations, such as the major oil and gas producers, to small companies offering specialised services. Owing to the diversity and geographical spread of the industry, it is not possible to describe an average career in mining and minerals engineering. You could focus exclusively on coal or salt, for example, or you could travel extensively - anywhere from Antarctica to Zambia with spells in the UK - gaining experience of mining for, say, copper, zinc, lead or gold.

Related Occupations

You might also consider: petroleum, chemical, civil, mechanical, energy or nuclear engineer, materials scientist/metallurgist or geologist.

Impact on Lifestyle

If you want to stay involved in mining operations, you have to go where the mines are. Given that many mines are in remote locations, you can't always live where you would ideally like. You may sometimes work normal office hours in a relatively clean environment but you may equally work highly irregular hours, outdoors or deep underground, in conditions that could be difficult, dirty and at times dangerous.

Earnings Potential

Salary levels vary widely according to employer and sector. In the UK, starting salaries range from £20,000 to £25,000. With five years' experience this can increase to between £30,000 and £40,000. By the age of 40, UK mining engineers generally earn between £50,000 and £65,000. Salaries tend to be higher overseas, with Australia, Canada and the US generally providing the best levels of pay. Salaries in South Africa, on the other hand, are relatively low. More demanding work locations may pay better salaries.

Further Information

Institute of Materials Minerals and Mining, London SW1Y 5DB
Website: www.iom3.org
Website: www.uk-rocks.net

Engineering Council UK, London WC2R 3ER
Website: www.engc.org.uk

International Council on Mining and Metals
Website: www.icmm.com

Alternative/equivalent entrance requirements can include: ILC, IB, EB, NC/ND and many other similar international systems. For further details see the Equivalent Qualifications section in the Introduction.

Museum Keeper - Art Gallery Curator

What is Involved?

As a curator or keeper, you would usually manage a section of a large museum or art gallery (exhibiting, for example, paintings/sculpture, archaeological objects, historically important documents and artefacts or furniture), and would be responsible for the acquisition, identification, display and care of the exhibits. This would include seeing that they are kept in appropriate lighting and atmospheric conditions and arranging for any necessary restoration or conservation. You may also find yourself involved in the design of exhibitions and in administrative tasks: including cataloguing, preparing exhibition catalogues, articles and poster displays; giving talks and looking after members of the public.

In a large gallery or museum, jobs can be highly departmentalised and you might specialise in, say, 16th Century Italian art, 19th Century sculpture, Egyptian artefacts, Greek vases or the paintings of JMW Turner. In a small museum or art gallery, you could be responsible for everything from developing an acquisition policy, working with school groups, preparing a touring exhibition and managing volunteers to raising sponsorship and writing press releases.

Opportunities for Training

There is no formal training route in this very small, competitive and highly academic field. You should have a good degree in a relevant subject area - which could mean anything from history, anthropology or history of art to ceramics, textile design or a science or technology subject - followed by a postgraduate course in museum or heritage studies. The Courtauld Institute, University of London or University of East Anglia are among universities offering relevant postgraduate provision. Many other opportunities are available and could even include a doctorate at an overseas university such as Harvard, Stamford or Rome.

You would need to show your commitment by undertaking voluntary work experience in a museum or gallery and you would find that some employers run formal schemes leading to National/Scottish Vocational Qualifications in cultural heritage management. You might find it useful to work over a period of several years towards Associateship and then Fellowship of the Museums Association.

Requirements for Entry

You would normally need two or three A level/Advanced Higher, three or four Higher or equivalent qualifications for degree entry, together with a broad platform of GCSE/S Grade passes at A-C/1-3. For a postgraduate course, you should have a relevant first degree and evidence of your commitment (usually in the form of voluntary experience).

Kind of Person

You would need to have a genuine interest in art and historical artefacts, good organisational skills and the ability to explain and arrange exhibits in an imaginative way for visitors to enjoy. You might well be expected to have very detailed knowledge of a particular subject area. Good communication skills would be essential both for giving talks on your specialism and for writing associated articles and catalogues or even books.

Broad Outlook

This is not an easy career route to follow: there is increasingly intense competition for jobs, the pay would generally be described as poor and the level of qualifications and experience demanded is extremely high. In addition, career progression can be difficult - you would have to be willing to move anywhere in the country to widen your experience and gain promotion - and short-term contracts are often seen as the norm.

The Museums Association website contains details of current opportunities. Potential employers include independent museums and galleries, universities, local authority museums and galleries and national museums and galleries. There is also some scope for overseas work, especially in Commonwealth countries.

Related Occupations

You may also wish to consider: archaeologist, archivist, art auctioneer, conservator, art restorer, or fine arts/antiques dealer.

Impact on Lifestyle

While you would generally work around 36 hours per week, you should expect some weekend commitment in line with the opening hours of the museum or gallery. You may find yourself working late into the evening when a new exhibition is being launched, usually with an opening reception for friends of the museum or gallery or for local counsellors and sponsors. As noted above, you would almost certainly have to move home from time to time to pursue opportunities for promotion.

Earnings Potential

Low pay is widely recognised as a major problem, with museum pay falling behind that of comparable sectors. To address this issue, the Museums Association produce annually updated best practice salary guidelines. The current recommendation for graduate entry is £16,000 to £19,000, rising to £19,500 to £23,500 for a candidate with a postgraduate qualification and/or relevant experience. A Director of a large establishment could earn up to £75,000.

Further Information

Creative and Cultural Skills: the Sector Skills Council for the Creative and Cultural Industries, London SE1 3HN
Website: www.ccskills.org.uk

Museums Association, London E1 6NW
Website: www.museumsassociation.org

National Museum Wales, Cardiff CF10 3NP
Website: www.museumwales.ac.uk

National Museums Scotland, Edinburgh, Scotland EH1 1JF
Website: www.nms.ac.uk

Cultural Leadership Programme
Website: www.culturalleadership.org.uk

Alternative/equivalent entrance requirements can include: ILC, IB, EB, NC/ND and many other similar international systems. For further details see the Equivalent Qualifications section in the Introduction.

Musician

What is Involved?

As a professional musician, in classical or popular music, you would play one or more instruments and/or sing. You could be a performer or composer, a teacher working from home or in a school, college or university, an administrator, publisher, record company executive, instrument manufacturer, librarian, broadcaster or journalist. Many musicians combine some of these activities, especially those who both perform and teach. As an orchestral player, you may spend many years with one orchestra or work freelance, taking session work for concerts, recordings, backings and jingles. You could also join the armed forces or the police for service with a regimental or police band.

In popular music, you might combine singing with playing an instrument either as a soloist or in a small group. Your main contact with the public would be through performing, perhaps supported with recordings and videos.

Opportunities for Training

Whatever area of music you choose, there is no standard training programme and no fixed career path. Any performing career would demand very high standards, simply because the competition is so intense. For classical musicians, the specialist music colleges and conservatoires offer three- or four-year degree courses with the emphasis on performance. Alternatively, you could study music to degree level at university, where courses may have more academic content, before taking a postgraduate course to concentrate on technique and performance. Music therapy training is also at postgraduate level.

The armed services train musicians (including string players) for military bands. Recruits are brought in from the age of 16 and are given two-and-a-half years of professional training. There is limited formal training for popular music, although there are some courses. You should gain as much performing experience as possible, while trying to get noticed by a recording company.

Requirements for Entry

For degree course entry, you would need at least two A level/Advanced Higher, three Higher or equivalent passes plus supporting GCSE/S Grade passes (A-C/1-3), and you would need to have reached an advanced level of instrumental or vocal performance (at least grade 8). To teach in a maintained school, you would need a recognised professional qualification for teaching as distinct from training in music. See our separate article for 'Teacher'.

Kind of Person

Qualities such as artistry, determination and dedication must be combined with general musicianship and technical mastery of your instrument or voice. As a performer, you must be confident in your ability and enjoy being in front of an audience. As a private teacher, you should like working with people and would need good communication skills, patience, perseverance and the ability to run your own business. To work in a school, you must like and understand young people and want to teach them, no matter what their ability.

Broad Outlook

Competition is fierce and the pay is generally below that of other jobs requiring similar levels of skill, training and expertise. To succeed, you must have more than talent alone; you must also have absolute dedication and determination. To get work, you have to be known and this means taking every opportunity - concerts, auditions, awards, bursaries and competitions - to show that you are worth engaging. Even after becoming established, you would find that earning a living as a performer - out of recordings, broadcasts and concerts - is hard work. Many performers combine a performing career with teaching or other work in the community, perhaps as a music therapist.

Job prospects for classroom teachers are good, since the demand for music teachers exceeds the supply. Pop musicians often start informally as a group of students at school or college, usually with a manager to organise gigs and recording contracts. Some become rich and famous but many others work more or less full-time in pubs, clubs and concert halls.

Related Occupations

You might also consider: teacher, music therapist, recording engineer or radio/TV producer.

IImpact on Lifestyle

Working hours can be long and irregular, with evening and weekend performances and rehearsals during the day, often linked with extensive travel to concerts or gigs. As a music teacher, you would work more regular hours but would usually be expected to organise evening and weekend events.

Earnings Potential

Top performers command extremely high fees but, for the majority, earnings are moderate. The Incorporated Society of Musicians publishes on its website recommended rates for most types of musical activity. Music teachers, permanent members of major orchestras and musicians in the armed forces are among the few to enjoy the luxury of a regular income, although many musicians make a reasonable living.

Further Information

Incorporated Society of Musicians, London, W1C 1AA
Website: www.ism.org

Musicians' Union, London SW9 0JJ
Website: www.musiciansunion.org.uk

Association of British Orchestras, London W1D 6DF
Website: www.abo.org.uk

Alternative/equivalent entrance requirements can include: ILC, IB, EB, NC/ND and many other similar international systems. For further details see the Equivalent Qualifications section in the Introduction.

Naval Architect

What is Involved?

As a naval architect, you would be a professional engineer responsible for the design, construction and repair of ships, boats and other marine vessels and offshore structures. You could be involved with merchant ships, passenger ferries, naval warships, offshore drilling platforms or yachts, powerboats and other recreational craft. Given the size and complexity of many of these vessels, you would work as a member of a team containing many specialist engineers. Part of your role as a naval architect would be to integrate their activities and take overall control of a project. You would also have a specialist role in ensuring that the final product is safe, efficient and seaworthy.

Apart from the architectural aspects of ship form and layout, you must be able to use complex mathematical and physical models to ensure that your design is satisfactory technically and that it meets the relevant safety rules and standards. Alternatively, you may specialise in construction, usually taking responsibility for the management of a yard or for sections of it such as planning, production or fitting out. There is a continuous striving to make savings on existing techniques and equipment through the adoption of new processes and practices and by better training for the work force. You would also organise the supply of materials and components, inspection and testing as well as the vital resources of manpower.

Opportunities for Training

You would normally undertake a degree course in Naval Architecture, Marine Technology, Offshore Engineering or Ship Science. The course should be accredited by the Royal Institution of Naval Architects (RINA) and lead to registration with the Engineering Council UK as a Chartered Engineer (CEng) or Incorporated Engineer (IEng). There is also scope to qualify below degree level as an Engineering Technician (EngTech). You must have an aggregate of seven years of education, approved training and responsible experience in industry after reaching the age of 18 years before you can achieve full RINA membership and CEng status.

Requirements for Entry

You should take a broad range of subjects at GCSE/S Grade, covering both the arts and sciences and including maths, physics and English. You should then add three A level/Advanced Higher, five Higher or equivalent qualifications, including good pass grades in maths and/or physics. These studies should lead to qualifications satisfying the entry requirements for either an accredited masters degree (MEng) course if you want to become a chartered engineer, or a degree (BEng) course if you are intending to become an incorporated engineer. (See the separate article on engineering qualifications in the introduction).

Kind of Person

You would need a creative, practical, enquiring and logical mind, excellent communication skills in speech and writing, mature judgement and evidence of leadership ability. A keen interest in sailing, windsurfing or other maritime pursuits can be extremely helpful. You must have a broad understanding of many different branches of engineering together with advanced skills in computer-aided design.

Broad Outlook

Naval architecture is a truly global profession and you should find that your qualifications and experience would open up career opportunities all over the world once the global economy picks up again after the downturn of 2009. You may become a specialist in one particular aspect of ship design or construction or you may use your professional skills in project management to develop a broader management career, possibly outside the maritime field.

Potential employers include ship and boat builders and repairers, offshore constructors, design consultants and, for the ships and submarines of the Royal Navy, the Ministry of Defence. Major equipment manufacturers also employ teams of engineers, including naval architects, on the design of such products as propulsion systems, auxiliary systems, sub sea production systems and control systems.

Continuing professional development (CPD) is essential and can be achieved through courses and conferences organised by the RINA and other engineering professional institutions or organisations on new technologies, management systems, communication, business and many other topics.

Related Occupations

You may wish to consider: mechanical engineer, electrical/electronic engineer, civil engineer, offshore engineer, officer in the Royal or Merchant Navy, architect or systems analyst.

Impact on Lifestyle

Achieving CEng status can mean considerable extra work in the years immediately following your degree but this should be a good long-term investment. You may have to travel extensively as you seek to develop your career.

Earnings Potential

While you would probably start on around £21,000 to £27,500, you should see your salary increase with experience to £35,000 to £45,000. Higher earners can make £50,000 to £75,000 a year. Salaries vary between employers according to geographical location and specialisation.

Further Information

Royal Institution of Naval Architects, London SW1X 8BQ
Website: www.rina.org.uk

Defence Engineering and Science Group, Bath BA1 5AB
Website: www.desg.mod.uk

Engineering Council UK, London WC2R 3ER
Website: www.engc.org.uk

Alternative/equivalent entrance requirements can include: ILC, IB, EB, NC/ND and many other similar international systems. For further details see the Equivalent Qualifications section in the Introduction.

Nurse

What is Involved?

As a registered nurse, you would be working as part of a multi-disciplinary team providing health care in hospitals, specialist clinics and the community. You would specialise in one of four main branches:

In the adult branch, your main focus would be patients from the age of 16 upwards.

As a children's nurse, you might be looking after a very sick baby on a life support machine, a 10 year-old needing urgent surgery to repair a broken leg and a 14 year-old with a damaged liver.

As a mental health or psychiatric nurse, you would be working with patients suffering from problems such as depression, anxiety, alcohol dependency and severe eating disorders.

As a learning disability nurse, you would be least likely to work in a hospital and could spend most of your time with patients in their own homes or in residential care centres.

Opportunities for Training

You would have to undertake a university-based diploma or degree programme, leading to registration with the Nursing and Midwifery Council (NMC). Training usually lasts three years (some degrees take four years) and includes equal amounts of theory and practice. You would gain experience in a variety of care settings, including hospitals, nursing homes and the community.

The three-year course is divided into two distinct parts:

●   the first year, the "Common Foundation Programme" or CFP, is undertaken by all students, regardless of branch choice. It includes core issues and topics, together with experience of a wide variety of care environments

●   the second part, the branch programme, concentrates on specific branch subjects and practice placements

You should investigate the area of nursing which you would like to study and ultimately work in, as the choice of branch for the second part usually has to be made upon application. However, some universities enable you to make a more informed choice after you have started.

Requirements for Entry

There are no national minimum entry requirements for entry into nursing, as each higher education institution set its own criteria. However, these are generally around five GCSE/S Grade passes A-C/1-3, or equivalent for a diploma course. You should contact the university of your choice to check on the exact requirements. For a degree course in nursing, you would normally need at least two A level/Advanced Higher, three Higher or equivalent qualifications, together with supporting GCSE/S Grade passes. The more scientific courses may specify science subjects at AS or A level, Advanced Higher or Higher, with biology being the most popular. Admissions officers are usually looking for commitment, motivation and experience as well as academic qualifications, so it is a good idea to get some relevant work experience.

Kind of Person

You would need to be very resilient, both physically and mentally, to face the many challenges involved in caring for people who are ill or disabled. You would be constantly interacting with other people, so would need to be good at both talking and listening. You would need to be able to inspire trust and confidence, displaying tact, sensitivity and maturity. At times, you would have to put people at ease in stressful situations. You would also have to work closely with others as part of the healthcare team.

Broad Outlook

For many years, nursing has been on the list of recognised shortage professions, with the result that employment prospects have been excellent. However, financial problems in the NHS three years ago led to a recruitment freeze in many NHS Trusts and a survey of universities indicated a shortage of opportunities for nurses qualifying that year. The position has since improved and the Department of Health insists that jobs still exist. It accepts, however, that competition for posts has intensified and that graduates need to be flexible on where they are willing to work. The Royal College of Nursing campaigns vigorously on behalf of the nursing workforce and publishes an annual labour market review. You may wish to check the latest information on its website.

Related Occupations

You may wish to consider physiotherapist, occupational therapist, radiographer, dietitian or speech and language therapist. Alternatively, you might develop your career as a midwife or health visitor.

Impact on Lifestyle

Depending on your chosen branch, you might have to work on a shift basis, including nights, weekends and public holidays, although not usually more than 37.5 hours per week in total. There is currently such a shortage of nurses that many employers would be prepared to discuss all types of flexible working arrangements.

Earnings Potential

Qualified nurses in the NHS usually start in Band 5, on a scale currently ranging from £20,710 to £26,839. Earnings can rise to £33,436 for a nurse specialist at the top of the scale and to over £65,000 for a nurse consultant. Additional allowances are paid for appointments in and around London, ranging from 20% of basic salary for Inner London, to 15% for Outer London and 5% for the London Fringe. Earnings in the private sector are generally likely to be higher, depending on where you live and the hours you are prepared to work Overtime is payable at time and a half when excess hours are worked over full-time hours (37.5).

Further Information

NHS Careers, Bristol BS99 3EY
Website: www.nhscareers.nhs.uk

Nursing and Midwifery Council, London W1B 1PZ
Website: www.nmc-uk.org

Royal College of Nursing, London W1G 0RN
Website: www.rcn.org.uk

Alternative/equivalent entrance requirements can include: ILC, IB, EB, NC/ND and many other similar international systems. For further details see the Equivalent Qualifications section in the Introduction.

Occupational Therapist

What is Involved?

As an occupational therapist, you are most likely to work as part of a multi-disciplinary team. Your job would be to assess and treat people of all ages with physical and mental health problems, to help them regain, develop or maintain an independent lifestyle. You may be involved with helping someone who has had a stroke or a person with an eating disorder return to a normal lifestyle.

Alternatively, you could find yourself helping burns victims recover from their injuries, work which may include applying make-up to camouflage any scarring. This rehabilitation can start before the patient leaves hospital and continues once they have been discharged, either in the patient's own home or in the occupational therapy department at the hospital. You might also work with long-stay patients in hospital, helping them maintain contact with 'normal' life, and you may become involved with supporting patients' families.

Opportunities for Training

You would need to be state registered with the Health Professions Council, which means in most cases that you must take a validated three-or four-year degree course in Occupational Therapy. All training courses are about two thirds academic, covering such areas as anatomy, physiology, psychiatry and orthopaedics, together with the particular skills and techniques used by occupational therapists, the organisation and management of occupational therapy departments and how to provide suitable aids and equipment for patients. The remaining third of the course is clinical and is spent in departments and hospital clinics learning about practical day-to-day occupational therapy. During this time, you would learn to assess and treat patients under the guidance of a registered therapist and then build up to treating your own small caseload under supervision.

An alternative route to qualification is the four-year, in-service, day-release course for people already working as assistants in occupational therapy departments. Accelerated postgraduate courses are also available, enabling graduates of other disciplines to obtain a licence to practise in two years.

Requirements for Entry

You would need a minimum of two A level/Advanced Higher, three Higher or equivalent qualifications, together with at least five GCSE/S Grade passes A-C/1-3. Normally, this requirement includes at least one science subject at GCSE/S Grade, while some courses look for A level/Advanced Higher or Higher biology. Demand for courses can be quite high, which means that applicants often need more than the minimum requirements. It is best to check with admissions tutors to be sure of meeting the entry requirements for particular courses.

Kind of Person

Since the job is very varied and you would have to meet and deal with a large number of people with different problems and needs, you would need to be creative and flexible. Each patient will require their own particular programme to work on and will make progress at their own rate. You will need to be able to gain the confidence of your patients both to find out what their needs are likely to be and to be able to encourage them to keep trying. At times progress can be frustratingly slow and hard work. As well as being able to establish supportive relationships with patients, you would have to be able to explain the treatment clearly and adjust the programme as necessary. You would have to keep good records on each patient and you would need to liaise with other healthcare professionals, sometimes taking part in case conferences.

Broad Outlook

Occupational therapists have been part of local authority social services since departments were first established and remain the only Allied Health Professionals to be employed in this setting. Occupational therapy staff make up between 1% and 2% of the social services workforce in the UK and yet they handle some 25% to 40% of the referrals to social services. There has been a shortage of suitably qualified candidates but vacancy rates are reducing in many parts of the country, with some areas unable to offer newly qualified occupational therapists posts.

There are opportunities for specialisation in areas such as burns and plastics, neuroscience or working with handicapped children. There are also increasingly openings for occupational therapists to promote safe procedures at work and in the home, in order to reduce the risk of injury.

There are opportunities to become self-employed or to work freelance or in private practice.

Related Occupations

You might consider social worker or other therapy-based professions in the medical field, such as radiographer, physiotherapist, speech and language therapist or nurse.

Impact on Lifestyle

The work can be demanding, stressful and, at times, frustrating so you need to have commitment and a real desire to help others to achieve their potential. You would have to keep up to date with what equipment or exercises are available to help your patients. Occupational therapists usually work a 36-hour week, although you might sometimes be required to work extra hours.

Earnings Potential

A newly qualified NHS occupational therapist would start in Band 5, on a scale ranging from £20,710 to £26,839. This could rise to £39,273 for a team manager at the top of the scale and to around £55,000 for a consultant. Additional allowances are paid for appointments in and around London, ranging from 20% of basic salary for Inner London, to 15% for Outer London and 5% for the London Fringe. Salaries in the private sector are often linked to NHS levels but may be higher.

Further Information

British Association/College of Occupational Therapists, London SE1 1LB
Website: www.cot.org.uk

Alternative/equivalent entrance requirements can include: ILC, IB, EB, NC/ND and many other similar international systems. For further details see the Equivalent Qualifications section in the Introduction.

Oceanographer

What is Involved?

As an oceanographer, you would be a scientist concerned with the chemistry, biology, physics or geology of the marine world. This could include studying coastlines, waves and tidal flow, the structure of the seabed, estuaries and coastal waters or organisms that live in the sea. You work could relate to the pollution of the seas or issues of climate change.

If your main interest is biology, you might study sustainable methods of seafood production; as a marine chemist, you might focus on how pesticides or nuclear waste enter and move through the oceans; if you are interested in physics, you might prefer to study the interaction between the wind and ocean currents; as a geologist, you could study the deposition of sediments in the oceans.

Whatever your principal science, the additional dimension of oceanography would give you a broad range of skills and knowledge relevant to understanding and managing the marine environment.

Opportunities for Training

An ocean science degree would give you a broad overview of all the disciplines of oceanography, so that you can understand how they combine to explain the ways in which the oceans interact with the earth and the atmosphere. Most courses are modular, giving you a chance to specialise if you wish to as your awareness grows. There are also universities offering degrees focusing on a particular area of oceanography, such as marine biology or marine chemistry. For postgraduate study, it is more common to specialise in one of these specific areas of oceanography.

Requirements for Entry

For entry to a degree course, you would need at least two A level/Advanced Higher, three Higher or equivalent qualifications, usually including passes in sciences related to your main interest. Some universities specify more than the minimum, so you should research admission requirements carefully. Employers of oceanographers often require postgraduate qualifications.

Kind of Person

You would need a strong interest in science and the sea, with an enquiring mind and a keen attention to detail and accuracy. You would probably need to spend extended periods of time on a boat gathering data. You may need to go down to the seabed in a submarine vehicle or by diving. You would need IT skills to carry out detailed calculations.

Some of your work is likely to be carried out on your own but you would also need to work as part of a team. You may need to write up reports and explain to people what you have found out or what you are aiming to explore. These may be other scientists but could also be people who do not share your technical knowledge, so you would need to be able to communicate clearly.

Broad Outlook

In oceanography, the majority of jobs currently available are filled by people from mathematics, physics or chemistry backgrounds, sometimes as joint honours degrees with oceanography. There are also opportunities for graduates in biology, marine biology, biochemistry, zoology, geology and geophysics.

While competition for posts is fierce, there are opportunities for oceanographers to work as researchers and the Natural Environment Research Council is a major employer. There are also opportunities to work in a commercial environment or for an organisation like the National Rivers Authority, a harbour authority or the Royal Navy. As environmental concerns become more important there is an increasing number of consultancies being set up, creating opportunities to work in private practice.

Related Occupations

You might also consider: hydrographic surveyor, geologist, meteorologist, biologist, chemist, physicist, microbiologist or biochemist.

Impact on Lifestyle

Oceanographers can expect to travel widely and, at the very least, to work alongside colleagues from many nations. You are likely find yourself working away from home, sometimes abroad or living on ships. When you are working out in the field you would be out in all sorts of weathers, sometimes cold and wet, sometimes basking in bright sunshine! You would generally work normal office hours but when you are at sea you may be expected to work long hours on a rota to finish your project in the time available.

Earnings Potential

Using government research and university rates as examples, you will find that typical starting salaries for recent graduates or MSc candidates range from £17,000 to £20,000, and from £19,000 to £29,000 for PhD candidates. Typical salaries for first time lecturers are £27,000 to £37,000, while experienced senior lecturers can earn £38,000 to £56,000 plus. Oceanographers who work in private industry would be on a similar scale or slightly higher. Consultancy pay can be higher still, although most consultants start on a rate ranging from £25,000 to £35,000, with pay levels increasing with suitable experience.

Further Information

Natural Environment Research Council, Swindon SN2 1EU
Website: www.nerc.ac.uk

National Oceanography Centre, Southampton SO14 3ZH
Website: www.soc.soton.ac.uk

Society for Underwater Technology, London EC2R 5BJ
Website: www.sut.org.uk

British Oceanographic Data Centre, Liverpool L3 5DA
Website: www.bodc.ac.uk

Alternative/equivalent entrance requirements can include: ILC, IB, EB, NC/ND and many other similar international systems. For further details see the Equivalent Qualifications section in the Introduction.

Office Manager

What is Involved?

All companies and organisations rely on well-run offices to maintain their profitability or success. As an office manager, you would be responsible for making sure that every aspect of the organisation's administration were carried out in the most efficient and satisfactory way. You could be dealing with the outgoing and incoming information and communication and its accurate storage and retrieval, in both paper and electronic form. You would probably have a team of clerical and administrative assistants to deal with the day-to-day office duties, such as answering queries (in person or on the telephone), typing letters or emails, taking and passing on messages, providing help at meetings and filing information. You should set the tone of the office.

Opportunities for Training

There is no single route into office management, but many managers gain promotion from other administrative positions and are employed because of their experience and proven success in other fields. Training is often carried out on-the-job. Another route would be to take a degree or higher national diploma (HND). There are a good number of university courses in subjects such as business studies or management and allied options; postgraduate courses are also available.

More specific training courses could include the OCR (Oxford, Cambridge and Royal Society of Arts) Diploma and Higher Diploma in Administrative and Secretarial Procedures or the Education Development International level 3 Certificate in Business Administration. There are also National/Scottish Vocational Qualifications in administration.

Requirements for Entry

While there are no particular educational requirements laid down for office managers, graduates are increasingly being employed. Most subjects are acceptable but it would be useful to be able to show that you are numerate and have some idea of what business organisation entails. You might consider a course in business studies (though they vary widely and you should look carefully at their content before making your choice) or another subject containing an option in some aspect of business. Just as important as the actual subject of the course, however, would be your personality, general interest and understanding of the business world. A sandwich course, which includes an industrial or business placement, could be useful.

For entry to a degree course, you would need two or three A level/Advanced Highers, three or four Higher or equivalent qualifications, together with five GCSE/S Grade passes A-C/1-3. The courses last three or four years. For the HND route, you would need one or two A level/Advanced Higher, two or three Higher or equivalent qualifications. The courses last two or three years.

Kind of Person

You should be organised, efficient and confident; you should also be willing to take responsibility and to make decisions quickly and fairly. As a manager, you should be happy working both as leader and member of a team, delegating sensibly and making sure that everything is working smoothly. Excellent communication skills would be important, as you would probably be in contact with a wide variety of people, both in the organisation and outside it. Computer literacy and a good standard of written language would be valuable.

Broad Outlook

While the numbers of clerical and administrative staff may have fallen with the arrival of computers, there is still a need throughout the country for skilled office managers. Increasingly, business is becoming internationally based, making office managers with some ability in foreign languages particularly in demand. Non-commercial areas, such as national and local government and higher education, also need efficient office managers.

Related Occupations

You might also consider: accountant, accounting technician, banking executive, chartered secretary, hospitality manager, leisure services manager, local government administrator, management consultant; personnel (human resources) manager; retail manager or civil service administrator.

Impact on Lifestyle

As an office manager you would normally work regular office hours but you might have to work overtime at certain times of the year. Weekend work would be unusual but, as the one in charge, you would be expected to take the lead if extra time should be needed.

Earnings Potential

There is considerable variety in salary scales, according to the size of the organisation and the amount of responsibility involved. In a large company or organisation, a skilful and ambitious manager could gain high rewards, with a possible share in company bonuses. Starting salaries of between £18,000 and £33,000 should be possible, rising with experience to £25,000 to £45,000.

Further Information

Institute of Customer Services, Essex CO1 1EW
Website: www.ics-nto.com

Association of Medical Secretaries, Practice Managers, Administrators and Receptionists, London WC1H 9LN
Website: www.amspar.co.uk

Council for Administration, London SE11 5EE
Website: www.cfa.uk.com

Institute of Administrative Management, London WC1V 6DX
Website: www.instam.org

OCR, Cambridge CB1 2EU
Website: www.ocr.org.uk

Institute for Professional Administrators, London SE11 5EE
Website: www.inprad.org

Education Development International
Website: www.ediplc.com

Alternative/equivalent entrance requirements can include: ILC, IB, EB, NC/ND and many other similar international systems. For further details see the Equivalent Qualifications section in the Introduction.

Operational Researcher/Management Scientist

What is Involved?

As an operational researcher, you would specialise in applying mathematical, statistical, computing and other analytical techniques to help organisations evaluate their operational procedures, improve their efficiency and devise strategies for future development. Operational research (OR) work can be very varied, giving you the opportunity to move around and experience many different business environments, ranging from central government, health, defence or transport to manufacturing industry, retailing, financial services or power, water and telecommunications supply companies. Within these, you might consider areas such as information storage, handling and access, management decision making, manufacturing processes, sales administration, accounting systems, logistics, forecasting or scheduling. In a rapidly developing economy, OR techniques are in great demand to keep organisations efficient, economically viable and competitive.

Your work would often involve visiting the workplace to talk to operational personnel and management in order to establish what changes need to be looked at, what kinds of problems arise regularly to disrupt efficient operation and where information bottlenecks are causing delays in, for example, the delivery of goods or in reordering raw materials. You would then apply appropriate OR techniques, such as mathematical modelling and computer simulations, to analyse the problems and come up with pragmatic solutions for the management team or company board to consider. Finally, you could be directly involved in the installation and testing out of new systems.

Opportunities for Training

Most people employed in OR are graduates and many would have followed courses with a significant mathematical, statistical or computing content. However, opportunities can exist for people from other disciplines and those who move into OR from other professions. Many undergraduate courses in mathematics, statistics, business studies and management include some OR, although it is not always necessary for entrants to the profession to have studied OR. Many employers would look firstly for quantitative, logical and communication skills and then provide any further appropriate training. In fact, graduates are recruited from many disciplines - and most OR groups have members contributing a variety of skills. After graduating, you could either seek employment straight away or follow a postgraduate course. Many significant employing organisations prefer candidates with an MSc in OR and a list of suitable courses can be found on the Operational Research Society website.

Requirements for Entry

For entry to an appropriate degree course, you would normally need to have at least two A level/Advanced Higher, three Higher passes or equivalent, in most cases including mathematics. After successfully completing your degree and demonstrating that you have the required analytical and business interest skills, you could progress to employment or postgraduate study.

Kind of Person

A solid grounding in maths, statistics and computing would be an important asset for a career in OR. However, before launching into data analysis, you would have to assemble and understand the information relating to the problem area. This would often involve in-depth discussions with people at all levels. Good communication skills and business awareness would, therefore, be crucial in winning co-operation, whilst literacy, numeracy and computer literacy would be vital in the execution of your work. You would need an excellent grasp of business operations, with an insight into management controls, communications, production and administration systems. You would have to pay careful attention to detail and you might need strong powers of persuasion to convince managers and directors that your proposals would solve their problems.

Broad Outlook

Opportunities for promotion often occur within a high demand field of this sort, both in your existing organisation and by moving to another. Some 250 companies, government departments, financial institutions, retailing, transport, health, management consultancy groups and university departments offer openings for OR staff. This is a field in which you can gain a remarkable overall grasp of organisational structures and is likely to open up many opportunities for rapid promotion to senior general management levels and even to board level, where your training would give you a considerable technical advantage.

Related Occupations

You might also consider: work study officer, management consultant, software engineer, statistician or actuary.

Impact on Lifestyle

Your work could involve a great deal of travel in the UK and abroad, with often lengthy periods spent away from home and therefore with some disruption of social and family life. Disentangling complex systems and coming up with better ones would often be accompanied by the pressure of meeting deadlines, writing reports and proposals and making presentations to managers or senior executives.

Earnings Potential

Typical starting salaries range from around £20,000 for a recent first-degree graduate to around £32,000 for an MSc/PhD holder in London. These figures should rise with experience to £40,000 to £80,000. In management consultancies, operational research specialists tend to start at around £25,000, progressing to a mid-career salary of between £60,000 and £80,000 and possibly going up to £100,000. Salaries tend to be highest in consultancy and lower in the public sector.

Further Information

Operational Research Society, Birmingham B1 2RX
Website: www.orsoc.org.uk

Association of European Operational Research Societies, London WC2A 2JT
Website: www.euro-online.org

Alternative/equivalent entrance requirements can include: ILC, IB, EB, NC/ND and many other similar international systems. For further details see the Equivalent Qualifications section in the Introduction.

Optometrist

What is Involved?

As an optometrist you would be responsible for caring for people's sight. Your job would include testing sight, examining eyes and giving advice on visual problems. This may involve prescribing and fitting spectacles or contact lenses or it may mean referring the patient to their GP if you find a problem involving disease or damage to the eye. You would start by talking to the client to establish the reason for their visit, noting any history of problems or illnesses and whether they drive or play sport. You would then use a series of tests to examine the eyes and determine whether there are problems you can deal with or more serious issues in need of referral for medical treatment.

Opportunities for Training

To become an optometrist, you would need to pass the General Optical Council (GOC) professional qualifying examination. This has two distinct parts:

- BSc Optometry (sometimes Ophthalmic Optics), a broadly based scientific degree combining theory with clinical work. The theoretical side includes anatomy and physiology, optics, optometry, pharmacology and the use of drugs, recognition of ocular abnormalities; the practical covers dispensing practice and management and professional studies.

- A Pre-Registration Period of training , including work based assessment and supervision by a registered optometrists, followed by a Final Assessment examination based on the GOC Stage 2 core competencies for optometry. This includes practical examinations and a clinical decision making section based on pre-written case scenarios.

Requirements for Entry

There are only eight British universities offering a first degree in optometry and there is a high demand for places. Most universities require two or three sciences at A level/Advanced Higher, three Higher or equivalent qualifications, some specifying biology as one of them; chemistry, maths and physics are other particularly useful subjects. It is advisable to check entry requirements with the individual institutions. Before applying, you should spend some time on a work experience or work-shadowing placement with a qualified optometrist.

Kind of Person

Optometry involves combining expert knowledge with good communication skills, patience and precision to achieve the best possible care for your clients' eyes. You need to be able to understand a complex and precise science and have sufficient mathematical aptitude to make the accurate measurements and calculations needed. The instruments used are delicate and you would need manual dexterity to use them correctly. As there are constant developments in this field, you would need to keep yourself up to date. You would be dealing with people from all walks of life, some of them worried about their sight or the prospect of wearing glasses or lenses. If you intend to work in private practice, you would also need good business sense and management skills. An interest in fashion and colour is helpful.

Broad Outlook

With more than half the UK population having a diagnosed visual defect, there is no shortage of work for the nation's 8,500 registered optometrists. Most work in general practice on their own, in partnership for a small independent firm or in one of the big high street chains. Excellent prospects for self-employment attract many people to the profession. There are also opportunities to work in hospitals alongside eye specialists and their teams. Some optometrists become specialists themselves in a particular field or else assist with eye tests and prescriptions following operations or other medical treatment. There are also chances for research and teaching.

Related Occupations

You may be interested in other professions concerned with maintaining or correcting people's vision, such as dispensing optician or orthoptist. You might also consider other medical related professions, such as speech and language therapist or radiographer.

Impact on Lifestyle

Most optometrists in private practice work a 37.5-hour week, although in some of the large practices you may have to work on a rota system in which days off vary. Saturdays are often busy in high street practices. If you set yourself up in practice you would have to work long and unsocial hours, at least to start with, in order to establish yourself. In the NHS, you would work a 35-hour week, although you may be on call at evenings and weekends. There is considerable scope for part-time work.

Earnings Potential

There is no set minimum salary for the pre-registration year in private practice but most practices offer salaries of around £16,500 per annum. Earnings should rise on qualification to approximately £22,000 to £26,000 The range of typical salaries for a senior optometrist in private practice is generally £40,000 to £50,000. Your earnings potential can be much higher if you set yourself up as an independent optometrist, with typical salaries for experienced practitioners sometimes exceeding £80,000. Hospital eye service salaries are initially graded in NHS Band 6, ranging from £24,831 to £33,436, with additional payments for specialist skills. A hospital principal can earn over £65,000 at the top of the scale.

Further Information

College of Optometrists, London WC2N 5NG
Website: www.college-optometrists.org

Association of Optometrists, London SE1 0HL
Website: www.assoc-optometrists.org

General Optical Council, London W1G 8DJ
Website: www.optical.org

Alternative/equivalent entrance requirements can include: ILC, IB, EB, NC/ND and many other similar international systems. For further details see the Equivalent Qualifications section in the Introduction.

Orthoptist

What is Involved?

As an orthoptist, you would carry out detailed eye testing, using advanced equipment, to diagnose the causes of your patients' eye problems. You could measure the extent of long or short vision, of misalignment of the eyes, astigmatism, loss of vision and detect glaucoma and other eye diseases. You would refer patients where necessary to doctors for further assessment, treatment or surgery. Then you would give your patients advice on suitable treatment and monitor their progress. This may involve exercises to 're-educate' the eye muscles in cases of lazy eyes or after strokes. You may be involved in helping patients with their recovery after operation.

You could also be involved with assessing the vision of older patients who have been affected by illness, injury or a stroke or of children, who are likely to be the majority of your patients, and who may have difficulty in explaining their difficulties. For example, you would use a computerised field analyser to find out where the patient is experiencing a blind spot. Each working day is likely to be different. As well as conducting clinics for outpatients, you would accompany consultants on ward rounds in hospitals. You could also work in private practice.

Opportunities for Training

You would need to study for a degree in orthoptics approved by the Orthoptists Board of the Health Professions Council. This is available at two universities in the UK: Liverpool and Sheffield. The degrees are of three-year duration, leading to BSc or BMedSci (orthoptics) qualifications. The first year covers general anatomy and physiology. It gives an understanding of the normal visual system as well as introducing optics and orthoptics. In years two and three, the investigation and management of disorders of vision are taught. In addition, you would learn about ophthalmology and pathology so that you can recognise disorders and diseases of the eye. You would be given practical experience with clinical placements in all three years of your course.

Requirements for Entry

To take a degree in orthoptics you would need three A level/Advanced Higher, four Higher or equivalent qualifications, including at least one science subject, preferably biology but physics or maths would be very helpful, together with five GCSE/S Grade passes A-C/1-3, which should include English, maths, and physics or dual science. It is advisable to arrange a visit to your local orthoptic department to see what the work involves before applying for a place.

Kind of Person

You would need a keen interest in biology, maths and physics, as well as having good interpersonal skills to deal with the wide range of people you would meet in this work. Some of your patients may be hard to communicate with because they are elderly or young children, so you would need to be patient and creative both in your explanations and to capture their attention. Much of the testing involves skilful measuring and the use of precision instruments. You would be expected to keep accurate records on your patients so you would have to be well organised. As well as working as part of a team, you would also need to be able to work responsibly on your own.

Broad Outlook

There is demand both for full-time and part-time orthoptists. The majority of orthoptists are employed in the National Health Service within a set grading structure. Opportunities exist for promotion to Head Orthoptist in clinical practice.

You could also study for a higher degree (MSc, MPhil or PhD) and/or consider a teaching career in orthoptics. The British qualification in orthoptics is respected throughout the world and there are opportunities for working abroad. There is great potential for future research within the orthoptic field and both universities are actively involved in the development of a large and productive research profile.

Related Occupations

You may be interested in other related professions such as dispensing optician or optometrist. Alternatively, you might like to consider another profession in the medical field, such as radiographer, podiatrist, speech and language therapist or physiotherapist.

Impact on Lifestyle

Most orthoptists work normal hours from Monday to Friday. Your social and family life would therefore be far less disturbed than that of other health professionals working in hospitals, who have to deal with emergencies and patient care on a 24-hour basis.

Earnings Potential

A newly qualified NHS orthoptist would start in Band 5, on a scale ranging from £20,710 to £26,839. This could rise for a specialist in Band 6 to £24,831 to £33,436 and for an advanced practitioner in Band 7 to £29,789 to £39,273. A head of department could earn up to £65, 657. Additional allowances are paid for appointments in and around London, ranging from 20% of basic salary for Inner London, to 15% for Outer London and 5% for the London Fringe. Salaries in the private sector are often linked to NHS levels but may be higher.

Further Information

British and Irish Orthoptic Society, London WC1H 9HX
Website: www.orthoptics.org.uk

General Optical Council, London W1G 8DJ
Website: www.optical.org

Health Professions Council, London SE11 4BU
Website: www.hpc-uk.org

Alternative/equivalent entrance requirements can include: ILC, IB, EB, NC/ND and many other similar international systems. For further details see the Equivalent Qualifications section in the Introduction.

Osteopath

What is Involved?

As an osteopath, you would be working as a practitioner in complementary medicine. Your skill would reside in your sensitivity of touch, which you would use to locate the source of problems presented by patients, and the manipulative skills of your hands as you apply the treatments. You would look for such things as tissue tension or variations in the movement of joints as indicators of underlying dysfunction. Using your hands to correct joint and tissue abnormalities, you would make it easier for a patient's body to function normally and use its own recuperative powers more effectively. Beyond diagnosing and treating the structural and mechanical problems of the body, you would look at each patient's diet, lifestyle and mental well being to restore the state of balance within their total bodily function.

You would start by listening to a patient's account of their problem and observing the way they stand, walk, and move. You would then use your hands to discover the underlying causes of pain. Sometimes you may make use of x-rays as well. On finding the source of the problem, you would ascertain that it could benefit from osteopathy and you would carry out treatment using a variety of manipulative techniques. You may need to refer the patient to their doctor or another healthcare professional if you feel the problem is not suitable for osteopathy.

Opportunities for Training

In order to practise as an osteopath you must be registered with the General Osteopathic Council, which means that you must have trained at an accredited osteopathic school. Courses vary from four to five years full-time or five years on a mixed-mode basis. There is also an 18-month course open only to medical practitioners.

All of these osteopathic courses offer BSc or BSc Honours degree programmes. You would learn basic medical sciences, including anatomy, physiology and pathology, in addition to osteopathic philosophy, concepts and techniques.

Requirements for Entry

While they may vary slightly between each school, the usual minimum entry requirements are three good A level/Advanced Higher, four Higher or equivalent passes, two of which should be chemistry and biology, together with five GCSE/S Grade passes A-C/1-3, including English and maths.

Osteopathy is not limited to school leavers. In fact, many practitioners choose osteopathy as a second career later in life.

Kind of Person

You would need excellent communication skills, especially in terms of listening to your patients, teasing out details of their problem and explaining your diagnosis. Having gathered the relevant information, you would need to be able to take a logical problem solving approach in order to assess the facts and decide on a course of action. You would need a caring attitude, with the ability to put nervous or shy patients at ease.

You should be in good health, with a high level of manual dexterity; osteopathy requires skill and technique rather than muscle power, with men and women having equal success as practitioners. To be self-employed or working for a small practice, you would need good organisational and business skills.

Broad Outlook

Over seven million people a year seek osteopathic treatment and demand is increasing. (There has been a 25% increase in demand since the introduction of statutory self-regulation for osteopaths in the 1990s). With most people feeling that they stand a better chance of obtaining relief for back pain outside conventional medicine, osteopathy is a growing profession. Each patient may require more than one treatment and it may be that some patients choose to come back once or twice a year to ensure that a problem does not recur.

Currently, most osteopaths work on a self-employed basis in the private sector, but there is a growing tendency towards multi-disciplinary environments and integration with the National Health Service. Occupational Health within private and public companies is also a key growth area for osteopathic practice.

Related Occupations

You may be interested in other professions in the field of complementary medicine such as chiropractor or reflexologist. Alternatively, you might consider a therapy-based profession in the medical field such as physiotherapist or occupational therapist.

Impact on Lifestyle

As a newly graduated osteopath, you would have a number of possible areas of practice to consider: set up on your own; join an established practice; work within the NHS; or join a multidisciplinary practice. As with all professions, you should reckon on it taking two to three years to become established and develop a full practice with the financial return that goes with it. Whilst London may appear to offer the greatest opportunity, it also has the largest number of practitioners and the most expensive premises. Setting up your practice further afield, where your premises would cost less and your services should be in greater demand, could make a lot of sense.

Earnings Potential

Since most osteopaths are self-employed, your income could vary considerably and would be determined by your reputation and the hours you are prepared to work. A typical charge is between £25 and £50 per session. You would need to meet a number of professional costs, including the retention fee for your professional body. Other business costs may include rental of your clinic, heating, lighting and any equipment plus wages for a receptionist or administrative staff. The British Osteopathic Association estimates that annual salaries can range from £16,000 to £65,000.

Further Information

General Osteopathic Council, London SE1 3LU
Website: www.osteopathy.org.uk

British Osteopathic Association, Luton LU1 2NA
Website: www.osteopathy.org

Alternative/equivalent entrance requirements can include: ILC, IB, EB, NC/ND and many other similar international systems. For further details see the Equivalent Qualifications section in the Introduction.

Patent Attorney

What is Involved?

As a patent attorney, also known as a patent agent, you would have a particular expertise in intellectual property rights, encompassing patents, industrial designs, design rights and related copyright areas. You would work in the patent department of a large industrial organisation, in a private firm of patent agents or in a government department. A patent is a right granted to inventors or companies, in return for disclosure of an invention, to stop other people using that invention for a certain period of time (maximum 20 years). In order to secure a patent, a full description of the invention needs to be filed with the Patent Office and you would develop special skills in the long and complex process of securing, maintaining and enforcing patent rights.

Patent agency is becoming an increasingly Europe-wide profession and you would be likely to have considerable contact with the European Patent Office in Munich.

Opportunities for Training

While it is possible to represent clients without being registered, you would normally obtain a post as a technical assistant to a patent agent, either in a firm of agents or in an industrial patent department, and study for the examinations leading to entry on the Register of Patent Agents. It is usual for a person entering the profession to take four or five years to qualify, with foundation papers usually taken after about a year in the profession, followed by the advanced papers two or three years later. Academic training is available, particularly through Certificate and Master's courses in intellectual property run by Queen Mary, University of London, Manchester University, Bournemouth University and Brunel University. These qualifications give exemption from some of the examinations.

Not giving an exemption, but providing valuable skills training, are several different courses available from Firecrest Tutors.

Most patent attorneys also become European patent attorneys, taking an examination similar to the advanced patent paper. You must be on the list of qualified practitioners if you wish to act before the European Patent Office. It is also possible to qualify as a patent attorney while working as a solicitor in a legal practice with an intellectual property department.

Requirements for Entry

You would usually need a science, technology or engineering degree, together with advanced writing skills, the ability to acquire legal skills and a reading knowledge of French and German.

Kind of Person

You would need to be a mixture of scientist, lawyer and linguist, with a reasonable level of skill in each of these areas. You must be able to write clearly and unambiguously and you would need a logical, analytical mind, combined with attention to detail and keen powers of recall. You may become heavily involved in litigation in the courts of the UK and other countries and would need personal qualities similar to those required by a solicitor or barrister/advocate. See our separate articles covering these occupations.

Broad Outlook

Career development opportunities are generally good and do not always end simply by being a partner in a firm of patent attorneys or the head of a patents department. Some patent attorneys move to executive or management positions, while others move abroad, particularly to English speaking countries or to multinational companies who work in English. Some choose to take UK solicitor qualifications as well or even become US attorneys.

You could concentrate on patent work or broaden your scope to work across the whole intellectual property field. Similarly, you might specialise in securing or enforcing intellectual property rights for your clients or employers, or you might branch into related areas such as licensing and contract arrangements based on such rights.

Related Occupations

You might also consider: patent examiner, solicitor, barrister/advocate, biochemist, pharmacologist, biotechnologist, physicist or engineering professions for example.

Impact on Lifestyle

You would always be working to meet specific deadlines and the work itself can be very mentally and intellectually demanding. Standard office times would usually apply but the Internet makes work away from base increasingly viable, both within and outside normal hours. You could be involved in considerable travel, especially within Europe.

Earnings Potential

For industry and private practice, the starting salary for a science graduate would be from £22,500 to £32,500, with a significant salary increase - to £50,000 to £70,000 - usually following qualification. This should rise with experience to £90,000 to £150,000 in industry and £90,000 to £400,000 in private practice.

Further Information

Chartered Institute of Patent Attorneys, London WC2A 1DT
Website: www.cipa.org.uk

European Patent Office, D-80331 Munich, Germany
Website: www.epo.org

Intellectual Property Institute, London WC1B 3QB
Website: www.ip-institute.org.uk

Firecrest Tutors, Dorset SP8 4TW
Website: www.firecrest-tutors.org.uk

Alternative/equivalent entrance requirements can include: ILC, IB, EB, NC/ND and many other similar international systems. For further details see the Equivalent Qualifications section in the Introduction.

Patent Examiner

What is Involved?

As a patent examiner, you would be employed by the UK Intellectual Property Office (IPO) to examine new patent claims before accepting them as valid for official registration. The patent system provides a stimulus to invention by granting innovators a monopoly (extendible up to 20 years in the UK) for the manufacture and sale of patented inventions. In exchange, the innovator discloses the nature of the invention, allowing others to build upon the discovery and avoiding duplication of research effort.

Your job would be to investigate each application to ascertain that the invention is clearly described and you would conduct a search through UK and foreign patent specifications to ascertain that the invention is truly novel. You would write a report of your initial search results and would use this to determine with the applicant or their agent whether to proceed to the second stage of substantive examination and detailed investigation of the claims made for the invention. Finally, the application would either proceed to grant of a patent or would be refused. If refused, the applicant may appeal to the Courts.

The IPO is based in modern premises on the outskirts of Newport, South Wales.

Opportunities for Training

Training begins with lectures and seminars on various aspects of Intellectual Property law and on the basic skills of the examining job. You would quickly move on to working on live applications alongside other newly recruited examiners, tutored by experienced senior examiners. You would be encouraged to study for a postgraduate diploma in Intellectual Property Law, facilitated by a university and taught in-house, with other training and development opportunities including foreign language training.

To enable you to keep abreast of the latest developments, you would be encouraged to visit laboratories, factories and exhibitions and to participate in seminars.

Requirements for Entry

You would need a degree in a mathematical, engineering or scientific subject. Suitable disciplines would include electrical/electronic, telecommunications, mechanical, civil or chemical engineering, physics, organic chemistry, chemistry, biotechnology, computer science and mathematics. See our separate articles on these subjects for details of degree entry requirements.

Kind of Person

You would need sound scientific and technical knowledge and the ability to exercise this knowledge within the concepts of patent law. You should be prepared for a mixture of the legal, the scientific, the technological and the commercial. You would also need excellent analytical and critical skills, coupled with the ability to express an argument cogently, both on paper and orally. To appreciate the level of innovation in patent applications, you would need a flexible and creative approach to problem solving. The work increasingly involves the use of computers, so you would need good IT skills.

Broad Outlook

The UK Intellectual Property Office regularly recruits between 20 and 40 engineers/scientists from university or industry. The programme is normally advertised from late autumn with the closing date for applications in early February. Interviews are held during March and April with successful candidates starting in September. Restricted discipline recruitment schemes may also be held at different times of the year. You may register your interest with the IPO in order to receive an application form for the next recruitment scheme.

The Patent Examiner career is structured, with opportunities for promotion after two to four years and again after five to nine to Senior Examiner. These promotions are 'non-competitive', meaning that you are promoted when your performance reaches the required level; it is not necessary to wait for a vacancy to occur. More senior positions to Deputy Director and above are, however, competitive.

The overwhelming majority of examiners complete their careers within the IPO, but there are opportunities for training in general management and for gaining experience in other areas of government. There is also the possibility of transferring to the European Patent Office in The Hague, Berlin or Munich, but your German and French must be strong as you would be working in a totally trilingual environment.

Related Occupations

You might also consider: electrical/electronic, telecommunications, mechanical, civil or chemical engineer, physicist, biotechnologist, mathematician or patent attorney.

Experience of patent examining work is regarded as qualifying for corporate membership of the Institution of Mechanical Engineers or the Institution of Engineering and Technology.

Impact on Lifestyle

You would usually work a five-day week from Monday to Friday and you would enjoy the normal benefits of the civil service, with a progressive salary scale, promotion prospects and excellent pension fund. The work itself can be very mentally and intellectually demanding. There would be deadlines to meet and you would have to be sure that your decisions on the validity of a patent could not later prove to be incorrect.

Earnings Potential

Patent examiners currently start on a scale running from £22,364 to £25,412 per year. Promotion to senior examiner (typically after seven years) should lead to a salary of more than £50,000. More senior posts are paid at Senior Civil Service rates.

European Patent Office salaries are very competitive, depending on the level of your relevant work experience, and include an allowance for expatriates who do not live in their home country and a household allowance for those who are married and/or have children.

Further Information

UK Intellectual Property Office, Newport, S Wales NP10 8QQ
Website: www.ipo.gov.uk/career.htm

European Patent Office, D-80331 Munich, Germany
Website: www.epo.org

Alternative/equivalent entrance requirements can include: ILC, IB, EB, NC/ND and many other similar international systems. For further details see the Equivalent Qualifications section in the Introduction.

PE Teacher/Instructor

What is Involved?

As a PE teacher or instructor, you would be fulfilling a very specialised role in a school, in the armed services or in many other community activities including health clubs and fitness centres. Your job would be to help people to develop all-round physical fitness, coordination of hand and eye, awareness of the need for exercise, to develop their strength and endurance, to improve their performance in sports generally and to maintain healthy lifestyles.

In a school your job would, in the main, be performed outside the classroom in the gymnasium, sports hall or on the playing fields. You must become aware of the special demands which physical education poses in terms of commitment and dedication, especially, as often happens, when PE staff are responsible for the running of the school's major games, with often very demanding fixture commitments.

In the armed forces, either as an officer or a non-commissioned instructor, yours would be a very specialised function. Royal Marine instructors develop and supervise PT in training centres and commando units. The Army Physical Training Corps operates on similar lines, whereas the RAF equivalent also embraces specialist training in parachuting, leadership, outdoor pursuits and survival techniques.

Opportunities for Training

See our separate article 'Teacher' for details of routes to qualification. You could specialise in PE on the BEd route or you could take a degree in a sports-related subject and follow it with the PGCE. PE is one of the main exceptions to the broad rule that the BEd route is for people who want to specialise in primary education. A sports-related degree could also incorporate specific coaching awards as part of your qualification. You should check prospectuses for details.

In the armed forces, the Royal Air Force recruits people specifically as physical training instructors and physical education officers but the Army and Royal Navy normally appoint PE specialists internally.

Requirements for Entry

For entry to teacher training or to a sports-related degree, you would normally need two or three A level/Advanced Higher, three or four Higher or equivalent passes, together with a good spread of GCSE/S Grade passes at A-C/1-3, or equivalent including English, maths and a science.

You would need to be very fit and many courses would look for evidence of sporting achievement.

Kind of Person

You would need to be enthusiastic about sport and all manner of physical activity. You would be expected to comply with the code of conduct set down by the governing body of any sport with which you are involved and you should try to establish professional standards of behaviour. You should be able to motivate and inspire people and would need to be patient with those who are slow to learn or who do not share your passion for sporting activity. Good organisational and communication skills would be essential.

Broad Outlook

With more and more people becoming aware of the value of exercise and sporting participation, opportunities in the exercise and health club sector are steadily increasing. In education, the Association for Physical Education has expressed concern that training places for new PE teachers are to be cut by a third over the next three years, despite government plans to more than double the sport being played by pupils.

Related Occupations

You might also wish to consider: leisure services manager, professional sportsperson or sports coach.

Impact on Lifestyle

As a PE teacher, you would be spared most of the daily round of marking and administration but you may be expected to organise and lead a great number of out-of-school activities. You could be involved during the holidays with school trips or visits, such as skiing, water-sports and outdoor adventure activities. In the armed services, you would have to be available for duty at any time and could be called upon to organise or participate in particularly demanding exercises or operations.

Earnings Potential

A Newly Qualified Teacher (NQT) in England and Wales can expect to start on a scale ranging from £20,627 to £30,148 or £25,000 to £34,768 in Inner London. If you are a career changer or mature entrant you may, depending on your previous experience, start at a higher level. If you take on a leadership role, for example by becoming a headteacher, a deputy or an assistant headteacher, you will be on a pay range extending from £40,494 to £100,424 (£107,192 in Inner London). The larger and more challenging the school, the higher up the pay scale a headteacher's salary will be. In the armed services, you would be paid on the normal scale for your force, with the starting point determined by your age and qualifications.

Further Information

Training and Development Agency for Schools, London SW1E 5TT
Website: www.tda.gov.uk

General Teaching Council for Scotland, Edinburgh EH12 6UT
Website: www.gtcs.org.uk

Association for Physical Education
Website: www.afpe.org.uk

SkillsActive, Sector Skills Council for Active Leisure and Learning
Website: www.skillsactive.com

Armed Services Websites:
Website: www.rafcareers.com
Website: www.army.mod.uk
Website: www.royal-navy.mod.uk
Website: www.royalnavy.mod.uk/royalmarines

Alternative/equivalent entrance requirements can include: ILC, IB, EB, NC/ND and many other similar international systems. For further details see the Equivalent Qualifications section in the Introduction.

Petroleum Engineer

What is Involved?

As a petroleum engineer, you would be working in a specialised field of mining engineering concerned with exploration to find reservoirs of oil and gas in the earth. Once the exploration team has located a suitable source of oil and gas, you would determine how to set about the process of extraction. This would mean that you would liaise with other experts, such as geologists, to decide on the best method of drilling, bearing in mind the overall geography and geology of the area and particularly the types of rock involved. You would also need to consider the likely costs of extracting the optimum quantity from the reservoir. This process is likely to involve you in using computer technology to simulate the extraction process and so decide on the most appropriate equipment and processes needed.

Production, the process of getting the oil out of the ground, would be your specialist area as a petroleum engineer but you would be part of a team of engineers of every sort involved in designing, building, maintaining and running the complex structures and equipment on land or at sea.

Back in the research and development laboratories, you might work with scientists and chemical and mechanical engineers to improve products, create new ones, find new ways to extract oil and make the petroleum industry as environmentally friendly as possible.

Opportunities for Training

You should study for a degree at university, with specialist petroleum engineering courses available at Aberdeen, Leeds, London South Bank and Manchester. It is also possible to study petroleum engineering as a postgraduate course, possibly focusing on the Centre for Petroleum Studies at Imperial College in London, which has strong links with the industry. In order to become a chartered engineer, you would need to complete an approved four-year MEng course or a three-year BEng degree course plus at least an extra year of postgraduate study. See our separate article on engineering qualifications.

Requirements for Entry

You would normally need A level/Advanced Higher, Higher or equivalent qualifications to study at the universities listed above, including at least two subjects from maths, physics and chemistry. If not actually required, then they will be strongly preferred. You would need a good first degree in science or engineering for admission to the MSc at Imperial.

Kind of Person

You would need a strong interest in maths, science and technology and should enjoy solving problems. Your work would involve you in using sophisticated computer technology, not only to model the possible drilling options but also to sift through the mass of complex information than needs to be considered. You would be working as a member of a small team, some of whom would have different specialised knowledge. You would need to communicate clearly with other team members and also to take account of their views. At times you may need to be flexible and to modify your proposals to fit in with other people's ideas.

Broad Outlook

The major petroleum companies were riding high on the commodities boom, enjoying record prices and record profits. All this has come to a juddering halt with the world recession of 2009. Prices have plummeted and expansion plans have been put on hold. The major companies are no doubt big enough to survive without serious damage, although the immediate prospects for new graduates are not encouraging. The global outlook is predicted to improve again from 2010 onwards.

There is likely to be a continued demand for oil and gas, which means that there will always be a need for petroleum engineers to discover new petroleum sources on land or under the sea and to optimise the extraction process. It is important to be realistic about your chances of a career in the oil industry. In any one year, the opportunities are limited and they go to the people with the best qualifications and personal qualities for the work.

Engineers can be found in managerial, technical and non-technical roles in all parts of the petroleum business. Most oil companies operate throughout the world and every area of the industry offers a wide choice of jobs for engineers.

Related Occupations

You might also consider: mining, chemical, nuclear, energy or manufacturing engineer. Alternatively, you may prefer to consider: metallurgist, materials scientist, geologist or oceanographer.

Impact on Lifestyle

You are likely to spend a great deal of your time monitoring drilling production on locations as far afield as the North Sea or Alaska. This might involve you working in difficult, dirty or dangerous conditions, perhaps on an oilrig at sea or in arctic or desert conditions. You would, therefore, be expected to travel extensively as part of your job and this could have an impact on your family and social life.

Earnings Potential

You are likely to be well paid, starting on around £29,000 to £35,000 as a recent graduate, although salaries at the higher end of the scale are more likely to be available to those with a relevant PhD. Your salary should rise quite quickly as you gain in experience and achieve chartered status. After 10 to15 years, your earnings should be in the region of £52,000 to £90,000. Location and assignments have a considerable influence on salary. There can be generous benefits packages and overseas allowances, together with bonuses for offshore work. An experienced freelance engineer can earn over £1,000 per day. For more detailed information, explore the *Salary and Benefits Survey 2009* on the Energy Institute website.

Further Information

Energy Institute, London W1G 7AR
Website: www.energyinst.org.uk

Institute of Materials Minerals and Mining, London SW1Y 5DB
Website: www.iom3.org

Engineering Council UK, London WC2R 3ER.
Website: www.engc.org.uk

Society of Petroleum Engineers, London W1W 8QJ
Website: www.spe.org

Alternative/equivalent entrance requirements can include: ILC, IB, EB, NC/ND and many other similar international systems. For further details see the Equivalent Qualifications section in the Introduction.

Pharmacist

What is Involved?

Your job as a pharmacist would involve working with drugs and medicines. You would either prepare and dispense medicines or you would work in researching and developing medicinal products. The majority of pharmacists work in the community, usually in a pharmacy. This means that you would work directly with the public, preparing and dispensing medicines according to doctors' prescriptions and also offering advice. Alternatively, you may work in a hospital dispensing drugs, medicines and other preparations such as special feeding solutions or diagnostic materials. Some pharmacists choose to work in industry and become involved in the manufacture of drugs.

The roles and services of pharmacists are developing to serve the nation's health in the 21st century. Working with other healthcare professionals, pharmacists help to ensure that people with acute and long-term illnesses can use their medicines safely and effectively. Pharmacists provide a first port of call to customers for self care of minor ailments and also help people maintain a healthy lifestyle by providing useful advice. It is also the pharmacist's responsibility to make sure that the pharmacy is well run and that staff are properly trained.

There are about 21,000 community pharmacists and around 12,000 community pharmacies in Great Britain located in cities, towns and villages. Community pharmacies are visited by members of the public over two billion times each year.

Opportunities for Training

In order to work in a hospital or in the retail trade you must be registered with the Royal Pharmaceutical Society. This means that you will have to undertake a four-year Master of Pharmacy degree at a school of pharmacy, which includes some clinical experience as well as the theoretical study of pharmaceutics and pharmacology. There is also a five-year sandwich course, which includes blocks of practical training. At the end of your degree, you would need to complete one year of pre-registration training and then pass the Society's registration exam.

Requirements for Entry

For the degree in pharmacy, you would need three good A level/Advanced Higher, four Higher or equivalent qualifications, one of which must be chemistry. Most universities would want or prefer your other subjects to be chosen from maths, biology and physics.

Kind of Person

You would need a strong interest in science and in medicine, with a logical mind and a methodical approach to your work. Accuracy would be very important, as you would be handling potentially dangerous medicines, and you would need good concentration and organisational ability. In addition, you would have to enjoy dealing with people. You may be working with customers or patients, acting as a link between them and the doctor, and this could involve explaining how their prescribed drugs should be administered and detailing possible side effects. If you choose to work in industry, you would be working as part of a team involved in painstaking research and production processes.

Broad Outlook

The changing nature of community pharmacy makes it difficult to be specific about future prospects. There should be attractive opportunities for qualified pharmacists to work in primary care centres or to operate needle exchange services but traditional community outlets are suffering from growing competition from supermarkets. However, opportunities currently abound in both hospital and industrial pharmacy.

Of all the healthcare professionals, pharmacists have the widest education and training in the use of medicines for the prevention and treatment of disease. Community pharmacists make a key contribution to the safety and effectiveness of medicinal treatment.

Related Occupations

You might consider another profession in a scientific or medical field, such as doctor, dentist, pharmacologist, research biologist, or biochemist.

Impact on Lifestyle

Whether you work in a pharmacy, a hospital or in a laboratory, you would be working in clean and sometimes sterile conditions. Hygiene is always important and you may need to wear protective clothing. Pharmacists are among the most accessible healthcare professionals because the public do not need to make an appointment to see them and many shops are open extended hours. You may therefore have to work unsocial hours, which could mean working on a rota or shift system, including evening and weekend cover. Industrial pharmacists usually work regular hours, Monday to Friday.

Earnings Potential

Present salaries for pharmacy graduates during their pre-registration year start at about £16,500, rising to £20,000 to £30,000 in a community pharmacy. Newly qualified pharmacists in the NHS start in Band 5 on a salary range from £20,710 to £26,839. Salaries increase as you progress through the grades, and the top NHS pharmacist salary is currently over £65,000. In all cases, additional allowances are paid for posts in and around London. Such amounts can also be gained by having regional management responsibility in community pharmacy or a senior management post in industry. The ABPI website says that, in 2008, new graduates were likely to start on a salary of about £25,000, those with a relevant postgraduate MSc could expect about £28,000. Starting salaries for recruits with a PhD were about £31 to £32,000.

Further Information

Royal Pharmaceutical Society of Great Britain, London SE1 7JN
Website: www.rpsgb.org.uk

Association of the British Pharmaceutical Industry, London SW1A 2DY
Website: www.abpi.org.uk

National Pharmacy Association, St Albans AL1 3NP
Website: www.npa.co.uk

Alternative/equivalent entrance requirements can include: ILC, IB, EB, NC/ND and many other similar international systems. For further details see the Equivalent Qualifications section in the Introduction.

Pharmacologist

What is Involved?

As a pharmacologist, you would be involved in the discovery and evaluation of new pharmaceutical drugs and associated treatments needed to arrest or cure human and animal diseases. Your work may be based in a hospital or in a laboratory or office within a pharmaceutical company. Having isolated or synthesised a promising bioactive substance, you would conduct experiments to discover its effectiveness, side-effects and safe dosages.

Later you would work with other medical professionals, pharmacists and doctors, to carry our clinical trials on human beings or animals, when it is considered safe to do so. Most of the life-saving drugs used every day by doctors or vets have been tested out in this way and include thousands of different substances, including antibiotics, anti-malarial and chemotherapy drugs used in cancer treatments.

But still millions of lives are lost each year and the search continues for drugs which will be effective against AIDS, CJD, Alzheimer's and Parkinson's diseases. Pharmacologists will be faced with these challenges for a long time to come, although recent advances in genetic engineering are having a significant impact on the rate of progress in these areas.

Opportunities for Training

You would need a degree in pharmacology, which could focus on pharmacology alone or combine it with another subject, such as biochemistry, immunology, toxicology or cell biology. You might start by reading another subject, such as biomedical sciences or medicine itself, and then decide to specialise in pharmacology during your course. There are some sandwich courses available, which allow you to gain practical experience whilst studying. However you organise it, your degree in pharmacology should cover topics such as the causes of disease, the normal functioning of the body, how drugs work and their development.

Having completed their first degree in pharmacology, many graduates, choose to pursue a postgraduate course. This may be either a taught Masters in a specialist subject, such as toxicology or clinical pharmacology, or a research degree leading to a PhD.

Requirements for Entry

To gain admission to a degree course in pharmacology, you would need three A level/Advanced Higher, Higher or equivalent passes, usually including chemistry and two from biology, physics or maths. You would also need a good spread of GCSE/S Grade passes at A-C/1-3.

Kind of Person

You would need a keen interest and proven ability in chemical and biological research, particularly in scientific and medical discovery. Whilst you would probably have the opportunity to follow your own interests, you would also be working as part of a closely-knit team.

You would report your findings/experimental results at weekly or monthly meetings, so good verbal and written communication skills would be essential. You would need considerable determination to overcome many of the difficulties likely to arise in this work.

New drugs frequently exhibit side effects and it can take months or even years to monitor the effects on patients in clinical trials. It is here that you would work most closely with pharmacists and other health professionals, in order to avoid making serious and sometimes irreversible mistakes.

Broad Outlook

"There are still many diseases we need to find treatments and cures for, such as AIDS, cancer, cystic fibrosis, malaria. Pharmacologists are going to be busy for a long time," say the British Pharmacological Society.

Pharmacology graduates often enter the pharmaceutical industry; others enter careers including teaching, the scientific or other branches of the civil service, business and publishing. The degree is a good starting point for several positions in pharmaceuticals, such as marketing, medical information and product registration, as well as research.

Your future prospects can be further improved by mobility: in order to advance your career you may find it helpful to work in other European countries and in the USA.

Related Occupations

You might be interested in other medical careers, such as pharmacist or doctor. Alternatively, you might consider other scientific careers such as clinical biochemist, forensic scientist or research chemist/biologist.

Impact on Lifestyle

You are likely to work normal hours from Monday to Friday. However, you may need to be prepared to work into the evenings researching a specialist topic or to meet deadlines. There would always be a need to keep up with this rapidly advancing subject and some of your private time in the evening and at weekends would doubtless be spent reading relevant professional journals and scientific publications.

Earnings Potential

Typical starting salaries range from £21,500 to £26,000, rising after 10 to 15 years to £30,000 to £100,000. Salaries in the pharmaceutical industry tend to be higher than those in universities and public organisations. The possession of a PhD can secure up to 25% extra on your starting salary.

Further Information

British Pharmacological Society, London EC1V 2PT
Website: www.bps.ac.uk

British Toxicology Society, Macclesfield SK11 6FT
Website: www.thebts.org

Association of the British Pharmaceutical Industry, London SW1A 2DY
Website: www.abpi-careers.org.uk

Alternative/equivalent entrance requirements can include: ILC, IB, EB, NC/ND and many other similar international systems. For further details see the Equivalent Qualifications section in the Introduction.

Photographer

What is Involved?

As a professional photographer, you would most likely specialise in one particular area of work, such as fashion, newspaper, medical or high street photography. 'Photographer' tends to be a blanket term covering several different occupations in which the common factor is that you would be using a camera to record specialist information. The exact nature of your work, not to mention your work environment, would depend very much on your specialism and would determine the subject matter of the photographs being taken. As a medical photographer, for example, you would be likely to work in a hospital; as a newspaper photographer, you would work largely on location, going out to record newsworthy events; as a high street photographer, you would take portraits in a studio but would also go out to cover weddings or to take school photographs. The work would generally involve selecting the right location, setting up the lighting and choosing the appropriate equipment. It is important to decide as early as possible which specialisation interests you most and to develop your career within that area.

Opportunities for Training

Training can be formal or informal, depending on your specialist area. As a medical or newspaper photographer, for example, you would have to take relevant college degree/higher national diploma (HND) courses and sit examinations. On the other hand, your training as an advertising or fashion photographer could be entirely on-the-job, starting with odd jobs in the studio such as messenger work or coffee making.

Colleges offer a range of courses in photography every bit as varied as the range of specialisms in the work itself. There is no guaranteed route to suitable employment from the majority of courses. British Institute of Professional Photography (BIPP) professional photography qualifications are highly regarded and are recognised across the world as a benchmark of excellence. There are three levels of qualification, each reflecting increasing levels of experience, skill and achievement: licentiateship (LBIPP) is the entry level, which represents an established level of skill and competence; associateship (ABIPP) denotes a high standard of craftsmanship and individual creative ability; fellowship (FBIPP) is the highest qualification attainable and recognises distinguished individual ability and exceptional standards of excellence.

Requirements for Entry

Whether you are applying for a job or a college course, a good portfolio is essential to prove your interest and motivation. It is likely to be the main discussion point of your interview. The subject matter should reflect the specialist professional area for which you are applying, so you should avoid such things as holiday snaps, sunsets and family photographs. A dozen or so well-presented prints or transparencies should be enough at this stage. To become a medical illustrator/clinical photographer, training is by a full-time degree in clinical photography including work placements. If you have a first degree in photography, you may be able to take a postgraduate course in clinical photography. There is no absolute educational requirement for press photographer training, although degree/HND level standard is in many cases advisable.

Kind of Person

Most professional photographers are self-employed and you would need a high level of self-confidence, allied to exceptional talent and driving ambition, to survive in such fiercely competitive areas as advertising or fashion photography. Even in a high street studio, you would need good business skills and the ability to communicate effectively.

While you need a good eye for colour and composition, qualities such as punctuality, patience and reliability are also important. You should have some interest in digital imaging technology and the use of computers, as photography is rapidly changing to accommodate these developments. As a medical photographer, you would need knowledge of anatomy and physiology.

Broad Outlook

Some areas of photography are exceptionally competitive and overcrowded. It is particularly hard to find an opening in fashion, advertising or press photography and vacancies are rarely advertised. Starting as an assistant and gradually building up a network of personal contacts is often the only way to proceed. Once you are established in the profession, a combination of talent and perseverance can open the door to lucrative contracts. If you crave the security of a structured career path, medical photography may be the route to pursue.

Related Occupations

You may wish to consider: TV and film camera operator, graphic designer, illustrator, journalist or multimedia specialist.

Impact on Lifestyle

The impact of the work on your lifestyle would depend on your specialisation. In press and fashion, you could expect to work long and irregular hours. High street photographers are often busiest at weekends, covering weddings and christenings. Medical and industrial photographers would keep much more regular hours.

Earnings Potential

This would vary enormously especially, depending for example on how hard you are prepared to work as a freelance and how good your pictures are. You may have to start as an assistant photographer on an extremely low starting salary, perhaps earning in the region of £10,000 to £11,000. The usual range of entry level salaries is between £12,000 and £22,000, although successful photographers in fashion, advertising or working for the national press can earn much more. Salaries at the top end of the profession range from £35,000 to £70,000 and considerably more for those few photographers who become household names or who are published as photographers.

Further Information

British Institute of Professional Photography, Ware, SG12 9HN
Website: www.bipp.com

Skillset, Sector Skills Council for the Audio Visual Industries
Website: www.skillset.org/photo/careers

Institute of Medical Illustrators, Nottingham NG1 4JA
Website: www.imi.org.uk

National Council for the Training of Journalists, Saffron Walden CB11 3PL
Website: www.nctj.com

Association of Photographers, London EC2A 4QS
Website: www.the-aop.org

Alternative/equivalent entrance requirements can include: ILC, IB, EB, NC/ND and many other similar international systems. For further details see the Equivalent Qualifications section in the Introduction.

Physicist

What is Involved?

As a physicist, you would be looking at the nature of matter and of energy. Your work could cover areas such as light, sound, heat, electricity, magnetism, the planets and the forces of gravity and atomic bonding. You could become involved with atomic physics, electronics, computing the uses of laser optics or quantum physics. Your work could form the basis for much of present and future technology.

Current work in nanotechnology, for example, is predicted to transform our lives over the next two decades to a far greater extent than silicon microelectronics did in the 20th century. One application of this technology - nanotubes - can behave like metals or semiconductors, can conduct electricity better than copper, can transmit heat better than diamonds and rank among the strongest materials known, yet they are just a few nanometres across.

Opportunities for Training

If you wish to work as a professional physicist, you should look for a four-year first degree leading to MSci or MPhys. This would provide for study of physics in greater depth than a three-year BSc and should not be confused with postgraduate MSc courses Most universities offer the option of switching from BSc to MSci/MPhys and vice versa but you should check prospectuses carefully before applying. Look for a course accredited by the Institute of Physics. You should also investigate the possibility of working towards chartered physicist status.

The Institute of Physics gives bursaries of around £1000 a year to selected undergraduates studying physics in the UK and Ireland.

Requirements for Entry

Entry to most degree courses requires two to three A level/Advanced Higher, three to five Higher or equivalent qualifications, together with a good platform of GCSE/S Grade passes at A-C/1-3. Since there is a shortage of applicants, grade requirements in some universities are not high but all departments would be looking for good grades in physics and maths. For postgraduate study, you would usually need a first degree passed with first or upper second class honours.

Kind of Person

You would need to have a very strong interest in physics and you should be able to handle the numerical and theoretical aspects of the subject. You should enjoy the practical laboratory work that you do at school, as you are likely to be involved with analysing and monitoring experimental work in a laboratory. You would need good attention to detail and accuracy in taking measurements and readings. You are likely to use powerful computers to help you with the analysis of results, so you would need a high standard of IT skill.

There are likely to be rapid developments in your field and you would need to keep up to date with these and with new technology as it is developed. You would need to enjoy a challenge and have a logical and creative approach to problem solving.

In addition to your scientific interest and ability, you are also likely to need good communication skills. You would probably be working as part of a team and may need to instruct technicians who are helping you as well as keeping other team members up to date with your work. In addition, you may need to explain your work to others who do not share your academic and scientific background.

Broad Outlook

Your career structure would depend very much on the type of work you undertake. In academic research, for example, a PhD is usually followed by short-term postdoctoral research contracts of up to three years in length. These may be based in laboratories worldwide, so geographical mobility can be helpful for progression. Future promotion would depend on your research achievement, normally measured by the quality and quantity of original papers you publish and by your ability to attract funding. You might then progress to a lectureship and ultimately to a professorial post with management responsibilities. In industrial research, a small, specialist organisation may offer early responsibility and the chance to focus on a specific area of physics, whereas your career development in a larger organisation might take you more towards a managerial or commercial role.

Related Occupations

You might also consider: computer scientist, systems analyst, geophysicist or telecommunications, electrical, electronic or mechanical engineer.

Impact on Lifestyle

You would mainly work normal office hours from Monday to Friday, although you might occasionally need to work overtime to meet a tight deadline. In addition, you may have to spend some out of work time studying and reading to keep up to date with your subject. You may need to travel to conferences and meetings and could have to move in order to find a suitable job.

Earnings Potential

Physics World publishes details of salaries every three years, listed by job sector, job function and qualification. However, the data refer to median salaries and do not relate to the starting salaries that students often want to know about. There are financial benefits to extra study: the 45% of physicists who go on to study a PhD earn appreciably more than first graduates and the few that gain a DSc do especially well financially.

A typical starting salary in industry would be around £21,000 to £30,000. At a more senior level, after 10-15 years' experience, this might rise to £30,000 to £45,000. University professors earn in the region of £60,000 a year.

Further Information

Institute of Physics, London W1B 1NT
Website: www.iop.org

Institute of Physics In Ireland
Website: http://ireland.iop.org

Physics on the web
Website: www.physics.org

Alternative/equivalent entrance requirements can include: ILC, IB, EB, NC/ND and many other similar international systems. For further details see the Equivalent Qualifications section in the Introduction.

Physiotherapist

What is Involved?

As a physiotherapist, you would use movement, exercise, electrotherapy, manipulation and massage to treat pain, injury and damage to the body and to enhance the well being of the body. In addition, you would have to take into account any psychological, social and cultural factors that would affect your patients' ability to help themselves.

You may work in hospitals or in the community, rehabilitating sick or injured individuals, or helping the elderly or disabled to live as independently as possible. Alternatively, you may work as a specialist sports physiotherapist, repairing and trying to prevent injuries as well as helping people maintain levels of fitness.

Opportunities for Training

For membership of the Chartered Society of Physiotherapy (CSP) and state registration as a physiotherapist, you would need to take a three- or four-year course leading to an honours degree. The course is a mixture of theory and practical work, with a good deal of time spent working with qualified physiotherapists on placement in a clinical setting. You would at times find yourself training alongside other healthcare professionals, which is good experience for the workplace. Your clinical experience should cover areas such as outpatients, intensive care, rehabilitation, care of the older person, mental illness and work in the community. The academic side would include topics such as anatomy, pathology and psychology. In addition, you would learn the practical skills required in the workplace.

Requirements for Entry

The minimum entry requirements are the same as those for all degree programmes. However, competition for places means that conditional offers of a place are often set higher than the minimum. In England, Wales and Northern Ireland, for example, you would normally need three A2 subjects at a minimum of grade C and above (one should be biological science) and four A1 levels at grade B including a biological science, together with a minimum of five GCSEs at grade C and above. The latter should be taken at one sitting and include mathematics, English language and a spread of science subjects.

In Scotland, a typical student profile is five SCE Highers at grades AABBB taken at one sitting (minimum of two science subjects). In the Republic of Ireland, you should have an Irish Leaving Certificate with a minimum of four passes in subjects at higher level - two at B grade and two at C grade.

Many physiotherapy schools interview applicants, looking for genuine interest in physiotherapy, work experience involving caring for others and the experience of having watched a physiotherapist at work.

Kind of Person

You would have to establish a relationship with a wide range of people, most of whom would be ill, frightened or in pain. You would need to maintain a cheerful and positive outlook in order to reassure them and then encourage them to help themselves. At times, it would be necessary to be firm to make the patient persevere with difficult or uncomfortable exercises. Patience and tact are also needed, as progress made by patients can be very slow.

As well as getting on well with people, you should be able to give clear instructions so that the patient understands what each exercise requires. At the same time, you must be able to work alongside others as part of a team. You should be well organised and able to maintain detailed records of each patient.

Broad Outlook

Physiotherapist numbers have risen significantly for the first time in recent years, according to government workforce statistics for England published at the end of March 2009. The Department of Health census results show that the number of qualified physiotherapists has risen by 968 (4.8 per cent) from September 2007 to September 2008, bringing the total to 21,114. This follows a 0.9 per cent fall between 2005 and 2006 and only a slight increase the following year.

These signs of a clear increase in demand for physiotherapists after a period of negative or minimal growth are most welcome, indicating that the problems with NHS finances that brought about job freezes and very little graduate recruitment around 2006 have at last eased. There is still, however, some concern that the economic downturn of 2009 could affect employment prospects and bring about a reduction in the number of training places.

Having completed a period of junior rotations in the NHS, you could choose to stay in the service and progress to the senior grades, move into private practice or specialise in the private sector in areas such as health farms, occupational health or sport.

Related Occupations

You may be interested in other therapy-based professions in the medical field, such as occupational therapist, radiographer or speech and language therapist.

Impact on Lifestyle

NHS physiotherapists work a 36-hour week, which can include some unsocial or on-call hours. Physiotherapists in the sport and leisure sector often have to work during evenings and at weekends.

Earnings Potential

A newly qualified NHS physiotherapist would start in Band 5, on a scale ranging from £20,710 to £26,839. This could rise to £39,273 for a team manager at the top of the scale and to over £65,000 for a consultant. Additional allowances are paid for appointments in and around London, ranging from 20% of basic salary for Inner London, to 15% for Outer London and 5% for the London Fringe. Salaries in the private sector are often linked to NHS levels but may be higher.

Further Information

Chartered Society of Physiotherapy, London WC1R 4ED
Website: www.csp.org.uk

Alternative/equivalent entrance requirements can include: ILC, IB, EB, NC/ND and many other similar international systems. For further details see the Equivalent Qualifications section in the Introduction.

What is Involved?

Podiatrist is the internationally recognised name for a specialist who cares for feet and chiropodists are in the process of changing their title to match. As a podiatrist, you would be responsible for maintaining feet and the lower leg in a healthy condition; you would be qualified to diagnose, advise on and treat problems; you would have the chance to work in a number of different environments - hospitals, clinics and in people's homes, for example - and with a range of different people.

There are four main areas of work:

• **General clinics**, the starting point for many newly qualified podiatrists. The job involves assessing, evaluating and advising on foot care for a wide range of patients. You listen to a history of the patient's health and hear about any foot problems; you then examine the foot, possibly using specialised equipment, and discuss possible treatments with the patient.

• **Biomechanics**, concerning the very complex structure and function of the foot. Podiatrists working in this area are concerned to preserve this mechanism, restore it when it is damaged and ensure that it is capable of working at its maximum capacity. One of the main areas is orthotics or specially designed insoles, fitted inside shoes to help solve structural problems such as fallen arches or to correct problems with children's feet.

• **High Risk**, concerned with patients who have an underlying illness or condition that puts their lower limbs and/or feet at high risk of damage. Examples include problems with circulation or people who have lost the feeling in their feet or lower limbs.

• **Surgery**, involving routine surgical procedures such as treating in-growing toenails or cutting away soft tissue problems. This may involve the use of local anaesthetics, ultrasonics or freezing techniques. Some podiatrists opt for further study to enable them to work on more invasive surgery.

Opportunities for Training

To practise in the NHS, you must be state registered, which means that you must take a recognised degree course. These courses, offered at some 13 universities in the UK, take three or four years to complete on a full-time basis. They are modular in structure, comprising a mixture of theoretical and clinical modules, although the exact format and method of teaching varies between institutions. The theoretical subjects covered during the course include dermatology, anatomy, physiology, pharmacology, biomechanics and pathology as well as local anaesthesia and surgery.

Requirements for Entry

You would need two A level/Advanced Higher, three Higher or equivalent qualifications, one of which should be a science subject (ideally biology or chemistry), although some universities accept PE as an alternative. You should also have at least five GCSE/S Grade passes at A-C/1-3, including English Language and two sciences. It is best to check direct with the university admissions office in each case to be sure of specific requirements.

Some podiatry courses offer access courses for students who do not have the necessary science background or post-graduate courses for students with a relevant first degree. With only a limited number of places available to read podiatry, admissions tutors look for evidence that you understand what is involved. Work shadowing of a podiatrist is a very good idea and usually quite easy to arrange.

Kind of Person

Many podiatrists are self-employed and for this you need to have a good business sense, organisational skills and the ability to inspire confidence in your clients. Communication skills are important both in dealing with patients and with co-ordinating with other professionals. In addition, you need to have a keen scientific interest and would need to keep up to date with new developments and techniques.

Broad Outlook

There are good opportunities for work in this area, including private practice and some areas of specialisation. Podiatrists often start their career in the NHS, where they encounter a broad range of problems and patients, before deciding to set up in private practice or to specialise.

The Society of Chiropodists and Podiatrists claims that 83% of students seeking employment secure a job within six months of graduation and 100% within the first year. This compares very favourably with many other graduate employment rates.

Related Occupations

You might also consider: doctor, physiotherapist, occupational therapist, radiographer, speech and language therapist or nurse.

Impact on Lifestyle

In the NHS, podiatrists usually work a 36-hour week. However, in private practice, where the potential for earning is higher, the hours worked are likely to be longer and more unsocial, especially in the early days of establishing your business.

Earnings Potential

Podiatrists in the NHS usually start in Band 5, on a scale currently ranging from £20,710 to £26,839. Earnings can rise to £24,831 to £33,436 for a specialist and to £29,789 to £39,273 for an advanced practitioner. Additional allowances are paid for appointments in and around London, ranging from 20% of basic salary for Inner London, to 15% for Outer London and 5% for the London Fringe. Earnings in the private sector are generally likely to be higher, depending on where you live and the hours you are prepared to work. Many podiatrists who work in the NHS also run part-time private practices.

Further Information

Society of Chiropodists and Podiatrists, London SE1 3LY
Website: www.feetforlife.org

Alternative/equivalent entrance requirements can include: ILC, IB, EB, NC/ND and many other similar international systems. For further details see the Equivalent Qualifications section in the Introduction.

Police Officer

What is Involved?

As a police officer, you would serve the local community by working to protect people and property against crime, detecting offenders and taking a lead in dealing with emergencies. You would start your career, after initial training, as a uniformed constable on the beat. This may be on foot or in a patrol car. You must be prepared to deal with whatever comes along, from attending scenes of accidents, searching for missing people and responding to emergency calls, to making arrests, sorting out street fights, taking statements and attending large public gatherings. The work can mean being outside in all weathers, sometimes in unpleasant and potentially dangerous situations. You would also be involved in some office and court-related work, including preparing reports and taking statements, escorting prisoners and giving evidence. You may find it useful to join a voluntary cadet scheme if there is one in your area.

Opportunities for Training

All new police officers undertake an extensive and professional training programme known as the Initial Police Learning and Development Programme (IPLDP) during their first two years of service. Individual forces are responsible for the local implementation and delivery of IPLDP, with the emphasis upon local community involvement and a flexible timetable. IPLDP is divided into four training phases which cover the completion of the NVQ in Policing (levels 3 and 4):

- phase 1 - Induction (two to five weeks): general introduction to the organisation with training in first aid, health and safety, officer safety, ICT, race and diversity, human rights and community safety strategy
- phase 2 - Community (two to four weeks): training in crime and disorder reduction and a community placement
- phase 3 - Basic Police Skills (week seven for 28 weeks): workplace practice supported by class-based learning, learning in a 'replicated work environment' and work-based learning under supervised patrol
- phase 4 - Independent Patrol (weeks 35 to 104): combines operational duties with independent and distance learning.

Requirements for Entry

Applicants from all backgrounds and ethnic groups are encouraged to apply. The minimum age to apply is 18, and there is no upper age limit. You must be in excellent health and physically fit and you would have to pass the Police Initial Recruitment Test. You must be a British citizen, a Commonwealth citizen with unrestricted right of residence in the UK or a citizen of the Irish Republic.

There are no height restrictions and no specific educational requirements but you must have good eyesight, including normal colour vision. Glasses or contact lenses may be acceptable but you must have reasonable unaided vision. If you are ambitious, you may find that a degree level qualification will improve your career development prospects.

Please note you can only apply to one force at a time.

Kind of Person

Police work is tough on the body, taxing on the brain, draining on emotion and makes demands of your whole life. You would need to be socially aware, self-disciplined and without prejudice, mature and honest. You would be called on to make instant decisions and may face hostility and danger, so courage and self-confidence are very important qualities. You need to be able to stay calm yet able to weigh up a situation quickly. A sense of humour and a degree of flexibility are advantages. It is particularly important that you have good communication skills and can be assertive but courteous in your contact with the general public.

Broad Outlook

There are many more applicants than there are vacancies at present, which means that competition is fierce and standards are high. The role of the police force and the problems it faces are ever changing, as politicians grapple with increasing demands for more funding for the service in order to combat new and continuing difficulties in society.

All promotion is on merit and you may be recommended for your first promotion - to sergeant - after about five years. The police service is under constant scrutiny to ensure that senior posts are allocated fairly in relation to gender and race.

Related Occupations

You may consider other branches of the police service, including British Transport, UK Atomic Energy and the Ministry of Defence police. Other options might include: fire officer, prison officer, army, navy and air force personnel, security officer, health and safety inspector.

Impact on Lifestyle

As with all the emergency services, your hours of work would often be determined by the circumstances prevailing and you would regularly have to work over weekends and holidays.

Because the police force is locally organised, you are likely in your first few years of service to be based either in the area of your choice or your own home area. Later, promotion may depend upon your willingness to move area and be relocated on a regular basis.

Earnings Potential

Rates of pay vary by force but you a typical salary would be £21,534 when you start, rising to £24,039 when you have finished initial training and £33,810 to £37,071 if you gain promotion to sergeant. Inspectors can earn £42,264 to £45,843. Uniform is provided and occasionally help with accommodation or subsidised police housing. Additional allowances are paid for appointments in and around London.

Further Information

England and Wales Police
Website: www.policecouldyou.co.uk
National Policing Improvement Agency
Website: www.npia.police.uk
Police Service of Northern Ireland
Website: www.psni.police.uk
Scotland Police
Websites: www.centralscotland.police.uk, www.dumfriesandgalloway.police.uk,
www.fife.police.uk, www.grampian.police.uk, www.lbp.police.uk,
www.northern.police.uk, www.strathclyde.police.uk
Home Office Police
Website: http://police.homeoffice.gov.uk

Alternative/equivalent entrance requirements can include: ILC, IB, EB, NC/ND and many other similar international systems. For further details see the Equivalent Qualifications section in the Introduction.

Probation Officer

What is Involved?

Working as a probation officer in England or Wales, you would be part of the National Offender Management Service, supervising offenders in the community and engaging with the victims of serious violent crimes. A lot of your time would be spent trying to help offenders change their behaviour by identifying and challenging what causes them to offend. In Scotland, similar work is carried out by criminal justice social workers as part of local authority social services.

You might be attached to a crown court, involved in drawing up pre-sentence reports to help determine the best way to deal with offenders, providing details about their personalities, the circumstances of crimes, the likelihood of re-offending and the level of risk posed to the public. You might be involved with supervising community rehabilitation or punishment; or on drug treatment and testing orders, trying to break the link between drug addiction and offending, or you could work with prisoners before and after their release from prison.

Opportunities for Training

As we go to press in late April 2009, the National Probation Service says that the training of probation officers is under review and the existing training programme has been suspended until final decisions are made about the shape of the new arrangements.

It is not yet clear whether trainees in England and Wales will continue with the current programme of academic study and practice-based work, leading to the award of the BA (Hons) in Community Justice Studies and the NVQ Level 4 in Offending Behaviour, which together make up the Diploma in Probation Studies (DipPS). The degree is awarded by the University of Portsmouth and delivered via a distance learning route.

In Scotland, the Honours or postgraduate degree in Social Work is the recognised qualification for probation work.

Requirements for Entry

You would normally need to meet the university entry requirements for the BA (Hons) in Community Justice Studies, although the University of Portsmouth welcomes applications from highly motivated candidates irrespective of their backgrounds and recognises that individuals who may lack formal educational qualifications can nevertheless study successfully at undergraduate level.

See our separate article on 'Social Worker' for Scottish entry requirements for the degree in social work. Competition for training places is fierce and it is virtually essential to show experience of voluntary or other work in a field related to helping people in difficulty.

Kind of Person

You would have to deal with offenders, some of whom could be aggressive, violent, distressed or withdrawn. You would need to gain trust and develop a constructive relationship with people from a variety of backgrounds and with a number of problems. Your work would include listening to their stories, resolving conflicts and finding ways to move forward. This would need good communication skills, together with patience, authority and persuasive power. You would be involved with researching and writing reports and letters so written communication would be important. You must be able to speak convincingly in court. You would be working as part of a team and handling a lot of confidential and sensitive information about people, so your integrity would be essential.

Broad Outlook

There is stiff competition for trainee posts. Once through the training programme, you would find that opportunities are plentiful. If you want promotion, you may have to move into a management role, although many probation officers prefer to remain at practitioner level.

The National Association of Probation Officers is currently campaigning against what it says will be around 2,500 job losses between 2009 and 2012.

Related Occupations

You might also consider: social worker, teacher, psychologist, prison officer, police officer or youth and community worker.

Impact on Lifestyle

Your normal working week would be 37 hours but you would often be able to arrange your own working hours to some extent, and this could involve something quite different from the nine to five routine. You might need to provide cover at night and at weekends, working on a rota basis, but you would probably be given time off to compensate. You might have to move around the UK to find a suitable job. At times you would be expected to deal with stressful situations, which you could not simply leave in the office and not think about again until the next morning.

Earnings Potential

Pay negotiations are not yet complete for 2009 but, as a guide, the 2008 rate was from £17,191 to £18,406 while training, rising to £26,229 to £34,239 on qualification. There is a pay spine covering more senior probation officer appointments. In all cases, Inner or Outer London allowances are paid in addition to basic salary.

Further Information

National Probation Service, London SW1P 4LH
Website: www.probation.homeoffice.gov.uk

National Association of Probation Officers, London, SW11 1HT.
Website: www.napo.org.uk

Scottish Social Services Council, Dundee DD1 4NY
Website: www.sssc.uk.com

Probation Board for Northern Ireland
Website: www.pbni.org.uk

Skills for Justice Sector Skills Council
Website: www.skillsforjustice.com

Criminal Justice System Online
Website: www.cjsonline.org

Alternative/equivalent entrance requirements can include: ILC, IB, EB, NC/ND and many other similar international systems. For further details see the Equivalent Qualifications section in the Introduction.

Professional Sportsperson

What is Involved?

In most professional sports, you would be required to focus single-mindedly on your training, fitness and performance levels, shutting out most other demands on your time and energy. Every aspect of your life, diet, sleep, social relaxation and psychological strength would need to be subordinated to or controlled by the demands of your sport, and your career would become in many ways your principal way of life. A career as a professional sportsperson is frequently short, often ending by 35, especially in physical contact or physically demanding sports, and is vulnerable to termination through injury or loss of form. Dedication of vast amounts of time to training and preparation puts stress on both body and mind, which you would need to learn to control. The ability to work with others in teams is increasingly vital, not just in team sports, but in individualised sports where agents, trainers, dietitians, psychologists and physiotherapists are likely to be constant assistants and companions.

Opportunities for Training

An academic qualification is not necessary but is increasingly considered a sensible insurance against the unpredictable pitfalls in a sportsperson's life. Many sports bodies attempt to synchronise sporting participation and development of a career with educational or vocational training and, wherever possible, it is important to achieve whatever academic levels are within reach and do not clash impossibly with sporting demands. Preparation for a future role as coach, manager or administrator is a route followed by many sports performers to guarantee an effective career path.

It is vital to realise that, in most money-making sports, ability would be recognised at an increasingly early age, with footballers as young as nine encouraged into academies and schools of excellence by premiership clubs, cricketers absorbed into colts teams by county cricket clubs, rugby players enrolled in apprentice schemes and training set-ups by rugby premiership sides, and other sports having their own schemes for identifying and exploiting talent. Even if you are an outstanding school player, it is highly unlikely that at 17 or 18 you are going to be able to break into a major sports scene.

An Apprenticeship in Sporting Excellence is available, aimed at young people with realistic potential to reach the highest levels in their sport. It is currently offered by selected clubs in some sports, including football, golf and rugby union.

Requirements for Entry

There are no formal entrance qualifications to professional sport but it is sensible not to neglect your education and to take the opportunity to go on to higher education if appropriate. You could often continue to take part in your sport at university, national or even Commonwealth or Olympic levels. Because of the extremely young age of entry, your parents would need to be supportive in both care and financing, though sponsorship might be available in some sports.

Kind of Person

Commitment, talent and a competitive streak seem common to all professional sportspeople. The resilience to overcome disappointment, defeat or injury is essential, along with an ability to adjust to the demands of travel, practice and performance. You would need total dedication to practising and improving your sport, maintaining your fitness at a peak level and monitoring your diet.

Broad Outlook

There are huge sums of money involved in major sports like soccer, rugby, snooker, boxing and tennis, but the high-earning superstars are relatively few in number and it is easy to be misled by appearances. It is certain that sport will continue to attract and entertain huge sections of society in the coming decades, but that may be accompanied by a spreading and thinning of the rewards. The participation of women, especially where there is a growth in their involvement in sports like tennis and golf, should open more doors to them in the future.

Related Occupations

You might also consider: sports coach, PE teacher/instructor, physiotherapist, chiropractor, osteopath, or leisure services manager.

Impact on Lifestyle

As indicated above, the full impact on your life is likely to be all-consuming and intense, taking over many aspects of it. Practice, training, travel away from home in the UK and abroad can all create pressure on family and social life.

Earnings Potential

It is impossible to specify what you might reasonably expect to earn, given the great range of sports and the unpredictability of fitness and performance. The greater the popularity of the sport and the higher the level attained, the greater the rewards you can achieve. In addition to salaried team players, earnings would include appearance money, fees, advertising and endorsements. For those in less popular sports, a supporting job is often necessary.

As a very rough guide, a professional sportsperson on an Apprenticeship may start on around £6,000 a year, with accommodation and subsistence sometimes provided.

Earnings for established professionals may start at around £20,000 a year, while the most successful professionals in high-profile sports may earn anything from £100,000 to £10 million a year.

Further Information

SkillsActive, London WC1A 1PX
Website: www.skillsactive.com

Sports Coach UK, Leeds LS6 3BJ.
Website: www.sportscoachuk.org

UK Sport, London WC1N 1ST
Website: www.uksport.gov.uk

Apprenticeship in Sporting Excellence
Website: www.apprenticeships.org.uk

Alternative/equivalent entrance requirements can include: ILC, IB, EB, NC/ND and many other similar international systems. For further details see the Equivalent Qualifications section in the Introduction.

Psychologist

What is Involved?

As a psychologist, you would study the processes and nature of the human mind in order to understand how people behave, how they react to stimuli or circumstances and how they interact in small or large groups. You would use scientific methods to gather information and try to measure what constitutes normal or abnormal behaviour. You would be concerned not just with understanding human behaviour but also with using this understanding to help people and to bring about change.

There are several main specialisms for professional psychologists:

• *Clinical psychologists* work with people with mental or physical health problems - which might include anxiety and depression, serious and enduring mental illness, adjustment to physical illness, neurological disorders, addictive behaviours, childhood behaviour disorders or personal and family relationships;

• *Counselling psychologists* help people manage difficult life events such as bereavement, past and present relationships and working with mental health issues and disorders;

• *Educational psychologists* are concerned with children's learning and development, working primarily in schools with teachers and parents;

• *Forensic psychologists* undertake their work in the criminal and civil justice field, working with academic institutions, prison services, the National Health Service, probation services and social services;

• *Health psychologists* are concerned with the application of psychological methods to the study of behaviour relevant to health, illness and health care. For example, why and when people seek professional advice about their health, how patients and health care professionals interact or how patients adapt to illness;

• *Occupational psychologists* are concerned with the performance of people at work and in training, how organisations function and how individuals and small groups behave at work.

Other areas include neuropsychology and sport and exercise psychology.

Opportunities for Training

To become a chartered psychologist, you must have a degree in psychology or equivalent qualification accredited by the British Psychological Society. This is often referred to by employers as the GBR or Graduate Basis for Registration. Your degree would usually offer a broad introduction to the subject but, if you wish to work as professional psychologist, you would normally undertake postgraduate study in one of the specialist areas.

Requirements for Entry

University admissions requirements for a degree in psychology are usually two or three A level/Advanced Higher, three or four Higher or equivalent qualifications, together with a good spread of GCSE/S Grade passes A-C/1-3, including English and maths. There is no need to take psychology as a pre-university subject, although you should be able to demonstrate that you have an understanding of what is involved. Entry is competitive and you should research the exact requirements of each course that interests you.

Kind of Person

You would have to work with a wide range of people. Depending on what type of psychologist you become, you could find yourself dealing with children or adults with learning difficulties, patients with brain damage or disease, prisoners or people at work. You would need good communication skills and an ability to mix with people. In addition, you should have keen investigative skills and should be sufficiently numerate to understand statistical methods.

Broad Outlook

Employment prospects in most areas of psychology are good, especially for educational and clinical psychologists. There are opportunities to work for a number of different organisations, for the government and in private practice, although you may have to move several times to develop your career. It has been calculated that only 15 to 20% of psychology graduates end up working as professional psychologists.

Related Occupations

You may be particularly interested in other professions concerned with helping people, such as careers/personal adviser, speech and language therapist, teacher, human resources manager, probation officer or social worker.

Impact on Lifestyle

This is very dependent on the type of psychology that you choose to pursue as a career. An occupational psychologist working with companies in industry and commerce would usually work normal office hours; an educational psychologist dealing mainly with schoolchildren would be busiest during term time. On the other hand, a forensic psychologist may be called out to collaborate with the police at unsocial hours.

Earnings Potential

Earnings vary considerably between the different branches of psychology and between the different countries of the United Kingdom.

As a psychologist working in the National Health Service, you would start in Band 7 at £29,789 and could eventually earn over £95,000 as head of a large department. As an assistant educational psychologist, you would start at £25,200 to £28,281, rising to £30,546 to £40,111 on Scale A and to £40,111 to £54,486 as a senior or principal educational psychologist on Scale B. As an occupational psychologist, you might generally start at around £20,000 to £30,000 but this could rise to over £100,000 with experience and with fees negotiated for consultancy work.

Further Information

British Psychological Society, Leicester LE1 7DR
Website: www.bps.org.uk

Association of Educational Psychologists, Durham DH1 4ED
Website: www.aep.org.uk

Alternative/equivalent entrance requirements can include: ILC, IB, EB, NC/ND and many other similar international systems. For further details see the Equivalent Qualifications section in the Introduction.

Public Relations Executive

What is Involved?

As a public relations (PR) executive, you would specialise in the business of looking after the reputation of your clients, making a planned and sustained effort to establish goodwill and mutual understanding between them and the public. Your clients might include a business, a profession, a government department, a public service or an organisation concerned with health, culture or education. You would aim to find out the concerns and expectations of a client's customers, employees, suppliers, investors or other audience and feed these back to the management.

A large organisation might have its own in-house PR department, whilst smaller organisations would use an independent PR consultancy. You could find yourself organising receptions, entertaining clients at sporting events or gauging public reaction to a government initiative. At its best, PR helps an organisation to see its own role more clearly and helps it to react effectively to public perception of its performance.

Opportunities for Training

There are a number of routes into PR. You might enter the profession after working in another area, such as journalism, law, advertising or any industry of which you have experience. If you are looking to go into PR as your first job, you would almost certainly need a relevant qualification and work experience.

It is not essential but you could consider a first degree course specifically in public relations, approved by the Chartered Institute of Public Relations (CIPR). Alternatively, you could take a postgraduate course. Once you have a job in PR, you could work towards CIPR or CAM (Communication, Advertising and Marketing Education Foundation) professional qualifications.

Requirements for Entry

To gain admission to a degree course, you would need two or three A level/Advanced Higher, three or four Higher or equivalent qualifications, together with a good spread of GCSE/S Grade passes at A-C/1-3. The minimum requirement for the CAM exams is five GCSE/S Grade passes at A-C/1-3, including maths and English but the vast majority of new entrants are graduates. Relevant work experience would be essential.

Kind of Person

Exceptionally good 'people' skills are needed here. You would need to be able to communicate and to remember that this is a two-way process. You would need flexibility to cope with a variety of projects at the same time, together with thorough attention to detail. The ability to get on with a variety of people and work with others as part of a team would be essential.

You would have to be assertive and determined, able to you cope with pressure and tight deadlines and to make your point in discussions without alienating people. You would also need to be very well organised, with good IT and literacy skills. You would probably be expected to give presentations.

Broad Outlook

PR has a glamorous image and entry has become very competitive. It is now one of the top three most popular career choices for graduates, with an estimated 48,000 people working within PR in the UK today. Talent is still in demand and, once you have been accepted by a consultancy, you could progress to become a manager and then a director or start your own consultancy.

There is no standard promotion pattern in PR but, on successful completion of an initial training programme, you might expect to spend one to two years as a junior account executive, two or three years as an account executive and two to three years as a senior account executive or account manager before moving to associate or account director. You might need to seek promotion by moving companies.

Over half of all people employed in PR work in-house for large companies, local authorities, government departments, professional bodies and charities.

Related Occupations

You might also consider: journalist, solicitor, advertising copywriter, marketing executive, market researcher or events manager.

Impact on Lifestyle

You would be mainly office based and work normal office hours. However, when necessary you would be expected to work longer hours to meet deadlines. Depending on the nature of the work, you could find yourself travelling around the country or abroad on promotional tours or attending conferences. You might have to give presentations or organise functions in the evening or at weekends.

Earnings Potential

A typical salary for a PR account executive is likely to be around £19,000, while an account manager may expect to earn on average around £28,000. PR salaries at more senior levels vary from £36,000 for a senior account manager to £39,000 for an account director, £53,000 for a creative director, £75,000 for a Director and £100,000+ for a Chief Executive Officer.

Further Information

Chartered Institute of Public Relations, London SW1Y 4JR
Website: www.cipr.co.uk

CAM Foundation, Maidenhead SL6 9QH
Website: www.camfoundation.com

Public Relations Consultants Association, London SW1P 1JH
Website: www.prca.org.uk

Alternative/equivalent entrance requirements can include: ILC, IB, EB, NC/ND and many other similar international systems. For further details see the Equivalent Qualifications section in the Introduction.

Publisher

What is Involved?

The publishing industry includes books, newspapers, magazines, journals, directories and electronic media, although this article is concerned primarily with the editorial side of publishing books. Of the many thousands of books published each year, a small percentage are mass-market titles, while others include educational textbooks, academic research works or STM (scientific, technical and medical) publications. Your role as a publisher would involve working with colleagues in selecting or commissioning new books, revising existing titles, in design, marketing and sales to ensure that each publication makes maximum impact in its particular market, reaching as many readers as possible and recouping the initial investment made in it.

As a *commissioning editor*, you would decide whether to accept manuscripts submitted by literary agents or authors or whether to use your specialist knowledge of a particular market to commission specific books and projects. All manuscripts passing through your hands would need to be read and given an initial assessment, often by *readers* employed for the purpose; a number would then need a second opinion, perhaps from a specialist. You would have to weigh up the opinions of your readers, plus, in many cases, sales and marketing colleagues, before making a commitment to proceed.

You might also become concerned with the *contractual* side of publishing, including the drawing up of the initial contract between the publisher and the author, and the handling of subsidiary rights, such as translation, book club and serial rights.

As a *copy editor*, you would concentrate on preparing accepted manuscripts for the printers. You would need an exact eye for details such as repetition, contradiction, spelling mistakes, punctuation and grammar, and would have to discuss and agree all changes with the author. You might also have to discuss details of manufacture and presentation with the production, design and marketing departments.

Opportunities for Training

Some publishing houses run their own in-house training schemes or send new recruits on short courses run by specialist agencies but there are no universally recognised approaches to training and qualification. It is possible at a number of United Kingdom universities and colleges to take a first degree in publishing or a broader arts/humanities degree with a publishing option. There are also a small number of postgraduate courses, which could follow almost any first degree.

Requirements for Entry

New entrants are often graduates but there are no absolute entry requirements and you could be successful without formal qualifications if you can demonstrate sufficient technical ability, commitment, enthusiasm and commercial awareness. Even with a degree, the actual subject is often unimportant, although you would usually be expected to have specialist qualifications on the design side (see our separate article on Graphic Designer) and a business course would be a useful preparation for marketing.

Kind of Person

You would need an interest in people, places and events, knowledge of current affairs and a love of words. That includes understanding grammar, spelling and punctuation, especially for work as a copy editor. In all areas of publishing, computer and web skills are at the very least a definite asset and usually essential. Knowledge of foreign languages can be a particular asset in dealing with translation rights.

Adaptability can often be the key to developing a career in book publishing: it is worth trying - and working hard at - whatever is available in order to gain experience, taking on general duties within a small publishing house in order to learn the business.

Broad Outlook

Most opportunities tend to be in London and the south east, with many more openings in non-editorial than editorial specialisms. Indeed, competition for editorial posts is so intense that you would be well advised to develop skills, perhaps through specialist training, individual initiative or work experience, that make you stand out from the crowd. Good personal contacts are important, together with detailed knowledge of the sector in which you choose to develop your career.

Related Occupations

You might also consider: magazine publisher, journalist, broadcasting researcher, graphic designer or marketing or sales executive.

Impact on Lifestyle

Many people in publishing work a standard Monday to Friday, nine-to-five week, although additional hours are often required as publication deadlines approach. If your work involves dealing with international clients, you may be expected to travel extensively or to make telephone contacts at the appropriate time for the Far East or the United States.

Earnings Potential

Salaries vary widely in publishing, with editorial trainees starting on around £18,000 to £20,000 and working their way up through the system to £45,000 or more. Freelance copy editors currently earn £20 to £30 per hour.

Further Information

Publishers Association, London WC1B 5BW
Website: www.publishers.org.uk

Association of Learned and Professional Society Publishers, Brighton BN1 1AU
Website: www.alpsp.org

Publishing Training Centre, London SW18 2QZ
Website: www.train4publishing.co.uk

Society for Editors and Proofreaders, London SW6 3JD
Website: www.sfep.org.uk

Society of Young Publishers, London WC2H 8TJ
Website: www.thesyp.org.uk

Alternative/equivalent entrance requirements can include: ILC, IB, EB, NC/ND and many other similar international systems. For further details see the Equivalent Qualifications section in the Introduction.

Quantity Surveying Technician

What is Involved?

As a quantity surveying technician, you would work under the overall supervision of a quantity surveyor, builder, architect or civil engineer on the costing and management of all types of building work. This could involve you in office work or in travelling out to building sites. In the office you might be concerned with studying plans or drawings and costing all the items of labour and materials that would be needed. In this way you would be concerned to draw up estimates of the costs of the projected work in a Bill of Quantities. You might also be involved in the conversion of these measurements into the actual quantities of materials that the construction workers would need.

When you are out on site, you might be involved with valuing work done and in progress, so that necessary payments can be made to contractors or suppliers. You could also be concerned with discussing the cost implications of alterations to the work required by the client or forced by a change of circumstances.

Opportunities for Training

There are two main ways to start in this work:

• work towards N/SVQ Level 4 in Quantity Surveying Practice, usually while in employment

• take an HNC/D or Foundation degree course, either full- or part-time

Training may be available in your area via the Apprenticeships programme.

Requirements for Entry

Applicants for HNC/HND courses normally need one A level, or a BTEC/SQA national certificate/diploma. There are no set entry requirements for Foundation degrees, but applicants are likely to have completed an advanced apprenticeship with Level 3 qualifications, A levels, N/SVQs or other Level 3 qualifications.

Evidence of skills in maths, science and ICT is important.

The Chartered Surveyors Training Trust offers work-based routes. Applicants must have at least four GCSEs (A-C), or equivalent qualifications.

Kind of Person

You would need to have a methodical approach to your work and to be very accurate with a sharp eye for detail. You could find yourself handling complex measuring equipment, which would require some degree of technical knowledge. You would need to be confident in using maths and operating computers. You would be expected to liaise with a wide range of different people, clients, chartered surveyors/senior management, architects and also construction workers on the sites.

You might need to explain your points of view to clients, persuading them to accept your opinion. You could be negotiating with contractors about the amount of materials required for a job. Alternatively, you might find yourself encouraging the workforce to complete a particular job more quickly. You would need to be confident and articulate in both written and verbal communication.

Broad Outlook

The demand for quantity surveying technicians depends to a great extent on the state of the building trade and it must be said that the picture in early 2009 is far from encouraging, as the housing market continues to weaken and demand for industrial, office, retail and leisure facilities declines considerably. Forecasts suggest, however, that construction will pick up again in 2010.

Related Occupations

You might also consider: estate agent, architectural technologist, town planner or construction manger.

Impact on Lifestyle

If you were involved with working in an office you could expect to work regular office hours. However, you might also need to be on site and then the hours would probably be longer, particularly in the summer when there are more daylight hours. On site you would need to be prepared to get dirty and to wear protective clothing. To achieve promotion, you might need to move around the country.

Earnings Potential

As a school leaver studying part-time, you could expect to earn around £16,000, rising to around £25,000 once you have qualified and gained some experience. You could expect your salary to rise to £30,000 if you progress to a senior position. There is a difference in salary depending on where you work and also on how great the demand is for quantity surveying technicians in your particular area.

Further Information

Royal Institution of Chartered Surveyors, Coventry CV4 8JE
Website: www.rics.org

Society of Chartered Surveyors, Ireland
Website: www.scs.ie

Construction Skills
Website: www.constructionskills.net

Chartered Surveyors Training Trust, London SE1 9BG
Website: www.cstt.org.uk

Apprenticeships
Website: www.apprenticeships.org.uk

Quantity Surveyor

What is Involved?

As a quantity surveyor you would be concerned with the financial and contractual aspects of construction projects. You would be involved at all stages of the project and would usually be appointed by the architect or engineer who has designed the construction. You would be acting as the financial overseer of a particular project, translating the plans into detailed costs. This would involve working out the timings of each process and the materials needed.

You might advise on alterations to the initial designs; you could be involved in obtaining funding for a particular project; you might be asked to draw up a feasibility study of a project and advise on how to reduce the risks involved. During the construction phase you are likely to be responsible for making sure that the contractors keep to the specification and to the quoted price.

Opportunities for Training

You would need to take a degree course approved by the Royal Institution of Chartered Surveyors (RICS), followed by the RICS Assessment of Professional Competence (APC). This involves two years of structured, practical training with an employer, ending with an RICS professional assessment.

There are some four-year sandwich courses available, which include a year spent working in a quantity surveying practice. This year can count towards your required training period, provided that it has been approved in advance by the RICS. There are also some courses accredited by the Chartered Institute of Building.

Requirements for Entry

For a degree course, the minimum stated requirements are at least three A level/Advanced Higher, four Higher or equivalent qualifications, together with five GCSE/S Grade passes at A-C/1-3. These should usually include English and maths.

Kind of Person

To be a successful quantity surveyor you would need to be a practical person with a logical and methodical approach to problem solving. You would need a high standard of numeracy, together with the ability to analyse the content of complicated documents. A good understanding both of construction techniques and technology and of the relevant laws and health and safety requirements would be essential.

You should have good communications skills as you could be required to express your views and opinions both verbally and on paper. You are also likely to be involved in negotiating with a wide variety of people. This means that you would have to listen to the points of view of others as well as expressing your own opinion. In addition, you are likely to be working as a member of a team, which may require you to motivate and lead people on site. Finally, you would have to be familiar with specific computer programmes.

Broad Outlook

The demand for quantity surveyors depends to a great extent on the state of the building trade and it must be said that the picture in early 2009 is far from encouraging, as the housing market continues to weaken and demand for industrial, office, retail and leisure facilities declines considerably. Forecasts suggest, however, that construction will pick up again in 2010.

There are three main areas in which you could find employment: private practice; with a large building or civil engineering contractor or with local and central government. There may be opportunities to work in mainland Europe with some of the large consultancies and contractors, although you must have the relevant language skills.

Related Occupations

You might consider another specialism as a surveyor or perhaps another profession allied to the building industry, such as architect, town planner, housing manager or civil engineer.

Impact on Lifestyle

You are likely to spend the majority of your time indoors, working regular office hours. You would also have to spend at least some time on site and you may have to start early or finish late to match the daylight hours usually worked by site contractors.

You could be out in all weathers, sometimes exposed to wet, cold and muddy conditions. Buildings under construction are likely to be dirty and potentially dangerous places. You would need to wear protective clothing at times and be prepared to climb ladders or scaffolding.

Earnings Potential

When you first start working you could expect to earn between £18,000 and £30,000. If you start working for a large contractor, you could earn more as you may get paid for working site hours: £22,000+ is a more typical starting salary in such cases. Your salary could easily rise with experience to £32,000 to £75,000, and you could earn substantially more if you become a principal partner in private practice. The average salary across the UK for quantity surveyors with seven or more years' experience is £44,538.

Further Information

Royal Institution of Chartered Surveyors, Coventry CV4 8JE
Website: www.rics.org

Society of Chartered Surveyors, Ireland
Website: www.scs.ie

Chartered Institute of Building, Berkshire SL5 7TB
Website: www.ciob.org.uk

Chartered Surveyors Training Trust, London SE1 9BG
Website: www.cstt.org.uk

Alternative/equivalent entrance requirements can include: ILC, IB, EB, NC/ND and many other similar international systems. For further details see the Equivalent Qualifications section in the Introduction.

Radiographer

What is Involved?

There are two types of radiography: diagnostic and therapeutic. As a diagnostic radiographer, you would produce and interpret high quality images of the body to diagnose injury and disease; as a therapeutic radiographer, you would plan and deliver prescribed treatment using X-radiation and other radioactive sources. Your work as a diagnostic radiographer would normally encompass a wide range of different imaging investigations, such as ultrasound, magnetic resonance imaging and x-rays, although you might later specialise in one particular area.

You would provide a service for most departments within a hospital, including Accident and Emergency, outpatients, operating theatres and wards. Therapeutic radiographers work closely with doctors, nurses, physicists and other members of the oncology team to treat patients with cancer. You would use ionising radiation (mostly high-energy X-rays) to deliver an accurate dose of radiation to the tumour/cancer whilst minimising the dose received by the surrounding tissues. The work would often involve the care of the cancer patient from the initial referral clinic stage, where pre-treatment information is given, through the planning process and treatment to the post-treatment review (follow-up) stages.

Opportunities for Training

You would need to complete a qualifying radiography course at honours degree level. In England and Wales, these courses are three years full-time whereas in Scotland and Northern Ireland they are normally four years full-time. You would usually spend equal amounts of time in your university and in hospital departments. Alternatively, you could qualify as a therapeutic radiographer at postgraduate level if you have a relevant first degree or another professional healthcare qualification. Qualifying courses in diagnostic radiography are currently offered at 24 higher education institutions in the UK and in therapeutic radiography at 17.

Requirements for Entry

Entry requirements vary between universities but you would usually need two or three A level/Advanced Higher, three or four Higher or equivalent qualifications including a science subject, together with three GCSE/S Grade passes A-C/1-3, including maths and a science subject. A visit to a radiography department or radiotherapy centre is advisable before applying. There are no age limits in either diagnostic or therapeutic radiography, and mature students are especially welcome.

Kind of Person

Both diagnostic and therapeutic radiographers need good interpersonal skills to deal with patients of all types and ages, many of whom require reassurance and counselling as well as an explanation of the radiographic procedure with which they are being examined or treated. You would also need to be able to communicate well with the other professionals in the healthcare team to ensure that the most appropriate treatment is given to each patient. You must be confident about working with complex high-technology equipment and would need to give great attention to detail while remaining flexible enough to treat each patient as an individual case. The continuing development of radiographic techniques and treatments means that you would be constantly learning new skills. You would need to be able to think quickly and to be prepared to make decisions yourself.

Broad Outlook

The NHS employs most radiographers, although there are also opportunities to work within the armed forces and in the private sector. Within the NHS there is a career structure that gives the opportunity to take on management responsibilities or specialist skills. This means that you could develop a wide range of transferable skills that would equip you for management at all levels within the NHS, industry or higher education.

There is currently a worldwide shortage of both diagnostic and therapeutic radiographers and the UK qualification is normally transferable to most overseas countries. State registration is the most important factor for your career development, indicating that you meet the high ethical standards required, have achieved educational and professional excellence and are committed to duty of care.

Related Occupations

You might also consider: doctor, nurse, medical physicist, biomedical scientist, occupational therapist, physiotherapist or photographer.

Impact on Lifestyle

It is normal to work a 35-hour week but, for diagnostic radiographers, this would include night and weekend shifts for emergency cover. Allowances are given for this flexible working. Therapeutic radiographers work more regular hours, seeing patients by appointment in a radiotherapy or oncology centre, although pressure to reduce waiting lists can involve overtime working. Exposure to x-rays can be dangerous and there is always a need to meet strict health and safety requirements.

Earnings Potential

A newly qualified NHS radiographer would start in Band 5, on a scale ranging from £20,710 to £26,839. This could rise to £39,273 for a specialist at the top of the scale and to over £65,000 for a consultant. Additional allowances are paid for appointments in and around London, ranging from 20% of basic salary for Inner London, to 15% for Outer London and 5% for the London Fringe. Salaries in the private sector are often linked to NHS levels but may be higher.

Further Information

Society of Radiographers, London SE1 2EW
Website: www.sor.org

British Institute of Radiology, London W1B 1AT
Website: www.bir.org.uk

Irish Institute of Radiography and Radiation Therapy
Website: www.iirrt.ie

Radiography careers
Website: www.radiographycareers.co.uk

Alternative/equivalent entrance requirements can include: ILC, IB, EB, NC/ND and many other similar international systems. For further details see the Equivalent Qualifications section in the Introduction.

Research Biologist

What is Involved?

Biology is the study of living organisms of all types. As a research biologist you might choose to work with plants, animals or micro-organisms. A relatively new and expanding area of biology is biotechnology, which combines biology with technical developments such as genetic engineering.

Working as a research biologist, you would be at the cutting edge of your chosen specialised area, trying to discover new information and identify solutions to specific problems. In addition to working in universities in a pure research role, there are opportunities to work in food research institutions, in medicine-related areas or in such industries as pharmaceuticals or food production and brewing.

Opportunities for Training

To become a research biologist, you would need a good degree in biology. Most universities have relevant three- or four-year courses, offering biology as a single subject or in combination with a range of other subjects. There are also sandwich courses available which allow you to spend some time working in industry whilst you are studying. Some employers and large companies might sponsor you. Most research biologists would carry out postgraduate study and go on to take a PhD. You should consider working towards Chartered Biologist status.

Requirements for Entry

Degree entry requirements vary between universities. Most would specify biology at A level/Advanced Higher/Higher or equivalent and some would also want chemistry at a similar standard. The minimum requirements are normally stated as two A level/Advanced Higher, three Higher or equivalent qualifications, together with GCSE/S Grade passes A-C/1-3 in five subjects. Sometimes maths and English are specified.

To be accepted for postgraduate study leading to a career in research, you would normally need a degree passed with first or upper second class honours.

Kind of Person

As a research biologist you would need to have a deep interest in your subject and to be prepared to continue your academic study for many years. You would be working at the forefront of your specialised area of biology and as such could be moving the subject forward. In order to do this you would need an enquiring mind and an imaginative and creative approach to problem solving. If you do not find practical laboratory work interesting at the moment, this would probably not be the career for you. You would be expected to show accuracy and precision in recording your experimental results.

You are likely to be part of a team of scientists and to be involved with discussing your ideas and findings with other scientists. In addition, you may be expected to explain your research or developments in your field to others who do not have the same scientific background as you. You would almost certainly need to use computer technology both for your research and to communicate with other in the field.

Broad Outlook

There are opportunities for laboratory-based researchers in both the private and public sectors. Some researchers move away from pure research into technical marketing and information services or take on management roles. Even if you choose to work in a laboratory, you are unlikely to be working alone and may have support staff and technicians to manage. You may have to move around the country in order to develop your career.

Related Occupations

You may be interested in other careers based in the field of biology, such as microbiologist, forensic scientist or conservation officer. Alternatively, a career based in another science might appeal to you, including biochemist or pharmacologist.

Impact on Lifestyle

You are likely to be working regular office hours for five days a week most of the time. However, there may be occasions when you are under pressure to meet deadlines and would have to work late. You may need to read or write papers or journal articles in your free time. If you choose to work in an environment that is attached to a university, you may find yourself involved in some sort of lecturing role as well as being a researcher. In addition, you would be expected to travel to conferences and to other laboratories to keep up to date with your subject

Earnings Potential

As a research biologist assistant, you are likely to earn in the region of £22,000 to £27,500 with an MSc or MPhil. This should rise to £26,500 to £35,000 for a postdoctoral research associate and £33,000 to £57,000 for a research fellow. Professors can achieve salaries of £50,000 and beyond. Industry salaries, especially in the biotechnology and pharmaceutical sectors, are generally greater than those paid by the academic and public sectors.

Further Information

Institute of Biology, London EC4A 3EF
Website: www.iob.org

Biotechnology and Biological Sciences Research Council, Swindon SN2 1UH
Website: www.bbsrc.ac.uk

Bioscience @ Work
Website: www.biocareers.org.uk

Alternative/equivalent entrance requirements can include: ILC, IB, EB, NC/ND and many other similar international systems. For further details see the Equivalent Qualifications section in the Introduction.

Research Chemist

What is Involved?

As a research chemist, you would deal with the nature of atomic and molecular substances, their properties, chemical bonding and interaction. You might work in industry - in pharmaceuticals, foodstuffs, agriculture, oil and chemical manufacture or polymers, for example - or you might choose to stay within a university environment and carry out research that is primarily academic but could have major commercial potential. Increasingly, universities and their staff are patenting and licensing their discoveries - which can significantly increase their available revenues. As an **environmental chemist**, you would use your expertise to research the effects of certain chemicals on animals, people, or plants. Rapid industrialisation has spread pollutants and contaminants, which can affect the water we drink, the food we eat and the air we breathe.

Opportunities for Training

The Royal Society of Chemistry (RSC) accredits chemistry courses which are of a high standard in terms of intellectual challenge and content. These are usually integrated Masters degree courses, designated MChem or MSci rather than BSc. These are extended programmes that last four years, whilst BSc courses last three years. The first two years are usually identical to those of the Chemistry BSc course at the same institution. Students then take different routes in year 3 or 4.

Accredited courses satisfy the academic requirements for the award of Chartered Chemist (CChem). Graduates who are awarded an RSC accredited degree and are RSC members are automatically eligible to apply for CChem once they have gained several years of chemistry related work experience. Achieving chartered status in any profession indicates to the wider community a high level of subject specific knowledge and professional competence.

Having a PhD can be a great asset in a research career, so you would need to be prepared for further postgraduate study. This can be expensive but some companies might be prepared to help fund your studies.

Requirements for Entry

A level/Advanced Higher or Higher qualifications in chemistry and ideally in maths or another science are likely to be required for entry to a chemistry degree. However, if you choose to combine chemistry with a very popular subject, such as law, you may need to obtain higher grades than are required for chemistry alone. It is possible for students without these qualifications to take a foundation course before starting their degree, either at a university or a college of further education. The entry requirements for the MChem/MSci courses are generally a little higher than those for the corresponding BSc courses.

Kind of Person

As a chemical researcher you would need to have a very keen interest in your subject and an enquiring mind, constantly asking why reactions occur and examining the effects of chemical changes. You would be expected to keep yourself up to date with overall developments in the field and to show an analytic and logical approach to problem solving.

Accuracy and precision would be very important in making observations and in recording data. At times you would need to persevere in order to solve a particular problem and to be technically imaginative in your thinking. You would also need to work with other people as part of a research team and to be able to explain your ideas, theories and discoveries to others who may not be as expert as you.

Broad Outlook

This is a competitive field and you would always be under pressure to complete work on time and to publish your results in regular departmental reports or in learned papers. You may find that you will need to study further in order to gain recognition and promotion. Many researchers in industry move onto the sales, administration or management areas of their companies.

There are generally good prospects of employment for chemists, although all of industry is affected by the economic downturn in early 2009. As a graduating chemical scientist, you could choose to work in a field vital to the future, such as addressing climate change, providing energy, securing food and water or developing new technologies in healthcare, communication and security.

Related Occupations

You may be interested in other careers in the field of chemistry, such as pharmacologist, biochemist, or chemistry technician. Alternatively, you might like to think about another scientific career such as metallurgist, research biologist or forensic scientist.

Impact on Lifestyle

You are likely to be working regular office hours on weekdays most of the time. You should be prepared to travel for conferences and other meetings. Your work would always involve reading journals and other papers outside your normal work hours to keep up to date in your own field. At times, when you are making especially good progress or are under pressure to find a solution to a problem, you may need to work extra hours to meet deadlines.

If you choose to work in a university, carrying out research, you are likely to be involved in some sort of supervision of laboratory work and even to lecture to undergraduates at times.

Earnings Potential

You are likely to earn in the region of £22,000 to £30,000 when you first start as a chemical research assistant. This could rise to £60,000 and beyond, with larger salaries available for senior staff in some large manufacturing companies. Larger companies usually pay research scientists higher salaries than smaller, specialist employers, although the latter may offer you earlier responsibility and opportunities to remain in your preferred scientific area.

Further Information

Royal Society of Chemistry, London W1J 0BA
Website: www.rsc.org

Society of Chemical Industry, London SW1X 8PS
Website: www.soci.org

Engineering and Physical Sciences Research Council, Swindon SN2 1ET
Website: www.epsrc.ac.uk

Alternative/equivalent entrance requirements can include: ILC, IB, EB, NC/ND and many other similar international systems. For further details see the Equivalent Qualifications section in the Introduction.

Residential Care Home Manager

What is Involved?

As a residential care home manager, you would be responsible for looking after long- or short-stay residents in a particular home or hostel. You are likely to find yourself caring for children, elderly people or adults with physical disabilities, mental health or behavioural problems. Your job would be to help clients come to terms with their problems and, if possible, to become independent.

You could find yourself teaching, giving one-to-one counselling sessions, running group therapy classes and, at times, offering basic support such as help with dressing or feeding. You are likely to be involved with supervising the daily routine of the home and also with providing educational and recreational activities as appropriate. Other duties might include attending meetings and writing reports, dealing with staffing issues and checking the budget. You may not be resident yourself but you would usually be expected to sleep in for a certain number of nights on a rota basis.

Opportunities for Training

You would need to have or work towards a relevant qualification, such as:

- a professional social work qualification
- a nursing diploma or degree
- a relevant N/SVQ at Level 4, such as health and social care (adults) or health and social care (children and young people) and
- a competency-based management qualification, such as the N/SVQ Level 4 in leadership and management for care services

If you want to work as a manager in a registered home for older people or younger adults, a professional qualification in nursing or social work is required, together with a management qualification. Where the home is not registered, this is best practice rather than a requirement.

Requirements for Entry

Entrants to care home management need experience of working in social or medical care. Many managers have worked as care home assistants or deputy managers, and for many jobs there is a specified minimum length of experience.

You must be registered with the relevant General Social Care or Social Services Council and you must have your background checked by the Criminal Records Bureau. Further background checks are often required. For example, if you are working with vulnerable adults in England, you must meet the requirements set out in the Protection of Vulnerable Adults Act.

Kind of Person

You would need to be extremely flexible and adaptable, showing great patience and tact in building relationships with residents. You would be involved with helping them to realise their potential and try to regain control of their lives. This can make your work environment quite tense and stressful, so you would need to be emotionally stable and resilient in order to cope. You are likely to be motivated by a desire to help people to make more of themselves and to be content with sometimes very slow progress towards that goal. You would need to be a good listener who can accept a wide variety of people without judgement. Your job would involve working with a number of other people as part of a team.

Broad Outlook

There is generally a strong demand for qualified residential care home managers. Most homes or hostels are run by local authorities, voluntary organisations or the private sector. There are opportunities to specialise in a particular field and it may be possible to move into other fields of social work, depending on your experience and qualifications. In order to gain promotion, you would need to get as much experience as possible, perhaps transferring from the public or voluntary sector to the private.

Related Occupations

You might consider: field social worker, nurse, probation officer or youth and community worker.

Impact on Lifestyle

Spending some nights sleeping in, often in self-contained accommodation attached to the unit, including weekend and holiday period shifts, can severely disrupt your family and social life.

Earnings Potential

Salaries for residential care home managers vary according to the type and size of home and the level of responsibility involved. Starting salaries are usually around £21,000 to £27,000 a year, rising with experience to between £30,000 and £40,000 a year. Some managers may earn over £45,000 a year.

Further Information

Social Work Careers
Website: www.socialworkandcare.co.uk/socialwork

General Social Care Council (England)
Website: www.gscc.org.uk

Scottish Social Services Council
Website: www.sssc.uk.com

Care Council for Wales
Website: www.ccwales.org.uk

Northern Ireland Social Care Council
Website: www.niscc.info

British Association of Social Workers, Birmingham B5 6RD
Website: www.basw.co.uk

Irish Association of Social Workers
Website: www.iasw.ie

Children's Workforce Development Council, Leeds LS1 5ES
Website: www.cwdcouncil.org.uk

Alternative/equivalent entrance requirements can include: ILC, IB, EB, NC/ND and many other similar international systems. For further details see the Equivalent Qualifications section in the Introduction.

Restaurant Manager

What is Involved?

As a restaurant manager, you could work in locations from small exclusive dining establishments or wine bars to fast food outlets, mass-appeal eating-houses, hotels, clubs and branches of major chain organisations. As well as having a working knowledge of food and wine, you would need to meet the expectations of your customers and ensure that they return in the future.

If you work for a national chain organisation, you would have to fit in with company menu policies; in other areas, your chef or catering manager would be responsible for selecting the items on the menu but you would have an overview. You would have overall responsibility for cleanliness and hygiene, health and safety, air pollution and compliance with by-laws together with recruitment, training and staff motivation.

Budgetary control would normally be an important part of your job, including ordering supplies, publicising the business, paying staff, banking each day's takings and investing for future development.

Opportunities for Training

There are many possible avenues for training. You could start as a chef or food service assistant, for example, and work your way through progressive levels of National or Scottish Vocational Qualifications (N/SVQ). You might at the same time study part-time or by distance learning for the professional qualifications of the Institute of Hospitality.

You could take a national diploma course at a local college or you could continue into higher education for a degree or higher national diploma (HND) in a subject such as hospitality or catering. At this level, you may secure a place on a management training scheme run by one of the large hotel or restaurant groups.

Another possible training route would be to join an Apprenticeship training programme.

Requirements for Entry

Experience, motivation and commitment would generally count for much more than examination success. Depending on the training route you choose, you could enter the restaurant industry with no examination passes at all, with GCSE/S Grade passes at A-C/1-3, with A level/Advanced Higher, Higher or equivalent qualifications, with a degree or HND. You should research options carefully and talk them through with your careers or personal adviser.

Kind of Person

You would need a bright, extrovert personality and the ability to communicate well with everyone you meet. You should by nature be customer-orientated and service-focused, with a solid base of common sense and a resistance to pressure and stress, together with a sense of humour and tact, business flair and administrative thoroughness. Crises can often occur in the heat of a busy kitchen and you would need to be able to think quickly and act decisively to solve problems, while maintaining an atmosphere of unhurried and unflappable professionalism in the dining area. You should have a reasonable standard of numeracy to cope with the financial side of the business and sufficient IT skills to use specialist software packages for restaurants.

Broad Outlook

The restaurant business has undoubtedly suffered in the recession of 2009. Eating out is, after all, a luxury that most people feel they can cut back on when the going gets tough. It is almost certainly the case that not all restaurants will survive the current downturn but there will be no shortage of opportunity for those remaining when the predicted recovery starts to take effect.

Related Occupations

You might also consider: hospitality/hotel or catering manager, or chef.

Impact on Lifestyle

Demands on your personal time would be substantial, with long hours, split shifts and late working, including evenings, weekends and public holidays. Indeed, the better you are at your job, the longer into the night your clients might want to stay. Your working hours would start long before the first customers arrive and finish after the last ones leave. Clearly your social and family life would be affected to such an extent that everything else would have to revolve around your work.

Earnings Potential

The range of remuneration is wide. As an assistant restaurant manager, you might start at around £16,000 to £23,000, rising with experience to between £30,000 and £40,000. A senior manager in a large restaurant could earn in excess of £50,000, possibly up to £70,000. If you set up your own restaurant, your income would depend entirely on your own ability to establish a profitable business.

Further Information

Institute of Hospitality, Surrey SM1 1SH
Website: www.instituteofhospitality.org

People 1st for Skills, Uxbridge UB8 1LH
Website: www.people1st.co.uk

Springboard, London WC2H 8LP
Website: www.springboarduk.org.uk

British Hospitality Association, London WC2A 3BH
Website: www.bha.org.uk

Irish Hospitality Institute
Website: www.ihi.ie

Alternative/equivalent entrance requirements can include: ILC, IB, EB, NC/ND and many other similar international systems. For further details see the Equivalent Qualifications section in the Introduction.

Retail Manager

What is Involved?

Your role as a retail manager would depend very much on the type of retailing in which you were involved. You could be selling goods and services on-line, in a retail park, shopping mall or high street; you might work in a supermarket, a large department store or a specialist boutique. If you were the manager of a large department store, you might have a large team of assistant managers dealing with, for example, individual departments, customer services, finance, buying and human resources.

In a smaller organisation, you might take on many of these functions yourself. The basic principles would remain the same: to maximise profits by setting and reaching sales targets, persuading customers to choose your outlet and training and getting the best out of all members of staff. You would expect to spend some of your time on the shop floor, to see how customers are reacting to your latest range of products and to check that customers are being properly handled by staff. You would attend meetings with your staff and deal with administrative matters in your office.

Opportunities for Training

You could work your way to the top through sheer hard work and talent. However, more emphasis is now being placed on qualifications. Many large stores and chains have their own training schemes, for both graduates and non-graduates, and the competition for places on these schemes can be fierce. Diploma courses in retail management are available at different levels for candidates with GCSEs/S grades, A levels/Advanced Highers/Highers or equivalent qualifications. Universities and other institutions of higher education offer relevant degree and higher national diploma courses.

Requirements for Entry

While there are no precise educational requirements laid down for entry into retail management, employers are increasingly looking for staff who have reached a certain educational level or have completed a period of training. Graduates are generally offered places on fast-track management schemes.

The actual subject of your degree would not be crucial, since the training would cover all the necessary topics, but subjects allied to retailing, including business studies, would obviously be helpful. For entry into other relevant marketing, retail management, and other degree courses you would need two A level/Advanced Higher, three to four Higher or equivalent qualifications.

Kind of Person

You would need an outgoing personality, together with excellent communication skills, both spoken and written, since you would be dealing with a wide variety of people, including staff, suppliers and customers. Quick thinking and problem solving ability would also be necessary in a busy environment where many different things are happening at once. Physical and mental stamina would be important, as the hours could be long, and as manager you would be expected to be on hand to deal with anything that cropped up. A smart appearance would be necessary. You should be numerate and have a good eye for business.

Broad Outlook

The retail industry employs around three million people, or 11% of the UK's workforce, and there are usually vacancies to be filled, although several retail chains have already disappeared in the recession of 2009. Entry into management schemes can be competitive but promotion can come quite quickly if you show determination and flair.

Some managers gain promotion to the board of their company, while others may choose to go into allied occupations such as marketing or management consultancy. You could even be head-hunted by a competitor.

Related Occupations

You might also like to consider: advertising account executive, buying executive, hospitality/hotel manager, management consultant, marketing manager, office manager, operational researcher, personnel (human resources) manager or public relations officer.

Impact on Lifestyle

Retail management can be a demanding occupation and store opening hours are becoming ever longer (even 24 hours). While you would not be expected to be present all the time, you would probably have to work some evenings and certainly some weekends.

Earnings Potential

Pay scales vary enormously, depending on the size and scope of the organisation, and the amount of responsibility undertaken. Trainee managers in multiple stores could start at anything from £18,000 to £26,000, rising with experience to £30,000 to £70,000. There would also be other benefits offered by larger employers, such as bonuses, commission, enhanced pension scheme, staff discount and good social facilities. Small retail organisations tend to pay less.

Further Information

British Retail Consortium, London SW1H 9BP
Website: www.brc.org.uk

Institute of Grocery Distribution, Watford WD25 8GD
Website: www.igd.org.uk

Skillsmart, Sector Skills Council for Retail
Website: www.skillsmartretail.com

British Shops and Stores Association
Website: www.british-shops.co.uk

Irish Management Institute
Website: www.imi.ie

Retail Academy, York YO1 6WA
Website: www.retailacademy.org

Alternative/equivalent entrance requirements can include: ILC, IB, EB, NC/ND and many other similar international systems. For further details see the Equivalent Qualifications section in the Introduction.

Royal Air Force Officer

What is Involved?

As an officer in the RAF, you would be part of the service which guards the airspace of the UK and other areas for which Britain has responsibilities, including its operations under NATO. You would be responsible for leading and managing other non-commissioned personnel on bases at home and overseas, either in an active role in flying or in any of the numerous support services on which pilots depend. RAF aircraft are divided into three groups: fast jets, multi-engine and helicopters. If you were a pilot, you would specialise in one of these and would devote most of your time to flying duties.

Apart from pilots, officers in the RAF are employed in a variety of specialised areas, including: navigators who plan routes and guide pilots; fighter controllers who use radar to direct pilots in action; air traffic controllers who provide pilots with flight information and help them take off and land safely; intelligence officers who interpret photographic and other images from reconnaissance aircraft; engineers who keep aircraft in operation; RAF Regiment officers who defend airfields and other installations; administrators, physical training personnel, training officers, police officers, lawyers, chaplains, doctors, dentists and nurses.

Opportunities for Training

Initial Officer Training takes place at the RAF College Cranwell in Lincolnshire, the world's first military air academy. Over three ten-week terms, you would receive an introduction to military life and to the principles of leadership; you would build up your leadership skills and learn, in simulated military operations, how to gain trust and command respect; you would shadow RAF personnel to see leadership skills in practice; and undertake further practical exercises to put your own skills into action. Once commissioned, you would proceed to the specialist training of your choice. For pilots, you would be selected for training on fast jets, multi-engine planes or helicopters on the basis of your performance after a short period of initial training and flying with an instructor.

Requirements for Entry

For basic entry, you must have at least two A level/Advanced Higher, three Higher or equivalent qualifications, together with five GCSE/S Grade passes at A-C/1-3 including English and maths. You must also meet RAF nationality and residence requirements and pass a series of selection tests - including aptitude and initiative tests, interviews and a medical - held at the RAF College at Cranwell. Many posts - but not all - have rigorous eyesight requirements.

If you want to go to university first, you will find that graduates are welcome in all branches of the service, particularly if your degree is in a technological or other relevant discipline. Currently about 40% of applicants are graduates.

You can seek financial support through a sixth form scholarship or sponsorship at university. A Flying Scholarship could provide some free flying training.

Kind of Person

You must be confident and capable as a leader, able to work in a team but also able to stand apart and make decisions, often very quickly. You must be physically fit and prepared to accept responsibility for both personnel and very expensive equipment. Good communication skills are vital.

Each branch of the RAF requires its own mix of personal qualities: thinking and reacting quickly for a pilot or air traffic controller; working logically for an engineer, for example. Most branches need officers with a keen interest in the operation of advanced technical equipment.

Broad Outlook

The RAF is still recruiting, despite reports that it is changing to become a smaller, faster and more flexible fighting force.

Provided you complete your training programmes successfully and serve satisfactorily, promotion can be expected. However, promotion beyond flight lieutenant to squadron leader and above depends upon merit and performance. It is very competitive and dependent on vacancies. As an officer with a Permanent Commission, you would normally serve until you are 38 or for 16 years from the age of 21; a Short Service Commission is usually 12 years for a pilot or navigator and considerably less for ground-based work.

Related Occupations

You may also consider: Royal Navy/Royal Marines officer, Army officer, civil airline pilot, air traffic controller, aircraft engineer.

Impact on Lifestyle

You would have to be available for duty 24 hours a day, 7 days a week, but for much of the time you would work normal office hours from Monday to Friday, extended occasionally into weekends. During operations and in emergency situations, you would be expected to work whatever hours the circumstances demand. This and overseas commitments could take you away from family and friends, often for extended periods of time.

There is special provision for female officers who become pregnant either to seek early release from their commission or to take maternity leave before resuming their commission.

Earnings Potential

Your officer rank and pay scale would depend on your qualifications and chosen specialist area. As a Pilot Officer, for example, you would start on £23,475, rising to £28,216 to £31,188 as a Flying Officer, £36,160 to £43,002 as a Flight Lieutenant and £45,548 to £54,550 as a Squadron Leader.

There are different pay scales for some specialist officers and professionally qualified entrants can receive credits which determine their rank and starting salary. For instance, if you join as a fully qualified dentist, your pay range after training would start at £51,100.

Further Information

School and university careers and liaison service or local Armed Forces Careers Office
Website: www.rafcareers.com

Alternative/equivalent entrance requirements can include: ILC, IB, EB, NC/ND and many other similar international systems. For further details see the Equivalent Qualifications section in the Introduction.

Royal Navy/Royal Marines Officer

What is Involved?

As a young naval officer, you would have a management responsibility for people and for state-of-the-art equipment. Eventually you might find yourself in command of a warship, flying a helicopter, supervising the safe operation of a submarine nuclear propulsion plant or providing emergency medical care. You would be trained as a specialist to perform key operational roles, working together with the Royal Marines to carry out vital work in ships, submarines, aircraft, naval air stations and shore establishments. Officer specialisms include warfare, aviation, diving, Royal Marines, hydrographic surveying, meteorology, engineering, supply and training management. Then there are medical and dental officers, nurses and chaplains. Closely linked to the Royal Navy, the Royal Marines are a specialist amphibious commando force able to operate at very short notice in a variety of terrains, often under considerable threat.

Opportunities for Training

Initial training is at Britannia Royal Naval College, Dartmouth, which is like a university, specialising in leadership, professional training and higher education across a broad range of subjects. Your general training would include an introduction to seamanship and naval warfare, plus technical subjects such as marine engineering and weapons and sensors; naval studies would add an understanding of modern naval technology, strategy and associated background subjects; leadership training would give you practical experience and assessment and you would have a period of sea training. Nurse officers train at the Royal Naval Hospitals at Portsmouth and Plymouth, although they also spend some time at Dartmouth.

Requirements for Entry

With five GCSEs or equivalent (including Maths and English) and 140 UCAS points (see the Introduction for an explanation), you could join direct as an officer, starting as a midshipman and rising to sub-lieutenant after two years. If you are studying maths and science subjects, you could apply to read for an engineering degree. Seventy-five per cent of officers enter as graduates or obtain degrees during training. You would have to go through a rigorous selection process known as the Admiralty Interview Board (AIB). This gives both you and the navy a chance to assess whether a career in the Royal Navy is right for you. The main aim of the AIB is to assess your potential. It lasts two days and takes place at HMS Sultan, a Naval base near Gosport in Hampshire. There are nationality and residence requirements as well as strict eyesight standards. You must also be male if you want to take part in mine clearance diving, serve in submarines or join the Royal Marines.

Kind of Person

Life on board ship and in submarines requires very particular qualities of officers. You must be able to live and work under the pressures of confined space with large numbers of other people. This requires broadmindedness and high levels of self-discipline. As an officer responsible for the men and women under your command, you need good management, communication and interpersonal skills. You need to be quick thinking and resourceful, able to show initiative in sudden events which may be of a 'life or death nature' in the event of combat. Long spells working away from home require qualities of self-sufficiency and drive to get on with the job. An interest in science and technology is important in many areas of work. The hard physical nature of the commando training of the Royal Marines requires a very special level of fitness, stamina and determination.

Broad Outlook

Opportunities for promotion are good and all officers have an equal opportunity to demonstrate their future potential within a highly structured system. You should be able to expect a new appointment every two or three years. Serving in the Royal Marines offers the opportunity to be on instant alert to serve as a first response service anywhere in the world where trouble may flare up.

The Royal Navy recruits around 500 officers and 4,500 ratings each year.

Related Occupations

You may consider: army officer, merchant navy officer, RAF officer, air traffic controller.

Impact on Lifestyle

You would be working in an environment where much is expected of you and where you would be on call 24 hours a day. On exercise and operational duty, shifts and hours can be long and demanding, both physically and mentally. Communal living in often cramped conditions away from families for various periods of time requires a calm outlook on life and a high level of tolerance. You must be prepared to serve anywhere in the world.

All officers join on an initial twelve-year commission (Royal Marines eight years), although there are options to leave early in certain cases.

Earnings Potential

Graduates entering as Sub-lieutenants (Royal Marines 2nd Lieutenant) receive £28,216 to £31,188 at 21, rising to £36,160 to £43,002 for lieutenants (Royal Marines Captain). Salaries rise significantly on further promotion and officers receive additional allowances for such things as flying, serving in submarines or being at sea. A Captain (Royal Marines Colonel) currently earns from £77,545 to £85,268.

Further Information

Look up local Armed Forces Careers Offices in the telephone directory
Website: www.royal-navy.mod.uk

Britannia Royal Navy College
Website: www.britannia.ac.uk

Alternative/equivalent entrance requirements can include: ILC, IB, EB, NC/ND and many other similar international systems. For further details see the Equivalent Qualifications section in the Introduction.

Rural Practice Surveyor

What is Involved?

As a rural practice surveyor, you would be involved in offering advice on a range of aspects of countryside management and development. You might undertake the sale or purchase of rural holdings, value land, property and livestock and organise auctions; you might issue shooting or fishing permits or advise on leisure activities such as golf courses, outward-bound activities or tourist accommodation; you might be involved with managing an estate or large farming enterprise.

You could be employed as a consultant offering advice to farmers or landowners on such things as buildings, livestock, and investment in machinery or other possible uses for farmland. You could become involved with insurance, tax or compensation issues. Another area that is becoming increasingly important is that of conservation and the environment. As these examples show, this can be a very varied job, concerned with a full range of countryside issues.

Opportunities for Training

There are several possible routes to qualification, including distance learning, taking an accredited degree or following a relevant postgraduate course. Whatever academic route you follow, you can work towards chartered membership of the Royal Institution of Chartered Surveyors (RICS) by completing a period of structured practical training with an employer, ending with the RICS Assessment of Professional Competence. There are also some courses accredited by the Central Association of Agricultural Valuers.

Requirements for Entry

For entry to a degree course you are likely to be asked for two or three A level/Advanced Higher, three or four Higher or equivalent qualifications, together with supporting GCSE/S Grade passes at A-C/1-3, including English and maths. Some courses will accept more practical qualifications in place of the above.

Kind of Person

You would need to have a good basic understanding of the countryside and of rural matters. In addition to your agricultural interests, you should have a sound knowledge of the law and of financial matters. You could be involved with such things as valuations, managing accounting systems and budgeting, so you would need to be numerate. You should enjoy solving problems and applying your knowledge to find practical and logical solutions.

You could find yourself working for or with a wide range of different people and you would need to be able to communicate with them all clearly and with authority. You would need to enjoy being part of a rural community and out in the countryside in all weathers. You are likely to be walking some distance and clambering around buildings, which means that you would need to be reasonably fit and agile.

Broad Outlook

There are a number of different areas of employment for rural practice surveyors. You might work in the public sector for a local authority or a government department, such as the Ministry of Defence or the Department for the Environment, Food and Rural Affairs. You might equally find work with a major rural charity such as the Royal Society for the Protection of Birds or the National Trust. However, the major area of employment is the private sector, where you might be employed directly by an estate or large farm, indirectly by a group of smaller properties or within the rural department of a firm of general practice surveyors. There is increasingly work involving conservation issues and the diversification of use of rural land.

Related Occupations

You might also consider: farm or horticultural manager, landscape architect, town and country planner, conservationist or land, hydrographic, building or quantity surveyor.

Impact on Lifestyle

This is certainly not a Monday to Friday, nine to five job. The hours would depend greatly on the season and the consequent demands of the countryside. You would be working outside in all sorts of weather and at times likely to get wet, cold and muddy. You would need to spend a lot of time talking to farmers and other rural clients, listening to their problems and worries. You may be expected to travel quite long distances to get to your work.

Earnings Potential

Traditionally, this is not the best-paid branch of surveying, the compensation being that it offers an attractive lifestyle if you enjoy the country life. If you enter the profession as a graduate, you may start on £18,000 to £22,000. This is likely to rise to around £30,000 when you achieve full professional status and gain experience. The current average salary of rural practice surveyors working in the UK is £31,900, compared with the average for all RICS members of £49,366. Sometimes you may be offered accommodation as part of the payment package.

Further Information

Royal Institution of Chartered Surveyors, Coventry CV4 8JE
Website: www.rics.org

College of Estate Management, Reading RG6 6AW
Website: www.cem.ac.uk

Society of Chartered Surveyors, Ireland
Website: www.scs.ie

Chartered Institute of Building, Berkshire SL5 7TB
Website: www.ciob.org.uk

Central Association of Agricultural Valuers, Gloucestershire GL16 8AA
Website: www.caav.org.uk

Alternative/equivalent entrance requirements can include: ILC, IB, EB, NC/ND and many other similar international systems. For further details see the Equivalent Qualifications section in the Introduction.

Sales Executive

What is Involved?

As a member of a sales team (you might also be known as a sales representative or sales manager), you would be involved in selling products or services and ensuring that your clients are fully aware of your organisation's presence in the market place. You would usually be responsible for a range of products or services and might travel widely to meet customers and establish good relationships with them. Your work could include dealing with enquiries regarding specifications or prices, helping to solve any problems of supply or quality, seeking advice on technical issues and reporting any information on competitor activities to your sales and marketing colleagues.

You would usually work within a framework laid down by your head office marketing and sales department, who would generate enquiries from potential buyers by means of advertising, sales literature, the Internet and press and television announcements. You would normally have to meet revenue targets and generate new business in addition to maintaining relationships with existing customers.

Opportunities for Training

Many companies operate their own in-house courses for trainee sales staff, usually covering product knowledge, sales techniques and company sales policy. There are also relevant part- and full-time courses available at colleges and training centres and by distance learning, while bodies such as the Institute of Sales and Marketing Management, the Managing and Marketing Sales Association and the Chartered Institute of Marketing offer qualifications linked to grades of membership.

Increasingly, degree courses are available covering sales and related aspects of business management. These could provide a sound foundation for a future career in sales, although graduate opportunities are usually open to students of any discipline. You might need a degree in, say, IT or engineering for some specific technical sales areas.

Requirements for Entry

While there are no specific entry requirements for a career in sales management, employers often recruit graduates and people with experience in relevant fields. You would generally enhance your prospects with a broad platform of GCSE/S Grade passes at A-C/1-3, including maths and English, and would have even greater choice - including degree course entry - with A level/Advanced Higher, Higher or equivalent qualifications.

Kind of Person

You should have a confident, outgoing personality, a readiness to make new contacts, sensitivity to others and the ability to listen carefully to comments or requests. You would need to believe in your own products or services and to know enough about your clients to be able to suggest the right products to meet their needs.

You would have to be persuasive in explaining the special features of your products or services, aware of competition in the marketplace, efficient in handling orders and well organised in keeping appointments and maintaining your records. You would usually be expected to dress smartly. Other qualities needed would include numeracy, the ability to cope with rejection, patience to deal with awkward customers and the energy to keep going all day long.

Broad Outlook

There is usually no shortage of sales executive opportunities anywhere in the UK, although the 2009 recession is currently having a severely negative effect on selling activity. Promotion would normally depend on your track record to date and could lead to regional or national sales manager posts and eventually to a position as sales or export director. You may find that you need to move fairly regularly to other companies or parts of the country if you want to progress more rapidly, broaden your experience or take on more responsibility.

Related Occupations

You might also consider: buying executive, marketing manager, advertising executive, retail manager or public relations officer.

Impact on Lifestyle

You would work under a great deal of pressure to meet targets and you might be expected to travel widely. Deadlines could intrude on your family and social life, and your customers would expect you to place them top in your priorities. In some jobs, you could spend days or even weeks away from home and you might have to write up your reports and prepare presentations in the evening or at weekends.

Earnings Potential

There are no set pay scales but you might expect to start on around £18,000 to £35,000 as a graduate trainee. This could rise to £22,000 to £45,000 with around five years' experience and to £40,000 to £100,000 plus for a senior sales manager. It is essential to check the full remuneration package before you join a company, as your earnings might be linked with commission, bonuses, a car or car allowance and travelling and accommodation expenses. Salaries are usually based on success in meeting sales targets, and may be advertised as OTE or 'on target earnings'. Salaries in specialised areas such as pharmaceuticals, chemicals and technological equipment tend to produce higher rewards.

Further Information

Institute of Sales and Marketing Management, Bedfordshire LU1 4DQ
Website: www.ismm.co.uk

Chartered Institute of Marketing, Berkshire SL6 9QH
Website: www.cim.co.uk

Management and Marketing Sales Association, Cheshire CW11 3GE
Website: www.mamsasbp.com

Marketing Institute, Ireland
Website: www.mii.ie

Alternative/equivalent entrance requirements can include: ILC, IB, EB, NC/ND and many other similar international systems. For further details see the Equivalent Qualifications section in the Introduction.

Science Technician

What is Involved?

As a science technician, you might work in industry, where you could be involved for example with quality control during the production process. Alternatively, you might work with scientists in a research and development department, investigating new products or manufacturing processes. This work could be in industries such as food and drinks, agriculture, pharmaceuticals or oil and chemical manufacture itself. There are also opportunities to work within the civil service as an assistant scientific officer, in the health service and in schools and universities.

Your work would tend to focus on the more routine tasks essential to support research and development. You might, for example, assemble, maintain and repair laboratory equipment, monitor and record results data, order chemicals to maintain stock levels and constantly look for ways of improving experimental results. You would spend most of your time in a laboratory or workshop, working under the direction of one or more senior research scientists.

Opportunities for Training

There are several possible training routes. You could, for example, work towards a suitable qualification via an Apprenticeship, studying part-time for a National or Scottish Vocational Qualification. These are available in laboratory operations specialising in water, chemicals and pharmaceuticals, metal industry laboratory services, forensic science, and for laboratory technicians specialising in education. Alternatively, you could continue your education with a higher national diploma (HND) or a degree, possibly considering a sandwich course to gain practical work experience whilst studying.

There is often in-service training available within large organisations. This may cover more advanced skills, specialised scientific equipment or aspects of management, purchasing and stock control. You could also expect regular updating training in such areas as new techniques and technology, health and safety procedures and computer systems.

Requirements for Entry

The minimum requirements for training are usually four GCSE/S Grade passes A-C/1-3, including English, a relevant science and maths. You would need at least one or two science A level/Higher/Advanced Higher, or two or three Higher or equivalent qualifications for admission to an HND course, while degree entry would require two or three A level/Advanced Higher, or three or to four Higher or equivalent passes.

Kind of Person

You would need a keen interest in your particular area of science. You are likely to be working in an environment that is developing and changing all the time, although your work could at times be quite methodical and repetitive, as you would be carrying out routine tests and applications.

You would need to be accurate and to show attention to detail. In addition to your scientific skills, you would have to work as part of a team and provide a fast and efficient service when asked to do so. You may have to explain your work clearly to your colleagues, so you would need reasonably good written and verbal communication.

Broad Outlook

There are normally always jobs for science technicians and a wide range of different organisations in which to find employment, although declining opportunities in manufacturing industry, especially during the economic downturn at the start of 2009, may make it necessary for you move to another sector to develop your career.

There are opportunities within the civil service, industrial research and educational establishments, pharmaceutical companies and hospitals, to name but a few. It should be possible, with appropriate experience, to use your scientific and technical knowledge to branch out into areas such as production or technical sales and marketing.

Related Occupations

You might be interested in other science-based careers such as biomedical scientist, biochemist or molecular biologist.

Impact on Lifestyle

Most technicians work normal office hours Monday to Friday, so this work should not disrupt your social or family life. It may be necessary to work overtime sometimes when there are tight deadlines to meet, when research is at a critical point, or if you undertake shift work on a 24-hour production unit. You could find it necessary to move around the country to get promotion and there may be opportunities to work abroad. It would pay to study to improve your qualifications and prospects.

Earnings Potential

Salaries vary between the private and public sectors. On average, you could expect to start earning between £14,000 and £20,000 as a technician, rising to around £20,000 to £35,000. In some industries, salaries for experienced, competent technicians can be much higher than this.

Further Information

Royal Society of Chemistry, London W1J 0BA
Website: www.rsc.org

Institute of Biology, London EC4A 3EF
Website: www.iob.org

Institute of Physics, London W1B 1NT
Website: www.iop.org

Institute of Physics in Ireland
Website: http://ireland.iop.org

Apprenticeships
England: www.apprenticeships.org.uk
Wales: http://new.wales.gov.uk
Scotland: www.modernapprenticeships.com
Northern Ireland: www.delni.gov.uk

Alternative/equivalent entrance requirements can include: ILC, IB, EB, NC/ND and many other similar international systems. For further details see the Equivalent Qualifications section in the Introduction.

Secretary - Personal Assistant

What is Involved?

The term Personal Assistant (PA) refers to a job involving more than the basic secretarial duties of typing letters, answering the telephone and dealing with routine administration. If you were a PA, your main role would be to act as a close support to a manager or executive, handling the day-to-day running of an office to allow them to make the most efficient use of their time.

Your work could involve dealing with correspondence and other communications, organising meetings, liaising with other departments, companies or customers, and sometimes even acting on behalf of the manager. With experience, you could become an office manager, often with your own administrative team.

Opportunities for Training

There is no single training route but employers would be looking for good keyboard skills and computer literacy, sometimes with shorthand. Specific training for a particular company would normally be carried out in-house, usually after you have completed a one- or two-year college course in office skills and management.

There are also university-level diploma and degree courses in secretarial studies and administration, together with some courses specifically designed for graduates. If you have the right level of training and experience, such as the Certificate in Professional PA and Secretarial Skills, you would have the option of becoming a member of the Institute for Professional Administrators.

Requirements for Entry

While there are generally no specific educational requirements laid down for becoming a PA, employers would expect a high level of numeracy and proficiency and accuracy in written English.

Entry to secretarial courses usually requires a minimum of some GCSE/S Grade subjects, while others look for A level/Advanced Higher, Higher or equivalent qualifications. If you are thinking of going to university, you might consider undertaking a course in secretarial and office skills first - it would never be wasted and you need never be unemployed.

Kind of Person

You would need to be very well organised, with an eye for detail and with excellent communication skills, both spoken and written. You should be tactful and discreet, possessing a talent for getting on well with people of all kinds. You would need to be a real team member, able to work both with and for other people, sometimes taking decisions and sometimes implementing the decisions of others. A smart appearance would be important, since you would probably be involved in dealing with customers or other visitors to your organisation.

Broad Outlook

With the increased use of computers in office administration, the role of the PA has changed, with less call for the traditional shorthand/typist but increased scope for well-qualified and ambitious administrators. There will always be opportunities for such people to make their mark, and a good PA can often make the transition to management. You may decide to specialise in a particular area of work, such as medicine or law, or you might set up your own businesses, such as a secretarial or recruitment agency. Traditionally, the role of the PA has been undertaken almost exclusively by women; now more men are coming forward.

Related Occupations

You might like also to consider: civil service administrator, hospitality/hotel manager, office manager, personnel/human resources manager, public relations officer, medical secretary, farm secretary or secretary linguist.

Impact on Lifestyle

You would probably work usual office hours, though with increased responsibility and seniority might come the need to stay later at particular times of the year or travel to business meetings. Depending upon the amount of responsibility you were given, and/or the personality of your particular boss, you might need deep reserves of tact and diplomacy because you would have extensive access to confidential information.

Earnings Potential

Pay scales would vary widely, according to the size of the organisation and the seniority of your position. In general, starting salaries range from about £18,000 to £24,000, rising with experience to £27,000 to £38,000. Top jobs in prestigious companies in London can command over £40,000.

Further Information

Institute for Professional Administrators, London SE11 5EE
Website: www.inprad.org

Institute of Agricultural Secretaries and Administrators, Warwickshire CV8 2LG
Website: www.iagsa.co.uk

Association of Medical Secretaries, Practice Administrators and Receptionists,
London WC1H 9LN
Website: www.amspar.co.uk

Careers in Business and Administration
Website: www.breakinto.biz

Alternative/equivalent entrance requirements can include: ILC, IB, EB, NC/ND and many other similar international systems. For further details see the Equivalent Qualifications section in the Introduction.

Secretary Linguist

What is Involved?

As a secretary linguist (or bilingual/trilingual secretary or bilingual PA), you would be able to offer practical speaking and writing skills in one or more foreign languages in addition to the full range of secretarial skills. The exact nature of your job would vary considerably from one employer to another but could include anything from word processing in your different languages, translating correspondence and making phone calls abroad to receiving and entertaining overseas visitors, making foreign travel arrangements and keeping up to date with the political or commercial climate in relevant countries.

You may receive occasional requests for translating or interpreting but it should be clear that you are not a specialist in either of these fields. (See our separate articles on these occupations.) You would normally be based in an office and should have access to keyboards, software packages and reference materials specific to the languages you would be using.

Opportunities for Training

You could develop your secretarial and language skills in many different ways but would probably wish to gain a recognised qualification from one of the major awarding bodies, such as Edexcel, OCR or the Scottish Qualifications Authority (SQA). Your course should include English language skills, word processing and commercial applications of your chosen languages. There may also be specialist in-house training provided by your employer.

Requirements for Entry

You would need to be fluent in writing and speaking the languages you offer, and it would be a distinct advantage to have a sound understanding of the cultural, economic and social situation in the countries where your languages are spoken. Depending on the level you are aiming at, you may need A level/Advanced Higher, Higher or equivalent passes in one or more languages and you could find a degree valuable. However, experience of travelling or living overseas and using foreign languages on a regular basis could count for as much as examination success. Whatever your linguistic background, you would need a high-level secretarial qualification.

Kind of Person

You would need excellent communication skills and the confidence to enter into multilingual conversations on the telephone or in face-to-face meetings. You should have a keen interest in keeping your language skills up to date and a willingness to learn specialist vocabulary. Attention to detail, advanced IT skills and good organisational ability would all be important.

You should be able to get on with people easily, especially if your work involves welcoming foreign visitors to your organisation and making them feel at ease. A willingness to travel would quite likely be part of your interest in using languages and could enhance your employment opportunities.

Broad Outlook

With accelerating globalisation and the continuing development of the European Union, demand is healthy for people with genuine bilingual or trilingual ability (as opposed to a superficial smattering of language awareness). Most opportunities relate to the major European languages, especially French, German and Spanish, but there are also openings for specialists in Russian, Arabic, Japanese, Chinese and Eastern European languages.

A career as a secretary linguist presents above-average openings for late start, career break, flexitime, temping and freelance initiatives. There are also many job opportunities abroad, including the option of working as an English language specialist in a country where you can communicate easily in the local language.

Related Occupations

You might also consider: secretary/personal assistant, teacher, translator, interpreter, or another specialist role such as farm, medical or legal secretary.

Impact on Lifestyle

Many posts would involve a normal business week from Monday to Friday, but you could have to work unsocial hours if you need to be in regular contact with people in other time zones or if you are looking after overseas visitors. You may be expected to travel abroad as part of your job.

Earnings Potential

Levels of pay would vary considerably from one job to another, depending on the location and your ability and experience, but you could expect a salary higher than the normal secretarial rate, perhaps between £20,000 and £26,000, with additional allowances for out-of-hours working and overseas travel. This should rise with experience to £27,000 to £38,000 and could be higher for a senior post in a large international organisation.

Further Information

Institute for Professional Administrators, London SE11 5EE
Website: www.inprad.org

CILT, the National Centre for Languages, London WC2N 4LB
Website: www.cilt.org.uk

Scottish Qualifications Authority, Glasgow G2 7NQ
Website: www.sqa.org.uk

Chartered Institute of Linguists, London SE1 1UN
Website: www.iol.org.uk

European Management Assistants, AT-4600 Wels, Austria
Website: www.euma.org

Scottish Centre for Information on Language Teaching and Research (Scottish CILT), Glasgow G13 1PP
Website: www.scilt.stir.ac.uk

Alternative/equivalent entrance requirements can include: ILC, IB, EB, NC/ND and many other similar international systems. For further details see the Equivalent Qualifications section in the Introduction.

Shipbroker

What is Involved?

As a shipbroker, your role would be to facilitate the business of international bulk shipping by bringing together ship owners with vessels to fill and charterers with cargoes to transport by sea. You would also be involved with the purchase and sale of very large ships such as bulk carriers, container vessels, oil tankers and specialist ships. The main centre of international shipbroking operations is the Baltic Exchange in London, with some 50% of all tanker broking and up to 40% of dry bulk chartering carried out by about 5,000 shipbrokers working in around 700 shipbroking companies (there are 20,000 shipbrokers worldwide).

Other major shipping markets are found in Tokyo, Singapore, Shanghai, Hong Kong and New York as well as in European centres like Hamburg, Copenhagen and Oslo. Your work would include making presentations to potential clients, negotiating the main terms of a contract or sale, providing your clients with market intelligence and advice, entering tonnage into the company's database, checking the technical nature of a cargo and building up your own personal contacts throughout the world of shipping. Good relationships are vital if you wish to succeed.

Opportunities for Training

While there are no specific qualifications required, you might wish to apply for membership of the Institute of Chartered Shipbrokers (ICS) and to undertake one of their diploma courses, which can be taken by correspondence course or day release. These courses cover maritime law, international shipping and trade, economics and bulk transport. The Baltic Exchange also runs regular training courses on many aspects of the shipbroking business.

Many new recruits are graduates entering shipbroking after completing a degree in maritime business, although any academic subject would be acceptable.

Requirements for Entry

There is no required shipbroking qualification but you would gain much relevant background information from a business degree with a shipping specialism.

Kind of Person

You should be prepared to take a high level of responsibility, to mix well socially, to express views clearly and logically in both written and oral format, to have well-honed negotiating skills with a flair for maintaining contacts. Your intellectual credentials would be tested in the tenacity required to push through deals. Physical demands can also be high, with long hours, a global timescale, frequent exhausting travel, 24-hour availability in times of urgency and an extremely competitive global arena.

The highest levels of reliability, accuracy and integrity are essential. The motto of the Baltic Exchange - 'Our Word Our Bond' - symbolises the importance of ethics in trading. Members need to rely on each other and, in turn, on their principals for many contracts verbally expressed and only subsequently confirmed in writing. You would need good IT skills to cope with the sophisticated online information system at the Exchange.

Broad Outlook

Shipping markets are facing difficult times in the global economic downturn of 2009. However, it is widely accepted that free trade between nations - and shipbrokers are at the heart of this - will be a cornerstone of world economic recovery in 2010. There will be stiff competition from other shipping centres but the London market looks likely to remain very significant.

The Baltic Exchange is becoming increasingly computerised and brokers acting for ship owners can place shipping information, including the technical details of ships, directly online. However, negotiation is still handled completely by the brokers personally, since this is too complex to be automated by computer. Every ship, port and cargo is different.

Related Occupations

You might also consider: logistics manager, freight forwarder, stockbroker, insurance underwriter or marketing manager.

Impact on Lifestyle

The global market ensures that shipbroking services spread over 24 hours a day, seven days a week. Periods of frenzied activity occur regularly when there is a need to find employment for a fleet and, as a broker, you would wish to prove the value for money of your services to the ship owners and charterers. Typically, your day could start early in the morning, in time to catch the important Far Eastern Markets, or could go on late into the night for the USA. You would be working by telephone, fax, email and mobile for much of the time and might need to make frequent trips abroad.

Earnings Potential

Medium to high levels of pay can be expected, with a starting salary of around £26,000, rising to £65,000 - £85,000 for an experienced shipbroker. In good years, bonuses can easily double these figures.

Further Information

Institute of Chartered Shipbrokers, London EC3V 0AA
Website: www.ics.org.uk

Baltic Exchange, London EC3A 8BH
Website: www.balticexchange.com

British International Freight Association, Middlesex TW13 7EP
Website: www.bifa.org

Chartered Institute of Logistics and Transport, London SW1E 6LB
Website: www.ciltuk.org.uk

Alternative/equivalent entrance requirements can include: ILC, IB, EB, NC/ND and many other similar international systems. For further details see the Equivalent Qualifications section in the Introduction.

Social Worker

What is Involved?

Social work is all about people. As a social worker, you would help people to live more successfully within their local communities by helping them find solutions to their problems. Your work would involve engaging not only with individual clients but also with their families and friends, as well as working closely with organisations including the police, NHS, schools and the probation service.

Much of your work would focus on assessing the needs of your clients and planning the individual packages of care and support that will best meet those needs.

Social workers tend to specialise in either adult or children's services. In the former, your role might include working with people with mental health problems or learning disabilities; working with people in residential care; working with offenders, by supervising them in the community and supporting them to find work; assisting people with HIV/AIDs and helping older people at home to sort out problems with health, housing or benefits. In the latter, you might provide assistance and advice to keep families together; work in children's homes; manage adoption and foster care processes; provide support to younger people leaving care, at risk or in trouble with the law; or help children facing difficulties brought on by illness in the family.

Opportunities for Training

Becoming a social worker in England involves taking an honours degree in social work and registering with the General Social Care Council. The main route is a three-year undergraduate (Bachelors) degree course although two-year postgraduate (Masters) programmes are also available. Some universities offer part-time courses. All students on all courses must successfully complete at least 200 days of assessed practice before being awarded the social work degree.

Similar routes to qualification exist in the other countries of the United Kingdom but you must research options very carefully and consider studying/training in the country where you intend to work.

Requirements for Entry

Entry to the degree course is open to people of all ages, from school-leavers onwards. However, universities will look for previous experience of work or volunteering in social care. You may be able to gain admission over the age of 21 without formal examination passes, although as a school or college leaver you would normally need at least two A level/Advanced Higher, three Higher or equivalent passes, together with five GCSE/S Grade passes at A-C/1-3.

All programmes require you to have some relevant paid or voluntary social work experience. Certain types of criminal conviction could prevent you from meeting the entry requirements.

Kind of Person

You would need to be open minded and prepared to examine and even change your attitudes and possible prejudices. You may need to deal with racism and other forms of discrimination. You would certainly require personal qualities such as patience, determination and the ability to help people face painful and distressing problems. Social work can be both physically and emotionally stressful and not everyone can stand back from situations and assess them in an objective but caring way. Good practice would rely on the intellectual skills of analysis, reflection and adopting a critical perspective.

Broad Outlook

The end of 2008 proved to be a fraught time for social workers working in children's services as a result of all the adverse publicity surrounding the cases of 'Baby P' in London and 'Baby A' in Doncaster. These prompted a serious review of child protection in England and highlighted problems with the 'unmanageable workloads' of social workers. There are serious pressures in many parts of the country in what is very demanding and difficult work, made harder by the economic downturn increasing workloads further, while public attention is focused on the profession. It seems inevitable that more resources will be directed towards social work, offering challenging prospects for future generations of social workers.

Related Occupations

You might also consider: probation officer, residential care home manager, teacher, nurse, occupational therapist, psychologist, police officer, prison governor or youth and community worker.

Impact on Lifestyle

Most social workers are involved in a system providing cover 24 hours a day, seven days a week. This means that your hours are likely to be long and irregular. You may well be required to work a rota system or to be on call at times after your official hours of work, for which you may get extra pay. You may find yourself facing difficult situations, which can be unpleasant and at times dangerous. For example, you may need to call on someone with a history of violence or visit clients living in a squat.

Earnings Potential

There are no fixed grades for social workers, as each employing organisation negotiates within certain guidance. A newly qualified social worker would probably be on a starting salary of about £20,000 (more in London) and this could increase to about £30,000 or above, as a senior practitioner or team leader.

Further Information

Social Work Careers (England)
Website: www.socialworkandcare.co.uk/socialwork

General Social Care Council (England)
Website: www.gscc.org.uk

Scottish Social Services Council
Website: www.sssc.uk.com

Care Council for Wales
Website: www.ccwales.org.uk

Northern Ireland Social Care Council
Website: www.niscc.info

Irish Association of Social Workers
Website: www.iasw.ie

Children's Workforce Development Council, Leeds LS1 5ES
Website: www.cwdcouncil.org.uk

Community Care
Website: www.communitycare.co.uk

Alternative/equivalent entrance requirements can include: ILC, IB, EB, NC/ND and many other similar international systems. For further details see the Equivalent Qualifications section in the Introduction.

Software Engineer

What is Involved?

Working as a software engineer, you would be responsible for creating the original programs needed to enable computers to carry out a very wide range of functions. Your programs (or software) could include complex automation control for industry, accounts packages for bookkeeping or sophisticated business management systems. You would work on the basis of specifications laid down and agreed with a client, usually via a systems analyst in your own company or organisation. You would often work on your own for small projects, or as a member of a team of software engineers for large projects. Having written the software, you would make sure it works properly, oversee its installation and test it out in its finished form. You could also write up installation instructions and user manuals and even run training courses for the client's staff.

Opportunities for Training

There are a great many computer-related courses available at universities and there are significant differences between them, so it is important to read prospectuses carefully. Some courses offer a mixture of options combining the study of software and hardware and you then choose to specialise in one of these at the end of the first year. It is also possible to combine software engineering with a range of other subjects, including electrical and electronic engineering or management. Most degree courses last three or four years and some include a sandwich element of industrial experience. There are also higher national diploma (HND) courses, which are generally a year shorter than corresponding degrees, and postgraduate courses.

When in employment, you would be able to work towards professional qualifications offered by bodies such as the British Computer Society, the Institute for the Management of Information Systems or the National Computing Centre. There is an IT Professional Development Programme run by e-skills UK. This Master's level programme has been designed by industry practitioners and is delivered through universities and participating employers.

Requirements for Entry

To gain admission to a relevant degree course, you would need two or three passes at A level/Advanced Higher, Higher or equivalent, almost certainly including maths and perhaps physics too, together with at least five GCSE/S Grade passes A-C/1-3 to include English, maths and a science subject. For an HND, you should have at least one A level/Advanced Higher, two Higher or equivalent passes.

A good first degree would normally be necessary for admission to a postgraduate course.

Kind of Person

You are likely to be interested in technology and computers and up to date with developments in this ever-changing field. You should be strong at maths, with a logical and practical approach to problem solving. In addition, you would have to listen to the requirements and ideas of others and to accommodate these in your plans. With tight deadlines to meet, this would require you to prioritise effectively.

Broad Outlook

There are apparent contradictions in labour market data for software engineers. On the one hand, e-skills UK cite the need for 140,000 new employees every year in the UK IT and telecommunications sector; on the other, applications to IT-related degrees have tumbled by 50% over the last five years. Whatever the explanation for this, there is a clear incentive for employers to entice the right candidates from a shrinking pool, leading the National Computing Centre to assert that employment in the IT sector is likely to weather the economic storm of 2009, although there will be losers in some areas. Nearly half of respondents to its 'Benchmark of Salaries and Employment Trends in IT 2009' survey said they expect the number of IT staff employed at their location to increase over the next two years. Similarly, e-skills UK describe many aspects of ICT as 'credit crunch resistant'.

Related Occupations

You might also consider training as an electrical, electronic, communications, biomedical, aeronautical or automotive engineer. Alternatively, you might like to work as a systems analyst, webmaster or cybernetics specialist.

Impact on Lifestyle

Whilst your standard working week might well be within normal office hours and confined to weekdays, you are a likely to find yourself occasionally working at the weekends or in the evenings, in order to meet deadlines or to sort out some problem that has arisen unexpectedly. You would also find yourself reading about your subject out of work time to ensure that you are up to date with new developments. You may find that you have to travel clients' premises.

Earnings Potential

You could expect to start on a salary of around £21,000 to £35,000 when you first graduate, with earnings at the higher end relating to work in management consultancy. This should rise as you gain experience over 10 to 15 years to £30,000 to £80,000, if you are reliable and can produce useful results. The size of installation, location and the nature of the employer's business will affect salary levels. Computer manufacturers and software houses usually pay higher salaries.

Further Information

British Computer Society, Swindon SN1 1HJ
Website: www.bcs.org.uk

National Computing Centre, Manchester M1 7ED
Website: www.ncc.co.uk

Institute for the Management of Information Systems, Kent BR5 3QG
Website: www.imis.org.uk

E-skills UK Ltd, London SW1E 6DR
Website: www.e-skills.com

Irish Computer Society
Website: www.ics.ie

Big Ambition
Website: www.bigambition.co.uk

Lero: Irish Software Engineering Research Centre
Website: www.lero.ie

Alternative/equivalent entrance requirements can include: ILC, IB, EB, NC/ND and many other similar international systems. For further details see the Equivalent Qualifications section in the Introduction.

Solicitor

What is Involved?

As a solicitor, your job would be to provide clients with skilled legal advice and representation, including representing them in court. You might, like most solicitors, work in a 'private practice' partnership or you might work as an employed solicitor for central or local government, the Crown Prosecution/Procurator Fiscal Service, the magistrates/district courts or a commercial or industrial organisation. Your work could be general in nature - wills, divorce settlements, property sales, criminal cases and compensation for injury - or you could become expert in, for example, company, criminal, taxation, European, international or environmental law.

You could concentrate on work with legally aided clients, who could not normally afford a solicitor's fees, or you could specialise in advising multi-national corporate clients on urgent, multi-million pound deals.

Opportunities for Training

The law is complex and your training as a solicitor would have to follow a set of rigorous rules. The quickest route to qualification is by means of a qualifying law degree. If you take a degree in a subject other than law, you would have to complete a one-year full-time (or two-year part-time) course leading to the Common Professional Examination (CPE) or the postgraduate Diploma in Law. After successful completion of your law degree, CPE or Diploma in Law, you would have to undertake a one-year (or two-year part-time) Legal Practice Course (LPC), before entering a two-year training contract with a firm of solicitors or other approved organisation (such as a local authority or the Crown Prosecution Service), gaining practical experience in a variety of areas of law. There are proposals to introduce changes to the structure of the LPC in 2009, so check for updates. An alternative route would be to train as a legal executive and use this as a stepping-stone to qualification as a solicitor. See our separate article on 'Legal Executive'.

In Scotland, you would need a degree in Scots Law or a three-year pre-Diploma training contract, together with the 26-week Diploma in Legal Practice. You would follow this with a two-year training contract with a practising solicitor in Scotland, towards the end of which you would have to sit a Test of Professional Competence to determine whether you are a 'fit and proper person' to enter the profession.

Requirements for Entry

Competition for places to read law is exceptionally strong and university admissions tutors expect high grades at A level/Advanced Higher, Higher or equivalent. No particular subjects are specified. You will have to take the National Admissions Test for Law (LNAT) to secure a place on a Law degree at 10 of the most prestigious UK universities.

Kind of Person

You would need excellent written, verbal and interpersonal skills, together with the ability to read widely and take in considerable amounts of information. You would spend a lot of time interviewing clients in order to establish the facts of a case and form an opinion. Much of what you are told by clients would be confidential and they would need to be sure that it should remain so. You may be involved with complex financial issues, including company accounts and taxation, so a good standard of numeracy would be important.

Broad Outlook

Like the rest of the world, the legal profession is facing a difficult time in 2009. This has a knock-on effect for junior lawyers, especially trainees and students, who currently find themselves facing an even tougher employment market than usual. In the short term, training contract places and newly-qualified positions will be very difficult to find.

Related Occupations

You might also consider: advocate/barrister, legal executive, legal accountant, or civil service administrator.

Impact on Lifestyle

The training can be very expensive, especially if you choose not to take a law degree, leaving you with even larger loans to repay when you start training than most other students. Most solicitors work normal office hours, although you may have to put in many additional hours to complete work on time. Sometimes you may be on call, in the evenings or at weekends, to deal with clients who have been taken to a police station. Legal aid work can be poorly paid and demanding but would give you valuable experience in dealing with a wide range of cases.

Earnings Potential

Law Society research shows that 27% of law students expect to earn more than £31,000 on qualification, indicating that many could be disappointed by their starting salary. The average salary for a trainee solicitor is £20,925 and the Law Society sets the minimum salary at £18,420 pa for Central London and £16,500 pa elsewhere. Similarly, 42% of respondents expect their peak earnings to exceed £70,000 and 3% believe that they will earn an annual income of over £500,000 at some point during their career. The average annual salary for a lawyer is £51,463. This is even starker in the credit crunch era, when partners may be unable to draw profits and salary freezes are the norm.

The Law Society of Scotland recommends that trainee solicitors be paid £15,000 in the first year of their traineeship and £18,000 in the second, although some of the larger commercial law firms are known to pay trainees significantly higher salaries. As a newly qualified solicitor, you might expect to be paid about £25,000 if you work for a small firm and about £30,000 or over if you work for one of the larger commercial firms in Edinburgh or Glasgow.

Further Information

Law Society, Worcestershire B98 OTD
Website: www.lawsociety.org.uk

Junior Lawyers
Website: http://juniorlawyers.lawsociety.org.uk

Law Society of Scotland, Edinburgh EH3 7YR
Website: www.lawscot.org.uk

Law Society of Ireland
Website: www.lawsociety.ie

National Admissions Test for Law
Website: www.lnat.ac.uk

Alternative/equivalent entrance requirements can include: ILC, IB, EB, NC/ND and many other similar international systems. For further details see the Equivalent Qualifications section in the Introduction.

Speech and Language Therapist

What is Involved?

As a speech and language therapist (SLT), you would be a specialist in communication disorders. The ability to communicate is central to all that we do: who we are, how we learn and how we relate to each other at home, at school and at work. Your aim would be to help the thousands of people who fail to access education, social, economic and career opportunities due to communication difficulties.

In your work, you would assess and diagnose the people under your care or who have been referred to you, developing a programme of care to maximize their communication potential. You would also work to support people with swallowing, eating and drinking difficulties. You would work directly with a person with communication difficulties but would also be involved in breaking down communication barriers by influencing and supporting other people in their communication environment.

You might work with: people who stammer or have hearing impairments; babies with cleft palates or cerebral palsy; children who need help in learning to understand language or putting words together; adults or children involved in road traffic accidents; and adults who have had strokes or other neurological disorders.

Opportunities for Training

All speech and language therapists must complete a recognised three- or four-year degree programme and register with the Health Professions Council before being able to practise.

Programmes combine academic study and practice/clinical placements. Many programmes welcome applications from suitably qualified mature students, although universities may require evidence of recent study. If you already have an honours or equivalent degree, you may be eligible to enter a two-year postgraduate qualifying programme. Subjects in related fields (for example, psychology, social sciences and linguistics) are often preferred.

You would study the normal development of language and production of speech sounds, as well as communication disorders. You would also cover aspects of psychology, particularly normal development, phonetics and linguistics, neurology, physiology and anatomy, together with acoustics and audiology (hearing), as problems in these areas can affect speech and language. The practical side of your training would involve at least 150 hours of clinical placement with a range of client groups (eg children with special needs or adults with acquired neurological disorders), in which you would work under the supervision of qualified colleagues.

Requirements for Entry

Most recognised degree programmes require three A level passes or five Scottish Highers as minimum entry qualifications. Some require specific GCSE and A levels, such as English and biology, so check the entry requirements with each university.

Competition for places is keen and requirements are generally higher than the minimum. All courses interview candidates and usually ask about clinical observations. Before interview, therefore, you should seek to arrange a visit to your local speech and language therapy service.

Kind of Person

Good interpersonal skills are essential. It is important that you can communicate clearly and are able to listen and so gain the trust of your patients. You would need skills in observation, analysis and problem solving as you work with patients and clients. You would need a flexible and creative approach because what works with one patient would not necessarily work with another. You should also have an interest in both science and language. It is important to keep records for each patient and monitor their progress. This demands organisational skill and the ability to work independently, as well as to be part of a team.

Broad Outlook

Once you are qualified, employment prospects are good, although there is more competition for posts in the London area. The majority of SLTs work for the NHS, although opportunities for private work are now growing. In the UK, approximately 2.5 million people have a communication disorder of some kind. Of these, 800,000 have a difficulty so severe that it is hard for anyone outside their immediate families to understand them.

Related Occupations

You may be interested in other therapy-based professions in the medical field, such as occupational therapist, radiographer, physiotherapist or podiatrist. Alternatively, you might be interested in becoming a teacher or an educational or clinical psychologist.

Impact on Lifestyle

NHS SLTs work a 36-hour week, usually Monday to Friday, but you should be prepared to work extra hours occasionally. In private practice, the hours may be longer and can involve some unsocial hours, but the earnings are likely to be higher. You may be required to travel to different locations during your working day.

Earnings Potential

A newly qualified NHS SLT would start in Band 5, on a scale ranging from £20,710 to £26,839. This could rise to £39,273 for an advanced SLT at the top of the scale and to over £65,000 for a consultant. Additional allowances are paid for appointments in and around London, ranging from 20% of basic salary for Inner London, to 15% for Outer London and 5% for the London Fringe. Salaries in the private sector are often linked to NHS levels but may be higher.

Further Information

Royal College of Speech and Language Therapists, London SE1 1NX
Website: www.rcslt.org

Irish Association of Speech and Language Therapists
Website: www.iaslt.com

Health Professions Council, London SE11 4BU
Website: www.hpc-uk.org

Alternative/equivalent entrance requirements can include: ILC, IB, EB, NC/ND and many other similar international systems. For further details see the Equivalent Qualifications section in the Introduction.

Sports Coach

What is Involved?

As a sports coach, you would provide coaching on the techniques of a sport to players under your tuition, assisting them to learn their sport, to enhance their skills and get the most out of their efforts. You would monitor their technique and performance; help them reach top physical and mental condition; confer, if necessary, with other specialists such as dietitians, physiotherapists or sports psychologists; and explain how the abilities of the individual should relate to those of the team. All areas of sport are covered by coaches, and more opportunities occur at a wider age range than ever before.

Coaches in exercise and fitness can be found in such activities as keep fit, yoga, weight training, circuit training, aerobics, aquafit, step and line dancing, and other movement and fitness classes. They are likely to be employed by leisure centres or to be self-employed. More and more they are setting up their own clubs and classes. Holiday camps, outward bound centres, cruise ships, private hotels and even large business organisations now employ their own resident trainers. The armed forces, security services, probation and prison services also have instructors to train in fitness and, if appropriate, in self-defence.

Opportunities for Training

The national governing bodies (NGB) often provide part- or full-time courses in their own sports areas. For example, bodies such as the LTA (Lawn Tennis Association), the PGA (Professional Golfers Association) and the RYA (Royal Yachting Association) offer courses for coaches and provide official recognition and registration. There is some higher education provision with higher national diploma (HND) courses and foundation degrees in leisure studies, and more especially degree courses in PE, movement studies, sports science or coaching.

The UK Coaching Certificate (UKCC) endorses NGB qualifications, giving coaches a nationally recognised qualification and also a progressive development pathway.

Requirements for Entry

The National Coaching Foundation offers a substantial range of options to would-be coaches in all areas. For entry to teacher training or to a sports-related degree, you would normally need two or three A level/Advanced Higher, three or four Higher or equivalent qualifications, together with a good spread of GCSE/S Grade passes A-C/1-3, including English, maths and a science for teacher training courses. HNDs would require one A level/Advanced Higher, two Higher or equivalent qualifications. You would need to be very fit and many courses would look for evidence of sporting achievement.

Kind of Person

In addition to physical fitness, you would need good verbal communication skills, sensitivity to others, the capacity to mix praise and criticism in acceptable doses, powers of analysis, persistence, organisation and stamina. As a professional representative of your sport, you would usually be expected to set an example to others in terms of your behaviour, appearance and adherence to the code of conduct laid down by your governing body.

Broad Outlook

The expanding leisure industry now employs three million people in the UK, 40,000 of whom specialise in sport. Hosting the Olympic and Paralympic Games in 2012 will have increased the investment in sport by £300 million. The potential for increased sporting and coaching opportunities into 2016 is very considerable. You would find, however, that this remains a very competitive and somewhat unpredictable world.

Coaches in professional sport are often ex-professional sportspeople who have gained coaching qualifications.

Related Occupations

You might also consider: PE teacher/instructor, professional sportsperson, youth worker, leisure services manager, teacher, physiotherapist, chiropractor or osteopath.

Impact on Lifestyle

This can be only slightly less involving than for the full-time sportsperson, but possibly without the same level of personal intensity. Nevertheless, it can involve working throughout the day, at weekends and, for indoor sports, during the evenings. This could be seen as one of the most sociable of career fields with the most unsocial of time schedules to meet the likely demands of clients.

Earnings Potential

The number of full-time, paid coaching positions is limited, with little standardisation in rates of pay. Salaries vary depending on the employer, whether the position is full or part-time and at what level coaching is required. In professional sport, you would be likely to receive a basic salary with bonuses, depending on how much prize money is earned or how well an individual or team performs. As a full-time coach, you might expect to start on £15,000 to £25,000. The hourly rate can depend on how many people are being coached and at what level, but usually ranges from £10 to £25. Experienced coaches working full-time may have the potential to earn up to £50,000, although those in professional soccer or tennis would anticipate considerably higher financial rewards.

Further Information

Sports Coach UK, Leeds LS6 3BJ
Website: www.sportscoachuk.org

Central Council for Physical Recreation, London SW1H 0QT
Website: www.ccpr.org.uk

Institute of Sport and Recreation Management, Loughborough LE11 3TU
Website: www.isrm.co.uk

Association for Physical Education, Reading RG1 5AQ
Website: www.afpe.org.uk

SkillsActive, Sector Skills Council for Active Leisure and Learning, London WC1A 1PX
Website: www.skillsactive.com

Sports Leaders UK, Milton Keynes MK14 6LY
Website: www.sportsleaders.org

Alternative/equivalent entrance requirements can include: ILC, IB, EB, NC/ND and many other similar international systems. For further details see the Equivalent Qualifications section in the Introduction.

Stage Manager

What is Involved?

As a stage manager, you would liaise with all the members of a theatrical production, including the producer, director, actors, theatre manager and sound, lighting, set and costume designers. You would be the practical co-ordinator, from the planning stage before the rehearsals to the taking down of the set. On tour, you would be in charge of organising travel and accommodation for the cast, and of booking rehearsal space and time. Whatever the production, you would work very closely with the director, helping to implement his or her ideas and stage directions, collecting props and arranging sound effects, relaying the director's ideas to the set designers and making sure that actors were in the right place at the right time for rehearsals. You would also make sure that safety procedures were being followed at all times. During the actual performances, you would be present at the side of the stage, overseeing the smooth running of the production. You would normally head a team including a deputy stage manager, one or more assistants and a number of stagehands, although you might combine all of these roles in a small touring company.

Opportunities for Training

Whilst it may be possible to join a repertory company without formal training, only a very small number of people now enter the profession in this way. The more usual route would be to take one of the many two-year diploma courses available at drama schools, or follow the option of a three-year degree course.

You may be able to take a creative apprenticeship in technical theatre and/or work towards National/Scottish Vocational Qualifications (N/SVQs) in stage management.

Requirements for Entry

Many of the courses on offer would result in a qualification of a degree or higher national diploma (HND). For a degree course you would need two or three A level/Advanced Higher, three or four Higher or equivalent qualifications, together with five GCSE/S Grade passes A-C/1-3. For entry to an HND course you would need a minimum of one A level/Advanced Higher, two Higher or equivalent passes, together with four GCSE/S Grade passes A-C/1-3. Relevant work experience or involvement in school or other amateur productions would prove as important as academic qualifications when applying for a drama school place.

Kind of Person

As the essential link between all the different people in a theatre company, you would need excellent communication skills and the ability to remain calm when others around you talk of crisis. Tact and diplomacy would be valuable, together with good organisation, an eye for detail, and accuracy in keeping records. The job often calls for a blend of leadership and the willingness to work as part of a team, which would enable you to liaise with confidence between a wide variety of people, often in stressful situations. Practical ability would be useful, and you would need to be interested in both the artistic and technical sides of productions. Physical, emotional and mental stamina would be of prime importance, allied to a strong sense of determination.

Broad Outlook

Employment prospects for graduates of technical courses at drama schools are extremely good, with surveys of recent graduates across the sector showing that virtually 100% achieve employment in the industry. Some people who train and work as stage managers choose to stay in stage management all their working lives, while others might move into administration or producing. Many cross from theatre to television, to trade shows or to the music industry. The skills needed are similar, whatever the area of work. Indeed, film and television producers often look for stage management experience when recruiting for new productions. However, even experienced stage managers have periods out of work.

Related Occupations

You might also consider: actor, floor manager (television), events and conferences manager or public relations officer.

Impact on Lifestyle

You would inevitably be working long and unsocial hours, perhaps rehearsing a new production during the day and managing the current performance each evening. There could also be a good deal of travelling involved, either on tour or moving around from one contract to another. The lifestyle of a stage manager would not necessarily fit well with family or social commitments.

Earnings Potential

A typical starting salary for an assistant stage manager would be around £14,500 to £17,000, rising to around £20,000 for a stage manager. This could grow with experience to £25,000 to £40,000. Your salary level would depend on the company and the type of contract under which you are employed. Subsistence and touring allowances may also be paid. Freelance stage managers tend to earn more, particularly in the West End theatres.

Minimum rates for stage managers are set by Equity, the performers' and entertainment workers' trade union.

Further Information

Association of British Theatre Technicians, London EC1M 3JB
Website: www.abtt.org.uk

National Council for Drama Training, London WC1H 0JJ
Website: www.ncdt.co.uk

Stage Management Association, London EC1M 3JB
Website: www.stagemanagementassociation.co.uk

Equity, London WC2H 9EG
Website: www.equity.org.uk

National Association for Youth Drama in Ireland
Website: www.youthdrama.ie

Skillset: sector skills council for creative media
Website: www.skillset.org/careers

Creative and Cultural Skills
Website: www.ccskills.org.uk

Creative Choices
Website: www.creative-choices.co.uk

Alternative/equivalent entrance requirements can include: ILC, IB, EB, NC/ND and many other similar international systems. For further details see the Equivalent Qualifications section in the Introduction.

Stockbroker

What is Involved?

Your role as a stockbroker would be to buy and sell securities on behalf of clients. Securities are bonds, stocks and shares, which are used by the government and companies when they wish to raise additional capital. Government bonds carry fixed rates of interest but company shares can fluctuate in value in accordance with the fortunes of the company and the shareholder can make a profit or loss on them.

It would be very important, therefore, for you to be aware of the details of a company's performance and state of health, together with the economic trends of the whole stocks and shares market, so that you can advise their clients satisfactorily about whether to invest their money, to hold or to sell those shares they already have. Your clients may be individuals, companies (for example insurance companies) or institutions, such as those acting on behalf of pension funds. Trading is carried out by telephone and computer at the London Stock Exchange.

Opportunities for Training

All firms employing stockbrokers must be members of the Stock Exchange and you would have to be registered as an 'authorised person' with the Financial Services Authority. To achieve this, you must pass the examinations administered by the Securities and Investment Institute or the CFA Society of the UK. You would normally be expected to study for the examinations at home, in your own time, but your employer would organise an in-house training programme, allowing you to gain experience over a period of time in different departments and perhaps develop a special interest.

Requirements for Entry

While there are no formal educational requirements laid down for entry into stockbroking, it has become virtually an all-graduate profession. Any degree subject could be acceptable but subjects such as economics, business studies, maths, statistics and law would be particularly relevant.

For entry to a degree course, you would need two or three A level/Advanced Higher, three or four Higher or equivalent qualifications, together with a minimum of five GCSE/S Grade passes at A-C/1-3. You might consider a sandwich course, which would include a business placement. You may wish to continue your studies with a postgraduate Master of Business Administration (MBA) course before you apply for a post.

Kind of Person

You should be able to cope with pressure and stress, sufficiently confident to back your own judgment and willing to take risks once you have analysed all the relevant data. You would need a high standard of computer literacy, as all your dealings would work through the Stock Exchange computerised settlement system. Good communication skills would be very important, in order to present detailed information to clients, and honesty and integrity are vital, as you could be dealing with large amounts of other people's money.

Advanced numeracy skills and an understanding of what can affect share prices are also of great importance. Dealing rooms can be fraught and busy places, with an atmosphere of tension and excitement as the brokers try to do their best for their clients by buying and selling at the most advantageous prices.

Broad Outlook

The global economic crisis of 2009 is blamed by most commentators on reckless investment in high-risk sectors by professionals who should have known better. In its most pessimistic forecast, the International Labour Organisation estimates that the downturn could lead to the loss of 51 million jobs worldwide by the end of the year, causing the world's richest countries to pump trillions of dollars into the markets in an effort to pull the world economy out of recession. Consequently, stockbroking, normally one of the most sought-after careers by the most ambitious graduates, has suddenly lost most of its allure. This is despite the fact that stockbrokers themselves say that, unlike banks, they do not act as market makers, liquidity providers, deposits takers or lenders. Their activities do not, therefore, give rise to systemic risk to the financial system and they should not be subject to the same level of regulatory reform.

Mindful of the predicted recovery in market confidence in 2010, some firms are looking to maintain their recruitment levels and continue to offer opportunities for young people.

Related Occupations

You might also consider: accountant, actuary, market maker, banking executive, economist, financial adviser, insurance broker or investment analyst.

Impact on Lifestyle

Probably the most obvious effect this career would have on your life would be the high pressure and long hours that it would involve. Global markets may require unsocial hours of work and this would have to be taken into consideration, although it may be a matter of starting early and finishing late rather than working through the night.

It is also quite likely that you would have to take work home with you over the weekend. You would have to be prepared to dress smartly.

Earnings Potential

You might earn £30,000 to £40,000 at the beginning of your career, and progress over the next few years to £50,000 to £80,000, depending on your performance and promotion. Higher earners can make around £140,000 a year, and some stockbrokers earn well in excess of these figures. You would be exceptionally well paid if you are successful.

Further Information

Securities and Investment Institute, London EC3M 1AE
Website: www.sii.org.uk

London Stock Exchange, London EC4M 7LS
Website: www.londonstockexchange.com

Financial Services Authority, London E14 5HS
Website: www.fsa.gov.uk

Association of Private Client Investment Managers and Stockbrokers, London E1 7JH
Website: www.apcims.co.uk

CFA Society of the UK, London EC2V 5AY
Website: www.cfauk.org

Alternative/equivalent entrance requirements can include: ILC, IB, EB, NC/ND and many other similar international systems. For further details see the Equivalent Qualifications section in the Introduction.

Structural Engineer

What is Involved?

Working as a structural engineer, you would be involved in a field closely related to civil engineering. You would be concerned with all aspects of the design and construction of structural frameworks, ranging from bridges, coastal defences, grandstands and airport hangars to the steel structures used in large buildings. In addition to the technical requirements of a particular project, you would be expected to consider environmental factors. The structures that you are creating could have a major impact on the surrounding countryside and local conditions may also influence the type of structure that would be viable and appropriate. You could find yourself involved with tackling problems involving pollution and infrastructure as well as selecting the most appropriate construction materials.

Opportunities for Training

There are relatively few universities offering specific degree courses in structural engineering. Sometimes the subject is combined with architectural studies or with civil engineering. There are also civil engineering courses on which you could choose to specialise in structural engineering after a year or two. In all cases, it would be important to make sure that you choose a course accredited by the Institution of Structural Engineers. Sandwich courses are available, giving you the opportunity to spend some time working in industry whilst studying.

In order to become a chartered engineer, responsible for research, design and development, you would need to spend at least four years in undergraduate study, followed by postgraduate study and supervised experience. The initial requirement can be achieved by taking a four-year degree course that leads directly to an MEng. Alternatively, you could take a three-year degree course leading to a BEng and follow this with a year of more specialised post-graduate study. To become an incorporated engineer, responsible more for the efficient day-to-day management of projects, you could take the BEng route and follow this with further study and on-the-job training.

Requirements for Entry

In order to be accepted for an MEng in structural engineering, you are likely to need three A level/Advanced Higher, four Higher or equivalent qualifications, including maths and physics, together with at least five GCSE/S Grade passes at A-C/1-3. Entry requirements for the BEng are usually slightly lower but would still normally include maths and physics or engineering at A level/Advanced Higher or Higher.

Kind of Person

Your job would be to solve structural problems in a sensible and practical way. For this you would need to enjoy using your technical knowledge, combined with sound common sense, to reach logical conclusions about the structures you are designing and constructing. You would need a rigorous approach to each project. Much of your work would involve using sophisticated computer technology to model structures and test different design solutions before going ahead with construction.

You would work in a team and would have to be reliable and efficient, able to take orders and carry them out without delay, to coordinate the work of others or to give presentations to clients. You would need to explain your ideas and plans clearly to others who often may not share your specialist knowledge.

Broad Outlook

There are usually good opportunities for structural engineers in the UK and abroad, as UK qualifications are recognised in many overseas countries. The industry is to a large extent dependent on the state of the economy, which determines how many new projects are likely to be started. Indeed, structural engineering projects have been severely affected by the economic downturn in 2009. However, forecasts indicate that the industry should start to pick up again in 2010.

Related Occupations

You might be interested in another branch of engineering, such as: civil, mechanical or marine engineer. Alternatively, you might consider: architect, town planner, naval architect, offshore engineer, surveyor or construction manager.

Impact on Lifestyle

You are likely to spend quite a lot of time working out of the office and on site, often out of doors in all kinds of weather. You might occasionally get dirty, wet and cold. When you are working on site you may be expected to work site hours, which can be longer than normal office hours, especially during the summer months. In addition, you may be expected to travel quite long distances within the UK and overseas, which could disrupt your social and family life.

Earnings Potential

Salaries for new graduate trainees are in the region of £22,000 to £30,000. After 10 to15 years in the job, with experience and seniority, you should see your earnings rise to £40,000 to £55,000.

Further Information

Institution of Structural Engineers, London SW1X 8BH
Website: www.istructe.org.uk

Engineering Council UK, London WC2R 3ER
Website: www.engc.org.uk

Construction Skills, King's Lynn PE31 6RH
Website: www.bconstructive.co.uk

Association for Consultancy and Engineering, London SW1H 0QL
Website: www.acenet.co.uk

Alternative/equivalent entrance requirements can include: ILC, IB, EB, NC/ND and many other similar international systems. For further details see the Equivalent Qualifications section in the Introduction.

Surveyor (Chartered)

What is Involved?

As a chartered surveyor you would be a specialist in understanding both the built and the natural environments, seeking to gauge the right balance between them, physically measuring them but also measuring their impact on people and business. The work may appear to revolve around building sites and mathematical calculations but the broader perspective is important.

You would find that a qualification in surveying can prepare you for many different jobs, ranging from valuing residential or commercial property, fine art or antiques, to exploring mineral deposits, reclaiming land from the sea, preserving historic buildings or managing environmentally sensitive land. In rural practice you could expect to deal with land, plant and livestock in addition to property; in planning and development, on the other hand, you might find yourself advising on issues such as the suitability of a new shopping precinct.

You could work in the private or public sector, based in an office for report-writing but more likely spending a lot of your time out of the office visiting sites, buildings, land and farms.

Opportunities for Training

The principal professional body is the Royal Institution of Chartered Surveyors (RICS), which offers many different routes to qualified status. You would most likely meet the academic requirement through a full- or part-time degree or diploma course in a relevant subject, although there are many other options, including postgraduate courses if your first degree is not approved.

On achieving the academic standard, you must complete at least two years structured on-the-job training in a surveyor's office (one year if you have already spent a year with a surveyor as part of a sandwich course) before attempting the Assessment of Professional Competence (APC). Whatever route you follow for the academic stage, it is successful completion of the APC which ultimately confers chartered status.

Requirements for Entry

You would normally need three A level/Advanced Higher, four Higher or equivalent qualifications for admission to an approved degree course. Many students opt for a more vocational route after GCSE/S Grade, following a relevant national award, for example, before progressing to higher education. Course titles include construction, land management or the built environment.

Kind of Person

The RICS stresses that good communication skills, both written and oral, are necessary for negotiating agreements, making presentations and submitting reports to clients. It also indicates that an aptitude for maths and science can be helpful for the more technical sides of the job and that a logical, practical mind is important.

You would need to be a practical person with good observation skills and you would almost certainly require the ability to drive.

Broad Outlook

The outlook for chartered surveyors can vary depending on your area of specialisation. For example, opportunities for surveyors working in property management and valuation of buildings tend be linked to the state of the commercial and residential property market, and the housing market has suffered a devastating year between April 2008 and March 2009, with a massive drop in sales, widespread redundancies, falling house prices and potential buyers finding great difficulty in securing mortgage finance. For a number of years before that, however, the market had been extremely buoyant and all the indicators suggest that it will be again in the near future. If you pursue a career in this sector, you must accept that this is a field that fluctuates and that your prospects and your pay will rise or fall in relation to market confidence. Similarly, the construction industry has been severely affected by the economic downturn, with a knock-on effect on demand for the building surveyor's expertise.

Surveying is an international profession and there are opportunities to work abroad.

Related Occupations

You might also consider: estate agent, civil engineer, architect, town planner, building surveyor, quantity surveyor and rural practice surveyor.

Impact on Lifestyle

Surveyors tend to work normal office hours, although a considerable amount of that time can be spent out of the office. Depending on your specialisation, you may have to travel considerable distances. If you are involved in estate agency, you may have to work at weekends and in the evenings in order to carry out surveys. It may prove necessary to move several times to build the right experience for your career development.

Earnings Potential

Graduate starting salaries are generally around £22,000, slightly higher in the London area. Salaries for qualified chartered surveyors range from around £32,000 to £44,000, while a principal might earn around £70,000. Top-end salaries can be over £100,000. Most surveyors receive additional benefits as part of their salary package. These may include a performance related bonus and a company car.

Further Information

Royal Institution of Chartered Surveyors, Coventry CV4 8JE
Website: www.rics.org

Society of Chartered Surveyors, Ireland
Website: www.scs.ie

Alternative/equivalent entrance requirements can include: ILC, IB, EB, NC/ND and many other similar international systems. For further details see the Equivalent Qualifications section in the Introduction.

Systems Analyst

What is Involved?

As a systems analyst, you would investigate problems related to the use of computers in business and other organisations. Having been called in to analyse a particular system, you would begin talking to the client to ensure that you understand exactly what is required. You would then prepare a feasibility study to see whether the organisation's present system can be adapted to meet the newly identified need. If it cannot be suitably modified, you would advise on a new system to overcome the problem. You may design the new system yourself or you may call in a software engineer to take your specification and turn it into a working solution. See our separate article on 'software engineer'.

Whoever designs the system, you would normally remain responsible for its successful implementation. You would have to cost the whole operation, draw up a detailed implementation plan, write relevant user manuals and set up staff training programmes.

Opportunities for Training

The computer industry is still developing at a rapid pace. Job titles and training routes are not always clearly defined and employers often focus more on experience and ability, frequently taking a fairly relaxed view of formal qualifications. A very large number of higher education courses can now provide the right sort of background but you would find that many people currently working in systems analysis have moved there after gaining experience in programming. They would not necessarily have a degree in computing, although most would have studied to degree or higher national diploma (HND) level. There are specialist postgraduate courses available for graduates of almost any discipline, while some employers provide their own analysis and design training.

You may be able, if you wish, to enter computer-related work straight from school or college, studying part-time for National/Scottish Vocational Qualifications through an Apprenticeship.

When in employment, you would be able to work towards professional qualifications offered by bodies such as the British Computer Society, the Institute for the Management of Information Systems or the National Computing Centre.

Requirements for Entry

To gain admission to a degree course, you would normally need two or three A level/Advanced Higher, four Higher or equivalent qualifications, which may include maths for courses such as software engineering or computer science. For HND entry, one A level/Advanced Higher, two Higher or equivalent would be the usual minimum requirement.

You would need a good first degree to gain a place on a postgraduate course.

Kind of Person

You should have a considerable knowledge of information technology and be able to think logically and creatively in this field. You must enjoy solving IT problems and implementing solutions. You would need to be able to explain problems and solutions clearly to others, so both verbal and written communication skills are vital. You would also need to be adaptable and continue to learn and implement new technology.

Broad Outlook

There are apparent contradictions in labour market data for IT specialists. On the one hand, e-skills UK cite the need for 140,000 new employees every year in the UK IT and telecommunications sector; on the other, applications to IT-related degrees have tumbled by 50% over the last five years. Whatever the explanation for this, there is a clear incentive for employers to entice the right candidates from a shrinking pool, leading the National Computing Centre to assert that employment in the IT sector is likely to weather the economic storm of 2009, although there will be losers in some areas. Nearly half of respondents to its 'Benchmark of Salaries and Employment Trends in IT 2009' survey said they expect the number of IT staff employed at their location to increase over the next two years. Similarly, e-skills UK describe many aspects of ICT as 'credit crunch resistant'.

The huge expansion of the use of information systems in business and commerce has resulted in an increasing demand for systems analysts. The introduction of fourth generation languages and object-oriented programs means that traditional boundaries between programmers and systems analysts have been eroded. Some analysts see themselves also as developers and project managers. You may be employed in the IT department of a large company, you may work for a company that manufactures IT hardware or software, or you may work as an agency or independent consultant. There are opportunities throughout the UK and in many countries overseas.

Related Occupations

You might also consider: software engineer, multimedia programmer, or webmaster.

Impact on Lifestyle

You would usually work a 37- to 40-hour week with weekends free. If deadlines have to be met, you may have to work at weekends or late into the evening. Travelling to clients and periods spent away from home would often be necessary, with an impact on your social and family life.

Earnings Potential

Typical starting salaries range from £24,000 to £26,000, rising with experience to £40,000 to £58,000. Salaries tend to be higher in some sectors, especially the financial sector, and in London, the South East and Midlands, where they may exceed £80,000.

Further Information

British Computer Society, Swindon SN2 1FA
Website: www.bcs.org.uk

National Computing Centre, Manchester M1 7ED
Website: www.ncc.co.uk

Institute for the Management of Information Systems, Kent BR5 3QG
Website: www.imis.org.uk

E-skills UK Ltd, London SW1E 6DR
Website: www.e-skills.com

Institution of Analysts and Programmers, London W13 9NH
Website: www.iap.org.uk

Irish Computer Society, Dublin 2
Website: www.ics.ie

Big Ambition
Website: www.bigambition.co.uk

Alternative/equivalent entrance requirements can include: ILC, IB, EB, NC/ND and many other similar international systems. For further details see the Equivalent Qualifications section in the Introduction.

Teacher

What is Involved?

As a teacher, you would enable pupils to develop their abilities and aptitudes and fulfil their own individual potential. Much of a typical school day would be concerned with specific subjects but you would also have a pastoral role to play - helping your pupils with personal problems and supporting them when they are faced with difficult decisions. You would also have links with parents, in particular at parents' meetings, which are usually held in the evening. Preparation of lessons and marking would take up a good deal of your time. As a nursery school teacher, you would work with children aged three to five. As a primary school teacher, you would work with children within the five to eleven age range. You would usually be responsible for a single class of children, though there might also be scope for teaching a particular subject to different classes within the school. As a secondary school teacher, you would specialise in one or two subjects, which you would teach throughout the school to different age groups from 11 to 16/18.

Opportunities for Training

Recognised training is essential for teaching posts in maintained schools. You would need to undertake Initial Teacher Training (ITT) and obtain Qualified Teacher Status (QTS) in England and Wales, with a similar requirement for Scotland. Once trained, you must register with the relevant General Teaching Council for England, Scotland or Wales. There are several different routes and courses involved and you should do some careful research to determine which one would be the best for you. Many of the courses are full-time but there are increasing opportunities for part-time and distance learning. Most of the routes take three or four years and involve spells of teaching practice in schools.

The two main routes to QTS (although there others) are as follows:

a   A first degree that includes a teaching qualification. Many of these courses are aimed at students who wish to work in primary schools, although there are others aimed at secondary school work.

b   A first degree followed by a postgraduate certificate in education. The first degree should normally be in a National Curriculum subject. This route is more commonly taken by students who wish to work in secondary schools.

Routes are similar in Scotland but are not described in terms of ITT/QTS and courses are geared to the specific needs of the Scottish education system.

Requirements for Entry

The minimum requirements for ITT in England/Wales are two A levels or equivalent and three GCSE Grades A-C or equivalent, including English and maths. (Some courses also require a science at GCSE Grade C or above).

In Scotland, you would need at least two Advanced Higher or three Higher, including English or equivalent, together with S Grades 1-3 in two other subjects, including maths at grade 1/2 or equivalent.

Kind of Person

You would need to enjoy working with children and young people and to be patient with those who find it difficult to learn. You also need to enjoy the subject or subjects that you are going to teach. Training may help you to handle difficult situations in the classroom but the enthusiasm for learning and helping others to learn must come from you. You would need to have very good communication skills, to be well organised, a good member of a team but confident enough to work on your own, and consistent and fair in your treatment of your pupils.

*B*road Outlook

There will always be a need for good teachers and there are often shortages, although the situation varies from subject to subject and area to area. With the expansion of nursery education, there may well be increased demand in this field.

Teachers can be promoted to posts of responsibility in academic, administrative and pastoral roles - as heads of department or year group, personal tutors, heads and deputy heads. Allowances can also be offered for additional teaching and learning responsibilities.

*R*elated Occupations

You might also consider: careers/personal adviser, educational psychologist, nursery nurse, social worker or youth worker.

*I*mpact on Lifestyle

Teachers are held in great esteem by some and blamed by others for many of the ills of society. Your life would probably be affected by the need to take work home with you, although good organisation and use of time in the holidays should help to cut this down. The holidays (particularly in the summer) are a great asset, though they should not be regarded as completely free - much organisation and forward planning goes on, both in and out of school.

*E*arnings Potential

Salary scales for newly qualified teachers in England and Wales currently start at £20,627 or £25,000 if you teach in Inner London, rising to £31,148 (£34,768 in Inner London). Advanced skills teachers are paid on a scale from £35,794 to £54, 417 (£42,559 to £61,188 in Inner London). Headteachers can earn anything from £40,494 to £100,424 a year (£47,265 to £107,192 in Inner London), depending on the size of the school.

*F*urther Information

Training and Development Agency for Schools, London SW1E 5TT
Website: www.tda.gov.uk

General Teaching Council for Scotland, Edinburgh EH12 6UT
Website: www.gtcs.org.uk

Department of Education Northern Ireland, Co Down BT19 7PR
Website: www.deni.gov.uk

Department of Education and Science, Ireland, Dublin 1
Website: www.education.ie

Alternative/equivalent entrance requirements can include: ILC, IB, EB, NC/ND and many other similar international systems. For further details see the Equivalent Qualifications section in the Introduction.

Textile Designer

What is Involved?

As a textile designer, you would be concerned with the design of a range of fabrics or textiles that would be used mainly for producing clothes, curtains, furnishing fabrics, carpets or wallpaper. You might work initially on paper but you are more likely to use a computer with a specialist software package allowing patterns and colours to be changed rapidly and the designs to be printed out in colour for consideration and approval by clients. You would then produce samples by weaving, knitting or screen printing, taking great care to ensure the right fabrics are used in each case.

Your work would be very much influenced by changing fashion and lifestyle trends. Clients need new ideas and colour schemes and furnishing fabrics change every year, so you must constantly think ahead and anticipate the current and future moods of manufacturers and buyers. You must also take account of the manufacturing processes involved, ensuring that your designs could actually be put into production without being prohibitively expensive and that you are not specifying unrealistic colours or yarns.

Opportunities for Training

You would need to have a formal training in textile design, usually via one of the specialist courses available at degree or higher national diploma (HND) level in universities and art schools throughout the UK. Some courses focus purely on design and artistic creativity, while others are more orientated towards the technology of manufacturing or the business of marketing. You must check prospectuses carefully when researching possible courses. You might decide to continue your studies to postgraduate level before you enter the labour market.

Requirements for Entry

The main entry requirement for study or employment is usually a portfolio of work. This might include samples of knitting, sewing, dyeing or weaving in addition to examples of your drawing skills. Talent and creativity are usually more highly regarded than examination success, although it is always helpful and sometimes essential to have a platform of GCSE/S Grade passes A-C/1-3 and A level/Advanced Higher, Higher or equivalent studies, including an art related subject.

In England and Wales, you would normally complete a one- or two-year foundation course before progressing to a three-year art and design degree. In Scotland, the foundation course is the first year of a four-year degree. The HND route is normally a year shorter and may be more closely linked to manufacturing processes.

Kind of Person

To be a successful textile designer you would need to combine artistic creativity, drawing skills and an acute awareness of colour and texture with a good understanding of the technical side of the business. You should have a keen interest in fashion and may spend some time visiting exhibitions and fashion shows to spot trends and see what other designers are doing.

You must be able to communicate your ideas visually and verbally to clients or colleagues and may need to persuade buyers to accept your work. You would also have to be prepared to see some of your ideas rejected. You would need good IT skills, especially in using computer design packages, and an understanding of how developments in technology could enhance your design concepts. Poor colour vision could present serious problems.

Broad Outlook

Textile design is a very competitive field. Even well established designers can go out of fashion and find that buyers lose interest in their work. However, the textile business is one of the largest in the world and there will always be a demand for creative and talented people. You could work for a large manufacturer or a smaller independent design house. You could set up your own business and might use an agent to market your collections to prospective buyers. British design training is valued abroad and you might choose to work overseas.

Women currently account for some 75% to 80% of the workforce.

Related Occupations

You might also consider: fashion, graphic or interior designer or photographer.

Impact on Lifestyle

This is a global industry which means that, as well as career opportunities abroad, you could find yourself having to travel fairly extensively in order to keep up to date with trends and to visit overseas fabric manufacturers. If you are employed by a large group, you would normally work office hours from nine to five, but could also work at trade shows, which could involve weekend and evening work. As a self-employed designer, you would often need to work very long hours, late into the evening and over weekends, to establish your business and meet the last-minute deadlines of clients.

Earnings Potential

Your pay would depend upon the nature of your employment, whether for a large or small company or self-employed. Junior designers working for a textile manufacturing company usually start at about £20,000 to £25,000, which could increase to £28,000 to £40,000 as they become experienced. Your earnings as a freelance designer would vary greatly, depending on your reputation. Paying commission to an agent would reduce your fee income but could help you establish a broad client base.

Further Information

Textile Institute, Manchester, M1 6FQ
Website: www.texi.org

Skillfast-UK, Leeds LS28 6BN
Website: www.skillfast-uk.org

Chartered Society of Designers, London SE1 3GA
Website: www.csd.org.uk

Your Creative Future
Website: www.yourcreativefuture.org

UK Fashion Exports, London W1B 1PW
Website: www.5portlandplace.org.uk

Alternative/equivalent entrance requirements can include: ILC, IB, EB, NC/ND and many other similar international systems. For further details see the Equivalent Qualifications section in the Introduction.

Tour Operator

What is Involved?

As a tour operator, you would organise the package holidays, leisure activities, tours, expeditions, cruises and coach trips on sale at travel agents. Details of these are publicised in sales brochures and advertisements, written about in newspapers and magazines and featured on radio and TV travel programmes. Working as a product manager for a tour operator, you might arrange expeditions by elephant or bicycle, journeys by Pullman train or cruise liner, flights by hot air balloon or Concorde.

You might organise accommodation in anything from a chalet to a chateau. As a contract manager, you would negotiate availability and prices with the airlines, hotels, local transport companies, attraction owners and others involved in the package. In addition, it would be vital to check the quality of food, sanitation, beaches and entertainment, usually in liaison with your local representatives.

Opportunities for Training

There is no single route to a head office position as a tour operator but many tour operators traditionally obtained the ABTA Tour Operators Certificate (ABTOC), which was generally accepted by the tour operating industry as a recognised commercial qualification. The ABTOC primary examination covered the knowledge you should have within about one year of starting work, including locational geography, emergency procedures, legislation, ticketing and administration.

The advanced examination would then take this level forward to encompass the wider range of skills and deeper knowledge required after two or more years' experience, such as providing complex holiday itineraries. These qualifications are now compiled from units in the City and Guilds First Diploma and Advanced Diploma in Travel and Tourism. People 1st, the sector skills council for the industry, is currently rewriting the vocational qualifications for tour operators. Check the website for details.

You might also work towards National or Scottish Vocational Qualifications (N/SVQ) in Travel Services (Tour Operations). Alternatively, you could consider a degree, foundation degree or higher national diploma (HND) in travel and tourism, hospitality management or leisure and recreation. You should look for a course having close links with the travel industry.

Requirements for Entry

Experience is generally regarded as far more important than academic success. There are no specific entry requirements for the ABTOC or N/SVQ routes, although individual employers might look for GCSE/S Grade passes A-C/1-3, including English, maths, geography and modern languages. You would need at least two A level/Advanced Higher, three Higher or equivalent qualifications for degree course entry, slightly less for the HND or foundation degree.

Kind of Person

You would need to combine very strong organisational and entrepreneurial qualities with the vision to put together holiday packages that appeal to the public, are competitively priced and demonstrate a concern for the overall comfort and enjoyment of customers. You should enjoy travelling, visiting resorts, making new contacts and establishing friendly and long-term relationships.

Your work would call for considerable attention to detail in such matters as the accuracy of descriptions in your promotional materials or exchange rate considerations and local taxes in determining precise costs. You would also need to write contracts to establish agreements and take out appropriate insurance cover. Marketing, business administration and finance and accountancy skills would all be important, especially an understanding of how to manage cash flow in what can be a highly seasonal business.

Broad Outlook

An early victim of the credit crunch, Britain's third-largest tour operator at the time went into administration in September 2008, grounding 21 planes and causing chaos for 85,000 customers actually on holiday and 200,000 more booked to travel in the future. There will almost certainly be more stories of this kind before the world economy begins its predicted recovery in 2010 and the sun shines once more on those seeking to make a career as tour operators.

Related Occupations

You might also consider: travel agent, events and conferences manager or marketing executive.

Impact on Lifestyle

While you might work fairly standard hours in a head office post, you would usually have experienced the complete absence of set hours for a resort representative. You would often have to sort out problems at any time of the day or night in such a post, and would be expected to work for as long as it takes to resolve the issues. Frequent travel and extended absence from home would normally be a significant feature of the work and could disrupt your family and social life.

Earnings Potential

Salaries vary greatly between agencies, with larger chains generally paying higher rates. As a recent graduate, you might start on around £14,500 to £25,000. Typical salaries at senior level range from £22,000 to £45,000.

Further Information

Institute of Travel and Tourism, Herts SG12 8WY
Website: www.itt.co.uk

Association of Independent Tour Operators, Twickenham TW1 1RG
Website: www.aito.co.uk

Tourism Management Institute, London NW1 1JD
Website: www.tmi.org.uk

People 1st: Sector Skills Council for Hospitality, Leisure, Travel and Tourism
Website: www.people1st.co.uk

City and Guilds
Website: www.cityandguilds.com

Alternative/equivalent entrance requirements can include: ILC, IB, EB, NC/ND and many other similar international systems. For further details see the Equivalent Qualifications section in the Introduction.

Town Planner

What is Involved?

Working as a town planner, your job would be to balance the demand for new development and buildings with the diminishing amount of land available. You would be responsible for maintaining an attractive environment that can also sustain the demands of the population who live there. You would be involved with listening to the views of a number of interested parties, including conservationists, builders, farmers and residents, before advising on planning decisions. You would need to consider future developments and demands on amenities as well as the current situation, taking into account such factors as design features, waste and environmental management, transport, urban renewal and employment or recreation demands.

You would sometimes be implementing national planning policy at a local level, such as, for example, the current government preference for building on brownfield sites. You would use various sources of information, including surveys, public opinion and existing legislation, and could be involved with large-scale projects or with decisions on home extensions. You would almost certainly be required to use a wide range of skills in order to produce your reports. Much of the work is based in an office and involves the use of a computer but you would also be expected to make site visits.

Opportunities for Training

In order to work as a town planner, a Royal Town Planning Institute (RTPI) accredited qualification is essential. To become a chartered town planner, the accredited academic qualifications must be supported by two years' work experience.

If you wish to study town planning as your first degree, there are specialist town and country planning or urban studies degrees, accredited by the RTPI. These courses provide the full planning education in four years (five if on a sandwich course), which includes a three-year undergraduate BA degree and a one-year Postgraduate Diploma. The courses are also available part-time. Graduates who are not from RTPI-accredited planning courses will need a recognised postgraduate qualification.

Requirements for Entry

For a first degree in town planning, you would need two or three subjects at A level/Advanced Higher, three or four Higher or equivalent qualifications, together with at least three GCSE/S Grade passes at A-C/1-3. A few universities specify particular subjects but most are looking for a combination of arts and science subjects. Geography can be a useful subject to offer. The content of the courses can vary considerably, so it is important to study the prospectus carefully to make sure that the course on offer covers areas of interest to you. Work experience is a good idea because it gives you a chance to find out about the range of options available.

Kind of Person

You should be committed to achieving the best possible quality of life in your area without causing undue damage to the environment. You would need to communicate effectively with a wide range different people and to listen to their views. Your job would involve writing clear reports in language that can be easily understood and you would at times be required to work under pressure to meet tight deadlines. You would have to speak at public meetings and would need to be persuasive or assertive if your audience is hostile. You would probably be responsible for managing other staff.

Broad Outlook

These are difficult times for all professionals connected with construction. The economic climate has created uncertainty for employed planners, those who run their own practice and graduates looking to gain employment, leaving no doubt that the jobs market will become more challenging during 2009.

Related Occupations

You might also consider: civil engineer, architect, landscape architect, surveyor or cartographer.

Impact on Lifestyle

You may have to travel quite large distances to get to planning sites, or find that you have to move around the country in order to find the job you want or to gain promotion. Most planners who work for local authorities work a 37-hour week although you might be expected to attend planning meetings in the evenings.

Earnings Potential

In the public sector, starting annual salaries average about £20,000. Senior planners can expect to earn between £25,000 and £37,000, with an average of about £29,000, and principal planners and team leaders can earn between £29,000 and £41,000, with an average of about £34,000. Chief planning officers, heads of departments and directors can earn between £55,000 and £80,000, with an average salary of about £64,000. The higher salaries in these ranges are paid by local authorities where there is a scarcity of planners, for example London boroughs or local authorities in the South East.

Pay in the private sector should be comparable to that in the public sector. There are no set scales and individual salaries are usually a matter for negotiation with the employer.

Further Information

Royal Town Planning Institute, London EC3R 8DL
Website: www.rtpi.org.uk

RTPI Ireland
Website: www.rtpi.org.uk/rtpi_ireland

Commission for Architecture and the Built Environment, London WC2B 4AN
Website: www.cabe.org.uk

Alternative/equivalent entrance requirements can include: ILC, IB, EB, NC/ND and many other similar international systems. For further details see the Equivalent Qualifications section in the Introduction.

Town Planning Support Worker

What is Involved?

In order to carry out their roles efficiently and effectively, town planners need a great deal of help from planning support staff. In this type of work, you would probably specialise in one of three main areas:

- As a *planning administrator* you could be searching various types of land and property files and plans to gather information, or perhaps helping at reception or on a 'help desk' to provide members of the public with advice on a range of planning matters.

- As one of the *technical support staff* your work might include carrying out surveys, mapping and recording information, the establishment and maintenance of databases or the production of illustrations and other graphics for documents and exhibitions. One specialist growth area is the application of computer technology to a range of planning tasks.

- As a *planning enforcement officer* your job would be to ensure that development has permission and that any conditions attaching to the permission are complied with. The work would involve monitoring a variety of sources, gathering and presenting evidence, field investigation and dialogue with property owners and developers.

Opportunities for Training

The generally accepted training route for town planning support staff is to work towards the National/Scottish Vocational Qualification (N/SVQ) at Level 3 in Town Planning Support and the higher national certificate (HNC) in Land Administration (Planning). The N/SVQ has pathways designed to meet the needs of different types of support staff: everyone studies the same core units and then there is a choice depending on whether you are a planning administrator, enforcer or working on the technical side. You can study for the HNC part-time at a number of colleges and it normally takes two to four years to complete.

There is also a distance learning foundation course in planning. This provides the underpinning knowledge for the N/SVQ but could be of interest to anyone pursuing a career in town planning support.

With one of the qualifications outlined above and at least two years relevant experience, you could be elected to technical membership of the Royal Town Planning Institute.

Requirements for Entry

There are no absolute minimum entry qualifications needed to obtain a job in town planning support, although you would normally be expected as a new entrant to have good GCSE/S Grade passes A-C/1-3 in English, maths and other appropriate subjects. Relevant experience might be a more important factor for more mature candidates. There are usually specific entry requirements for formal training programmes at college.

Kind of Person

Your work would require you to be both accurate and neat in your presentation. You would need to be computer literate as you may need to use specialised software to produce graphical presentations and relevant statistics. You should also be reasonably confident at maths, as you may need to explain the statistics involved in a report. You would find yourself working as part of a team but you are also likely to be responsible for your own particular work. At times you may have to work under pressure to meet a deadline. You should be able to express yourself clearly both in your written reports and when speaking to the public. You may be involved with a number of different projects at one time, so would need to be well organised. Enforcement work in particular requires diplomacy and maturity.

Broad Outlook

These are difficult times for all professionals connected with construction. The economic climate has created uncertainty for employed planners, those who run their own practice and graduates looking to gain employment, leaving no doubt that the jobs market will become more challenging during 2009.

The majority of planning support staff work in local government. Others work in central government departments - including regional offices and regional development agencies - in National Park authorities, local development and regeneration organisations. Smaller numbers of planning support staff are employed in the offices of major developers and planning consultants.

There is a clear promotion route in local authority planning departments, although it may be necessary to move in order to gain promotion. You could use your qualifications and experience to progress to professional town planner status.

With further study, town planning support staff may qualify to become town planners.

Related Occupations

You might consider: architectural technologist, chartered surveyor, town planner, estate agent, land agent or landscape architect.

Impact on Lifestyle

You are likely to be working a 37-hour week in an office, although there may be occasions when you are expected to work overtime in order to finish a project on time. Planning enforcement entails a lot of travelling to development sites and can involve confrontation with abusive and uncooperative people.

Earnings Potential

There is a pay scale for planning support staff and your entry point would depend on your age and qualifications. As a trainee you are likely to earn from around £13,000 to £15,600, rising with experience to between £17,000 and £25,000 a year. As a senior member of the planning support team you could earn £27,000 or more. Salaries in the London area are usually higher than elsewhere.

Further Information

Royal Town Planning Institute, London EC3R 8DL
Website: www.rtpi.org.uk

RTPI Ireland
Website: www.rtpi.org.uk/rtpi_ireland

Commission for Architecture and the Built Environment, London WC2B 4AN
Website: www.cabe.org.uk

Alternative/equivalent entrance requirements can include: ILC, IB, EB, NC/ND and many other similar international systems. For further details see the Equivalent Qualifications section in the Introduction.

Trading Standards Officer

What is Involved?

As a trading standards officer (TCO), you would work within local government enforcing the law and regulations that govern goods and services which we buy, hire and sell. You would be championing the rights of the consumer by making sure that they were not being cheated, which could involve anything from checking the scales of a local trader to testing the claims made about a product by its manufacturer or importer.

You might take samples of pre-packed food to ensure that the correct weight is shown; you might check weighing machines, beer and spirit measures and labelling. Another important aspect would be identifying potential hazards or unsafe products.

Sometimes a case may involve action in the criminal court, requiring you to investigate possible criminal offences and attend as a witness or present cases in the Magistrates Court. Although you would have to write up reports in an office, you would also be out in the local community.

The exact nature of the work would vary according to your location. In a rural area, you might spend much time on animal health ensuring, for example, proper transport of livestock to market. As a city-based officer, you could be more concerned with street traders and problems of counterfeit goods. In a port, you might work with customs to vet imported goods.

Opportunities for Training

The most direct entry route is via a degree accredited by the Trading Standards Institute and then a trainee trading standards officer post. Five universities offer approved degrees: Glasgow Caledonian, Manchester Metropolitan, Teesside, University of Wales Institute Cardiff, and Queen Margaret Edinburgh. Local authorities sometimes sponsor students on these courses. Trainee TSO vacancies with local authorities are also open to graduates of any subject via a postgraduate diploma course, although a degree in law, mathematics or a science subject may improve your chances. There is currently one accredited postgraduate diploma course offered full- and part-time at Manchester Metropolitan University.

In order to qualify as a TSO, you must hold the Diploma in Consumer and Trading Standards (DCATS), which normally takes 18 months to complete. There are four levels to this qualification, starting with the Foundation Certificate. The accredited degree/diploma route provides exemptions from the first three levels of examinations, but students without an accredited degree will need to have passed the foundation certificate and to have gained 40 points from the second level. The fourth level is the Higher Diploma.

Requirements for Entry

Entry to an approved specialist degree would require two or three A level/Advanced Higher, three Higher or equivalent qualifications, together with five GCSE/S Grade passes A-C/1-3. You could become an enforcement officer or consumer adviser with a degree in any other subject. Relevant experience would be an absolute requirement before you could take the DCATS examinations.

Kind of Person

You would need to be firm but tactful, not easily intimidated. You would need a good memory for all the relevant legislation and the ability for assessing the key facts in each situation. It would be vital to have a very keenly observant eye for possible deviations from the law. You would need the confidence and integrity to stand up for your views and make some unpopular decisions. This could involve explaining your cases with precision and clarity in courts of law, so some public speaking experience could help. You would also need to be able to write clear reports.

Broad Outlook

Trading standards officers are employed throughout the UK and there is a clear promotion structure, ie senior officer to section head, divisional officer and then to deputy or chief trading standards officer. Departments are usually small, however, so promotion often calls for mobility.

There are increasing controls and regulations and consumers are complaining more, so there is plenty of work available. Local authority budgets have, however, been reduced and finding a training place can be very difficult. You may choose to develop your career by moving into the private sector, where you might advise on quality control or consumer law in the food or retail sectors.

Related Occupations

You might also consider: environmental health officer, police officer or health and safety officer.

Impact on Lifestyle

You would normally expect to work regular office hours but the process of deregulation means that shops and public houses now have longer opening hours and can trade seven days a week. You may have to follow up certain complaints or queries during these 'non-traditional' times.

Earnings Potential

Local government trading standards officers might expect to earn around £24,000 to £34,000. Senior managers may earn considerably more. This salary information is a guide only and there may be local agreements in place. For further information about salaries for particular positions, contact your local council directly.

Private sector opportunities are usually paid at senior manager level and above.

Further Information

Trading Standards Institute, Essex SS15 6HT
Website: www.tradingstandards.gov.uk

Department of Enterprise, Trade and Investment for Northern Ireland, Belfast BT4 2JP
Website: www.detini.gov.uk

Improvement and Development Agency (I&DeA), London EC1M 5LG
Website: www.lgtalent.com and www.idea.gov.uk

Consumer Focus
Website: www.consumerfocus.org.uk

Local Better Regulation Office
Website: www.lbro.org.uk

Contact your local authority and ask to speak to the manager of the trading standards department.

Alternative/equivalent entrance requirements can include: ILC, IB, EB, NC/ND and many other similar international systems. For further details see the Equivalent Qualifications section in the Introduction.

Translator

What is Involved?

As a translator, you would be a highly skilled linguist specialising in the written word. You would normally translate into your mother tongue and would be required to produce authentic, idiomatic and accurate versions, which mirror the tone and levels of meaning of the originals. In literary areas, style and idiom would predominate, but most translation work is in commercial, legal, scientific or technical material, where accuracy and understanding are much more important. Your work may span a very broad spectrum, from medicine, tourism or engineering to law, politics or finance, and could include legal contracts, scientific articles, technical manuals, promotional brochures or business letters.

Opportunities for Training

You would normally be expected to study one or more foreign languages to degree level. It could be helpful if the course includes modules in translation or if you combine language studies with a subject such as business, law, computing or engineering. Almost all courses of this kind would give you the opportunity, which you should take, to spend at least a year abroad. You might then progress to a full- or part-time postgraduate diploma in translation. You may be expected to work towards the National/Scottish Vocational Qualifications (N/SVQ) level five in translating and you would usually need to join and pass the examinations of professional organisations such as the Chartered Institute of Linguists (IOL) and/or the Institute of Translation and Interpreting (ITI).

Requirements for Entry

For entry to a degree course, you would usually need two or three A levels/Advanced Highers, three or four Highers or equivalent, including a good pass in at least one foreign language. You would need a good first degree for progression to a postgraduate course. The N/SVQ route does not require any formal academic qualifications and could prove attractive if you have advanced linguistic skills, cultural awareness or technical knowledge but do not want to go to university. You may, for example, have come to translating through a bilingual upbringing, residence abroad or regular contact with speakers of your second language. You would have to provide evidence of your ability by maintaining a detailed record of texts translated and building a portfolio of your best work.

Kind of Person

You must be able to write impeccably in your mother tongue, preferably in a variety of styles. An enquiring mind would be essential, with a particular interest in researching and understanding commercial or technical issues. In addition to your mastery of at least one foreign language, you must have a thorough knowledge of the institutions, culture, attitudes and practices in the countries where that language is spoken, normally acquired through residence there.

You would need to be capable of working alone in front of a computer screen, armed with specialist dictionaries and reference books, working at speed to find the right words and phrases. Editing and IT skills would come together in the growing use of computerised translating programs, which produce fast but rough drafts for revision to an acceptable final standard.

Broad Outlook

While some international organisations, government departments, multinational companies and aid agencies employ their own translating teams, around 80% of translators work on a full- or part-time basis for a specialist language company or translation bureau. French, German and Japanese are the most sought-after languages, although it can be lucrative to add something more unusual. It is possible, but far from easy, to start up as a freelance translator. The competition is intense and you would need to be very skilled, professional and businesslike to succeed. A lot of work is passed on by the recommendation of colleagues, so it would be an advantage to make yourself known to others in the profession.

Related Occupations

You might also consider: teacher, secretary linguist, interpreter, tour operator or diplomat.

Impact on Lifestyle

You can choose your own hours if you are working from home, sending and receiving material by email. However, the work can be unpredictable and you may need to supplement your income with other activities, especially teaching. As a staff translator, you would be more likely to work normal office hours from Monday to Friday, with occasional overtime if a translation is needed urgently.

Earnings Potential

How much you earn could depend on your language combinations, your subject areas and your speed and reputation. You would normally quote a freelance rate based on every 1,000 words translated, ranging from around £75 to £100 per 1,000 words for French or German to £180 for every 1,000 Chinese characters. Translators often agree fees per project, based on a word count of around 2,000 to 3,000 words per day. Salaries for full-time employment vary considerably, starting at around £19,000 for a young graduate. Generalist translators earn between £25,000 and £30,000, and specialist translators between £30,000 and £35,000. Senior translators earn £50,000 plus. The European Commission and United Nations are the best paying employers of senior translators.

Further Information

Institute of Translation and Interpreting, Milton Keynes MK9 2EU
Website: www.iti.org.uk

CILT, the National Centre for Languages, London WC2N 4LB
Website: www.cilt.org.uk

Chartered Institute of Linguists, London SE1 1UN
Website: www.iol.org.uk

European Personnel Selection Office, B-1049 Brussels, Belgium
Website: www.eu-careers.eu

Association of Translation Companies, London W1B4 EH
Website: www.atc.org.uk

Alternative/equivalent entrance requirements can include: ILC, IB, EB, NC/ND and many other similar international systems. For further details see the Equivalent Qualifications section in the Introduction.

Travel Agent

What is Involved?

As a travel agent, you would sell holidays on behalf of tour operators, together with air, ferry, train and coach tickets, hotel reservations, car hire services, tours and expeditions, theatre seats and insurance. You might work with the general travelling public or specialise in services for business customers and you would sometimes be asked to arrange complete itineraries.

Some travel agencies are independently owned, while others are part of chains that market their own tours and package holidays as well as those of other tour operators. Most of the 7,300 travel agencies in the UK have high street, shop-front premises, where you would inform and negotiate with clients and check availability on computer systems before completing a sale.

Opportunities for Training

Many young people enter through Apprenticeships provided by national and local training providers. They work towards N/SVQs at Levels 2 and 3 in travel and tourism, together with other appropriate travel-related qualifications. Some gain qualifications in customer service.

It can be helpful to have qualifications in travel and tourism, gained through a college course and/or previous employment, but this is not essential. Useful qualifications include:

- AS or A levels in travel and tourism

- The new Diploma in Travel and Tourism, which will be available in schools and colleges from September 2010

- City and Guilds travel and tourism diploma

- BTEC Certificates and Diplomas in travel and tourism.

Some colleges also offer the Guild of Travel Management Companies (GTMC) Introductory Certificate in Business Travel for those who want to specialise in this area.

Alternatively, you might consider a degree, foundation degree or higher national diploma (HND) in travel and tourism or a related subject.

Requirements for Entry

Experience is generally regarded as far more important than academic success. There are no specific entry requirements, although individual employers might look for GCSE/S Grade passes A-C/1-3, including English, maths, geography and modern languages. You would need at least two A level/Advanced Higher, three Higher or equivalent qualifications for degree course entry, slightly less for the HND.

Kind of Person

To be a successful travel agent, you would need to be a good communicator and come across as friendly and helpful. You would be selling holidays and travel-related products and would therefore need to be enthusiastic and a good salesperson. A retentive memory and a thorough knowledge of hotels, resorts and travel possibilities would be very helpful in building trust and retaining your clients, together with a good working knowledge of geography for discussing possible destinations.

You would have to be very efficient and organised, as you would often be dealing with more than one client at a time and it would be essential not to make mistakes with reservations and tickets. You would be dealing with prices and overall costs of holidays, so you would need to be numerate. You should also have good IT skills, as computers are always used for making bookings and finding up-to-date information. You should have a smart appearance and you should have the ability both to listen carefully and to make suitable travel suggestions.

Broad Outlook

An early victim of the credit crunch, Britain's third-largest tour operator at the time went into administration in September 2008, grounding 21 planes and causing chaos for 85,000 customers actually on holiday and 200,000 more booked to travel in the future. There will almost certainly be more stories of this kind before the world economy begins its predicted recovery in 2010 and the sun shines once more on those seeking to make a career in travel and tourism.

Travel agencies differ greatly in size and there may be more scope for promotion to more senior positions in larger companies and chain stores. A growing number of travellers are using the Internet to make their own travel arrangements but many people continue to use travel agencies for their specialist knowledge and advice.

Related Occupations

You might also consider: tour operator, leisure/recreation services manager, or travel and tourism clerk.

Impact on Lifestyle

You would normally work shop hours from Monday to Saturday, although you may have to work some evenings and Sundays as well in a busy shopping centre. You may find that you are required to go to resorts abroad for research purposes but this would usually be seen as an occasional perk of the job.

Earnings Potential

Salaries vary greatly between agencies, with larger chains generally paying higher rates. As a recent graduate, you might start on around £14,500 to £25,000. Typical salaries at senior level range from £22,000 to £45,000.

Further Information

Institute of Travel and Tourism, Herts SG12 8WY
Website: www.itt.co.uk

Irish Travel Agents Association, Dublin 2
Website: www.itaa.ie

People 1st: Sector Skills Council for Hospitality, Leisure, Travel and Tourism
Website: www.people1st.co.uk

Guild of Travel Management Companies, London W1T 7PD
Website: www.gtmc.org

Apprenticeships
Website: www.apprenticeships.org.uk

Alternative/equivalent entrance requirements can include: ILC, IB, EB, NC/ND and many other similar international systems. For further details see the Equivalent Qualifications section in the Introduction.

TV/Film Camera Operator

What is Involved?

As a camera operator in the TV/film industry, you would use different types of camera to record action on film, videotape or digital media. You might work on large- or small-scale productions in a studio; you might be part of an outside broadcast team covering sports fixtures or public ceremonies; or you might use special lightweight equipment in a small newsgathering team.

You would mostly be expected to follow instructions from a director, although you would usually be invited to contribute ideas for camera positions and shots during rehearsals. Depending on the budget and resources of the project on which you are working, you may be part of a team or you may have to operate sound and other equipment in addition to your main work with the camera.

Opportunities for Training

Getting started in this industry is far from straightforward. Experience is what counts but TV companies like the BBC no longer run in-house training schemes. The BBC does, however, offer work experience placements across the UK. All placements are unpaid and last between a few days and four weeks. BSkyB also offers placements for young people through its Reach for the Sky project. Competition for both schemes is fierce.

Film and TV Freelance Training (ft2) provide apprentice-style technical courses for freelance entrants but you have to be over 18, based in London and unemployed to meet their entry criteria.

There may be limited training opportunities with Scottish Screen and CYFLE in Scotland and Wales respectively (some for Welsh speakers only). Beyond that are various college courses up to degree and postgraduate level but none of these formal qualifications is a guarantee of work. It is important to get practical experience in any way you can, even if it means initially working for nothing.

Requirements for Entry

While it is not essential, you would be able to build your experience by taking a degree in photography or film studies following successful completion of a foundation year in art and design with some specialisation in camera work. You should have a portfolio of photographs or film and you should be able to demonstrate a keen interest in film and television. It would help if you had A level/Advanced Higher, Higher or equivalent qualifications and enough understanding of maths and physics to appreciate the technical aspects of film-making and broadcasting. You would need to be physically fit to be able to move equipment that is often heavy.

Kind of Person

In order to succeed in this kind of work you would need to be passionately interested in film photography and prepared to put up with short-term contracts, uncertainty of employment, lots of pressure and long working hours. You must be a team player, with a good eye for colour and composition. The work can be creative but also requires a high standard of technical awareness. Good eyesight and normal colour vision are essential, together with good hand/eye co-ordination. Some camera positions call for a head for heights!

Broad Outlook

You would almost certainly work on a freelance basis, building up a network of personal contacts and establishing a reputation for certain types of work. Small independent production companies spring up on a regular basis, in addition to the established film and television organisations, usually offering new work opportunities but most often on short-term contracts. You will increase your chances of a successful career if you are prepared to go anywhere in the UK or overseas to work. It is common to get work by contacting companies yourself, networking and word of mouth, and using a crew directory or diary service to market yourself. Competition for work is fierce.

Related Occupations

You might wish to consider: photographer, production assistant, or - with sufficient experience - film director.

Impact on Lifestyle

Initially, you can expect long hours, low wages and endless pressure. The early jobs are not likely to be very glamorous although later on they may well be. In the world of film and television, the hours always tend to be irregular, starting early, finishing late and often involving waiting around for hours on standby. If you work as a news camera operator, you may find yourself abroad, sometimes in potentially dangerous situations.

Earnings Potential

You could find yourself sometimes working for next to nothing, gaining experience and hoping that you will receive a retrospective payout if the film turns out to be a commercial success. At other times, you might be on a daily or weekly rate, depending on the project. Working in TV drama may earn you around £1,500 for a full week's work. On a low-budget feature film, you may earn around £1,800 a week, rising to around £2,200 a week on a major feature film. On commercials, you may earn around £450 for 10 hours a day. You would need your own camera kit (which can cost thousands of pounds) or to hire equipment. You would also need to keep equipment up to date. BECTU (the Broadcasting Entertainment Cinematograph and Theatre Union) offers advice on its website about freelance rates.

Further Information

Skillset - Sector Skills Council for the Audio Visual Industries, London W1D 3TH
Website: www.skillset.org

FT2 - Film and TV Freelance Training, London SE1 1TJ
Website: www.ft2.org.uk/recruit

CYFLE, Gwynedd LL55 1NS
Website: www.cyfle.co.uk

Scottish Screen, Glasgow G2 4QE
Website: www.scottishscreen.com

BECTU (Broadcasting Entertainment Cinematograph and Theatre Union), London SW9 9BT
Website: www.bectu.org.uk

Guild of British Camera Technicians, Middlesex UB6 8GD
Website: www.gtc.org.uk

Alternative/equivalent entrance requirements can include: ILC, IB, EB, NC/ND and many other similar international systems. For further details see the Equivalent Qualifications section in the Introduction.

Veterinary Nurse

What is Involved?

As a veterinary nurse, you would be involved in caring for animals before, during and after treatment by a veterinary surgeon. You could be required to carry out treatments such as administering drugs, taking x-rays and preparing animals for surgery. You may also offer advice to owners, for example on post-operative care.

You would be working mainly with domestic pets but could be required to cope with horses, farm animals or even zoo animals.

Your job would also include clerical and administrative work in a veterinary practice, such as keeping records, filing reports, answering the telephone and dealing with reception.

Opportunities for Training

You must have a qualification recognised by the Royal College for Veterinary Surgeons and, for most people, the veterinary nurse training scheme is the established training route. It takes at least two years to complete and you must be currently working in a registered veterinary practice.   During the programme, you would build up a portfolio recording your work and you would have to pass two sets of examinations. The course covers areas such as basic anatomy and physiology, animal welfare and first aid, diagnostic and surgical skills, anaesthesia, x-ray techniques and laboratory procedures.   You would also learn about the care of animals, dietary requirements, pain assessment and handling techniques.

Alternative routes include degree, foundation degree and higher national diploma (HND) courses. One of these might prove particularly useful if you want to work as a practice manager or perhaps move into animal-related sales, marketing or product development.

Many of the programmes are also available on a part-time basis for qualified veterinary nurses who wish to 'top up' their initial qualification.

Requirements for Entry

You would need a minimum of five GCSE/S Grade passes A-C/1-3, including English and two of the following: a biological science, a physical science or maths. There is a pre-training course, available at college or by distance learning, if you do not have the required qualifications.

Entry to a degree course is usually with five GCSE/S grade passes A-C/1-3 and two A levels/three H grades. One A level/two H grades may be required for a foundation degree or HND course.

You should also have experience of pet ownership and/or voluntary work at kennels or with animal charities.

Kind of Person

You would need a genuine concern for animals and a wish to care for them. At the same time, you would need to take an unsentimental approach as, inevitably, you would be involved with putting animals down or with unsuccessful surgical procedures. The work is likely to be messy and unpleasant at times as it frequently involves clearing up after animals. In addition to handling a variety of animals, you would need to be able to communicate clearly and sympathetically with their owners. You would have to work as part of the team within the practice and you would need some office skills for keeping records and booking appointments.

Broad Outlook

Most veterinary nurses work for vets in a private practice but there are opportunities to work for animal welfare organisations or in zoos. There are also jobs within veterinary hospitals, universities, breeding establishments, laboratories and research centres, and there may be opportunities to work overseas.

In large veterinary practices or animal hospitals, there may be chances for promotion to supervisor, senior practice nurse or manager. Some veterinary nurses move into training, lecturing or working in animal pharmaceutical companies.

The British Veterinary Nursing Association maintains an employment register to help match job seekers with current vacancies.

Related Occupations

You may be interested in other occupations working with animals, such as RSPCA inspector, or zoo keeper.

Impact on Lifestyle

You may be involved in working long and unsocial hours, including evenings and weekends, perhaps on a shift basis. The work can be physically demanding and emotionally draining, not to mention smelly and unpleasant at times. You would wear a uniform and would add protective clothing when necessary. There may be opportunities for part-time work.

Earnings Potential

There are no set salary scales for veterinary nurses. However, pay can start at about £10,500 while you are training, rising to £15,000 to £18,000 when you are qualified. Senior veterinary nurses or supervisors may earn up to £22,000 or more. Some veterinary nurses are offered a share in the profits of the practice to compensate for a lower salary.

Further Information

British Veterinary Nursing Association, Harlow CM19 5QE
Website: www.bvna.org.uk

Royal College of Veterinary Surgeons, London SW1P 2AF
Website: www.rcvs.org.uk

College of Animal Welfare, Cambridgeshire PE29 2LJ
Website: www.caw.ac.uk

Alternative/equivalent entrance requirements can include: ILC, IB, EB, NC/ND and many other similar international systems. For further details see the Equivalent Qualifications section in the Introduction.

Veterinary Surgeon

What is Involved?

As a veterinary surgeon, you would be concerned with the health and welfare of animals, including household pets, zoo animals, farm animals and horses. This may involve diagnosing and treating them when they are unwell or injured or advising on their living conditions and on steps that can be taken to ensure they stay in good health.

Vets also offer advice on such topics as breeding stock, any government or EU regulations regarding animals and vaccination programmes. Some vets are concerned with research and others work for government agencies ensuring that standards are maintained, particularly in animals destined to join the food chain.

Opportunities for Training

You would have to be registered with the Royal College of Veterinary Surgeons (RCVS) before you could practise veterinary surgery in the UK. This means that you must complete an approved degree in Veterinary Science. The degree usually takes five years, with some students opting to take an additional science subject for a year. At Cambridge it is a six-year course for everyone. The degree courses combine theory and practical work.

Requirements for Entry

There are seven universities in the UK offering a degree in Veterinary Science, although you should note that the newest of these, Nottingham, has not yet received full RCVS accreditation. You are restricted to a maximum of four applications, competition for places is very intense and the grades required are high. There is also a course at University College Dublin. Generally, universities are looking for 3 A levels or equivalent at grades AAB or above (340-360 points). All veterinary schools require chemistry at A level/Advanced Higher/Higher, some specify biology as well, while others want one or two subjects from maths, biology or physics as well as chemistry. Some universities will accept a third A level/Advanced Higher/Higher in a non-science subject if it is considered to be an academic subject. You also need English GCSE/S Grade A-C/1-3. Scottish applicants without Advanced Highers would need Highers of AAABB or equivalent, including chemistry at grade A. It is important to check with individual veterinary schools to be sure of their requirements.

All university veterinary schools insist that you show evidence of your interest and commitment by having gained experience of working in a veterinary practice and working with and handling animals including livestock. However, practical experience is not a substitute for academic qualifications.

Kind of Person

You would need a lot of determination to get onto the course in the first place: only about a third of applicants are successful. You then have to be dedicated and prepared to work hard throughout your training and when you start your career. As well as having top academic credentials and a good scientific understanding, you must have a real interest in animals. You also need to be unsentimental about them and prepared to face some hard decisions. Dealing with the owners is also very important: you must appear confident, in control and able to explain clearly both the problems and the treatments. You would need to be compassionate when dealing with a sick but much-loved family pet; at other times, when you find evidence of neglect for example, you would need to be firm and insist on correct standards of care. Handling large animals requires a reasonable level of physical fitness.

Most vets need to spend at least some time travelling to see their clients so you should be able to drive. You would be likely to work as part of a team whilst at the same time having to take decisions for yourself. You may also need to have good business skills to handle the business side of the practice.

Broad Outlook

There is currently a decline in the need for large animal vets because of challenges within the farming industry; however, there is an increased demand for horse vets and small animal vets who look after people's pets. Buying a share in an established practice can be an expensive commitment for a young vet.

Related Occupations

In the medical field, you might consider training as a doctor, homoeopath, radiographer or physiotherapist.

Impact on Lifestyle

Every veterinary surgeon has an obligation to deal with emergencies in any species at any time. It is a 24-hour service, 365 days a year. Being a vet is not a job where it is possible to work regular hours as animals require attention at all times of the day and night. Conditions of work can be unpleasant, smelly, dirty and very physically demanding and can involve a great deal of travelling.

Earnings Potential

Once qualified, most vets start working in a general practice as a veterinary assistant. Starting salaries vary greatly. According to data from the Society of Practising Veterinary Surgeons, a remuneration package for a newly qualified vet could range from £28,990 to £46,000, which includes a car, fuel allowance, accommodation and training. Should you become a partner, your earnings would depend on the size and location of the practice but could be substantial.

Further Information

Royal College of Veterinary Surgeons, London, SW1P 2AF
Website: www.rcvs.org.uk

Society of Practising Veterinary Surgeons, Warwickshire CV34 5DL
Website: www.spvs.org.uk

British Veterinary Association, London W1G 9NQ
Website: www.bva.co.uk

Career as a Vet
Website: www.walksoflife.org.uk

Association of Veterinary Students
Website: www.avs-uk.org.uk

Alternative/equivalent entrance requirements can include: ILC, IB, EB, NC/ND and many other similar international systems. For further details see the Equivalent Qualifications section in the Introduction.

Webmaster

What is Involved?

Your main tasks as a webmaster would be to set up, run and maintain websites for companies, organisations or individuals. The websites might be used for such purposes as publicity, marketing or buying and selling on the internet and you would need to start by discussing in some detail the precise needs of your client. At this stage, you would advise on what could be included on the website, including graphics, text and sound, together with the possibility of links to other sites. If the company or organisation has its own intranet (an internal version of the internet), you would discuss how this could best be linked to the web. You would be expected to advise on the cost of the project, and either design and program the website pages yourself or supervise others to do this. Once the design is agreed and the site is up and running, you would make sure that it is kept up to date and any problems are dealt with. You might work on a freelance basis as an independent consultant or you might be employed full-time by a large company or organisation.

Opportunities for Training

There is no single route to becoming a webmaster. Experience and talent can be as important as qualifications in this relatively new field; if you have experimented with web design as a hobby this could prove of benefit. There are, however, many relevant courses available at different levels of entry and you should look very closely to find out which would be the best one for you to follow. You might well find that one of these qualifications could give you an advantage in getting your first job. Training ranges from short courses offered by local colleges or commercial companies in web design, development and authorship to higher national diploma (HND) and degree courses with titles such as Interactive Multimedia Design or Media Technology. Once in employment, you could work towards a professional qualification awarded by an organisation such as the British Computer Society or the National Computing Centre.

You could also look for employment with training via an Apprenticeship.

Requirements for Entry

While there is no educational requirement laid down for entry into the profession, and plenty of young people virtually teach themselves to design websites, many employers look favourably at the possession of certificates from some of the courses mentioned above. Some webmasters pursue courses based on art and design, while others choose more IT-oriented courses. Short courses usually need a minimum of GCSE/S Grade qualifications for entry, while A level/Advanced Higher, Higher or equivalent passes are needed for HND and degree courses. A good portfolio of current artwork is a necessity for most art-based courses.

Kind of Person

You would clearly need to enjoy working with computers and to be skilled at programming. You must be prepared to update your skills and knowledge on a regular basis in order to keep pace with rapid technological change. A talent for design would also be very important, since websites need to have instant appeal, in keeping with the image that your clients wish to project. Good communication skills would be necessary, both spoken and written, as you untangle your clients' needs and explain your proposed solutions. You should develop a good understanding of business and budgeting, and you must be able to deliver your work within tight deadlines.

Broad Outlook

"Only by embracing a digital Britain and taking a lead in the global digital economy can we maintain our competitiveness as one of the world's leading economic and industrial powers in years to come. I do think that the digital revolution lies at the heart of success for Britain in the years to come." Despite these encouraging words from Prime Minister Gordon Brown in April 2009, there are apparent contradictions in labour market data for IT specialists. On the one hand, e-skills UK cite the need for 140,000 new employees every year in the UK IT and telecommunications sector; on the other, applications to IT-related degrees have tumbled by 50% over the last five years. Whatever the explanation for this, there is a clear incentive for employers to entice the right candidates from a shrinking pool, leading the National Computing Centre to assert that employment in the IT sector is likely to weather the economic storm of 2009, although there will be losers in some areas. Nearly half of respondents to its 'Benchmark of Salaries and Employment Trends in IT 2009' survey said they expect the number of IT staff employed at their location to increase over the next two years. Similarly, e-skills UK describe many aspects of ICT as 'credit crunch resistant'.

Related Occupations

You might also like to consider: software engineer, multimedia programmer/specialist, computer games designer, database administrator, graphic designer or systems analyst.

Impact on Lifestyle

If you were employed full-time by a company or organisation you would probably work a normal five-day week, although there might be occasions when you would have to meet deadlines or deal with problems and, therefore, put in extra hours in the evening or over a weekend. As a freelance worker, you would almost certainly find yourself in this position from time to time.

Earnings Potential

Earnings can vary a great deal, depending on the terms of employment. A webmaster in full-time employment within a company might earn around £22,000 to £25,000 a year on starting, rising to more than £40,000. As a self-employed freelance webmaster, your earnings would depend on the number and size of your commissions.

Further Information

British Computer Society, Swindon SN1 1HJ
Website: www.bcs.org.uk

British Interactive Media Association, Essex CM11 2PR
Website: www.bima.co.uk

e-skills UK Ltd, London SW1E 6DR
Website: www.e-skills.com

National Computing Centre, Manchester M1 7ED
Website: www.ncc.co.uk

UK Web Design Association
Website: www.ukwda.org

Apprenticeships
Website: www.apprenticeships.org.uk

Alternative/equivalent entrance requirements can include: ILC, IB, EB, NC/ND and many other similar international systems. For further details see the Equivalent Qualifications section in the Introduction.

Youth Worker

What is Involved?

As a youth worker, you would work with young people aged between 11 and 25, particularly those aged between 13 and 19, to promote their personal and social development and enable them to have a voice, influence and place in their communities and society as a whole. Youth work is carried out in different situations and locations, using a range of approaches. You might, for example, operate from a youth club or centre, offering some activities for all young people in the area and some targeted at specific groups. You might be a detached or outreach youth worker, making contact with young people who do not use youth centres. You could work in a school or college, contributing in particular to PSHE (personal, social and health education), citizenship and study support programmes. You might be involved with young people who have been excluded from school, who persistently misuse drugs or alcohol, or who have been involved in crime.

You would often work with other services - such as social services, housing, leisure, and health - to develop and improve provision for young people.

Opportunities for Training

There are many different ways of training to become a professionally qualified youth worker, normally building on part-time or voluntary experience. Qualifications vary considerably from one United Kingdom country to another and you should research local requirements carefully. Professionally validated awards (diploma, foundation degree, degree, postgraduate courses/Masters) in youth work or youth and community work/studies are currently offered by around 30 English universities and colleges of higher education. Both full- and part-time courses are available and all require completion of substantial fieldwork placements. Since youth workers operate in a wide range of settings, courses at different institutions reflect different occupational needs and have a range of titles.

As from September 2010, all new professional qualifications in youth work will be at honours degree level or higher.

Requirements for Entry

Entry without qualification is possible, but only if you commit to a programme of training to achieve a qualification. A degree course would normally require at least two A level/Advanced Higher, three Higher or equivalent qualifications in any subject, together with five GCSE/S Grade passes at A-C/1-3. If you are a mature candidate with relevant experience, you may be admitted without meeting these academic requirements.

Kind of Person

You would need to build relationships with young people based on trust and respect, offering them new experiences and challenges and encouraging them to think critically about their lives and values. You would encourage young people to take on greater responsibility for themselves and others and to work effectively as a team, judging when to stand back and when to intervene. This may mean letting them make mistakes but ensuring that they learn from them. You would use a range of interpersonal skills such as counselling, advocacy and group work. You could not be expected to be an expert on everything affecting young people but you should be aware of other local agencies and what they offer, and to recognise when you need to involve people with specialist skills and knowledge, while continuing to support the young person concerned.

Broad Outlook

Youth work skills are in great demand and opportunities for qualified people are expanding. In addition to employment within local authority youth services, there are an increasing number of opportunities for employment in other settings. These include other local authority departments such as leisure, arts and housing, health authorities, youth justice teams, and a range of voluntary organisations.

Overall, expansion in this field of work is likely as a result of government policy and initiatives to increase the employability and tackle the social exclusion of young people. Youth worker targets in England are now framed by the five outcomes highlighted by the government's Every Child Matters (2006) report: that children and young people should be healthy; be safe; enjoy and achieve; make a positive contribution; and experience economic well being.

Related Occupations

You might consider: social worker, probation officer, teacher, careers/personal adviser or education welfare officer.

Impact on Lifestyle

As a full-time worker, you would be contracted to work a set number of hours, usually 35 to 37 a week. Your contract would almost certainly specify evening and weekend sessions.

Earnings Potential

Starting salaries depend on your qualifications and your employing organisation. The current professional range pay scale starts at around £20,000 and rises to over £35,000. A senior manager can earn around £60,000.

Further Information

National Youth Agency, Leicester LE5 3GJ
Website: www.nya.org.uk

Youth Council for Northern Ireland, Belfast BT8 7AR
Website: www.ycni.org

Youth Link Scotland, Edinburgh EH12 5EZ
Website: www.youthlink.co.uk

Community and Youth Workers Union, Birmingham B15 1AY
Website: www.cywu.org.uk

Alternative/equivalent entrance requirements can include: ILC, IB, EB, NC/ND and many other similar international systems. For further details see the Equivalent Qualifications section in the Introduction.

Additional Career Outlines

Lack of space prevents us from giving a complete WORKBRIEF analysis of every possible career idea but we do list in this section a range of further occupational titles.

Our top priority here is to include the majority of careers mentioned under 'Related Occupations' in the main section but not described in their own detailed chapters.

Acupuncturist

Acupuncturists treat a wide range of ailments by inserting very fine needles into key parts of a patient's body, often with the effect of relieving pain. In China, they often use acupuncture to anaesthetise patients before operations. Most applicants are graduates - and often are aged 30 or above - but adults with previous experience in a medical field are often admitted for a course without a previous degree, A level or similar qualification.

British Acupuncture Council, London W12 9HQ
Website: www.acupuncture.org.uk

British Medical Acupuncture Society, Northwich CW8 1AQ
Website: www.medical-acupuncture.co.uk

Agricultural Adviser

Agricultural Advisers work within the land based industries, providing consultancy and research to farmers, the horticultural industry, government and levy bodies, food processors, food retailers and the agricultural supply industry. They may also operate in the international sector.

Agricultural Development and Advisory Service, Wolverhampton WV6 8TQ
Website: www.adas.co.uk

Agricultural Biologist

Agricultural Biologists specialise in the application of modern biological techniques to the study of plants or animals, their reproduction, genetic make-up, nutrition, health and diseases. They work mainly in agricultural research laboratories. They are usually graduates with degrees in biology, biotechnology, cell biology, food science, genetics, microbiology or molecular biology - see Research Biologist.

Institute of Biology, London EC4A 3EF
Website: www.iob.org

Agricultural Chemist

Agricultural Chemists apply modern chemical research techniques to the study of plants or animals, their biochemistry, nutrition, soil science, effects of fertilisers and growth hormones, crop yields and so on. They work mainly in agricultural research laboratories and are graduates with degrees in chemistry-related subjects such as chemistry, biochemistry, biotechnology, genetics, molecular biology and pharmacology - see Research Chemist.

Royal Society of Chemistry, London W1J 0BA
Website: www.rsc.org

Agricultural Researcher

Agricultural Research may be undertaken at a university, agricultural college or research institution, or within a relevant commercial concern, such as a manufacturer of agricultural chemicals. The aim is to find ways of improving crop yields and agricultural practices or to breed new disease-resistant strains of, for example, grains, fruit or vegetables. You might also research such areas as turkey, chicken, pig and egg production. See also Research Biologist and Research Chemist, together with Agricultural Biologist, Agricultural Chemist and Agricultural Adviser.

Agrisearch UK, Melbourne DE73 8AG
Website: www.eurofins-agrisearch.com

Aircraft Maintenance Engineer

Aircraft maintenance engineers are technicians who inspect, maintain and repair civil and military aircraft. They may be mechanical engineers, specialising in airframes and engines, or avionics engineers concerned with electronic and electrical systems. Normal colour vision is essential.

Association of Licensed Aircraft Engineers, Bagshot GU19 5AQ
Website: www.alae.org

Royal Aeronautical Society, London, W1J 7BQ
Website: www.aerosociety.com

Royal Air Force
Website: www.rafcareers.com

Antiquarian Bookseller

Antiquarian Booksellers run specialist bookshops, dealing in valuable books, often buying or selling through the top auction houses, or by direct contact with collectors or other dealers. They need to develop a detailed knowledge of sales prices and of the levels of supply and demand, to avoid overbidding at auctions.

Antiquarian Booksellers Association, London W1J 0DR
Website: www.aba.org.uk

Antiques Dealer

Antiques dealers buy and sell antique furniture or other artefacts, such as ceramics, clocks or ancient firearms. Numerous other specialisms exist, each one calling for individuals with detailed knowledge and experience. Central to the work are auctions and fairs, where dealers may sell or buy in stock, observe levels of buyer interest and develop their expertise. They often buy for collectors and export to other countries. This is a relatively small field of employment and jobs are difficult to obtain, unless you have suitable connections with a firm of dealers.

British Antique Dealers' Association, London SW7 1BD
Website: www.bada.org

Applications Developer

Applications developers work in computing, writing or modifying programs for a variety of technical, commercial and business users. These applications may then be bought off the shelf or tailored to meet the needs of specific clients. The work requires a thorough knowledge of programming techniques and computer systems in order to develop effective programs in accordance with agreed specifications.

British Computer Society, Swindon SN2 1FA
Website: www.bcs.org

e-skills UK, London SW1E 6DR
Website: www.e-skills.com

Institution of Analysts and Programmers, London W13 9NH
Website: www.iap.org.uk

Arboriculturist

Arboriculturists work in both rural and urban settings, cultivating and managing trees and shrubs. They also provide information and advice on specific tree-related issues, and may specialise in a particular area, such as tree climbing and maintenance, tree preservation and conservation, parks and gardens, planning, or tree survey and inspection. Some people start at craft level and work up to positions such as technical manager or supervisor, while others choose to take a relevant course such as a BSc (Hons) or National Certificate in Arboriculture.

The International Society of Arboriculture provides an arborist certification programme, and the Royal Forestry Society (RFS) offers a professional diploma for practitioners (DipArb(RFS)) at NVQ Level 4.

Arboricultural Association, Hampshire SO51 9PA
Website: www.trees.org.uk

International Society of Arboriculture, IL 61821, USA
Website: www.isa-arbor.com

Royal Forestry Society, Hertfordshire HP23 4AF
Website: www.rfs.org.uk

Archaeological Illustrator/Surveyor

Archaeological illustrators and surveyors are concerned with the specialised surveying of archaeological sites and with recording the layouts of structures and artefacts unearthed during excavations.

Association of Archaeological Illustrators and Surveyors, Reading RG6 6AU
Website: www.aais.org.uk

Archivist

Archivists save and look after the records of the past. These may include official documents, newspaper cuttings, rare books, photographs, films, videos and tape recordings, and may be publicly or privately owned, in national or local collections. Archivists carry out research, indexing and cataloguing, and give help to scholars, research scientists and others seeking specialist information.

Society of Archivists, Taunton TA1 1SW
Website: www.archives.org.uk

Aromatherapist

Aromatherapy is a holistic therapy, combining the possibility of healing both mind and body at the same time with the use of essential oils. These oils have many healing properties and can work alongside other complementary or orthodox remedies. Aromatherapy can be particularly helpful for the release of mental or emotional tension, mood swings, nervousness, acute anxiety and some psychosomatic disorders.

International Federation of Aromatherapists, London W3 6AY
Website: www.ifaroma.org

Art Gallery/Museum Assistant

Art Gallery/Museum Assistants work with and for Curators and Keepers in museums and art galleries, on all aspects of the display, storage and administration of their collections.

Museums Association, London E1 6NW
Website: www.museumsassociation.org

Art Restorer/Conservator

Art restoration involves the cleaning, repair and renovation of damaged works of art. It requires a scientific knowledge of materials used in the past, the processes of their deterioration and of modern materials which must be compatible with the originals. Antiques conservation calls for similar skills.

British Association of Paintings Conservator-Restorers, Norwich NR13 4WY
Website: www.bapcr.org.uk

Art Therapist

Art therapists work with individuals and groups experiencing a range of medical and emotional conditions, using artistic activities as an opportunity for expression and communication. You would need to achieve a diploma in art therapy, usually after completing a degree level course in art. You might work with paints of all kinds, canvasses, papers, pastels, clay, fabrics, collages, carving, sculpture or weaving materials, to allow clients to express and share their innermost thoughts and feelings.

British Association of Art Therapists, London WC1A 2AJ
Website: www.baat.org

Arts Administrator

Arts administrators provide support for a wide range of cultural events and activities in theatres, galleries, museums, arts festivals, arts centres, dance companies, community arts organisations and so on. The work might involve programme planning, front of house management, public relations, marketing, education and sponsorship. Jobs in arts administration are highly competitive, and gaining substantial relevant experience is much more likely to be of benefit than any specific subject of study. However, a degree in a subject such as art and design, arts management, business studies, English and literary studies or performing arts could prove extremely useful.

Arts Council England, London SW1P 3NQ
Website: www.artscouncil.org.uk

Arts Council of Northern Ireland, Belfast BT9 6AQ
Website: www.artscouncil-ni.org

Scottish Arts Council, Edinburgh EH3 7DD
Website: www.scottisharts.org.uk

Arts Council of Wales, Cardiff CF10 5AL
Website: www.artswales.org.uk

Arts Marketing Association, Cambridge CB1 7BN
Website: www.a-m-a.co.uk

Theatrical Management Association, London WC2E 9ET
Website: www.tmauk.org

Astronomer/Astrophysicist

Astronomers/astrophysicists use a range of optical and radio telescopes to study the structure and nature of the universe and to discover the scientific principles upon which it is based. They use advanced physics, mathematics, computing and other technologies to coordinate and analyse their data. This is regarded as a branch of physics and requires a degree in physics, astrophysics or astronomy.

Royal Astronomical Society, London W1J 0BQ
Website: www.ras.org.uk

British National Space Centre, London SW1W 9SS
Website: www.bnsc.gov.uk

British Astronomical Association
Website: www.britastro.org

UK Students for the Exploration and Development of Space
Website: www.uk.seds.org

Astronomy Ireland
Website: www.astronomy.ie

Biophysicist

Biophysicists consider the physical, electrical and mechanical properties of living tissues and cells, their protein structures, and nerve impulse transmissions, and thus play an important part in biological and medical research in association with other research scientists.

Institute of Physics, London W1B 1NT
Website: www.iop.org

Institute of Biology, London EC4A 3EF
Website: www.iob.org

Bookseller

Booksellers need to be familiar with, and able to promote, a wide variety of books. They must be able to advise customers on what is available and help them find the publications they are looking for. They use mainly electronic search methods to locate and order books. Large bookshop chains offer their own in-house training.

Antiquarian Booksellers Association, London W1J 0DR
Website: www.aba.org.uk

Booksellers Association of the United Kingdom and Ireland, London SW1V 1BA
Website: www.booksellers.org.uk

International Booksellers Federation, Boite 1, B1060 Brussels, Belgium
Website: www.ibf-booksellers.org

Brewer (Technical)

Technical brewers are responsible for managing the process of brewing and packaging beer. The work includes sourcing raw materials, running the brewery efficiently and ensuring consistent quality of the final product. In large breweries, the technical brewer usually specialises in one area of production, whereas in small breweries the brewer can be responsible for all aspects of the process. Trainee brewers are usually people with a degree or postgraduate qualification in subjects such as brewing, chemistry, biochemistry, bioengineering or biotechnology. Pre-entry experience and evidence of specialist knowledge can be very useful, and is usually gained through work experience in a brewery or distillery.

Institute of Brewing and Distilling, London W1J 7EE
Website: www.ibd.org.uk

Building Contractor

Building Contractors are usually the managers or owners of building companies, who undertake building and construction contracts, often under the guidance of an architect, surveyor or engineer, or who undertake work directly with private clients, development companies or local authorities - see Construction Manager.

Chartered Institute of Building, Ascot SL5 7TB
Website: www.ciob.org.uk

Construction Skills, Bircham Newton, Kings Lynn PE31 6RH
Website: www.cskills.org

Building Control Surveyor

Building control surveyors ensure that building control regulations are observed in the planning and construction stages of new buildings and most property extensions and conversions. On complex projects they may be involved at the pre-application stage, to offer advice on acceptable solutions to meet the statutory requirements of regulations. After the work has commenced, they make site visits at different stages to ensure that the construction is being properly carried out.

Royal Institution of Chartered Surveyors, Coventry CV4 8JE
Website: www.rics.org

Construction Industry Council, London WC1E 7BT
Website: www.cic.org.uk

Building Society Manager

Building Societies attract and look after their investors' savings and arrange mortgages for house buyers. Their work is closely related to banking in nature.

Building Societies Association, London W1S 3PB
Website: www.bsa.org.uk

Cell Biologist

This new science field breaks down the boundaries between cell biology, biochemistry, genetics and microbiology, focusing on the DNA making up genes. Cell biologists study cell structure and function, cell metabolism, molecular organisation, biochemical regulatory mechanisms, immunology, genetics, evolutionary patterns and mechanisms of reproduction.

British Society for Cell Biology
Website: www.bscb.org

Biology4all
Website: www.biology4all.com

Chef

Trained to cook food, usually in the kitchens of a restaurant, and to produce food to a high standard, chefs may specialise in certain branches of cooking, such as French, Indian or Thai, or simply produce a wide range of menus of all kinds.

Institute of Hospitality, Sutton SM1 1SH
Website: www.instituteofhospitality.org

Chemical Analyst

Chemical Analysts test the chemical composition of substances, using an extensive range of modern analytical equipment and traditional methods. They develop special tests to detect minute traces of chemicals.

Royal Society of Chemistry, London W1J 0BA
Website: www.rsc.org

Biochemical Society, London WC1V 6NX
Website: www.biochemistry.org

Civil Aviation

Civil aviation is a broad term, covering a range of career opportunities associated with air transport. These could include flying as a pilot or cabin crew, working in engineering maintenance and repair of aircraft or providing services for passengers within airports.

Civil Aviation Authority, London WC2B 6TE
Website: www.caa.co.uk

GoSkills, West Midlands B37 7UQ
Website: www.goskills.org

Clothing/Textile Technologist

Clothing/textile technologists carry out technical, investigative and quality control work on clothing and textiles, ensuring that products perform to specifications. Their work includes the development of products, improvement of production efficiency and quality, and liaison with people involved in the production process.

British Textile Technology Group, Leeds LS16 6QI
Website: www.bttg.co.uk

Textile Institute, Manchester M1 6FQ
Website: www.textileinstitute.org

Commodity Broker

Commodity Brokers act on behalf of clients to buy and sell such goods as metals, grains, sugar and wool in world markets. Most operate in leading financial centres, including New York, London, Paris and Frankfurt.

Financial Services Authority, London E14 5HS
Website: www.fsa.gov.uk

Euronext
Website: www.euronext.com

London Metal Exchange, London EC3A 2DX
Website: www.lme.co.uk

Communications Engineer

Working in this field would usually require a basis of electronics engineering but concentrating on communications by means of fibre optics, audio, broadcasting, television, radio, video, satellite and telephone systems.

Institute of Telecommunications Professionals
Website: www.theitp.org

Institution of Engineering and Technology
Website: www.theiet.org

Community Development Worker

Community workers work with people - individuals, families or larger groups - in communities usually perceived to be disadvantaged, perhaps because of problems related to age, race, ability, drugs, poverty or geography. The aim of the work is to empower communities to regain control over the conditions and decisions affecting their lives and to improve the quality of life for all who live in them.

Community Development Foundation, London N5 2AG
Website: www.cdf.org.uk

General Social Care Council, London SE1 2HB
Website: www.gscc.org.uk

Scottish Community Development Centre, Glasgow G2 6HJ
Website: www.scdc.org.uk

Computer-Aided Designer

Working in the field of computer-aided design, you would use specialised computer software packages to produce 2-D or 3-D designs, 3-D computer models of proposed building structures or engineering products, engineering and architectural drawings, often with virtual reality features to allow people to explore a design on a 'walk through basis' before its final construction.

British Computer Society, Swindon SN2 1FA
Website: www.bcs.org.uk

New Media Knowledge
Website: www.nmk.co.uk

Computer Engineer/Scientist

Computer engineers/scientists are involved in the design, development and manufacture of new computer hardware and its integration with suitable software. They work closely with electronic engineers and information technologists. Opportunities in the UK have been overshadowed by overseas competition in recent years - however, this field remains one of vital importance to the UK for the long-term future.

British Computer Society, Swindon SN2 1FA
Website: www.bcs.org.uk

Institution of Engineering and Technology
Website: www.theiet.org

E-skills UK, London SW1E 6DR
Website: www.e-skills.com

Computer Games Designer

The computer games industry is now of very great economic global importance, with a need for highly gifted and skilled computer programmers able to use multimedia and animation techniques and to create challenges young people, in ever more imaginative and sophisticated ways.

British Computer Society, Swindon SN2 1FA
Website: www.bcs.org.uk

E-skills UK, London SW1E 6DR
Website: www.e-skills.com

Blitz Games: advice for people considering a career in the games industry
Website: www.blitzgames.com/gameon

Computer Services Manager

Computer Services Managers handle the management of the computing and IT resources within a company.

Institute for the Management of Information Systems, Orpington BR5 3QG
Website: www.imis.org.uk

British Computer Society, Swindon SN2 1FA
Website: www.bcs.org.uk

Conservationist (Nature)

Nature conservationists are concerned with the protection of plants and animals in the wild and with the wider impacts of herbicides, pesticides and pollutants on the environment as a whole. Some one hundred National Nature Reserves and thousands of sites of scientific interest require management by wardens and their assistants. Scientists - usually biologists, botanists, zoologists, and geographers - are employed as Assistant Regional Officers in researching and monitoring environmental issues.

British Ecological Society, London SWI5 2NU
Website: www.britishecologicalsociety.org

Conservator

Conservators are concerned with the conservation and restoration of historic objects such as ancient books, documents, oil paintings, watercolours and paper decorations (eg Chinese wallpapers and silks), and work within museums, art galleries, ancient houses, properties of the National Trust and the various national Heritage organisations, as well as in the private sector.

Institute of Conservation, London SE1 9BG
Website: www.icon.org.uk

Constituency Agent

Constituency Agents are responsible for the local organisation of their constituencies and checking electoral rolls, recruiting for party membership, fundraising and organising meetings for their MPs or parliamentary candidates. They are required to take a correspondence course and examination and work under the supervision of an experienced agent for about 18 months. For further information contact your local or central party organisation or visit their website.

BUBL Information Services, Glasgow G1 1HX (for full list of all UK political parties)
Website: www.bubl.ac.uk/uk/bublukpolitical.htm

Consumer Scientist

Consumer scientists, sometimes known as home economists, work in many fields: from the food industry to the media; from appliance manufacturers to housing associations; in retailing and in the public sector; but in most cases they are there to represent the consumer, acting as a communication point between consumers and manufacturers.

In food product development, for example, they might work for a food manufacturer or large supermarket chain, researching consumer tastes and designing new dishes and food products to interest shoppers. In the media they might write articles or present programmes on cookery, family health issues or new products on the market. As health education officers or health promotion specialists, they teach people how to lead healthier lives. If they have specialised in food or textiles, they may teach these subjects, in secondary schools or in further or higher education.

Improve Ltd, York YO10 5ZF
Website: www.improveltd.co.uk

Control and Instrumentation Engineer

Control and instrumentation engineers apply automation techniques and computer-aided processes to design, install, develop and maintain instrumentation, electronics and computer control systems within the process industry (manufacturing).

Institute of Measurement and Control, London WC1E 6AF
Website: www.instmc.org.uk

Counsellor

Counsellors work with individual clients on a one-to-one basis, in a private and confidential setting, to explore difficulties they are facing. The counsellor's role is not to make judgements, to give advice or to direct clients to a specific solution, but rather to listen to clients' stories and encourage them to think clearly about their situation and perhaps consider a new perspective in order to find a way forward. There are several different approaches to counselling, each with its own theoretical basis.

British Association for Counselling and Psychotherapy, Warwickshire CV21 2SG
Website: www.bacp.co.uk/

British Psychological Society, Leicester LE1 7DR
Website: www.bps.org.uk

Counselling and Psychotherapy in Scotland, Stirling FK8 1UA
Website: www.cosca.org.uk/

Cybernetics

Cybernetics is the study and application of computerised feedback control systems, for example, in industrial production units or on aircraft. Thus, if the temperature of a chemical process rises above a set limit, a message to reduce the input of heat to the system is triggered. Heating is increased again if the temperature falls. Such processes are similar to those which occur in the human body.

Cybernetics Society, Welwyn Garden City AL8 7NA
Website: www.cybsoc.org

Dancer

Dancers communicate ideas visually, physically and musically in ballet, contemporary dance and in entertainment generally, working in films, television, pantomime, cabaret and sometimes in education.

Council for Dance Education and Training, London WC2H 9UY
Website: www.cdet.org.uk

Database Administrator

Database administrators manage and supervise the creation and installation of computer databases. Their services are required by central and local government, universities, schools, research establishments, libraries, accounting practices, industrial, banking and other commercial or financial groups.

British Computer Society, Swindon SN2 1FA
Website: www.bcs.org.uk

Dental Hygienist

Dental hygienists work closely with dentists to clean and polish the teeth of patients - and thus help prevent dental decay. They try to educate people to take care of their gums and teeth, and often visit schools to check on the dental health of pupils.

British Society of Dental Hygiene and Therapy, Gloucester GL2 2AT
Website: www.bsdht.org.uk

Dental Nurse

A dental nurse is trained to assist a dentist in a dental surgery, ensuring that the dentist has the materials and instruments needed in treating patients at exactly the right moment. The nurse is responsible for the hygiene of the surgery and equipment.

British Association of Dental Nurses, Thornton-Cleveleys FY5 4QD
Website: www.badn.org.uk

Education Social Worker

Education social workers or education welfare officers are employed by local authorities to investigate the problems of children whose education is being threatened by a wide range of social, behavioural, financial, transport, diet or health factors. They visit schools and identify the causes of problems, talk to the children and their families and devise solutions to overcome them.

Children's Workforce Development Council
Website: www.cwdcouncil.org.uk

National Association of Social Workers in Education
Website: www.naswe.org.uk

Energy Engineer

Energy engineers are concerned with the uses and economic combustion of fuels, with atomic energy and developments in the use of water, wind, tide and sun as sources of energy. They study the relative costs of producing energy in industry, comparing the economic advantages of using fuels such as coal, oil, natural gas, nuclear- or wind- generated electric power. They also look at methods to conserve energy and reduce heat loss from buildings.

Energy Zone
Website: www.energyzone.net

Engineering Geologist

Engineering geologists assess the integrity of soil, rock, groundwater and other natural conditions prior to major construction schemes, such as tunnelling, laying of pipelines, planning of buildings, docks and harbours. They also advise on procedures required for such developments and the suitability of appropriate construction materials.

Association of Geotechnical and Geoenvironmental Specialists
Website: www.ags.org.uk

Geological Society of London, London W1J 0BG
Website: www.geolsoc.org.uk

Institute of Materials, Minerals and Mining, London SW1Y 5DB
Website: www.iom3.org

Engineering Physicist

Engineering Physicists use their understanding of the physical sciences and mathematics to analyse the behaviour of engineering materials, parts and components.

Institute of Physics, London W1B 1NT
Website: www.iop.org

Equine Manager

An equine manager is involved with the management of all aspects of the work associated with stables or studs. This might involve overseeing coaching, training and breeding programmes as well as nutrition, marketing and the business aspects of equine activities.

British Horse Society, Kenilworth CV8 2XZ
Website: www.bhs.org.uk

Association of British Riding Schools
Website: www.abrs-info.org

Association of Irish Riding Establishments
Website: www.aire.ie

Ergonomist

Ergonomists - sometimes known as human factors specialists - ensure that equipment, facilities and systems are designed and organised to the highest standards of comfort, efficiency, health and safety for the people using them. The work involves the scientific study of the relationship between people, environments and equipment and using the findings to improve human interaction with processes and systems. Areas of work include product/equipment design, production systems, information and advanced technology, and transport design.

Ergonomics Society, Loughborough LE11 1RG
Website: www.ergonomics.org.uk

Estate Manager

As an estate manager you would be qualified to manage estates, farms, amenity horticulture sites and forestry operations. You may at times be responsible for developing leisure and recreational facilities, such as fishing, shooting, golf and hill walking, and even to establish and market holiday accommodation for tourists. Estate managers usually have qualifications in farming/agriculture or in surveying. They need a sound understanding of costing, accounts and management. They were originally known as Factors in Scotland - but are nowadays usually described as rural practice surveyors. Land agents cover much of the same ground but often specialise in the valuation and sale of agricultural land, farm buildings and agricultural machinery. See Rural Practice Surveyor.

Royal Institution of Chartered Surveyors, Coventry CV4 8JE
Website: www.rics.org

Exhibition Designer

Exhibition designers specialise in creating attractive display stands for major exhibitions. You would need to be able to work in a variety of styles, using a wide range of materials and specialist lighting effects.

Your Creative Future
Website: www.yourcreativefuture.org

Creative & Cultural Skills
Website: www.creative-choices.co.uk

Exploration Geologist

Exploration Geologists use drilling, seismic, acoustic, aerial photography and other methods to collect and interpret geological data, thereby locating mineral deposits, such as oil, petroleum, gas, platinum, gold, copper and nickel. They use field-mapping techniques and make calculations to estimate the size and locations of the reserves.

Association of Geotechnical and Geoenvironmental Specialists
Website: www.ags.org.uk/aboutus/welcome.cfm

Geological Society of London, London W1J 0BG
Website: www.geolsoc.org.uk

Institute of Materials, Minerals and Mining, London SW1Y 5DB
Website: www.iom3.org

Farm Secretary

A farm secretary works in an agricultural environment, helping employers to complete forms, keep accounts, monitor crop and milk production and calculate employees' wages. A farm secretary may work for one employer, be freelance or be sent out by an agency to a number of farms.

Institute of Agricultural Secretaries and Administrators, Kenilworth CV8 2LZ
Website: www.iagsa.co.uk

Fashion Buyer

Fashion buyers specialise in buying attractive garments for sale within fashion and dress shops or large retail store groups. They attend exhibitions where fashion houses show their latest collections to UK, European and International buyers. There is no guaranteed entry or single training route to this sort of work. See Buying Executive.

Chartered Institute of Purchasing and Supply, Stamford PE9 3NZ
Website: www.cips.org

Skillsmart Retail
Website: www.skillsmartretail.com

Fashion Retail Academy
Website: www.fashionretailacademy.ac.uk

Fashion Editor

Fashion Editors are be responsible for commissioning and editing the feature articles for specialist fashion magazines. Alternatively, they might write or edit a fashion section in a newspaper. They report on all the latest trends, attend fashion shows, and keep up to date with and comment on fashion available in retail stores. See also: Fashion Designer, Fashion Journalist, Fashion Photographer, Journalist, Magazine Publisher.

The Fashion Spot
Website: www.thefashionspot.com

Fashion School Review
Website: www.fashionschoolreview.com

Fashion Journalist

Fashion is a subject which creates considerable interest from a clothes conscious market - and this calls for specialist journalists who are fully in touch with trends in fashion design. They need the ability to make value judgements in this very creative field and to write with professional authority, flair and insight. A degree in fashion design could provide a strong foundation but there is no guaranteed route into this relatively small career field. See Journalist.

National Council for the Training of Journalists, Saffron Walden CB11 3PL
Website: www.nctj.com

Fashion Photographer

Fashion Photographers take photographs of models displaying the latest clothes, accessories, hairstyles and make-up. This involves working with the editors of fashion magazines, with fashion houses for their publicity literature, choosing locations and arranging lighting. Fashion photography is seen as one of the most glamorous areas of photography and it is certainly one of the most competitive. The lure of exotic locations, foreign travel, and joining the celebrity circuit must be weighed against working long hours and having to meet tight deadlines. See also: Photographer.

Skillset, Sector Skills Council for the Audio Visual Industries
Website: www.skillset.org/photo/careers/photographers/article_3274_1.asp

Fashion Sales Executive

Fashion Sales Executives are involved with all aspects of fashion retail, including promoting the products of fashion houses/labels, store management, customer service, visual merchandising, buying, design, computer technology and marketing. See also: Fashion Designer, Fashion Buyer, Sales Executive.

Fashion Retail Academy
Website: www.fashionretailacademy.ac.uk

London Fashion Week
Website: www.londonfashionweek.co.uk

Film Director

Directors supervise and guide the actors and actresses taking part in plays, films and radio productions. They interpret the author's intentions and the stage, studio or outside effects and background scenes required.

British Film Institute, London W1T 1LN
Website: www.bfi.org.uk

Skillset
Website: www.skillset.org

UK Film Council
Website: www.ukfilmcouncil.org.uk

Film Set Designer

See Television/Theatre Set Designer.

British Film Institute, London W1T 1LN
Website: www.bfi.org.uk

Skillset
Website: www.skillset.org

UK Film Council
Website: www.ukfilmcouncil.org.uk

Fine Art Dealer

Art dealers display original paintings, sculptures and other works of art in their galleries for purchase by the public or by members of the art trade. They usually specialise in a particular type, field or period of painting, sculpture or ceramics. They attend art auctions or buy direct from the public and need to become expert in such areas as valuation, restoration and authentication.

Society of London Art Dealers, London SW1Y 6JP
Website: www.slad.org.uk

Fish Farmer

Fish farming is concerned with the healthy cultivation and harvesting of fish under scientifically controlled conditions, usually in specially constructed tanks. Fish such as salmon, trout, plaice and sole produced in this way are now available in shops and restaurants throughout the UK and mainland Europe. Much of the work is concerned with preventing disease, controlling temperature and oxygen levels and keeping water free from pollution.

Institute of Fisheries Management, Nottingham NG2 7LF
Website: www.ifm.org.uk

Fishery Technologist/Scientist

Fishery Scientists investigate the best methods for harvesting fish in the wild and for rearing them in captivity. Most of the positions for qualified staff go to biologists with specialist postgraduate training or fisheries experience.

Institute of Fisheries Management, Nottingham NG2 7LF
Website: www.ifm.org.uk

Floor Manager (TV)

Floor managers perform similar functions to stage managers but work within television or film studios and co-ordinate camera crews. They make sure that the director's instructions are passed on, give cues to make sure things happen on time and ensure that actors are available and in position. See Stage Manager.

Skillset, London WC1A 1HB
Website: www.skillset.org

Food Presenter/Demonstrator

Food Presenters/Demonstrators use cookery skills to demonstrate the preparation of dishes from recipes. They need to be able to communicate clearly and work in a very organised way in front of cameras and/or a live audience. They are often qualified chefs or may have trained as consumer scientists, nutritionists, food scientists, culinary managers, restaurateurs or caterers.

Improve Ltd, the Food and Drink Sector Skills Council
Website: www.improveltd.co.uk

Food/Restaurant Journalist

Food/restaurant journalists research and write articles on food and produce reviews of restaurants for specialist food or other magazines, newspapers, radio, television and websites. Journalists who specialise in this area may also have qualifications in an area such as food science, culinary management, nutrition or catering. See also: Catering Manager, Chef, Dietitian, Journalist.

National Council for the Training of Journalists, Saffron Walden, Essex CB11 3PL
Website: www.nctj.com

Foreign Correspondent

Foreign correspondents are journalists who seek out news for television, radio, newspapers, magazines and news agencies. They may be based in one country or travel around the world whenever a major news event occurs. They would normally need considerable experience and proven track records within their home country before being selected for this type of work. See Journalist.

National Council for the Training of Journalists, Saffron Walden CB11 3PL
Website: www.nctj.com

Broadcast Journalism Training Council, Rippingdale PE10 0TH
Website: www.bjtc.org.uk

Furniture Designer

Furniture designers use a range of skills to design furniture and related products for industrial, commercial and domestic clients. The work may involve anything from bespoke design for individual clients, to batch runs of particular items or mass production. Furniture designers need to strike a balance between innovative design, functional requirements and aesthetic appeal.

Chartered Society of Designers, London SE1 3UW
Website: www.csd.org.uk

Crafts Council, London N1 9BY
Website: www.craftscouncil.org.uk

Your Creative Future
Website: www.yourcreativefuture.org

Geneticist

A genetic scientist studies the ways in which animals and plants transmit their characteristics from generation to generation by means of their genes. Scientists also study how to carry out genetic modification of plants to improve their resistance to disease and to increase the yields of fruit or vegetables.

Genetics Society, Roslin EH25 9PS
Website: www.genetics.org.uk

British Society for Human Genetics, Birmingham B15 2TG
Website: www.bshg.org.uk

Geochemist

Geochemists use their knowledge of chemistry to locate and analyse minerals and extract them from the earth's crust. A degree in chemistry or geology/geoscience is usually required, and a postgraduate qualification can be an advantage. See also geologist, geophysicist.

British Geological Survey, Nottingham NG12 5GG
Website: www.bgs.ac.uk

Geological Society of London, London W1J 0BG
Website: www.geolsoc.org.uk

Petroleum Exploration Society of Great Britain, London W1J 8DW
Website: www.pesgb.org.uk

Geographer

Geographers study and analyse the physical world, the environment and the interaction of these with society. The subject provides an insight into a variety of related occupations and academic subjects.   There are very few jobs available in geographical work, except for university lecturers and schoolteachers.   However, geography graduates enter commercial, industrial and public sector management; business and finance; surveying; clerical and secretarial work; marketing and sales.

Royal Geographical Society, London SW7 2AR
Website: www.rgs.org

Geophysicist

Geophysicists use methods such as ground-penetrating radar to measure and assess the properties of the earth and its environment in order to manage exploration and development projects on land and at sea. There are four key roles: engineering geophysicists analyse the shallow structure of the earth in preparation for the development of buildings, pipelines and cables; exploration/development geophysicists explore and identify new mineral deposits and sources of energy such as oil and gas; interpretation/processing geophysicists analyse detailed information from sites on land or at sea; seismologists investigate earthquakes and use this information to develop seismic hazard maps. A degree in physics, geology or geophysics is usually required, together with a postgraduate qualification in geophysics or geosciences. See also geologist, geochemist.

British Geophysical Association
Website: www.geophysics.org.uk/bga.html

British Geological Survey, Nottingham NG12 5GG
Website: www.bgs.ac.uk

Petroleum Exploration Society of Great Britain, London W1J 8DW
Website: www.pesgb.org.uk

Society of Exploration Geophysicists
Website: www.seg.org

Health Visitor

The health visitor is a trained nurse who visits people in their own homes, often when they have been ill or are recovering from an operation and need supportive medical help.

Community Practitioners' and Health Visitors' Association, London EC1 8HA
Website: www.amicus-cphva.org

Herbalist

As a medical herbalist you would be trained in the diagnosis of human diseases and their cure using a very wide range of plant extracts, often known from antiquity to have medicinal effects. You would undertake a training course leading to a degree in herbal medicine - also called phytotherapy - at one of a small number of universities. There is also a one-year course for qualified doctors at the School of Herbal Medicine.

National Institute of Medical Herbalists, Exeter EX4 3BA
Website: www.nimh.org.uk

Historical Researcher

Historical researchers are concerned with exploring historical records, books and relevant documents in establishing facts and in confirming or challenging existing historical theories, and are usually university based.

Institute of Historical Research, University of London, London WC1E 7HU
Website: www.history.ac.uk

Horse Breeder

Horse Breeders are involved with the care, covering, raising, marketing and management of horses. The horses may be bred for racing, equestrian sports, riding clubs, working horses or stock horses. Supervisors oversee the operations of the stud and managers run the business operations. Breeders develop an extensive knowledge of the stallions and mares and their relative values at stud. See also: Equine Manager

British Horse Society, Kenilworth CV8 2XZ
Website: www.bhs.org.uk

Horse Riding Instructor

Horse Riding Instructors train people to learn and improve their riding skills. They coach beginners and advanced national and international competitors, depending on the levels of their own skills and experience.

British Horse Society, Kenilworth CV8 2XZ
Website: www.bhs.org.uk

Association of British Riding Schools
Website: www.abrs-info.org

Association of Irish Riding Establishments
Website: www.aire.ie

Housing Manager

Housing managers work for local authorities and housing associations to provide a service to tenants of rented properties, assessing their needs, allocating property and arranging transfers. They may also collect rents, inspect for damage and arrange repairs and redecoration.

Chartered Institute of Housing, Coventry CV4 8JP
Website: www.cih.org

Immunologist

Immunologists investigate the functions of the body's immune system and use this knowledge to work towards treating and controlling a range of diseases and disorders. The work includes understanding the processes and effects of inappropriate stimulation, which are associated with the development of autoimmune diseases, allergies and transplant rejection. Immunologists work within clinical and academic settings, as well as in industrial research.

British Society for Immunology, London SW8 4HX
Website: www.immunology.org

Medical Research Council, London W1B 1AL
Website: www.mrc.ac.uk

Industrial Manager

Industrial Management offers a wide range of opportunities and specialisations. These include managing the people, materials and machinery involved in converting raw materials into finished products.

Chartered Management Institute, Corby NN17 1TT
Website: www.managers.org.uk

Information Technology Specialist

Information technologists specialise in the use, modification and control of existing standard software to achieve the needs of organisations and to provide essential management information. IT systems are used in banks, stock exchanges, insurance companies, the Civil Service, Armed Services, air traffic control, retail, manufacturing control and automation/robotics. Financial packages can produce sales invoices and statements, tax and VAT statements, stock lists, for example. Many other types of IT software are widely available, requiring expert installation and training of personnel.

British Computer Society, Swindon SN2 1FA
Website: www.bcs.org.uk

Jewellery Designer

Jewellery designers use their skills to create a wide variety of jewellery, some hand-made, some mass-produced. These can include traditional pieces using precious metals and gems, cheaper costume jewellery using synthetic stones and less precious metals, and fashion accessories made from other materials. There is most scope for designers of less expensive items

British Jewellers Association, Birmingham B18 6LT
Website: www.bja.org.uk

Association of British Designer Silversmiths
Website: www.theabds.co.uk

Justices' Clerk

Justices' Clerks are the principal legal advisers to lay magistrates in England and Wales and are committed to improving the quality of justice in Magistrates' Courts.

Justices' Clerks' Society, Liverpool L3 1BY
Website: www.jc-society.co.uk

Land Agent

See Estate Manager.

Lecturer (Higher/Further Education)

Lecturers in higher education are employed by one of the many universities and colleges offering degree and other postgraduate or qualifying courses. They are likely to be involved in tutorial work in addition to lecturing and supervising the practical work of students. In universities they frequently undertake research in their own subject areas.

University and College Union
Website: www.ucu.org.uk

British Accreditation Council
Website www.the-bac.org

Higher Education Academy
Website: www.heacademy.ac.uk

Legal Accountant

Legal accountants are people employed to conduct financial work in the offices of lawyers.

Institute of Chartered Accountants, Central Milton Keynes MK9 2HL
Website: www.icaew.co.uk

Institute of Chartered Accountants of Scotland, Edinburgh EH12 5BH
Website: www.icas.org.uk

Lexicographer

Lexicographers are responsible for compiling, editing and updating dictionaries. They monitor and record uses of language and use databases to interrogate a wide range of evidence. The work includes considering both the meaning and usage of words and phrases before compiling authoritative definitions. Bilingual lexicographers translate words and expressions rather than defining them. There are very few publishers of dictionaries in the UK, and not all companies that publish dictionaries employ lexicographers.

Chambers Harrap Publishers, Edinburgh EH7 4AY
Website: www.chambers.co.uk

HarperCollins, London W6 8JB
Website: www.harpercollins.co.uk

Oxford University Press, Oxford OX2 6DP
Website: www.oup.co.uk

Society for Editors and Proofreaders, London SW6 3JD
Website: www.sfep.org.uk

Loss Adjuster

Loss adjusters are called in by insurance companies to examine large and complicated insurance claims and to establish fair settlements. They may be members of the Chartered Institute of Loss Adjusters or qualified in for example law, surveying, accountancy or engineering.

Chartered Institute of Loss Adjusters, London EC3R 8LJ
Website: www.cila.co.uk

Magazine Publisher

Magazine Publishing is completely different from book publishing. Magazines are usually specialised and may appear weekly, monthly or less frequently. The main career areas include writing/editing, design and advertisement sales - see also Publisher, Graphic Designer and Journalist.

Periodicals Training Council, London WC2B 6JR
Website: www.ppa.co.uk

Marine Geologist

Marine geologists use hydrographic, seismic and sonar technology, acoustic systems and other methods to conduct geological hazard, marine geology and oceanographic investigations. Governments and the oil industry use their interpretation of the data for forward planning. See also: Geologist, Engineering Geologist, Hydrographic Surveyor, Oceanographer.

International Federation of Hydrographic Societies, Plymouth PL4 7YP
Website: www.hydrographicsociety.org

Marine Geophysicist

Marine geophysicists study the physical properties of the earth's crust under the oceans. They often work on marine research vessels using seismic acoustic reflection and other methods to collect data relating to the seabed. They process this and can produce reports for petroleum companies, cable layers and others. See also: Geologist, Engineering Geologist, Hydrographic Surveyor, Oceanographer.

Society of Exploration Geophysicists, Tulsa, OK 74137-2740, USA
Website: www.seg.org

Market Maker (Finance)

As a market maker, you would be one of a team of people dealing in a range of financial products. You would use your specialist knowledge to buy and sell commodities such as foreign exchange, equities, crude oil, metals, gold, vegetable oils, and grains. You would be dealing with buyers and sellers on a global scale - almost always in a fully computerised dealing room, by email or telephone rather than face to face with people on the floor of an exchange. See also Commodity Broker and Stockbroker.

Securities and Investment Institute, London EC3R 8AQ
Website: www.sii.org.uk

Mathematician

Mathematicians use their specialist skills in abstract and applied mathematical concepts to define, quantify and predict almost any situation connected with teaching, science, technology, business logistics, manufacturing, computing, economics and finance.

Institute of Mathematics and its Applications, Southend-on-Sea SS1 1EF
Website: www.ima.org.uk

Media Researcher

See Broadcasting Researcher.

Medical Laboratory Scientific Officer

See Biomedical Scientist.

Medical Secretary

Medical secretaries keep the medical records of patients and handle medical correspondence and filing. They may work in hospitals or private practices, for individual doctors/consultants or in health centres, and are trained in the use of medical terminology.

Association of Medical Secretaries, Practice Managers, Administrators and Receptionists, London WC1H 9LN
Website: www.amspar.co.uk

Medical Technical Officer

Medical Technical Officers (MTOs) or Clinical/Medical Technologists work in a healthcare environment, maintaining and servicing complex, specialised equipment used to diagnose and treat patients. Hospitals use an increasingly wide range of cutting edge technology in various areas, such as radiotherapy, bioengineering and laser procedures. There is an increasing demand for people with the correct medical physics knowledge, usually around or just below the level of university entry, to service, check the performance and gauge any environmental effects of this equipment. MTOs often liaise with scientists and doctors, and have direct contact with patients. They must show great attention to detail, coupled with the ability to reassure patients who may be uncomfortable with such complex machinery.

Specific MTO roles include:

- *Critical Care Technologist* - providing operational and technical support to general and specialist Intensive Care or High Dependency Units, especially with equipment to maintain circulation, respiration and renal support function, often operating as part of a multi-disciplinary clinical team.

- *Medical Physics Technologist* - assisting clinical and scientific staff in the construction of medical devices; this can involve mechanical, electronic and computing design procedures. The MTO may also carry out calibration and quality assurance tests of x-ray and other electro-medical equipment.

- *Nuclear Medicine Technologist* - using radioactive pharmaceuticals in diagnosis and therapy by administering radioactive agents and imaging their distribution using gamma cameras. The MTO also performs laboratory tests and administers routine therapeutic doses of radioactive iodine.

- *Radiotherapy Technologist* - performing quality control on radiotherapy dosimetry equipment and treatment units, such as linear accelerators and brachytherapy equipment, and computing radiation treatment plans. The MTO might also maintain and service radiation therapy equipment and construct patient fixation devices.

- *Vascular Technologist* - performing and interpreting non-invasive diagnostic studies on patients with arterial and venous disease. These include ultrasound imaging and blood-flow waveform analysis, and blood pressure measurement at rest and after exercise. The MTO might also carry out vascular measurement during surgery.

- *Technologist in Equipment Management* - maintaining and servicing electro-medical equipment to ensure both performance and safety. Whilst the more sophisticated equipment is installed in acute hospitals, this technologist would also support equipment in primary care.

- *Rehabilitation Engineer* - working with the rehabilitation team to provide bio-mechanical assessment, monitoring of patient recovery and the custom manufacture of aids such as wheelchairs and speech synthesisers for individual patients.

- *Renal Dialysis Technician* - responsible for the safe and efficient working of renal dialysis equipment (haemodialysis, peritoneal dialysis, and water treatment) both in hospital and at the patient's home.

Institute of Physics and Engineering in Medicine, York YO24 1ES
Website: www.ipem.ac.uk

National Health Service Careers, Bristol BS99 3EY
Website: www.nhscareers.nhs.uk

Society of Critical Care Technologists
Website: www.criticalcaretech.org.uk

Member of European Parliament (MEP)

After the 2009 elections, there will be a total of 736 MEPs, of whom 72 will come from the UK. Most of the time, Parliament and the MEPs are based in Brussels where specialist committees meet to scrutinise proposals for new EU laws. Parliament also meets in Strasbourg to amend and vote draft legislation and policy. MEPs do not sit in national delegations in the Parliament, but in multinational political groups.

European Parliament
Website: www.europarl.europa.eu

Member of Parliament

Members of Parliament represent their constituents in government, ensuring that their interests are kept in mind. They spend much of their time consulting their constituents, dealing with their problems and debating issues both in their constituencies and in Parliament. Much time is also spent considering legislation in committee or as ministers.

BUBL Information Services, Glasgow G1 1XH (for full list of all UK political parties)
Website: http://bubl.ac.uk/uk/bublukpolitical.htm

Method Study Officer

Method study traditionally involved the analysis of clerical/administrative work, but nowadays is closely related to work study and can include the analysis of the production methods used in industry. It involves measuring time and the human effort put into tasks in the workplace and looks for improvements which can be made, especially in reducing delays, bottlenecks, quality rejection, frustration and component shortage.

Institute of Management Services, Lichfield WS13 6AB
Website: www.ims-productivity.com

Mining Surveyor

Mining surveyors explore and map mineral deposits and consider the feasibility of their safe and profitable extraction. You might survey for metal ores, coal, salt or building materials, and could also be made responsible for mine safety and for avoiding environmental damage. You could advise of the value of deposits, leasing of land or mines and on legal matters.

Institute of Materials, Minerals and Mining, London SW1Y 5DB
Website: www.iom3.org

Molecular Biologist

Molecular biologists specialise in the biology of protein structures, DNA and RNA and the large molecules which govern the functions of cells and are associated with genetic factors. This field is sometimes referred to as the 'new biology'.

Institute of Biology, London EC4A 3EF
Website: www.iob.org

Multimedia Programmer/Specialist

Multimedia programmers bring together a wide range of software, including the technologies of computer simulation, animation, illustration, sound, virtual reality, satellite communication, laser science, television production, telephone and microwave systems. This is a rapidly growing field influencing education, medicine, entertainment, leisure, science, engineering, technology, commerce, industry and government.

Skillset, London WC1A 1HB
Website: www.skillset.org

e-skills UK, London SW1E 6DR
Website: www.e-skills.com

Music Teacher

Music Teachers may be professional teachers specialising in music or specialist instrumentalists or singers who spend some of their time teaching. Many musicians combine performance and teaching commitments in varying proportions - see also Teacher and Musician.

Training and Development Agency for Schools, London SW1E 5TT
Website: www.tda.gov.uk

Incorporated Society of Musicians, London W1C 1AA
Website: www.ism.org

Music Therapist

Music therapists are usually trained musicians with a postgraduate qualification in music therapy. They work with people of all ages, using mainly improvised music as a form of self-expression for clients with a variety of mental health problems, communication disorders and serious physical illness.

British Society for Music Therapy, East Barnet, EN4 8SY
Website: www.bsmt.org

Musical Instrument Technologist

Musical Instrument Technologists specialise in the construction and repair of all types of musical instruments.

Institute of Musical Instrument Technology, Croydon CR2 0QR
Website: www.imit.org.uk

National Association of Musical Instrument Repairers, London SE25 4HP
Website: www.namir.org.uk

Naturopath

This branch of alternative medicine is based on the belief that the human body is self-regulatory and capable of self-repair if given the right conditions. Treatment can consist of special diets or fasting, coupled with hydrotherapy and osteopathic techniques. Degree and postgraduate courses are available.

General Council and Register of Naturopaths, Street BA16 0QS
Website: www.naturopathy.org.uk

Network Administrator

Network Administrators are responsible for the smooth running and continuity of computer networks, essential to the accessing of pooled information within organisations.

Institute for the Management of Information Systems, Orpington BR5 3QG
Website: www.imis.org.uk

British Computer Society, Swindon, SN2 1FA
Website: www.bcs.org.uk

Newspaper Publisher

Newspaper Publishing is undertaken both by large national newspaper groups and by smaller local organisations. Most openings are for journalists/reporters who can eventually become editors, sub-editors, feature writers or columnists. The industry also employs administrators, art editors, business managers, legal/copyright experts, accountants, printing managers and sales executives - see also Magazine Publisher, Publisher and Journalist.

Newspaper Society, London WC1B 3DA
Website: www.newspapersoc.org.uk

Nuclear Engineer

Nuclear engineers work on the production and use of nuclear fuels to generate electric power, and the design and construction, control and safety of nuclear reactors. Their field covers many other branches of engineering - mechanical, civil, electrical and electronic - but is adapted to the handling and control of highly dangerous radioactive materials.

World Nuclear Association, London SW1Y 4JH
Website: www.world-nuclear.org

Nursery Nurse

A nursery nurse cares for babies and young mainly healthy children, usually under eight years of age, working in hospitals, clinics, crèches, nurseries and schools. Nursery nurses talk to children, read to them, show interest in their activities and their play with other children, discuss their painting and art work, helping them to enjoy their nursery life and to become confident and well adjusted socially.

Council for Awards in Children's Care and Education, St. Albans, AL1 3AW
Website: www.cache.org.uk

Nutritional Therapist

Nutritional therapists advise clients on how to improve their overall health and wellbeing by careful assessment of what their bodies need in terms of food, vitamins and minerals. Nutritional therapy is considered a complementary therapy and is often used alongside orthodox medicine.

British Association for Applied Nutrition and Nutritional Therapy, London WC1N 3XX
Website: www.bant.org.uk

Nutritional Therapy Council, Bournemouth BH1 9BL
Website: www.nutritionaltherapycouncil.org.uk

Occupational Hygienist

Occupational hygienists assess potential risks to workforce safety in environments including factories, offices and building sites. They are responsible for recognising, evaluating and controlling environmental hazards resulting from physical, chemical or biological factors in the workplace. Often working within a team with other professionals, such as doctors, nurses and engineers, they enable organisations to respond effectively to the requirements of legislation on issues such as asbestos, noise and manual handling.

British Occupational Hygiene Society, Derby DE1 1LT
Website: www.bohs.org/

Institution of Occupational Safety and Health, Leicestershire LE18 1NN
Website: www.iosh.co.uk

Opera Singer
Opera Singers sing for companies such as national, regional or privately owned opera companies, and compete for places in new productions and for shorter-term assignments. Operatic soloists undertake contracts to sing internationally and to make records for recording companies. They need to be able to sing in a number of languages.

Incorporated Society of Musicians, London W1C 1AA
Website: www.ism.org

Making Music, London EC2A 3NW
Website: www.makingmusic.org.uk

Organic Farmer
Organic Farmers produce food for human consumption whilst avoiding the use of chemicals such as pesticides, herbicides and artificial fertilisers - see also Farm Manager, Agricultural Adviser and Agricultural Researcher.

Garden Organic, Coventry CV8 3LG
Website: www.gardenorganic.org.uk

Orthotist/Prosthetist
Orthotists fit surgical appliances to human beings to correct a wide range of physical disabilities or weaknesses. They fit plaster casts, leg and arm supports, cervical collars and finger splints. The majority work for manufacturing companies who supply the health service, but spend a great deal of time in health service hospitals with patients. Orthotists measure patients, take casts and write instructions for appliances to be manufactured to meet their individual requirements. They also train patients to use the appliances and check that they are working properly, leg appliances in particular.

Prosthetists measure and fit amputees who have lost mainly legs. A major part of their work involves people who have lost limbs in car accidents, in armed conflicts and so on. They must be able to deal with children, whose appliances will become too small as they grow.

British Association of Prosthetists and Orthotists, Paisley PA1 1TJ
Website: www.bapo.com

Outdoor Pursuits Manager
Outdoor pursuits managers run centres providing facilities for a variety of outdoor activities, including climbing, mountaineering, water sports, orienteering, horse riding and cycling. They are usually responsible for recruiting, training and monitoring a team of staff, including instructors, ensuring adherence at all times to strict safety regulations.

Institute for Outdoor Learning, Cumbria CA11 9NP
Website: www.outdoor-learning.org

Institute for Sport, Parks and Leisure, Reading RG8 9NE
Website: www.ispal.org.uk

Institute of Sport and Recreation Management, Loughborough LE11 3TU
Website: www.isrm.co.uk

Outward Bound Trust, Cumbria CA11 0JL
Website: www.outwardbound-uk.org

Pathologist

Pathologists study human and animal tissues and assess diseases which affect cell structures, often detecting clues to sickness and also the causes of death.

Association of Clinical Pathologists, Hove BN3 1TL
Website: www.pathologists.org.uk

Picture Researcher

Picture Researchers use their visual knowledge and experience to find the 'right' pictures for whatever project they are working on, whether for a book, a newspaper, a magazine, an advertisement, a television programme, an exhibition, a brochure, a CD-Rom or a page on a website.

Picture Research Association, London EC2A 4QB
Website: www.picture-research.org.uk

Political Party Researcher

Political party researchers assist with the formulation of their party's policies and campaigns. They advise politicians about policy decisions and generate new policies by researching issues and making appropriate contacts. They are also responsible for drafting speeches and articles for politicians to describe party policy, or to respond effectively to criticisms of policies or performance. They research for debates, undertake committee work and prepare for or draft parliamentary questions. A significant part of the role is to provide politicians with the necessary information to attack opponents' policies and performance.

Working for an MP
Website: www.w4mp.org

BUBL Information Services, Glasgow G1 1XH (for full list of all UK political parties)
Website: http://bubl.ac.uk/uk/bublukpolitical.htm

European Parliament
Website: www.europarl.europa.eu

Presenter

A television or radio presenter is someone who links together the different parts of broadcasting programmes, introducing correspondents and conducting interviews with selected people. Genuine flair and originality, charisma and a captivating personality are required. News presenters need skills in journalism and an excellent grasp of current affairs; other presenters require specialist knowledge, for example weather presenters need training at the Met office, while political/financial presenters need an up-to-date understanding of parliamentary and City developments. There is no formal route into this very competitive careers field.

Skillset, London WC1A 1HB
Website: www.skillset.org

Press/Information Officer

Information officers work in the Civil Service to inform and explain government legislation or policy. Press officers release this information to the media and often accompany ministers on official overseas visits, when they release information on negotiations or developments to journalists. Information/publicity officers also produce publicity materials in association with, for example, public relations and advertising agencies and arrange conferences, exhibitions and marketing campaigns to explain government policy. In industry, commerce and education, information officers are very closely associated with librarians and perform many of the same tasks of keeping their organisations aware of relevant information released in magazines, newspapers, on television, radio or in published books and reports of all kinds. See also Public Relations Officer.

Chartered Institute of Public Relations, London WC1B 4HP
Website: www.cipr.co.uk

National Council for the Training of Journalists, Saffron Walden CV11 3PL
Website: www.nctj.com

Civil Service Recruitment Gateway, London SW1A 2AS
Website: www.careers.civil-service.gov.uk

Printing Technologist/Manager

Print Management embraces a number of skills in the operation of modern printing equipment and the control of print production.

Institute of Paper, Printing and Publishing, Chertsey KT16 9AS
Website: www.ip3.org.uk

Prison Governor

A prison governor is in overall charge of a prison, responsible for prison staff, the inmates and for all of its services or activities. Governors liaise closely with the police, social services and Home Office and must control the activity of inmates, and ensure they are kept in secure but humane conditions.

HM Prison Service, London SW1P 4LN
Website: www.hmprisonservice.gov.uk

Scottish Prison Service, Edinburgh EH12 9HW
Website: www.sps.gov.uk

Northern Ireland Prison Service, Belfast BT4 3SU
Website: www.niprisonservice.gov.uk

Prison Officer

In day-to-day contact with prisoners, prison officers are responsible for all the arrangements for food, hygiene, accommodation and recreation. The main roles are security and the maintenance of discipline.

HM Prison Service, London SW1P 4LN
Website: www.hmprisonservice.gov.uk

Scottish Prison Service, Edinburgh EH12 9HW
Website: www.sps.gov.uk

Northern Ireland Prison Service, Belfast BT4 3SU
Website: www.niprisonservice.gov.uk

Process Engineer
Process engineers develop industrial processes to make the products on which modern society depends. These products include food and drink, fuel, artificial fibres, pharmaceuticals, chemicals, plastics, toiletries, energy and clean water. The work concerns large-scale chemical and biochemical processes in which raw materials undergo change. This involves scaling up the manufacture of products and processes from the laboratory to full production.

Engineering Council UK, London WC2R 3ER
Website: www.engc.org.uk

Institution of Chemical Engineers, Rugby CV21 3HQ
Website: http://cms.icheme.org

Production Assistant (Film/TV/Radio)
Production assistants work in television, radio and film production, providing administrative and secretarial support for the producer. This is a demanding job and first class secretarial skills are essential.

Skillset, London WC1A 1HB
Website: www.skillset.org

Production Manager
See Industrial Manager.

Prosecutor (Crown Prosecution Service)
Prosecutors are responsible for reviewing and, where appropriate, prosecuting criminal cases following investigation by the police in England and Wales. They also advise the police on matters relating to criminal cases. You must be a solicitor admitted in England and Wales with a full current practising certificate, or a barrister called to the English Bar who has completed pupillage - see also Solicitor and Barrister.

Crown Prosecution Service, London EC4M 7EX
Website: www.cps.gov.uk

Prosthetist
See Orthotist.

Psychotherapist
As a psychotherapist you would be concerned with helping patients with psychological problems, such as depression, behavioural problems or eating disorders. You would usually encourage them to talk about their feelings, thoughts and worries and to get them to speak freely in group or one-to-one situations. This work is closely linked with that of clinical psychologists and psychoanalysts.

British Association of Psychotherapists, London NW2 4HJ
Website: www.bap-psychotherapy.org

The British Psychoanalytic Council, London N6 6QS
Website: www.bcp.org.uk

Quality Assurance Manager
Quality Assurance Managers are responsible for ensuring that manufactured goods are produced to meet their technical and operational specifications and that safety reliability and overall quality are maintained.

Chartered Quality Institute, London SW1X 7EE
Website: www.thecqi.org

Radio/TV Producer

Producers are responsible for promoting theatrical, film and video productions, for selecting or commissioning plays or scripts, for hiring directors, actors, actresses and for ensuring money is available to pay bills.

Skillset, London WC1A 1HB
Website: www.skillset.org

Recording Engineer

Recording engineering is a specialised branch of electronic/radio engineering. Recording engineers are mainly employed by broadcasting authorities and recording studios for programmes to be transmitted later, or sold on tape or disc. Vacancies are limited.

Skillset, London WC1A 1HB
Website: www.skillset.org

Recruitment Consultant

Recruitment consultants advertise for candidates needed to fill employment vacancies at many different levels, from executives or directors to temping, secretarial or technical roles. They also maintain databases of available candidates for high demand positions. Some specialise, for example, in IT, nursing/medical or office vacancies.

Recruitment and Employment Confederation, London W1W 7RG
Website: www.rec.uk.com

Reflexologist

Reflexologists are complementary medicine practitioners, applying pressure to patients' feet and hands to treat a range of medical problems.

Association of Reflexologists, Taunton TA1 1HX
Website: www.aor.org.uk

Robotics

Robots have evolved over the last 50 years from mechanical devices operated remotely by humans. In the car industry, such robots have been used for some time in production lines, to perform the routine and repetitive mechanical tasks of mass assembly. From these beginnings, robots have developed rapidly through advances in microelectronic and computing technology. Robots can now 'see', sense, move and manipulate, executing complex and precise tasks at very high speeds. They have come a long way from the car assembly line and a recent development has been the application of robotics in the human body.

British Automation and Robot Association, Coventry CV4 7AL
Website: www.bara.org.uk

RSPCA/SSPCA Inspector

RSPCA/SSPCA inspectors provide 24-hour cover for animals in need, carry out rescues, investigate cruelty complaints, bring perpetrators of cruelty to court, inspect animal establishments, give advice and administer first aid. Entry is extremely competitive.

RSPCA, Horsham RH13 9RS
Website: www.rspca.org.uk

Scottish SPCA, Edinburgh EH4 6EA
Website: www.scottishspca.org

Scriptwriter

Scriptwriters produce scripts to be used in TV, radio, film or theatrical productions or performances and indicate the settings and effects that should accompany them. They may adapt existing works or create new ones.

Skillset, London WC1A 1HB
Website: www.skillset.org

Security Officer

Security officers protect people, money, property, documents and organisations from theft, industrial espionage, kidnapping for example - using modern electronic devices, special patrols and specially armoured vehicles. Over 200,000 people are employed in private security companies. They are usually adults with armed services, police, prison officer and fire services backgrounds - but experts in electronic security systems are now increasingly employed.

International Professional Security Association, London W5 4NG
Website: www.ipsa.org.uk

Shorthand Writer

Shorthand writers or court reporters work in Crown Courts, the House of Commons and the House of Lords, where they record proceedings in shorthand or by using stenography equipment (Civil courts use audio recording equipment). In Scotland, they work in the High Court, Court of Session and the Sheriff Court.

Skills for Justice
Website: www.skillsforjustice.com

Sorene Court Reporting and Training Services
Website: www.sorene.co.uk

Verbatim Reporters
Website: www.verbatim-reporters.com

British Institute of Verbatim Reporters
Website: www.bivr.org.uk

Soil Scientist

Soil scientists interpret and evaluate the biological, chemical and physical properties of soil, with the aim of understanding how soil resources contribute to agricultural production, environmental quality and human health issues. They may work in research for public and private sector institutions, consultancy, overseas development, archaeological excavations, landscape design and site restoration. Independent of sector, much of the work involves undertaking fieldwork activity, including the collection of soil samples from a range of environments, conducting laboratory analysis and writing research reports.

Agricultural Development and Advisory Service, Wolverhampton WV6 8TQ
Website: www.adas.co.uk

British Society of Soil Science, Aberdeen AB15 8QH
Website: www.soils.org.uk

Institute of Professional Soil Scientists, Aberdeen AB15 8QH
Website: www.soilscientist.org/

National Soil Resources Institute, Bedford MK45 4DT
Website: www.silsoe.cranfield.ac.uk/nsri

Sonographer

A sonographer uses ultrasound imaging to produce images of structures of the human body, which can then be observed on a monitor screen or printed as photographs. This is a specialist area within radiography.

Society of Radiographers, London SE1 2EW
Website: www.sor.org

Special Educational Needs Teacher

Special Educational Needs Teachers specialise in helping children with educational and learning difficulties, which can include reading problems, social adjustment, behavioural and emotional problems, deafness, blindness, physical incapacity and psychological disorders - see Teacher.

Training and Development Agency for Schools, London SW1E 5TT
Website: www.tda.gov.uk

General Teaching Council for Scotland, Edinburgh, EH12 6UT
Website: www.gtcs.org.uk

Department of Education, Bangor, Co Down BT19 7PR
Website: www.deni.gov.uk

Statistician

Statisticians work with a variety of quantitative data, organising and analysing it to produce information on which decisions can be made, for example in government, finance, market research, economics, production and insurance. The statistician uses specialised knowledge of probability theory to estimate the likelihood of future situations arising, as well as producing statistics of past events.

Royal Statistical Society, London EC1Y 8LX
Website: www.rss.org.uk/careers

Tax Inspector

Tax Inspectors work for HM Revenue and Customs services and are concerned with assessing income tax, corporation tax, capital gains, appeals for tax rebates, and cases of tax evasion or fraud.

HM Revenue and Customs, Graduate Recruitment
Website: www.hmrc.gov.uk/jobs

Telecommunications Engineer

Telecommunications engineers deal with the communication of sound, vision and written information of all types by telephone, radio, television, satellite and cable, optical fibre, electronic mail, fax and teletext. Development work is conducted by electronic engineers and computer scientists. Telecom engineers install, maintain and repair equipment.

Institute of Telecommunications Professionals
Website: www.theitp.org

Institution of Engineering and Technology
Website: www.theiet.org

Television/Theatre Set or Stage Designer

As a stage designer you would work closely with a TV or film director to create the required costumes and sets for theatrical, film or television performances. You could produce drawings and also scale models of costumes and scenery for the production staff to work on. You would usually have a qualification (Degree/HND) from an art school in this field.

Society of British Theatre Designers, London EC1M 3JB
Website: www.theatredesign.org.uk

Theatrical Costume Designer

Theatrical Costume Designers design costumes for performers to suit the roles being played and the interpretation of the production - See also Fashion Designer and Television/Theatre Set or Stage Designer.

Society of British Theatre Designers, London EC1M 3JB
Website: www.theatredesign.org.uk

Association of British Theatre Technicians, London SE1 3XT
Website: www.abtt.org.uk

Tourism Officer

Tourism Officers develop and promote tourism in order to attract visitors and produce significant economic benefits for a particular region or site. They often work for local authorities, but may also work within private companies or other public sector agencies. Key areas include marketing and the development of services and facilities.

Tourism is increasingly focused on economic development or urban and rural regeneration, particularly in local authorities. This means that a tourism officer usually works closely with the residents and businesses of a local community.

Institute of Travel and Tourism, Hertfordshire SG12 8WY
Website: www.itt.co.uk

Tourism Management Institute, London EC2N 2AT
Website: www.tmi.org.uk

Tourism Society, London E1W 3HA
Website: www.tourismsociety.org

World Travel and Tourism Council, London E1W 3HA
Website: www.wttc.org

Toxicologist

Toxicologists carry out laboratory and field studies to identify, monitor and evaluate the impact of toxic materials and radiation on human and animal health, and on the health and status of the environment. Typical work activities include isolating, identifying and quantifying toxic substances or radiation and/or any harmful effects they have on biological materials, animals, plants or ecosystems. The use in toxicology of laboratory animals (in vivo), once common, is now declining and being replaced by bacterial and cell culture (in vitro) systems.

Association for Clinical Biochemistry, London SE1 2TU
Website: www.acb.org.uk

British Toxicology Society, Macclesfield SK11 6FT
Website: www.thebts.org

Transport Manager

Transport Managers usually oversee a fleet of vehicles and their drivers, making sure that goods reach their destinations on time and in good condition. They can carry out similar functions in the fields of aircraft and shipping, when exporting or importing - see Logistics Manager.

Institute of Transport Administration, Horsham RH13 6EH
Website: www.iota.org.uk

Travel & Tourism Clerk

Travel agency clerks work at counters discussing holiday choices and checking availability of hotels and flights on their computers - which they also use to print out details and quotations.

People 1st: Sector Skills Council for Hospitality, Leisure, Travel and Tourism
Website: www.people1st.co.uk
Apprenticeships
Website: www.apprenticeships.org.uk

United Nations Work

The United Nations plays a major role in world politics, health and relief work and offers many career opportunities in its various departments, which are centred mainly in New York and Geneva.

United Nations
Website: www.un.org

Waste Management Officer

Waste management officers are responsible for the development, management, supervision and control of waste disposal and recycling facilities. Some posts combine waste management and recycling functions, whilst others split the functions into separate jobs. The UK produces over 400 million tonnes of waste a year. It is the responsibility of the waste management industry, working with local authorities, to dispose of waste safely, with due consideration for the environment.

Chartered Institution of Wastes Management, Northampton NN1 1SX
Website: www.ciwm.co.uk

Waste Management Industry Training and Advisory Board, Northampton NN4 7HE
Website: www.wamitab.org.uk

Work Study Officer

Work Study involves the analysis of industrial or administrative work, measuring time and human effort put into tasks in the workplace and looking for improvements which can be made especially in reducing delays, bottlenecks, quality rejection, frustration and component shortage. Traditionally work study was confined to production processes but can now include the study of office work and is closely linked with method study. See also Method Study Officer.

Institute of Management Services, Lichfield WS13 6AB
Website: www.ims-productivity.com

Zoo Keeper

Keepers look after animals in zoos, mucking out their living quarters, preparing their bedding, water and food. They work long hours - from early in the morning to late in the evening - much of the time out of doors, and the work is often physically demanding. They must keep public and animal safety in mind and be constantly alert to animal health, assisting vets when animals are treated.

Association of British Wild Animal Keepers
Website: www.abwak.co.uk

Zoologist

Zoology is the scientific study of animals, their anatomy, physiology, ecology, evolution, breeding/embryology. Zoological research takes place in government and agricultural research centres, university departments, fishery research units, veterinary schools and agricultural colleges and has wide advantages for agriculture, conservation, fisheries and animal breeding.
Institute of Biology, London SW7 2DZ
Website: www.iob.org

Religious Careers

If you have strong religious beliefs, you might wish to consider a career as a vicar, priest, rabbi, elder, imam or whatever is appropriate for your particular faith. Many different religions are practised in the United Kingdom and we cannot possibly do justice to them in a book of this kind. You are probably already an active member of a religious group and we suggest that you start by discussing your career aspirations with a local representative of your religion.

Each religion has its own training methods but most involve a period of college-based study in the United Kingdom or overseas. You can obtain further information by visiting relevant websites from the list below.

Baptist Union of Great Britain - Website: www.baptist.org.uk

Buddhism - Website: www.buddhism.org

Church of England - Website: www.cofe.anglican.org

Church of Ireland - Website: www.ireland.anglican.org

Church of Scotland - Website: www.churchofscotland.org.uk

Hindu Council UK - Website: www.hinducounciluk.org

Islam - Website: www.islamic.org.uk

Judaism - Website: www.jewfaq.org/judaism.htm

Methodist Church of Great Britain - Website: www.methodist.org.uk

Methodist Church in Ireland - Website: www.irishmethodist.org

Catholic Church in England & Wales - Website: www.catholic-ew.org.uk

Catholic Church in Ireland - Website: www.catholicireland.net

Catholic Church in Scotland - Website: www.bpsconfscot.com

Sikhism - Website: www.sikhs.org & www.sikhnet.com

Index